AF531206

passionate brushstrokes

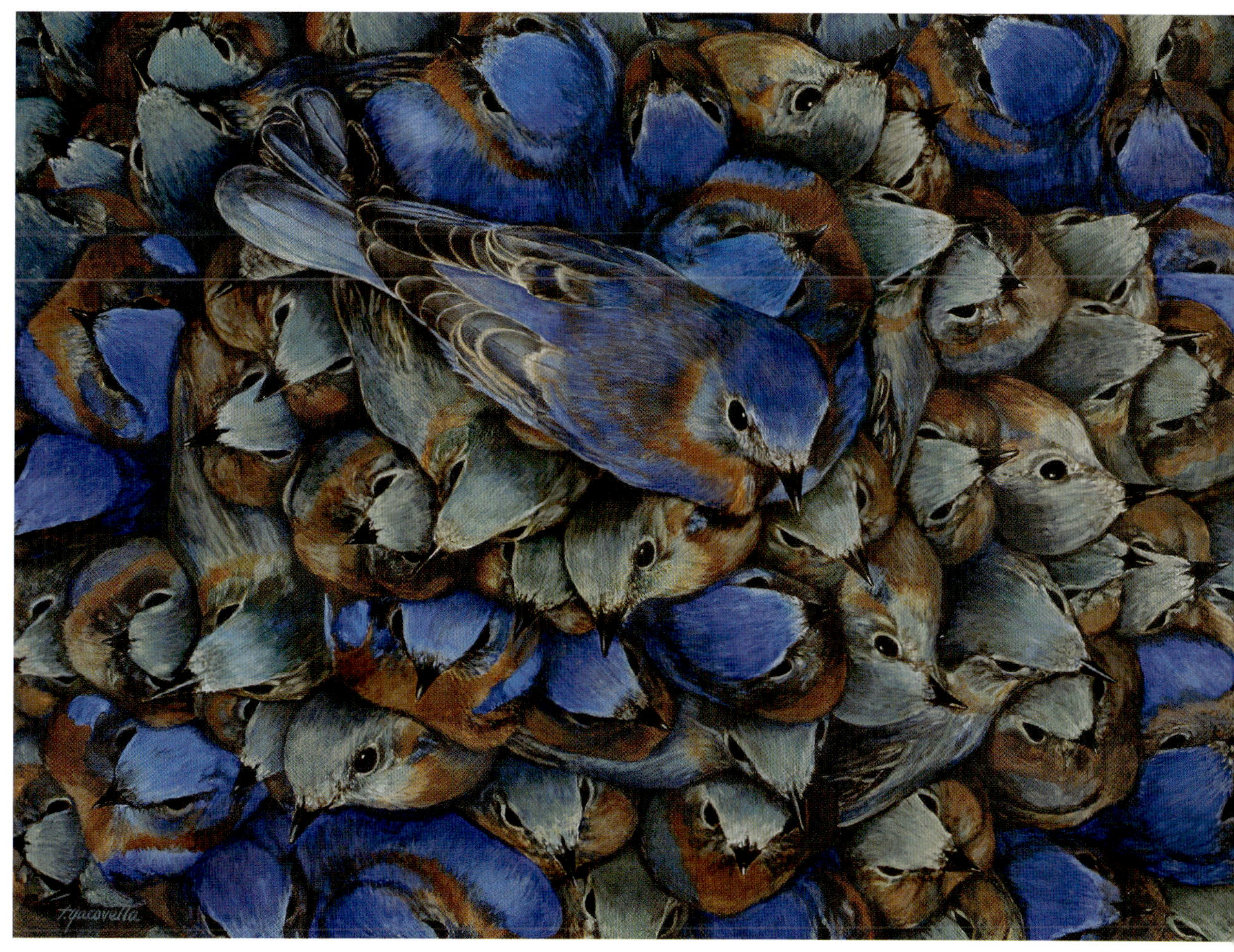

THE BEST OF WATERCOLOR

Splash 10

edited by Rachel Rubin Wolf

NORTH LIGHT BOOKS
CINCINNATI, OHIO
www.artistsnetwork.com

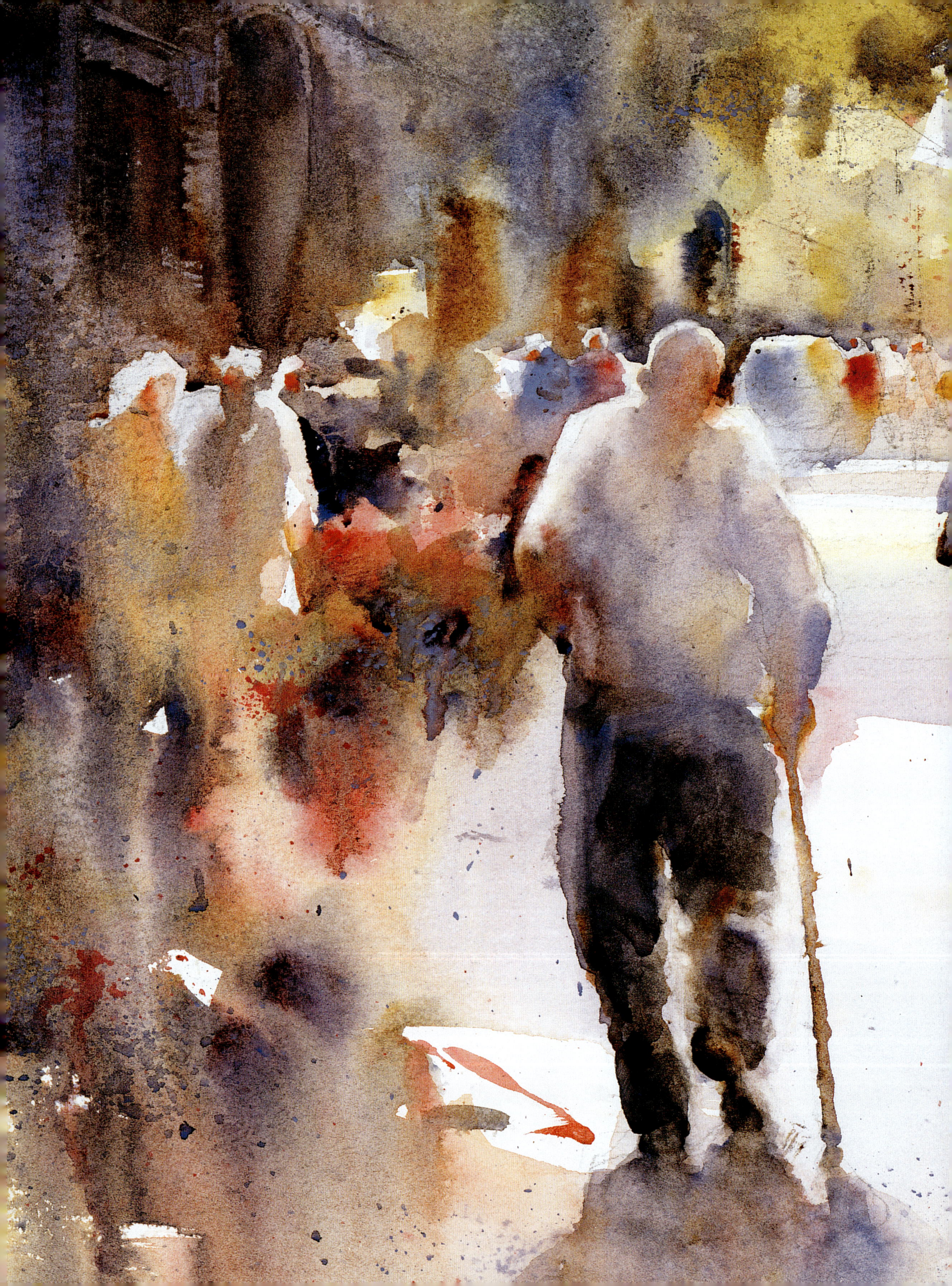

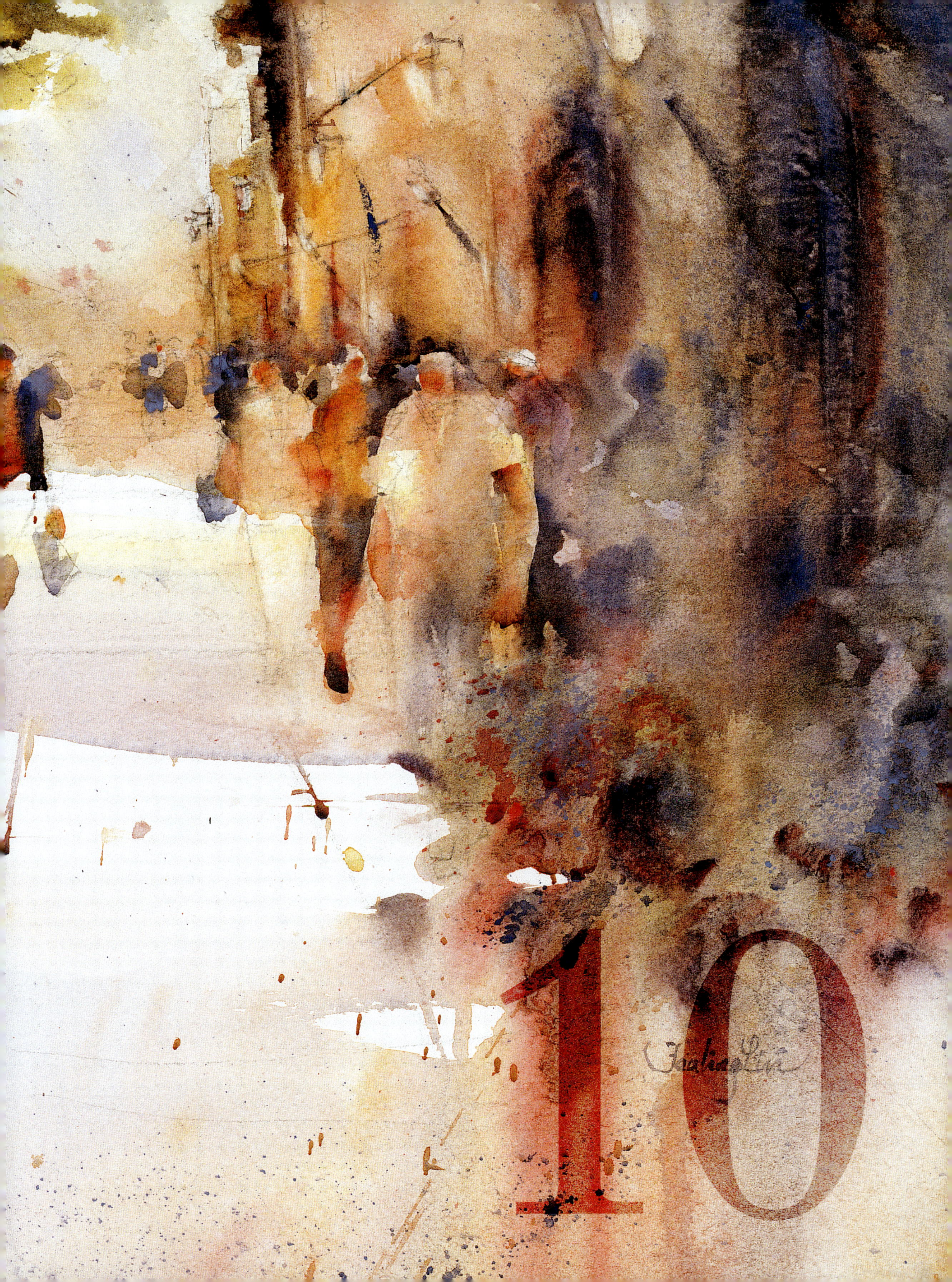
10

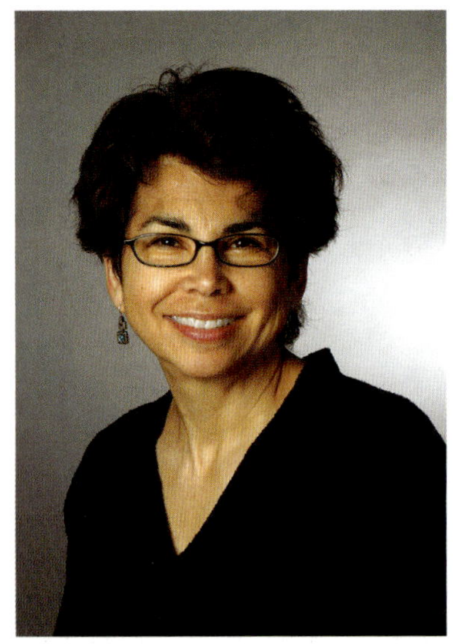

ABOUT THE EDITOR

Rachel Rubin Wolf is a freelance editor and artist. She edits and writes fine art books for North Light Books, including the *Splash* series (Best of Watercolor); *Strokes of Genius* series (Best of Drawing); *The Best of Wildlife Art* (editions 1 & 2); *The Best of Portrait Painting; The Best of Flower Painting 2; The Acrylic Painter's Book of Styles and Techniques; Painting Ships, Shores and the Sea*; and *Painting the Many Moods of Light.* She has also acquired numerous fine art book projects and authors for North Light Books and has contributed to magazines such as *Fine Art Connoisseur* and *Wildlife Art.*

 Published by North Light Books, an imprint of F+W Publications, Inc., 4700 East Galbraith Road, Cincinnati, Ohio, 45236. (800) 289-0963. First Edition.

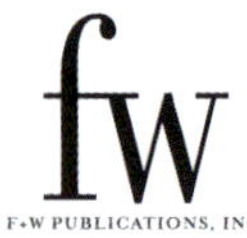

These books and other North Light titles are available from your local bookstore, art supply store or direct from the publisher at www.fwpublications.com.

12 11 10 09 08 5 4 3 2 1

DISTRIBUTED IN CANADA BY FRASER DIRECT
100 Armstrong Avenue
Georgetown, ON, Canada L7G 5S4
Tel: (905) 877-4411

DISTRIBUTED IN THE U.K. AND EUROPE BY DAVID & CHARLES
Brunel House, Newton Abbot, Devon, TQ12 4PU, England
Tel: (+44) 1626 323200, Fax: (+44) 1626 323319
Email: postmaster@davidandcharles.co.uk

DISTRIBUTED IN AUSTRALIA BY CAPRICORN LINK
P.O. Box 704, S. Windsor NSW, 2756 Australia
Tel: (02) 4577-3555

LIBRARY OF CONGRESS CATALOGING IN PUBLICATION DATA
Splash 10 : passionate brushstrokes. -- 1st ed.
p. cm.
Edited by Rachel Rubin Wolf and Vanessa Lyman.
ISBN-13: 978-1-58180-971-8 (alk. paper)
1. Watercolor painting--Technique. I. Rubin Wolf, Rachel, 1951-
II. Title: Splash ten : passionate brushstrokes.
ND2420.S65 2008
751.42'2--dc22
2007041976

EDITED BY **VANESSA LYMAN**
PRODUCTION EDITED BY **SARAH LAICHAS**
DESIGNED BY **JENNIFER HOFFMAN**
PRODUCTION COORDINATED BY **MATT WAGNER**

ART ON FRONT COVER
BREAKERS ON A ROCKY COAST
James Toogood • transparent watercolor • 23" × 17" (58cm × 43cm)

ART ON BACK COVER
MY PATIO DÉCOR
Alvin Joe • transparent watercolor • 28" × 20½" (71cm × 52cm)

ART ON PAGE 1
KEEP LOOKING FOR A BLUEBIRD
Tom Yacovella • transparent watercolor with acrylic accents • 18" × 24" (46cm × 61cm)

ART ON PAGE 2
AFTERNOON WALK
Fealing Lin • transparent watercolor on paper • 15" × 21" (38cm × 53cm)

metric conversion chart

TO CONVERT	TO	MULTIPLY BY
inches	centimeters	2.54
centimeters	inches	0.4
feet	centimeters	30.5
centimeters	feet	0.03
yards	meters	0.9
meters	yards	1.1

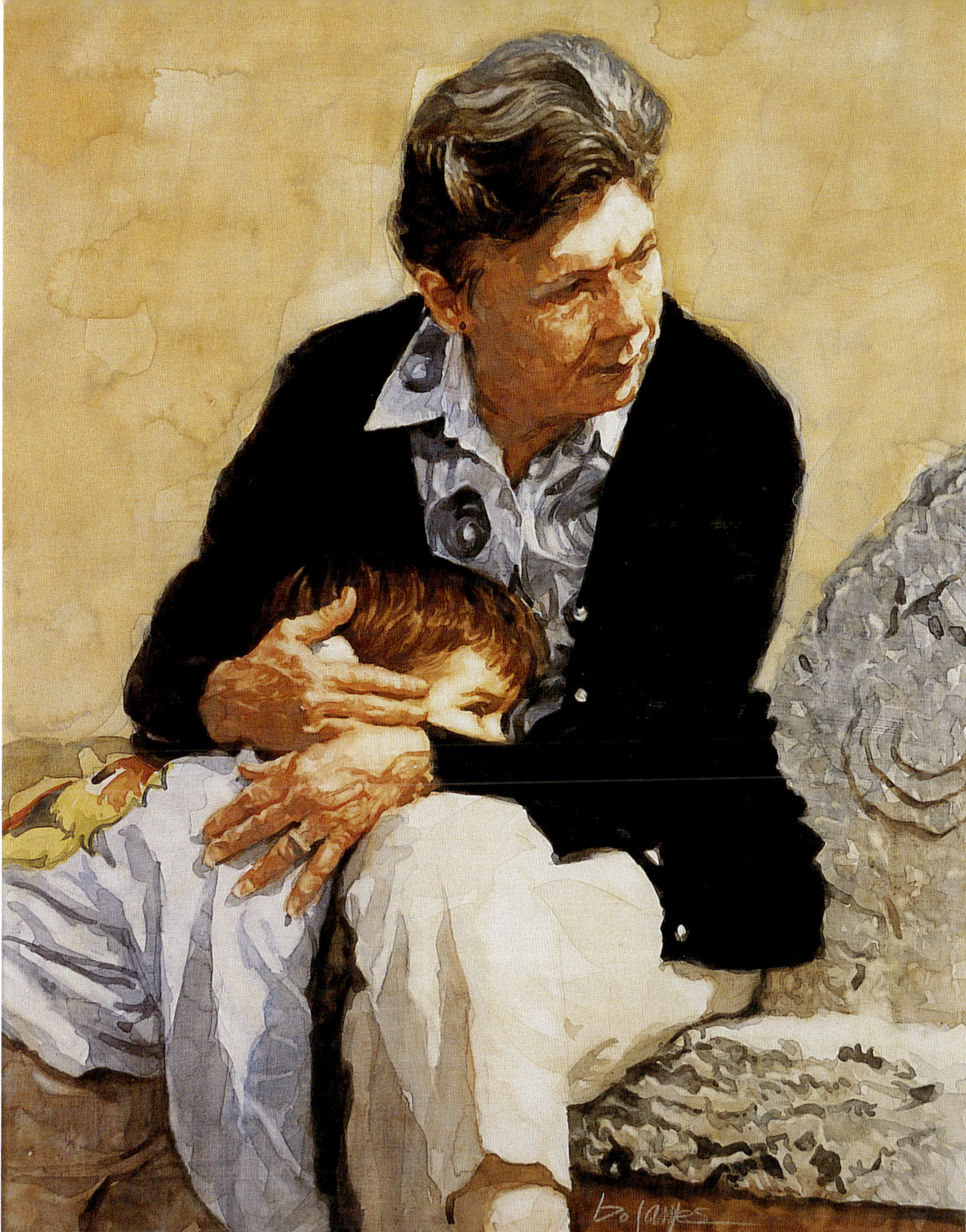

CUBAN GRANDMOTHER

Bill James • transparent gouache • 19" × 14" (48cm × 36cm)

ACKNOWLEDGMENTS

Much gratitude and credit goes to the editors, designers and staff at North Light Books who have done the work needed to make this into a beautiful book, including Megan Milstead, Sarah Laichas, Jennifer Hoffman, Vicki Adang, Roseann Biederman and Matt Wagner. There are many detailed stages to the creation of this book and many individual parts that have to be brought together. It is a job that "takes a village." Special thanks to Vanessa Lyman who has partnered with me from the beginning.

Another special thanks to the contributing artists, without whom this would be a rather dull white book! Your beautiful creations, as well as your unusually generous and friendly approach to life, make you a very special bunch indeed. Aren't you glad there is no forced retirement age for artists? Some of you are still going strong into your eighties and show no sign of putting down the brush!

table of contents

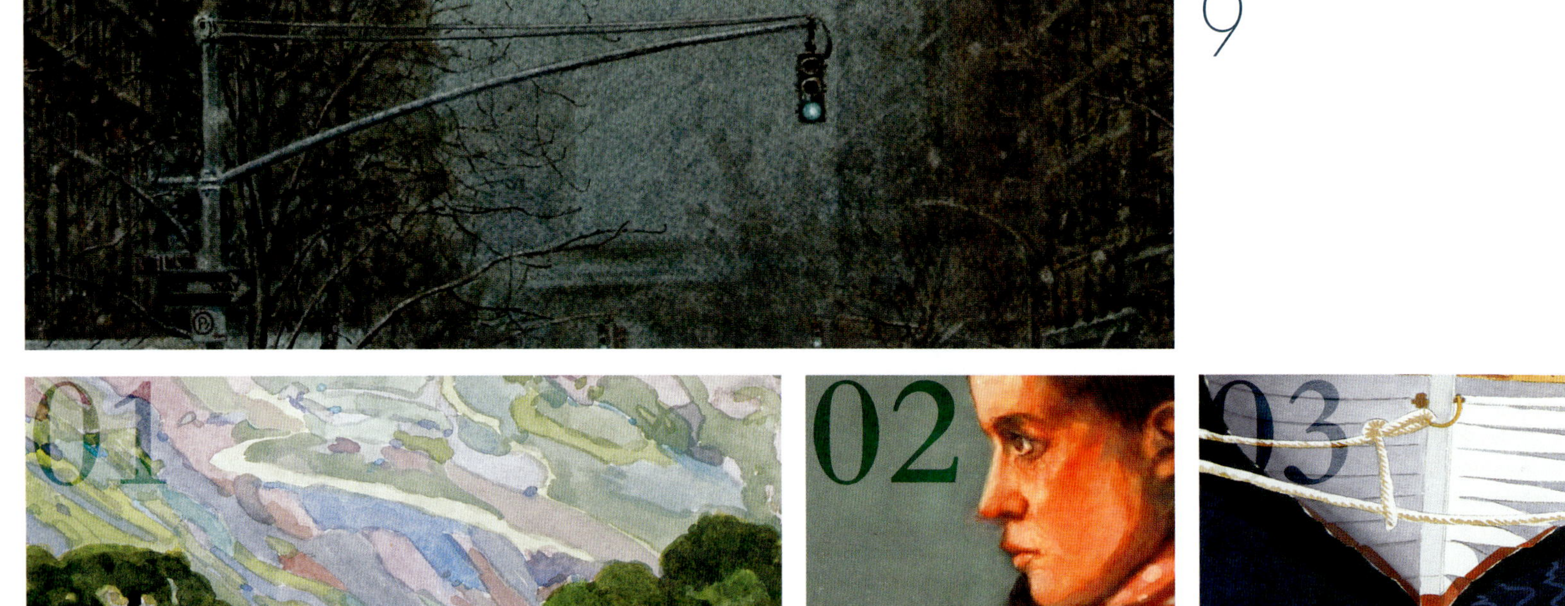

I love discovering landscape paintings. My passion is the magical process of turning the "That's a painting!" moment into a compelling image.

ROBIN PURCELL

With intense desire and passion, my paintings take me on a peaceful journey where time stands still and worries disappear.

CINDY AGAN

Pouring, spattering and freely splashing watercolor onto paper allows my passion to flow freely—from my heart, to my hand and through my brush.

JAIMIE CORDERO

Art is a platform to address one's passions.

MARY LOU FERBERT

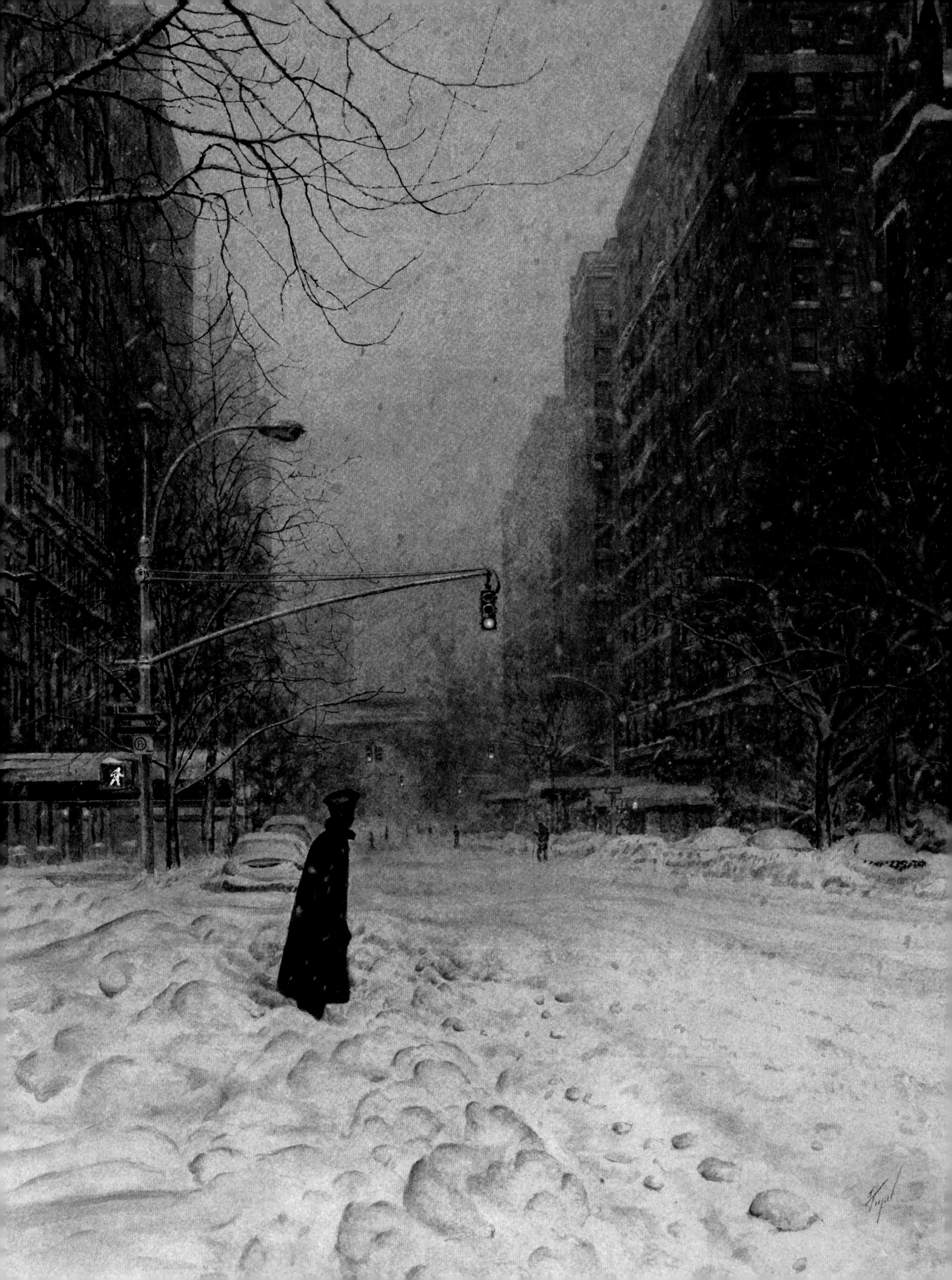

introduction

Well, fellow travelers, we have reached the tenth edition of this wonderful journey we call *Splash*. That is a benchmark worth noting. *Splash* has become a watercolor institution and has set a standard for tens of thousands of aspiring watercolor artists. Some of you will one day proudly see your work in *Splash*; many of you collect each edition that is published.

With the generosity of so many wonderful artists, *Splash* has been able to maintain the perfect balance between continuity and freshness. We see Margarat M. Martin's flower painting gracing the cover of the very first edition of *Splash*, published in the spring of 1991. And we see two of her new paintings, similar in style but with even more mastery, in this classic tenth edition. At least five other artists featured in this book—Neil Adamson, Mary Lou Ferbert, Kwan Jung, Don O'Neill and Pat San Soucie—also appeared in the first edition in 1991. Many others have been in multiple editions of *Splash*, including Mark Mehaffey and James Toogood, whose work you see here. But there are also many fresh new watercolorists who are making their first appearance in *Splash 10*.

It shouldn't have, but it surprised me just how passionate our artists were about our theme for this edition: passionate brushstrokes. Watercolor painters are unabashedly passionate about their painting—and, lucky for us, are happy to share that passion. Throughout the book we have scattered quotes by these artists in answer to two questions: In what way are you passionate about your painting? How do your brushstrokes express your passion?

All of the artists expressed how much watercolor painting is an integral part of their lives and very being. Joyce Roletto Faulknor sums it up simply by saying, "Paint with joy and happiness, and success will follow."

My hope, as always, is that this beautiful tenth volume of *Splash* brings you much joy and happiness. You can't have more success than that!

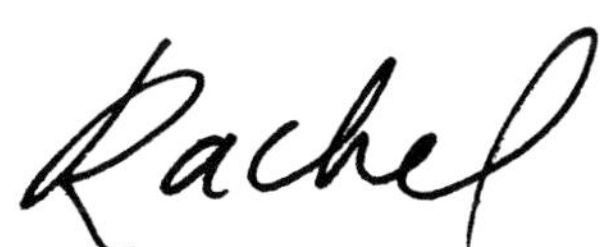

BLIZZARD IN THE VILLAGE

James Toogood • watercolor on paper • 24" × 18" (61cm × 46cm)

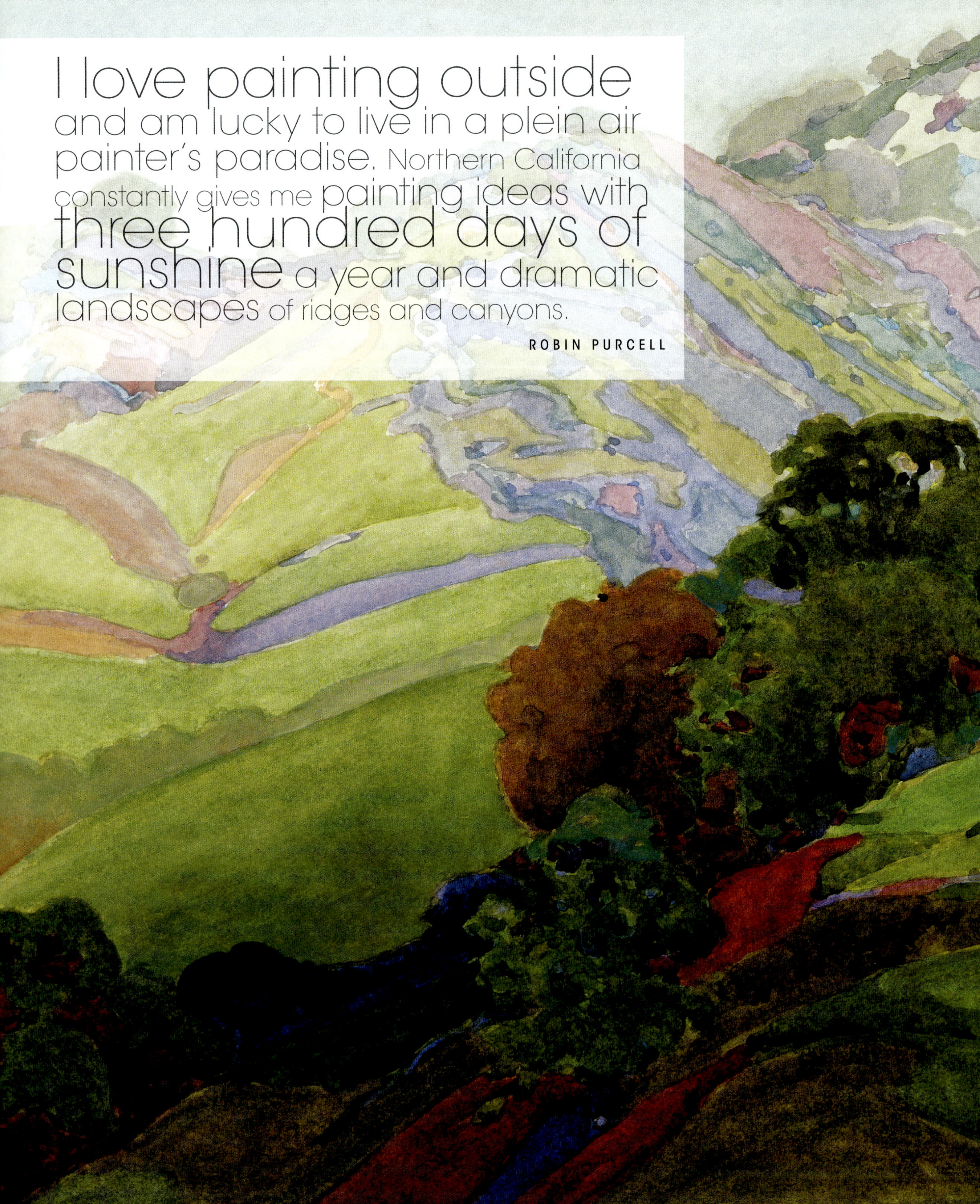

GREEN DAY

Robin Purcell • transparent watercolor on 300-lb. (640gsm) paper • 14" × 21" (36cm × 53cm)

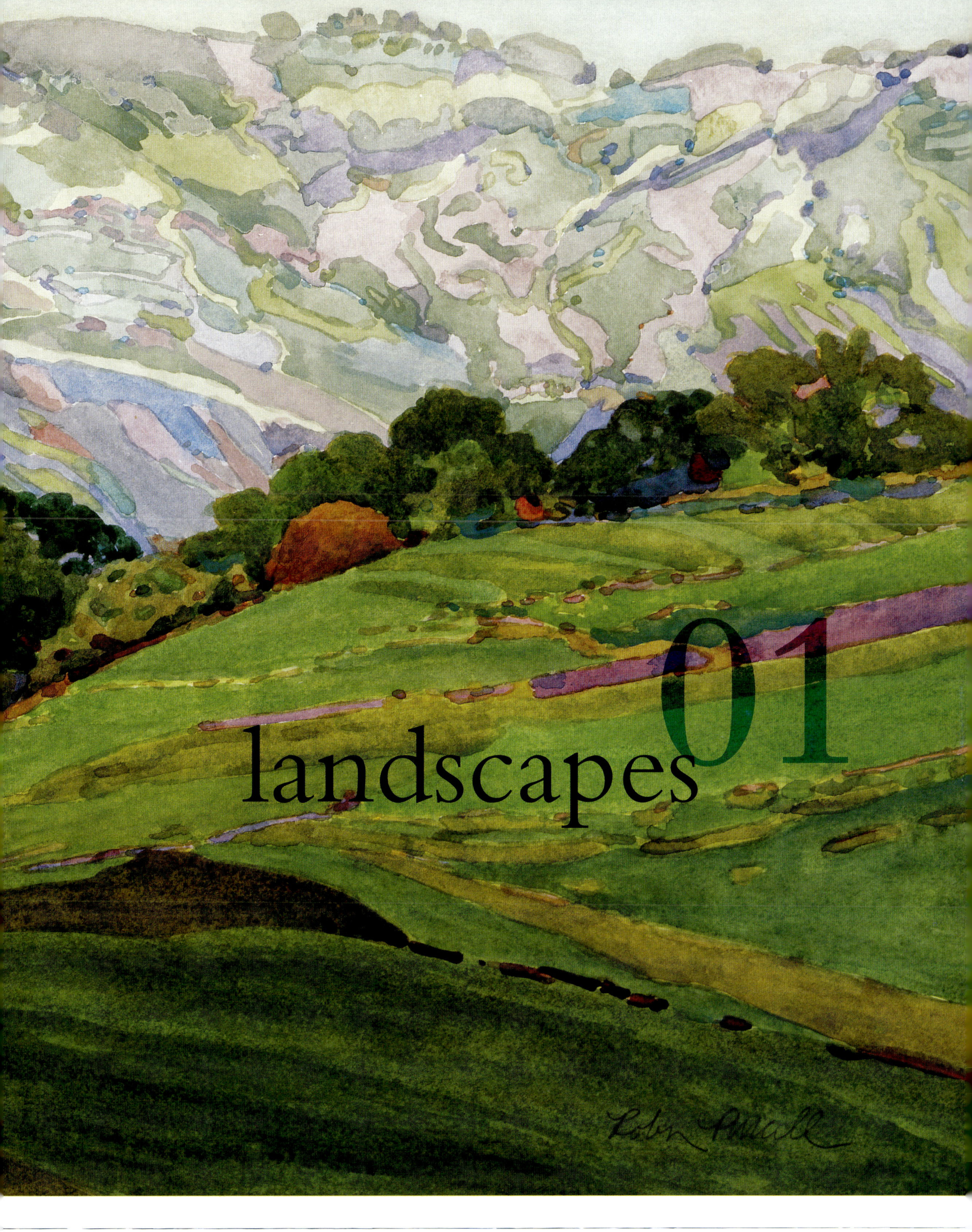

landscapes 01

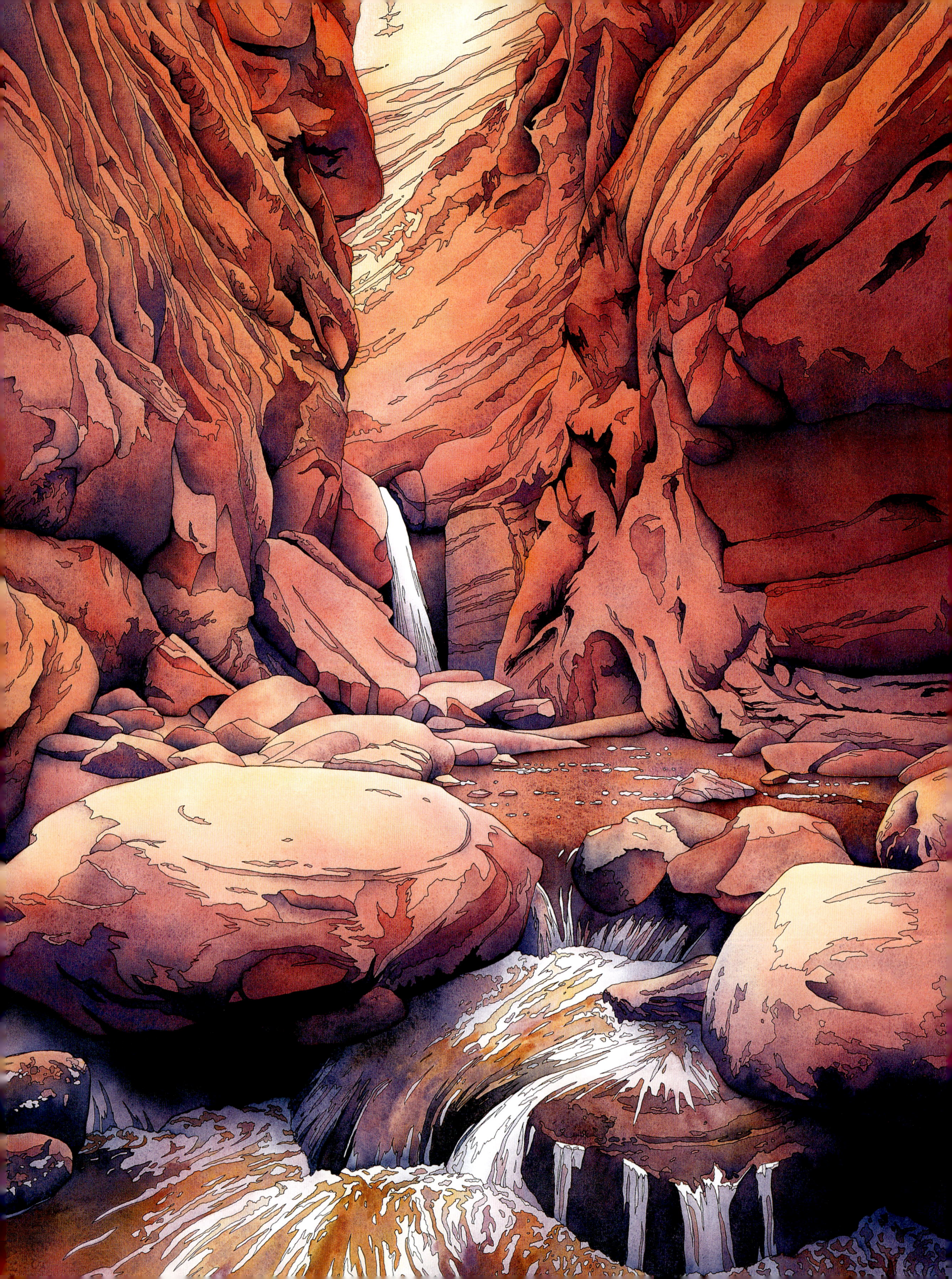

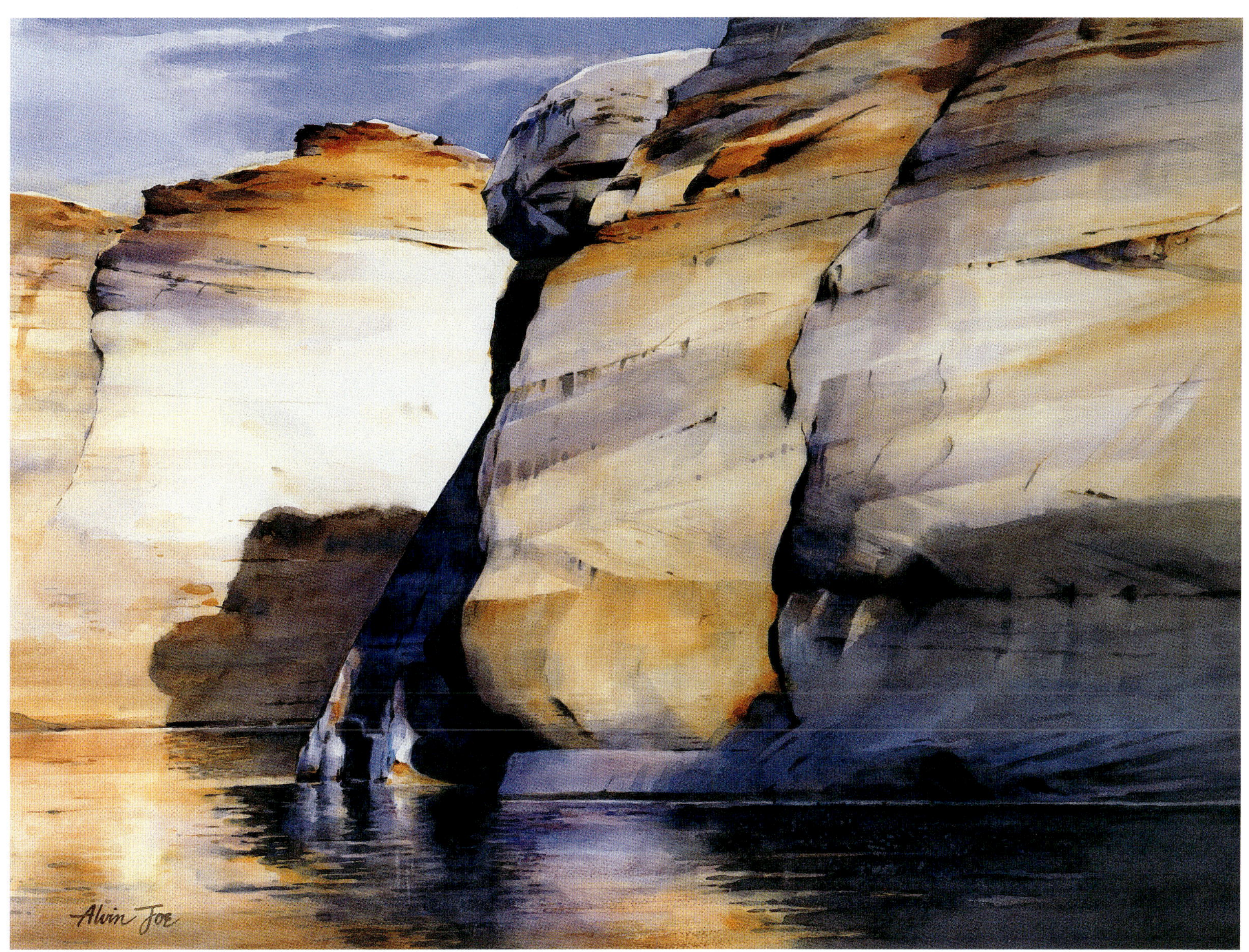

LAKE POWELL NARROW

Alvin Joe • transparent watercolor • 21" × 28" (53cm × 71cm)

In the late afternoon, the captain expertly maneuvered our ferryboat through this narrow part of Lake Powell located in the western U.S. The awesome rock formations tower above the lake, creating memorable shadows and reflections. My immediate desire was to capture this impressive display of nature in watercolor. I made 4" × 6" (10cm × 15cm) prints from the 35mm camera I carry on my trips. With additions and subtractions in the design, using 2-inch (51mm) and ¾-inch (19mm) flat brushes, I kept attacking with transparent layers of colors wet-into-wet from light to dark, warm to cool.

SUSTENANCE

Jonathan Frank • watercolor and India ink • 29" × 21½" (74cm × 55cm)

I photographed this scene in June. Several weeks later, I hiked back to the canyon to obtain further references, only to find this scene no longer exists. Two weeks after my first visit, a flash flood had washed away all the boulders and lowered the creek level by 5 feet (1.5m). Events such as this give me renewed awe and passionate interest in the effects of water in the desert. The painting is essentially a design of abstract shapes. Each one was painted with hard edges and multiple glazes to achieve rich color. After the painting is complete, I outline every shape I just painted. This unifies the painting, makes it clean and creates the effect of looking upon the scene with hyper-clarity, as if you could see everything perfectly.

Brushstrokes serve as the exclamation point for the whole painting process!

JONATHAN FRANK

I was born with a "thirsty brush" in my hand. My thirst for watercolor has never been satiated.

PAM STANLEY

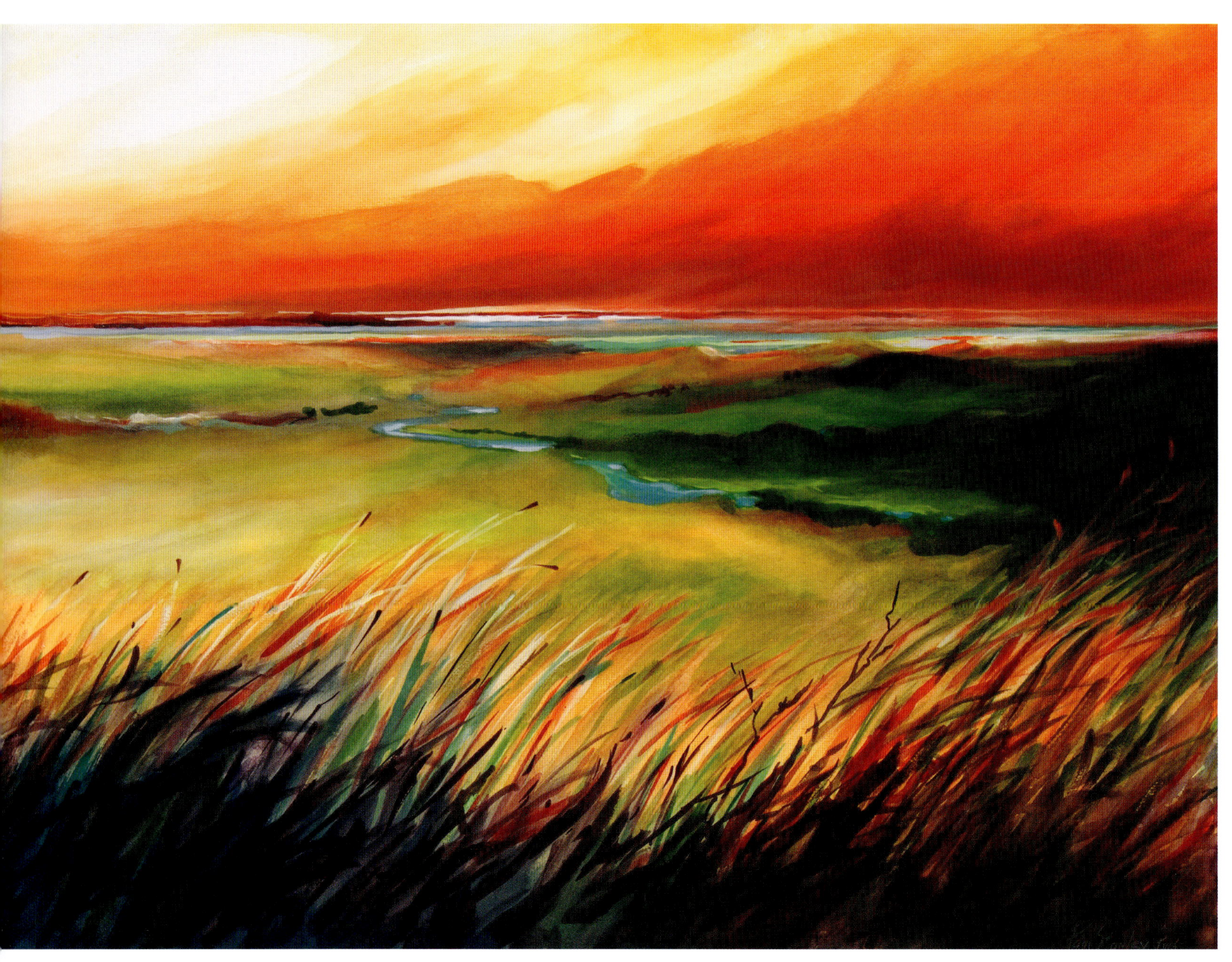

SEA SCAPE I

Pam Stanley • watercolor on 140-lb. (300gsm) cold-pressed paper • 20" × 30" (51cm × 76cm)

My paintings evolve in my bright, white studio. Beginning with random brushstrokes, I imagine early mornings at the beach—the intercoastal beyond the marshland, the movement of storm clouds—all treasured memories of my childhood on two coasts. These thoughts influence every brushstroke, from my 2-inch (51mm) gesso scrubber to my small, round, fabric dye brush. I prefer a "less water, more paint" approach.

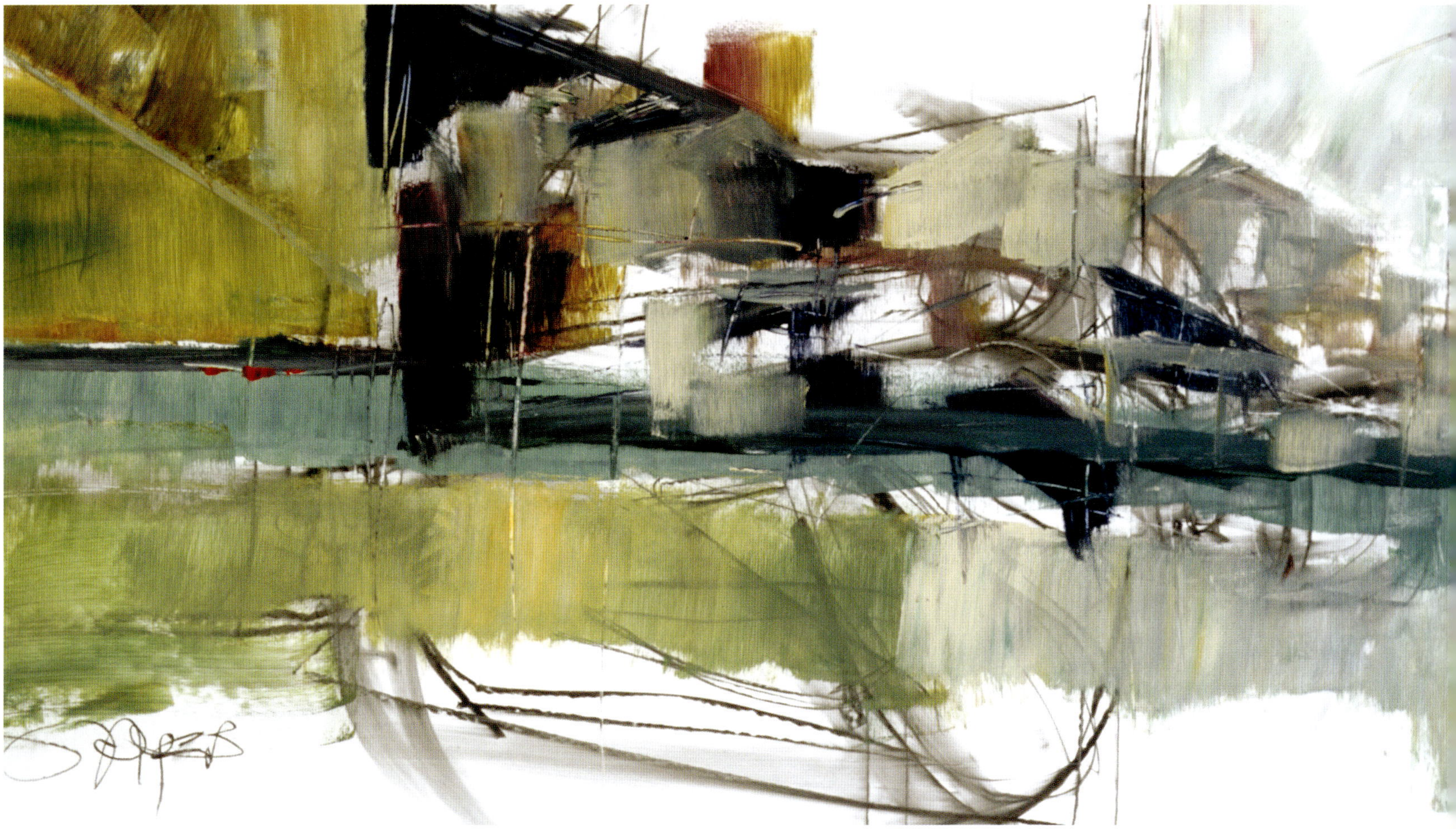

VILLAS Y MAR

Donald Sayers • acrylic on synthetic paper • 33" × 50" (84cm × 127cm)

For many years I attended Flying Colors Art workshops and retreats in Mexico. *Villas y Mar* was inspired by the Caleta Beach neighborhood of Acapulco. From a series of photos and memory, I did a quick sketch with compressed chalk. Then I laid in acrylic washes and pattern overlays with sponge brushes. Verticals were scratched out with a paintbrush handle. The impression of sand, sea and architecture express what I saw on walks to and from the beach. Drawing is the "bones" of my work, both tightly rendered and gestural elements. The composition is driven by the spin and visualization the drawing provides.

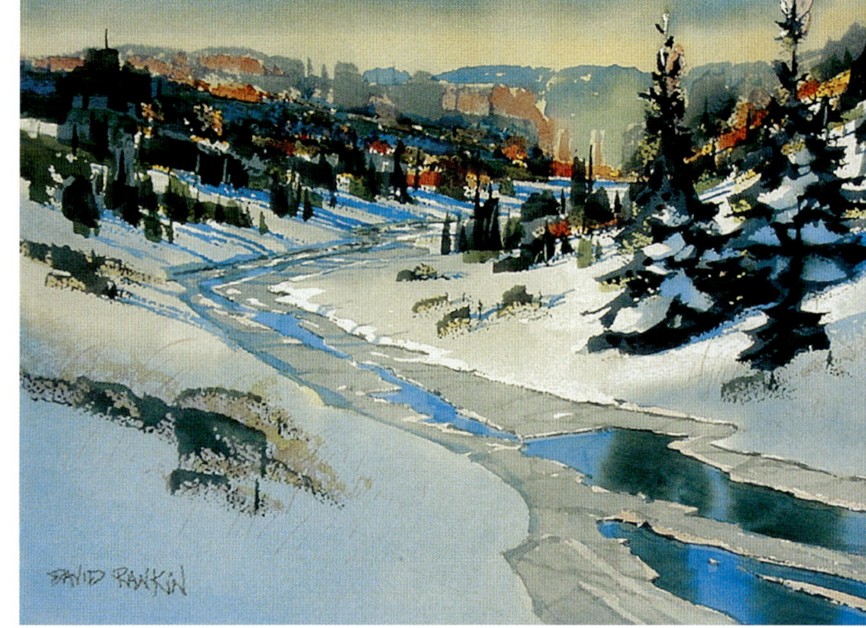

AFTERNOON LIGHT

David Rankin • transparent watercolor on 140-lb. (300gsm) rough paper • 12" × 14" (30cm × 36cm)

The intricate designs of winter streams cutting through deep snow are a subject that holds deep significance for me, representing the ever-present cycle of renewal within nature. Winter comes and we think she's killed off last season's harvest. But, in reality, she merely put the landscape to sleep, under a deep blanket of snow. No matter how deep the snow and ice, eventually these delicate and sinuous streams appear, cutting through the deepest snow and breaking the icy grip of winter—nature's symbol of renewed life and hope, the promise of spring.

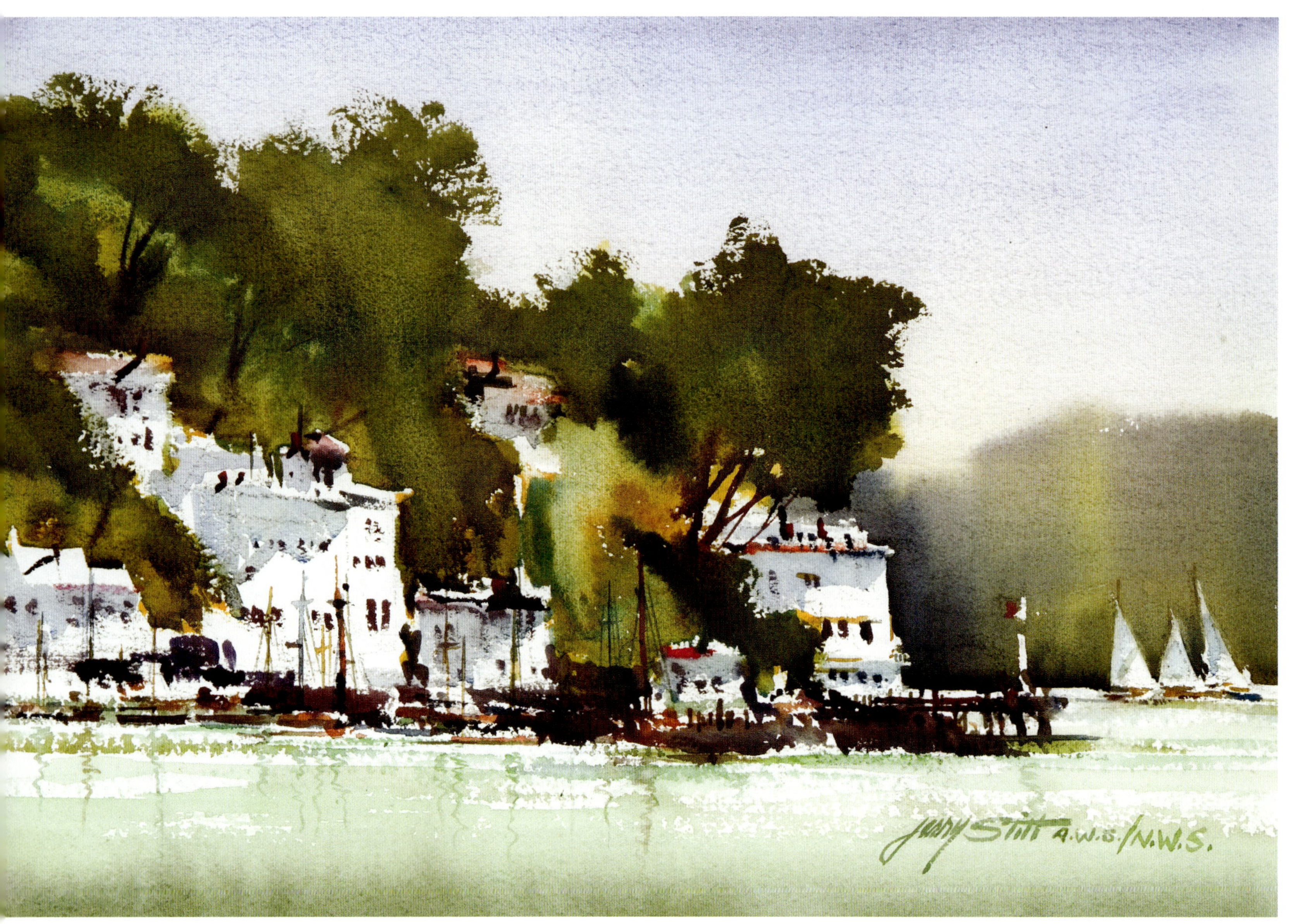

THE CORINTHIAN YACHT CLUB

Jerry Stitt • watercolor on 140-lb. (300gsm) cold-pressed paper • 14" × 20" (36cm × 51cm)

I would describe my style of painting as gestural. I don't paint what something is or how it looks; I paint what it is doing. A painting is good not because it looks like something, but because it feels like something. I select a color scheme to fit the mood I want to convey, for example, an atmospheric condition, early morning at the beach, or a wet, windy day. Because I use color to express the emotions and moods of these conditions, I like to paint on location. *The Corinthian Yacht Club* was painted on location in twenty-five minutes.

RED BARN COMPOSITION #5

Joseph Alleman • transparent watercolor on cold-pressed paper • 30" × 22" (76cm × 56cm)

This piece emerged from a series of sketches I did one evening at home. I had painted similar scenes both on location and from photos, but this was unique in that my imagination and past experience were the only actual sources. In doing so, I've drawn from the surroundings of where I live. When I create a scene like this, I feel a closeness to both the land and its inhabitants. It's as if I'm on the outside looking in, wanting to know more about this scene I've authored. The barn is a monument, a remnant of someone's past, standing for generations. The snow-lined paths, on the other hand, are fleeting in nature, creating a sense of being in the moment.

To see something familiar unfold with such newness through paint is a wonderful motivation for me.

JOSEPH ALLEMAN

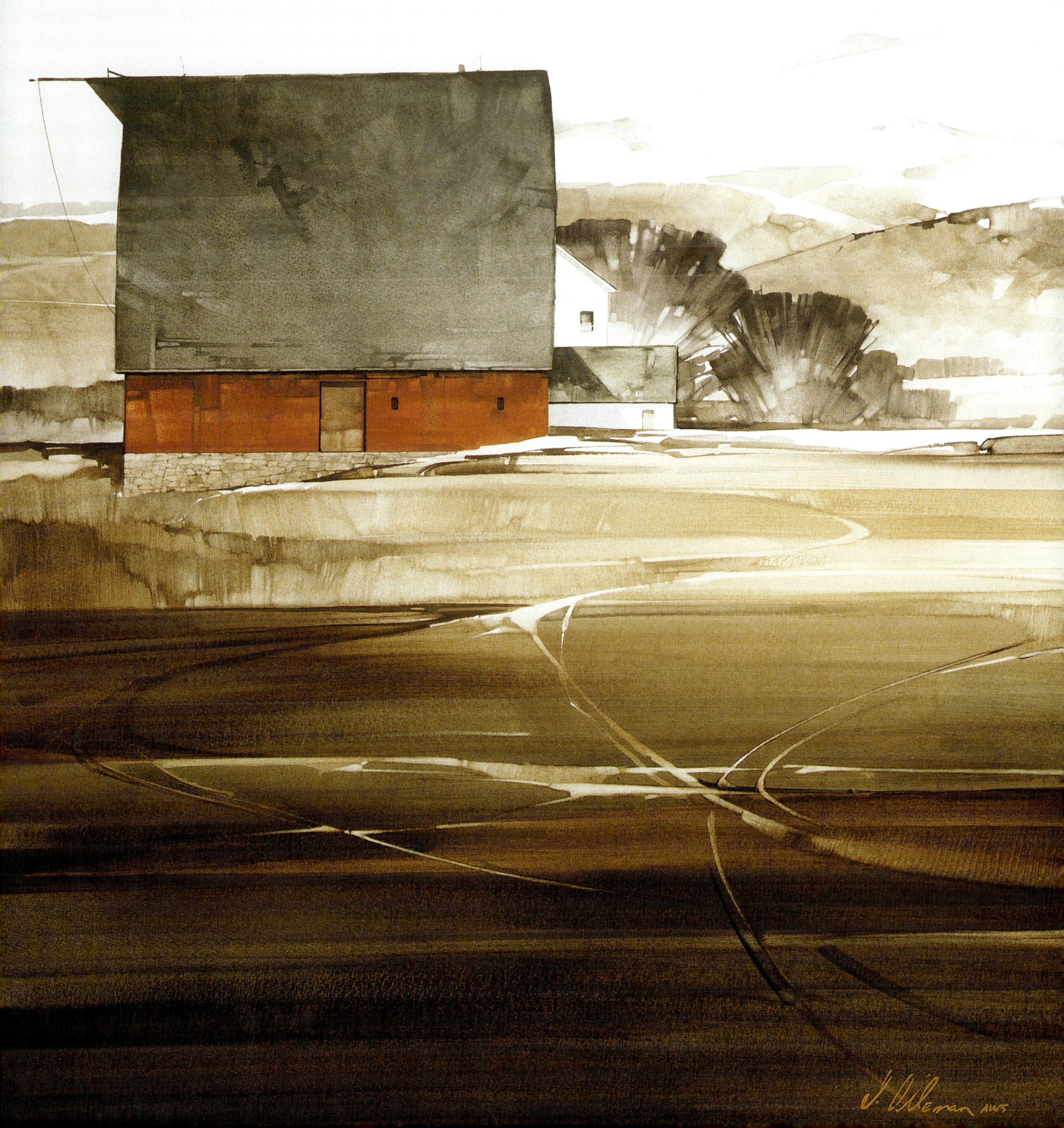

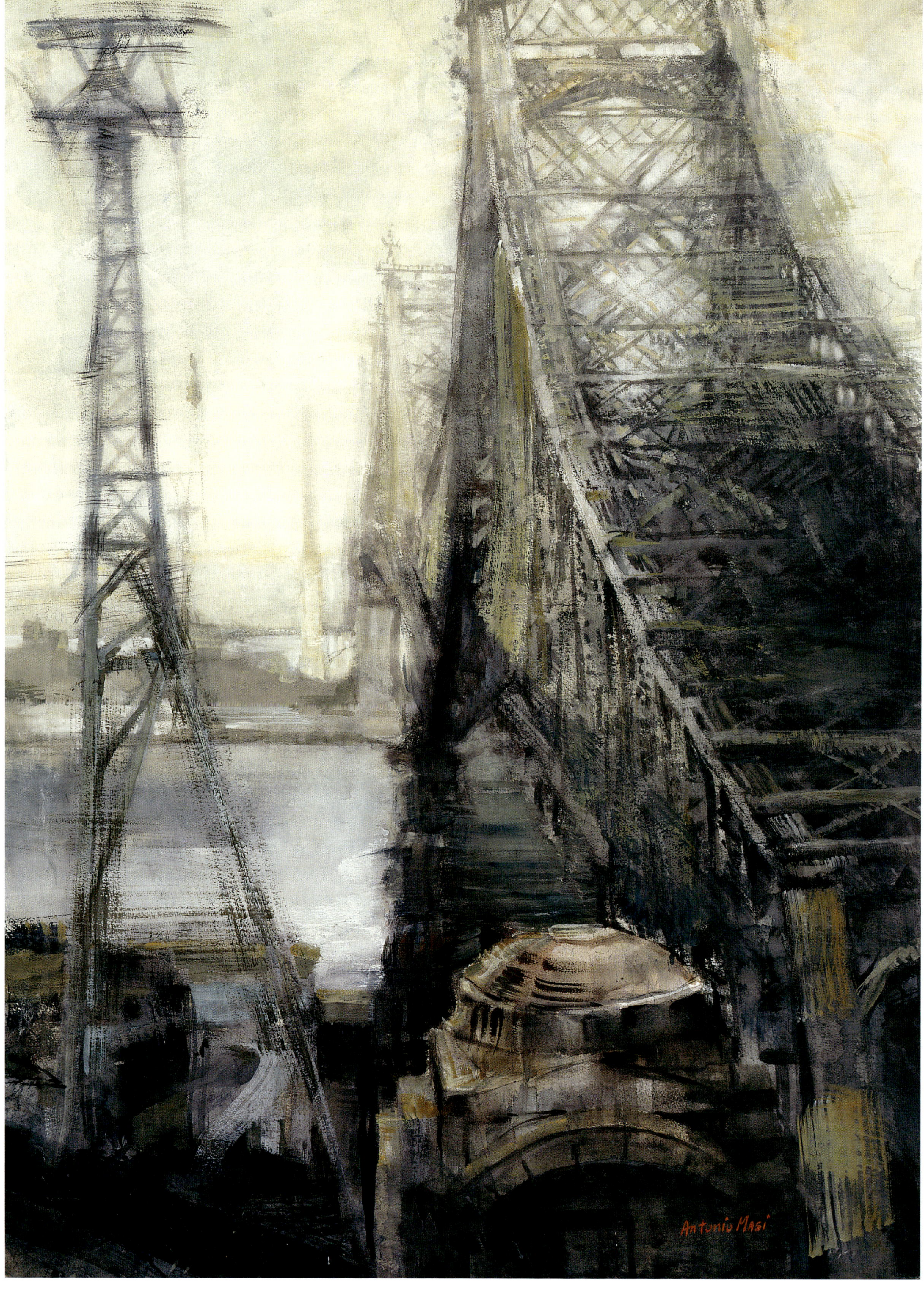
Antonio Masi

N.Y. TRAMWAY II

Antonio Masi • transparent watercolor with body color • 53" × 38" (135cm × 97cm)

The painting was done from riding on the tramway, on-site sketches, photographs and memory. Every stroke has its own inner life. I paint with quick and energetic strokes to create a textural surface. I contrast this with multiple glazes using 6-inch to 8-inch hake brushes on rough watercolor paper. This painting depicts the overpowering sensation of my first impression of the city. When I was seven, I came to New York City with my family from Italy. I have indelible impressions of Manhattan, of the boat docked that night, the immensity of the city and the thousands of glowing lights. I wanted to recreate that overwhelming sensation.

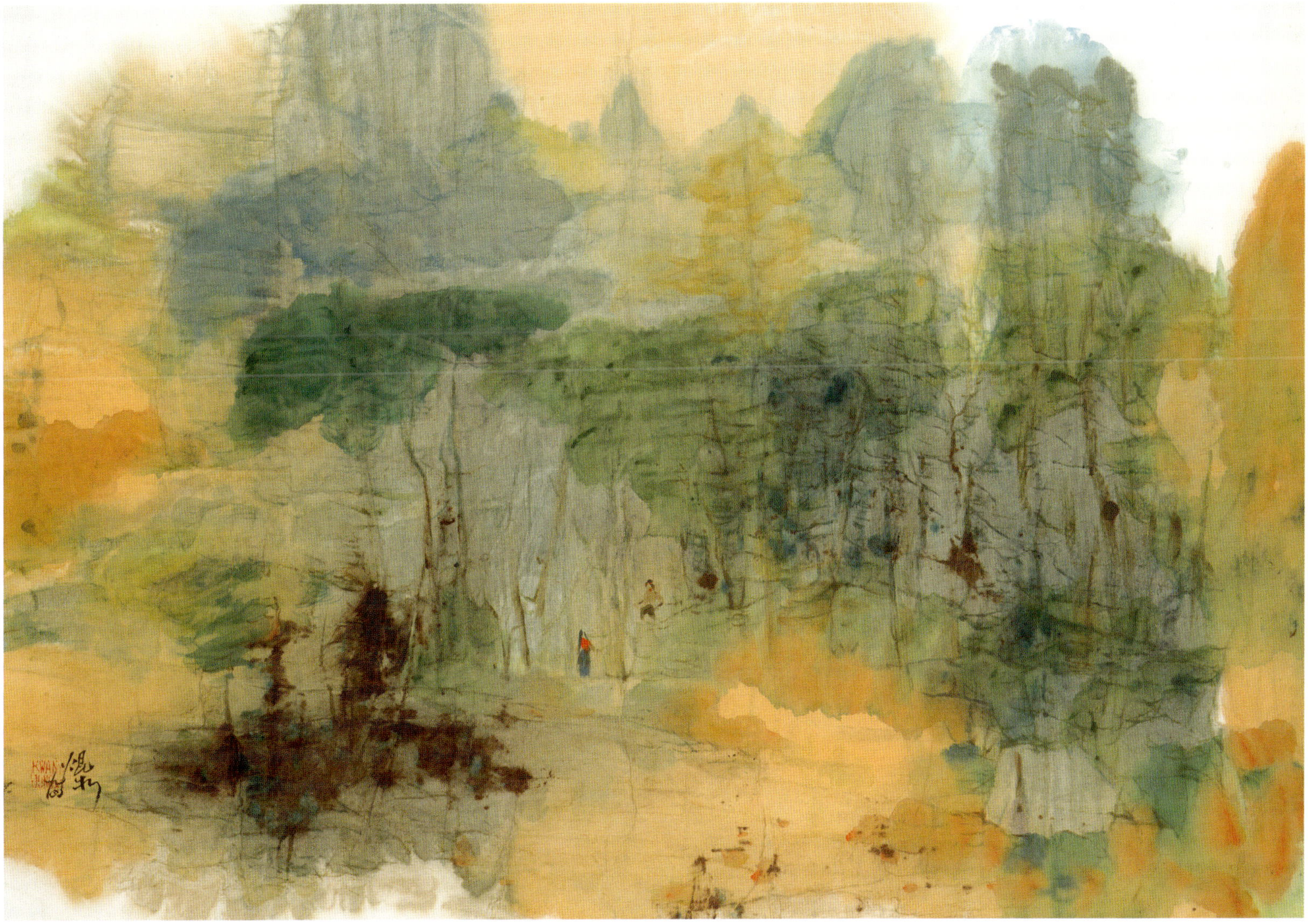

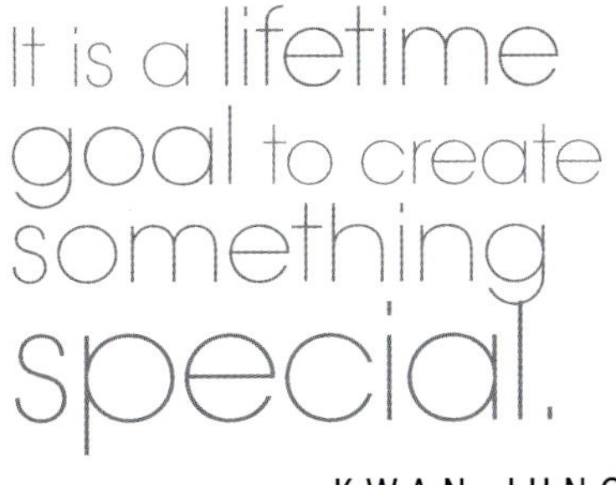

ENGAGEMENT IN THE PARK

Kwan Jung • acrylic on rice paper • 27" × 38" (69cm × 97cm)

I paint on rice paper with a difficult wet technique. I lay the rice paper flat on a table with absorbing paper underneath. I then select some color mixtures to pour on, and some strokes of brushwork follow. Usually the rice paper and the paper underneath turn into one wet piece, which is nearly impossible to separate by hand. I blot wet spots and then squeeze some water out by placing a bigger sheet of dry paper on top and wiping outward. I then carefully remove and discard this blotting paper. Finally, I place one large piece of dry paper on top of the rice paper. I line up one edge and start rolling from one end to the other to form a round tube. In doing so, the rice paper separates from the wet paper underneath. After cleaning the table, I put the tube down on a new sheet of dry paper and reverse the rolling process from the end to the beginning. I carefully separate the top paper from the rice paper, and the rice paper is ready for drying out and more brushwork.

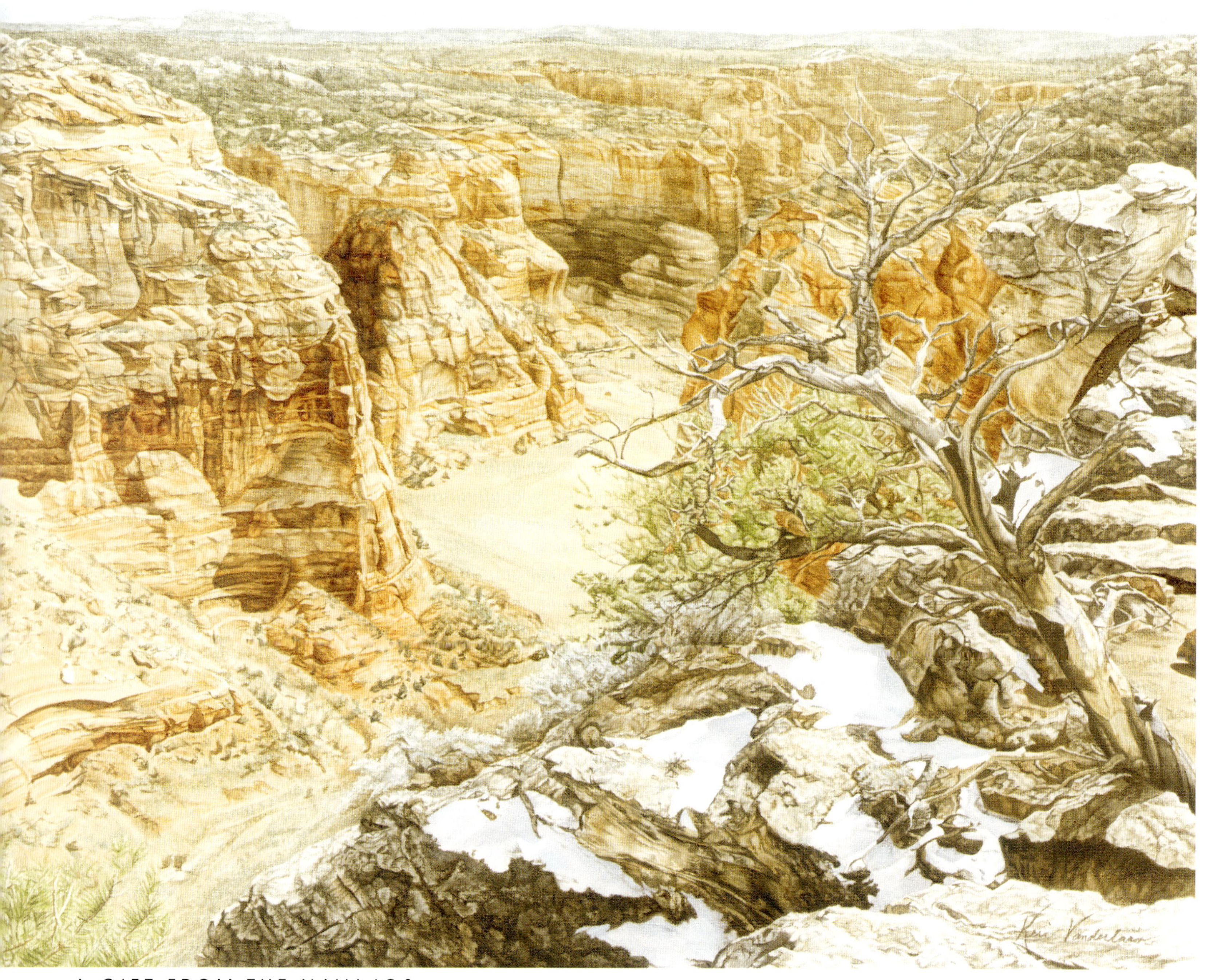

A GIFT FROM THE NAVAJOS

Keri Vanderlaan • transparent watercolor • 22" × 22" (56cm × 56cm)

This painting was done from photographs I took while visiting Canyon de Chelly National Monument, which is located in the Navajo Nation. I had been compelled to visit this park for years. I could only spend one day there and was very disappointed because the sky was heavily overcast and I wasn't able to get great photos. As I was about to leave the park, suddenly the clouds parted, revealing the vibrant reds and golds in the bright sunshine. I believe I was drawn to this place for a reason, and this painting is truly a gift from the Navajos. My painting strokes are very meticulous and every stroke counts. I painted an undertone of Raw Sienna to give the painting a warm glow and generally layered straight tube colors of transparent watercolors.

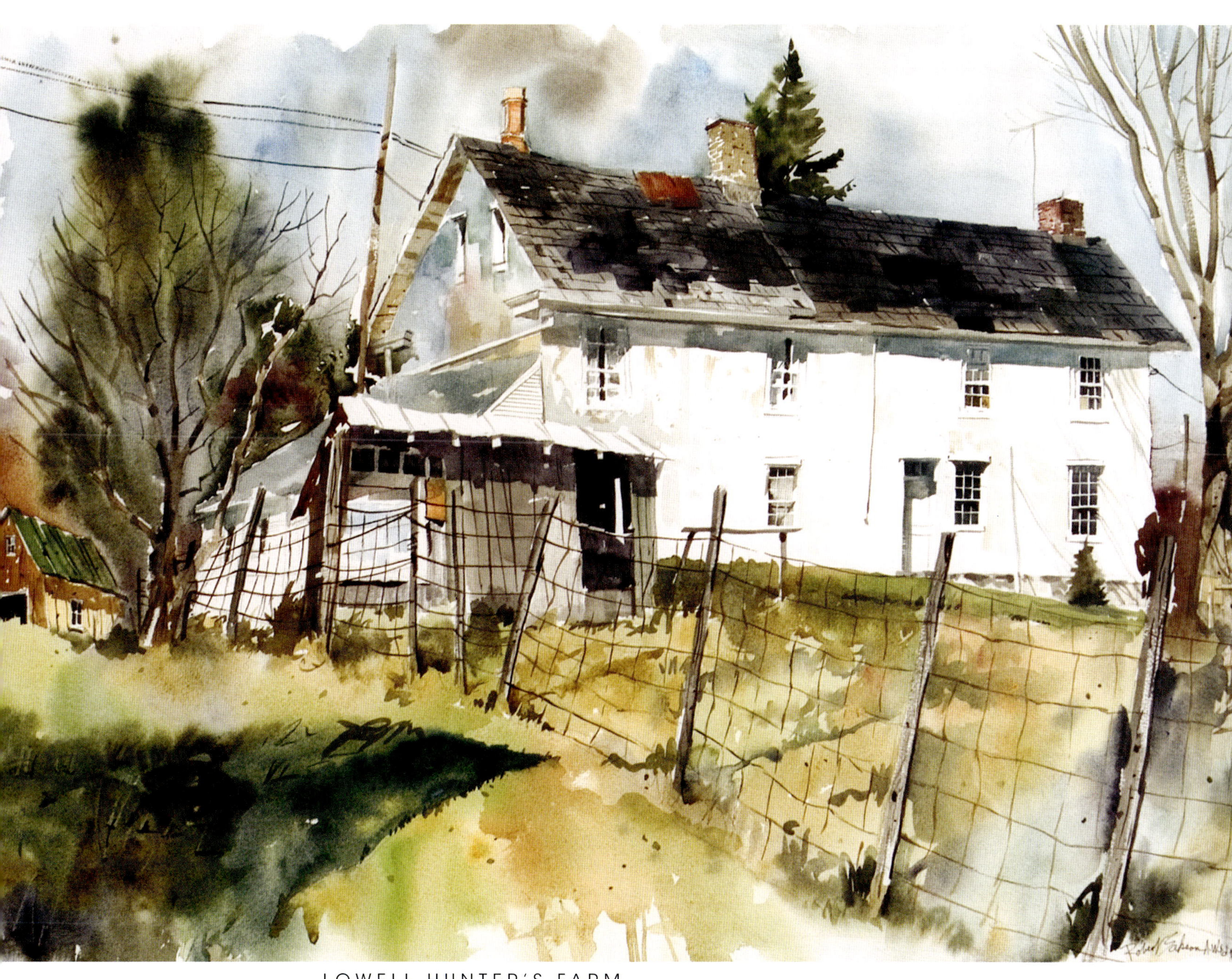

LOWELL HUNTER'S FARM

Robert Sakson • transparent watercolor • 22" × 30" (56cm × 76cm)

My artistic passion has always been the landscape. The various seasons with their ever-changing light and color fascinate me. This painting was done in the studio from a sketch and photos taken the same day. As a plein air painter, much of my work is done on 18" × 24" (46cm × 61cm) watercolor blocks on location and then developed in the studio. I try to capture the mood and spirit of the way the light plays on the subject. My interest in this place peaked when I met Lowell Hunter. Brought here at age nine, he hunted and farmed this land over eighty years. The house, built in the 1800s, has its original stone construction. This working farmhouse, painted from a low angle along the fence line, literally "explodes" from the surrounding land as the centerpiece of this painting. The history and color of this area has inspired my paintings for over forty years.

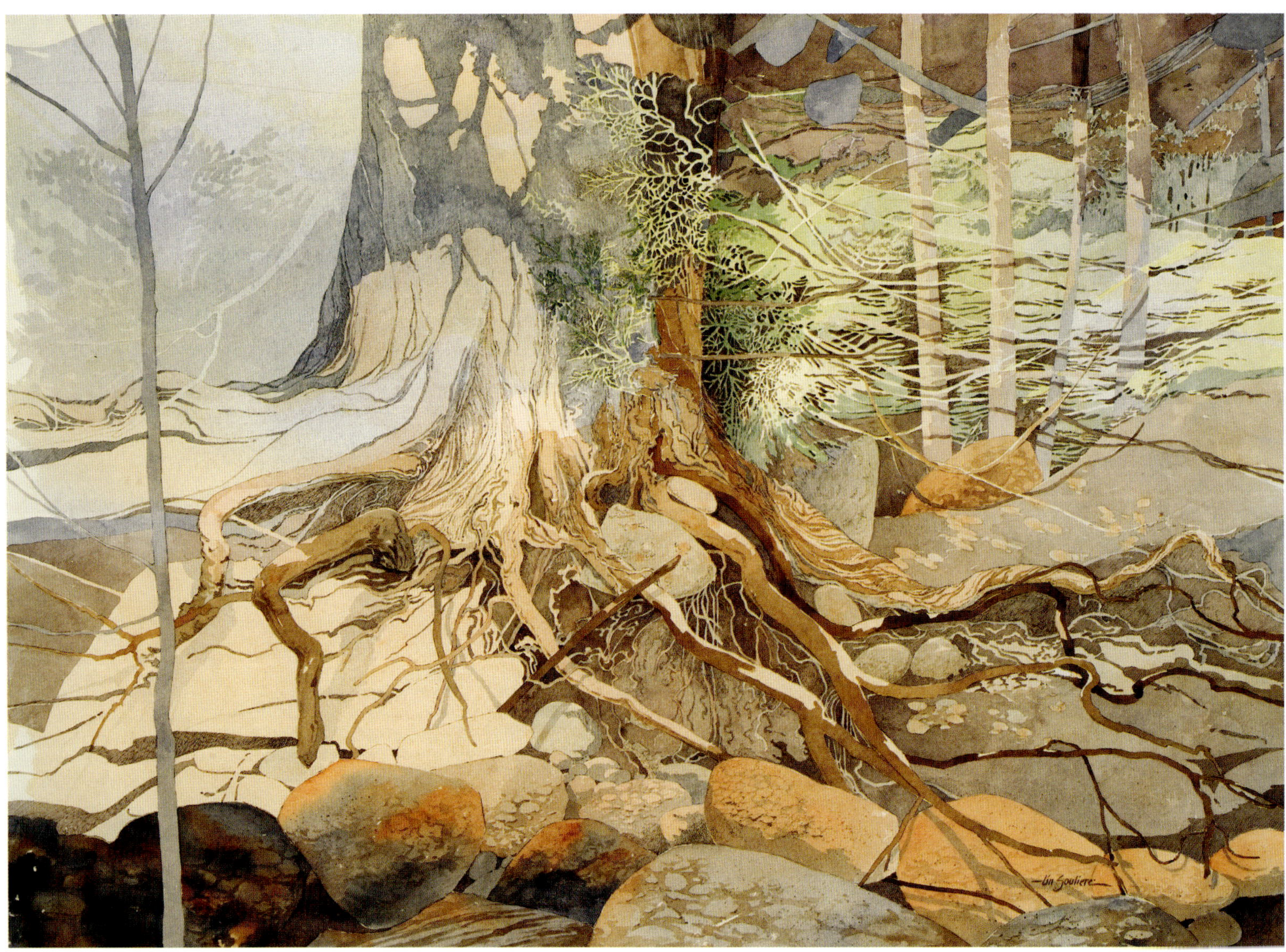

ANCIENT WITNESS II

Lin Souliere • transparent watercolor and ink on 300-lb. (640gsm) paper. • 22" × 30" (56cm × 76cm)

Ancient Witness is one of a series of paintings based on the Georgian Bay coastline where I live. The water holds a fascination for me—a world of hidden energy that bubbles to the surface to join the earth; a cycle of resurrection repeating itself, spring to summer, fall to winter. The old, twisted trees and rocks bear witness to it all. I paint to express this idea. Working from on-site sketches, reference photos, and bits of rock, fern and branches brought into my studio, I made the drawing with a fine-point ink pen. Then I poured saturated watercolor onto the drawing, gently moving the pigment around with my hands. This can all become mud if overworked. I finished the painting with expressive brushstrokes, creating negative shapes and intricate patterns, always allowing the light to glow through.

COLUMBIA GORGE

Kathy Collins • watercolor on paper • 40" × 34" (102cm × 86cm)

Pacific Northwest water and mountain views always inspire me, but one late afternoon's hike to a viewpoint above the Columbia River Gorge rewarded me with an especially stunning scene. Fifteen hundred feet below me, intense golden sunrays glanced off the backlit water as the river twisted and turned, disappearing into a brilliant haze. I pulled my sketchbook from my backpack and penned a quick drawing. Later in the studio, I tried to capture the feeling of that moment by splashing transparent Burnt Sienna and Crimson Lake directly onto the paper, wet-into-wet. I brushed in the land forms using darker earth tones and French Ultramarine while the edges were still damp, and then added thicker paint of the same hues for the darkest shadows. The resulting painting recalls for me that dramatic scene and the vivid impression it made.

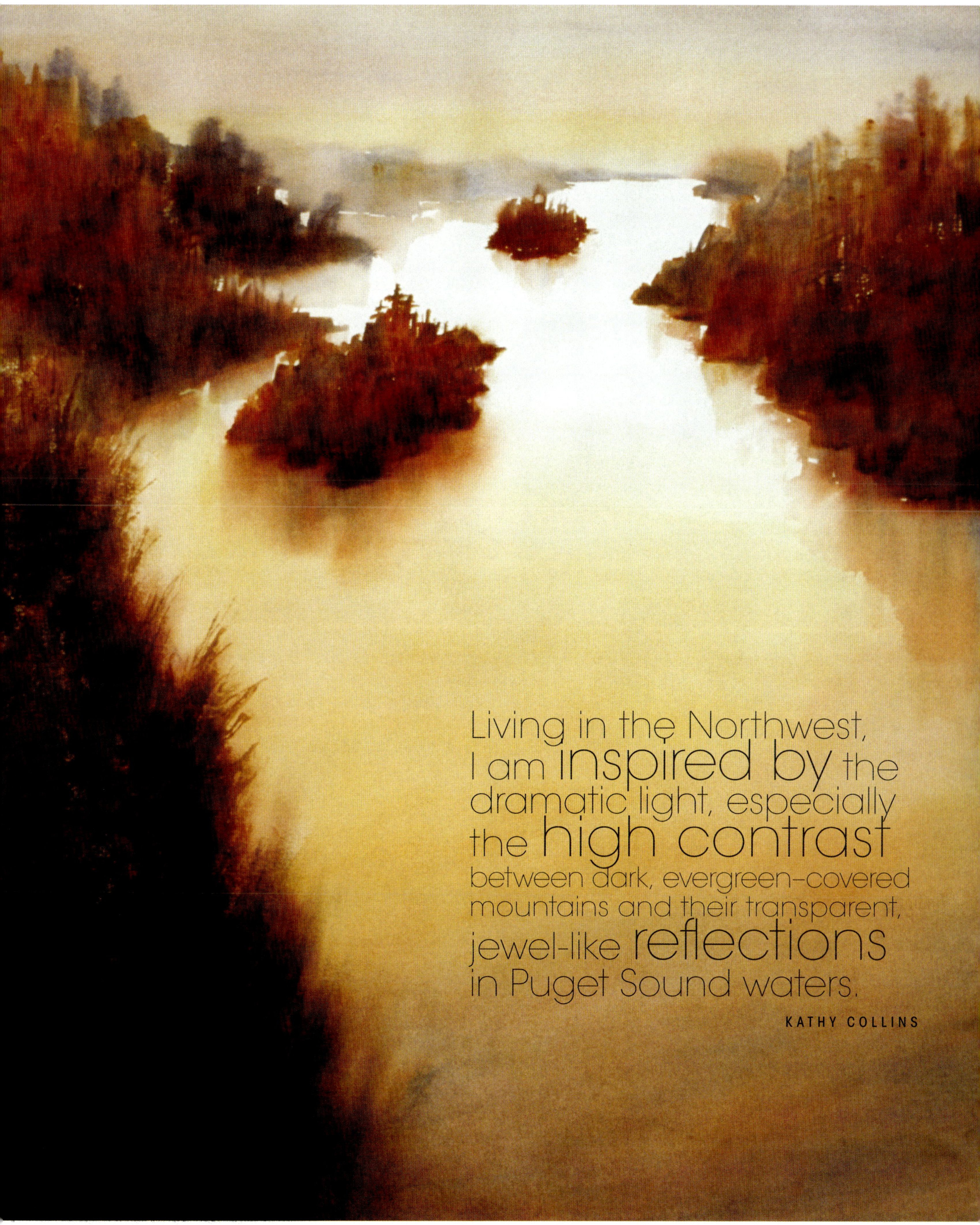
Living in the Northwest,
I am inspired by the
dramatic light, especially
the high contrast
between dark, evergreen–covered
mountains and their transparent,
jewel-like reflections
in Puget Sound waters.
KATHY COLLINS

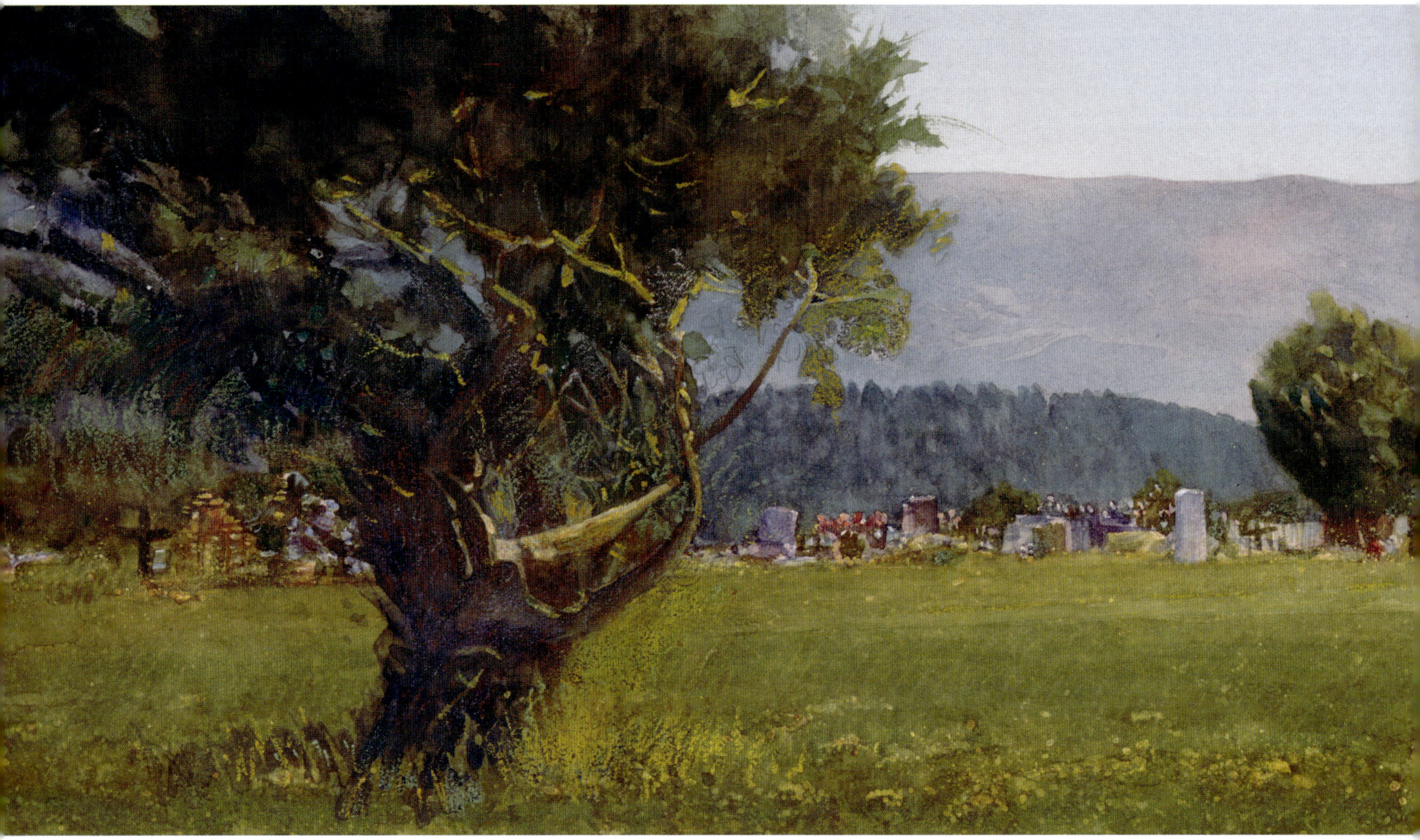

My reverence for nature imbues me to the core, and I simply must communicate this passion through my art.

DONALD W. PATTERSON

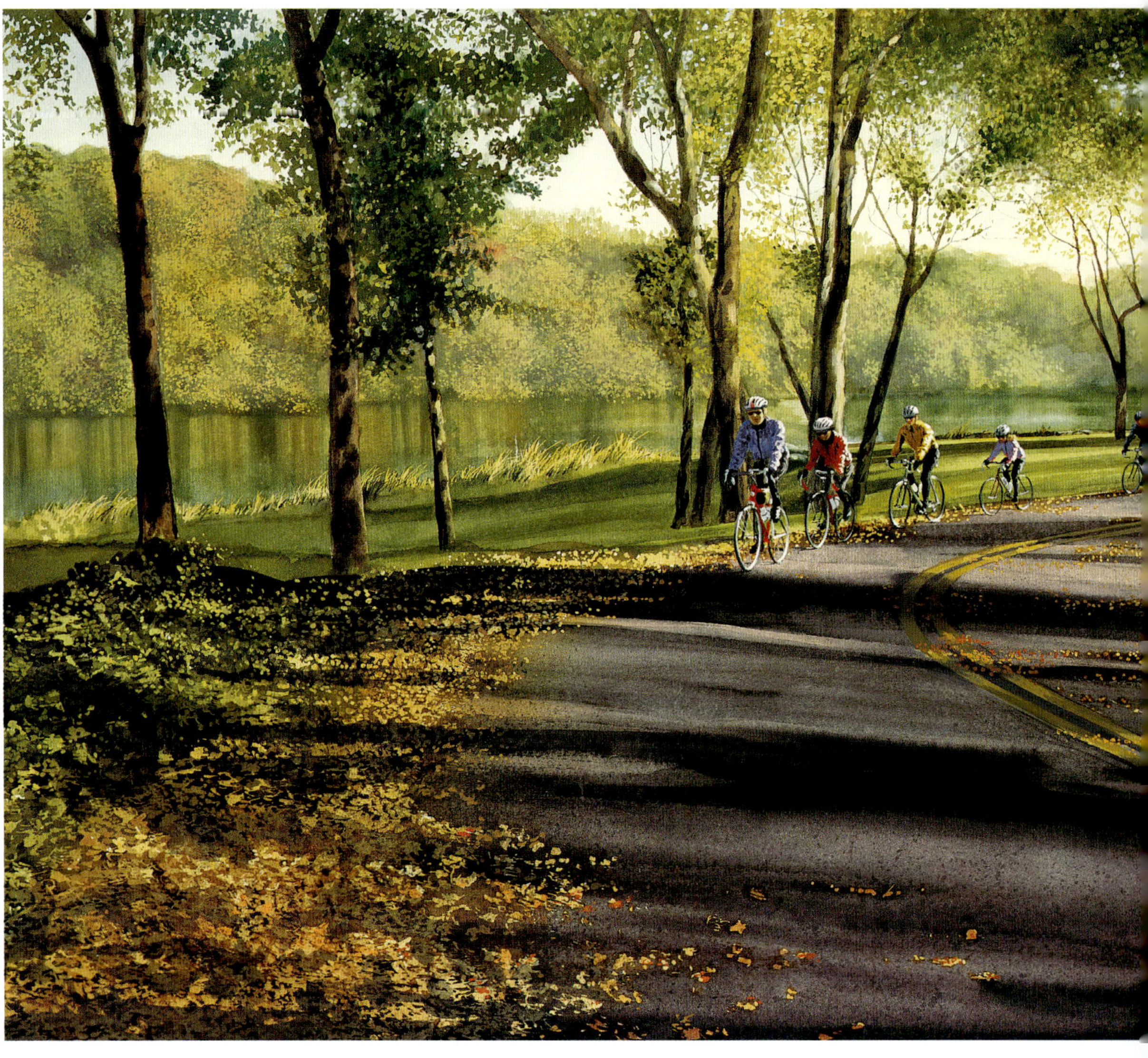

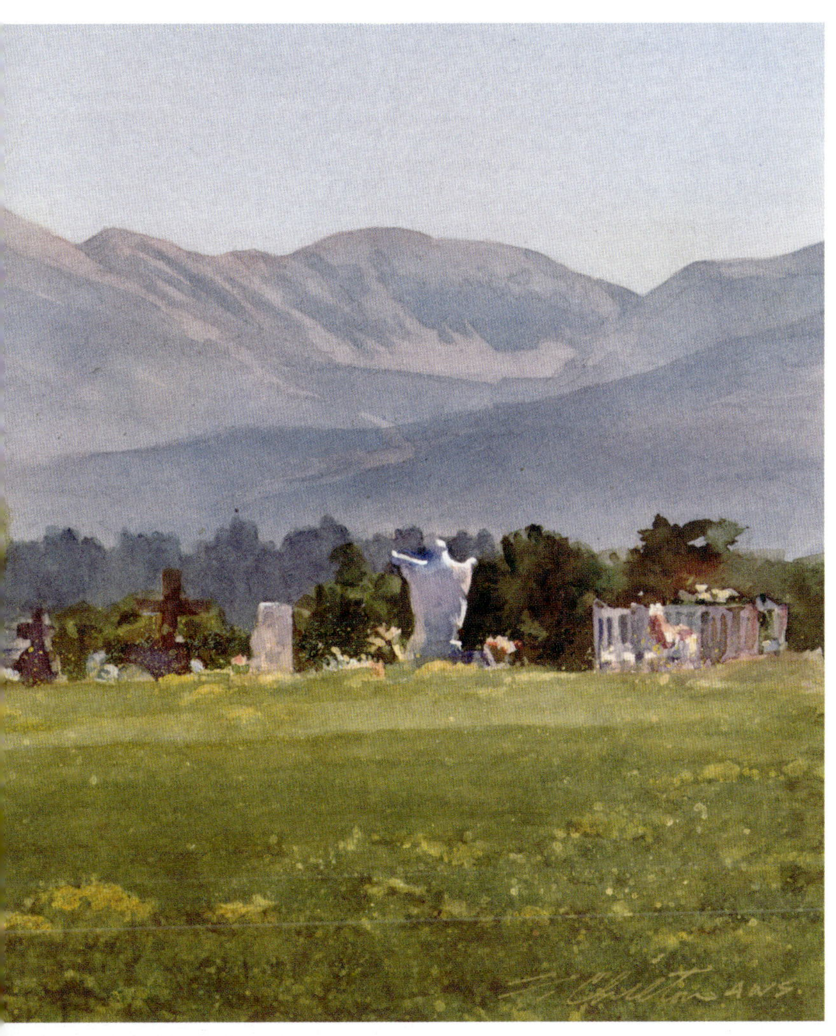

CEMETERY AT TRUCHAS

Fred Chilton • watercolor with pastel accents on cold-pressed paper • 12" × 32" (30cm × 81cm)

This cemetery is located on a flat, grassy plateau in the midst of pine-studded mountains of huge scale. The dramatic icon of Jesus seems as if he is blessing the whole world! Using photographic references in my studio, the statue of Christ and other features of light value were masked with liquid masking fluid while the sky was painted in a gradated wet wash. A variety of brushstrokes and textures were used on the headstones and other small features. Pastel was used to indicate grass around the foreground tree and to add texture and color to the tree itself.

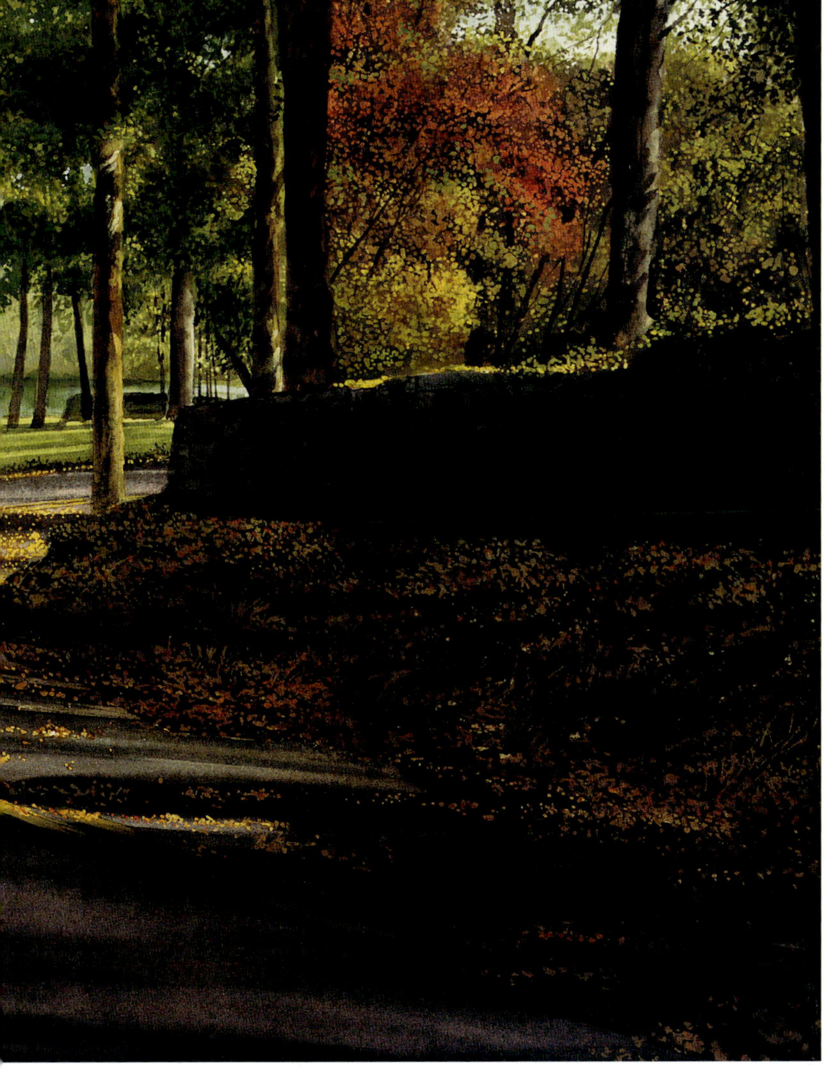

RIVER ROAD

Donald W. Patterson • transparent watercolor with gouache • 19¼" × 36¼" (49cm × 92cm)

One summer morning as I rounded a curve on my bicycle, I was confronted by this breathtaking scene of the Delaware River. Returning in the fall, I recorded the scene with my camera. I began the painting with transparent watercolor and then added gouache accents to the fallen leaves, foliage and road lines. Upon completion, I instantly realized I had to include cyclists to fully convey my passion for this scene. Soon after, I photographed my cycling friends on-site so that the light and perspective would match. Using gouache, I painted in the cyclists, and my passion was finally rewarded!

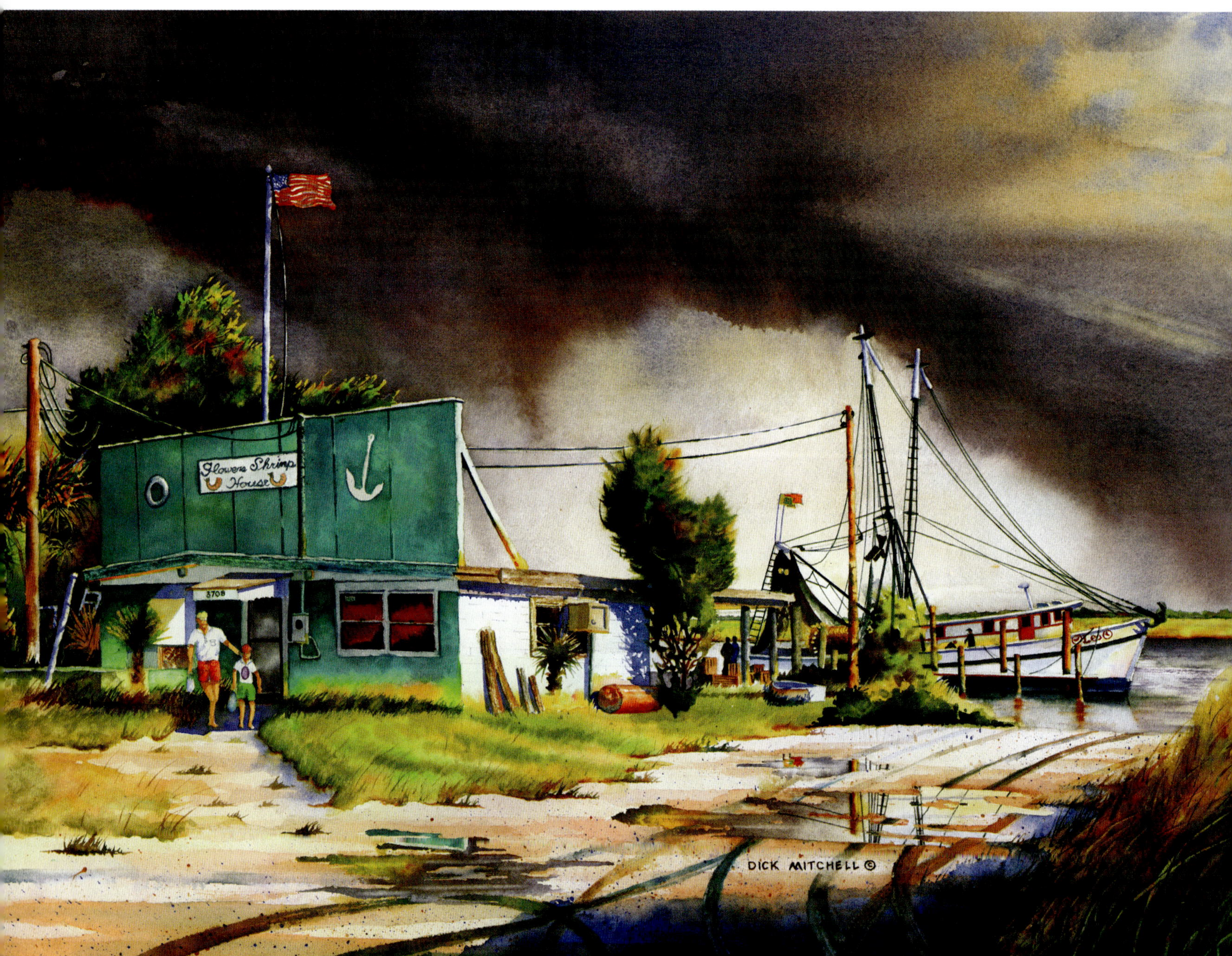

SCENT FROM HEAVEN

Dick Mitchell • transparent watercolor • 22" × 30" (56cm × 76cm)

My subject is located on a noncommercialized barrier island 40 miles south of Charleston, South Carolina, where we have spent numerous summer vacations. Buying fresh shrimp for dinner is the first order of business upon arrival. I tried to capture the total experience of the smells of salt water, marsh grass, shrimp hauls and the rapidly approaching storm, which will only add to the already high humidity. The outstretched flag suggests the welcome wind associated with the storm. The main challenge was to depict the thundercloud. A very light gray wash was laid down for the sky and allowed to dry. The sky was rewet with clear water, and then the heavy, darker clouds were dropped in from the top and allowed to wash into the lower, lighter portion of the sky.

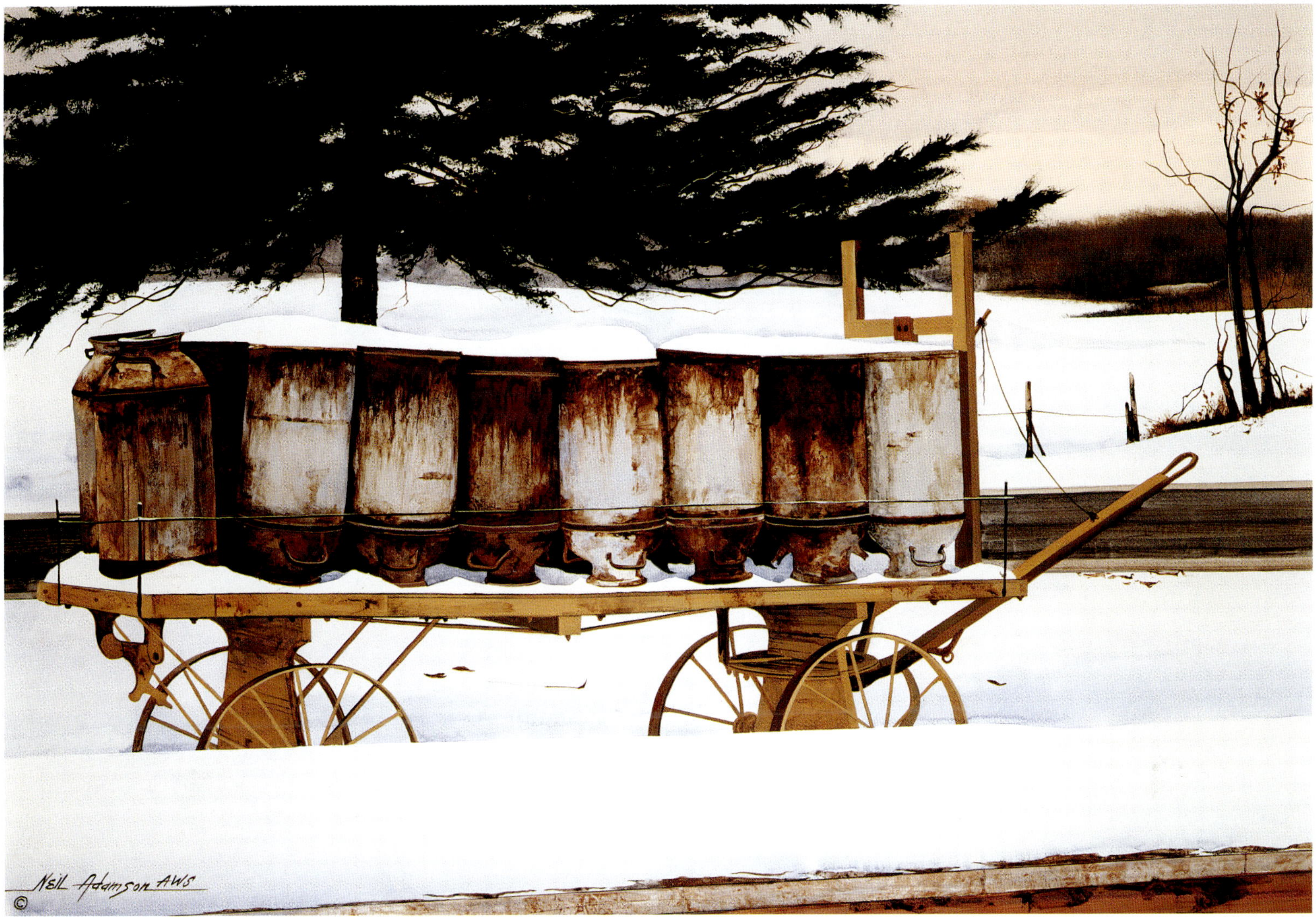

MILK CANS

Neil H. Adamson • acrylic on smooth paper • 16" × 28" (41cm × 71cm)

These milk cans were long survivors of the cold. Each has its story to tell of the bumps, dents and rust proudly displayed. After finishing an accurate drawing, I applied washes of Burnt Umber and Ultramarine Blue. When dry, I used various reds and earth tones for semi-opaque washes. Many techniques were used for the texture, including stippling, spatter, the sides of the brush and my finger. *Tropical Sanctuary* grabbed my interest because here was a bit of "old Florida" that had escaped development. The rich, lush foliage in shades of green and blue, along with its reflection, was achieved using flat, pointed and fan brushes and sponges.

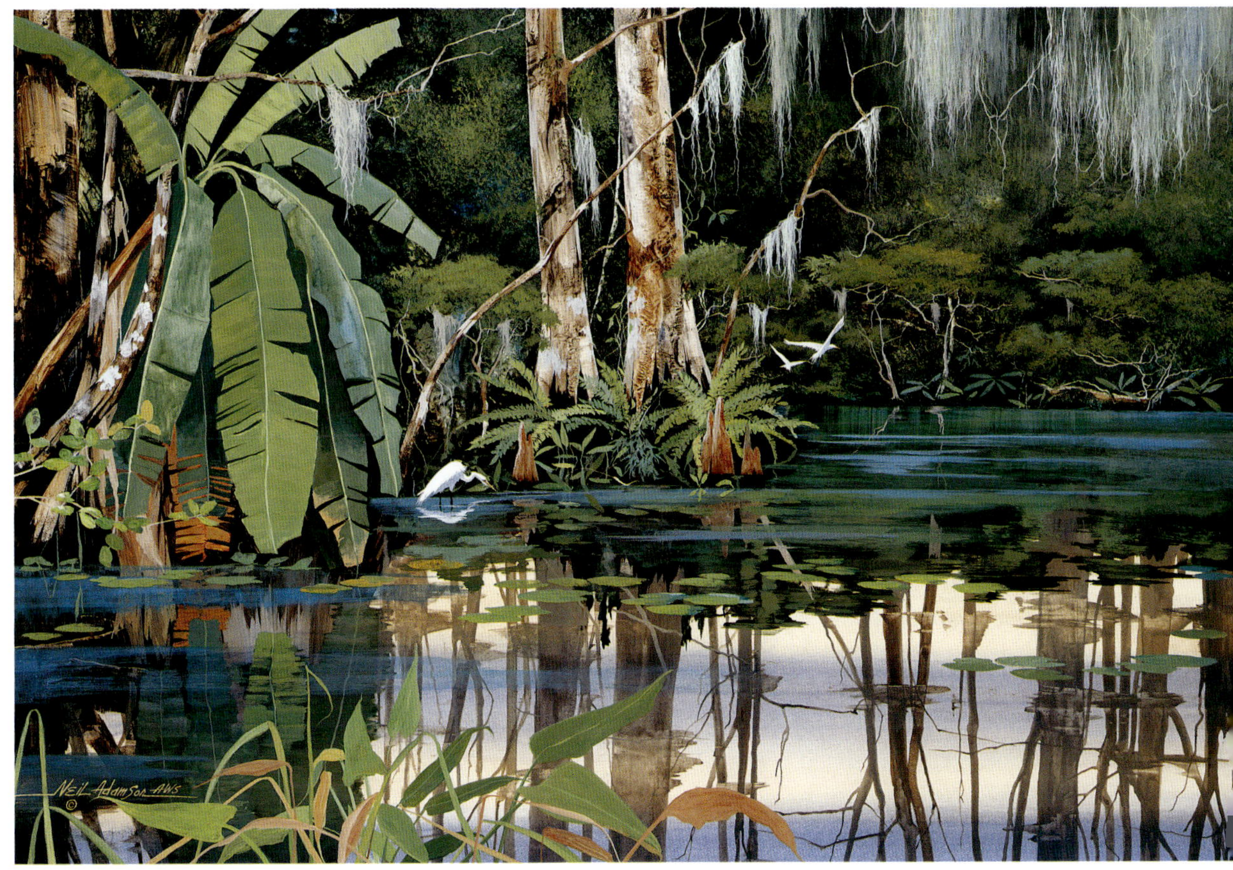

TROPICAL SANCTUARY

Neil H. Adamson • acrylic on smooth paper • 21" × 30½" (53cm × 77cm)

I paint when I look at a painting in progress; I paint when I look at people's faces; I paint in my sleep. I never stop painting—it simply is not always done on paper.

AL ZERRIES

THE GODDESS OF DENIAL

Al Zerries • transparent watercolor • 22" × 27" (56cm × 69cm)

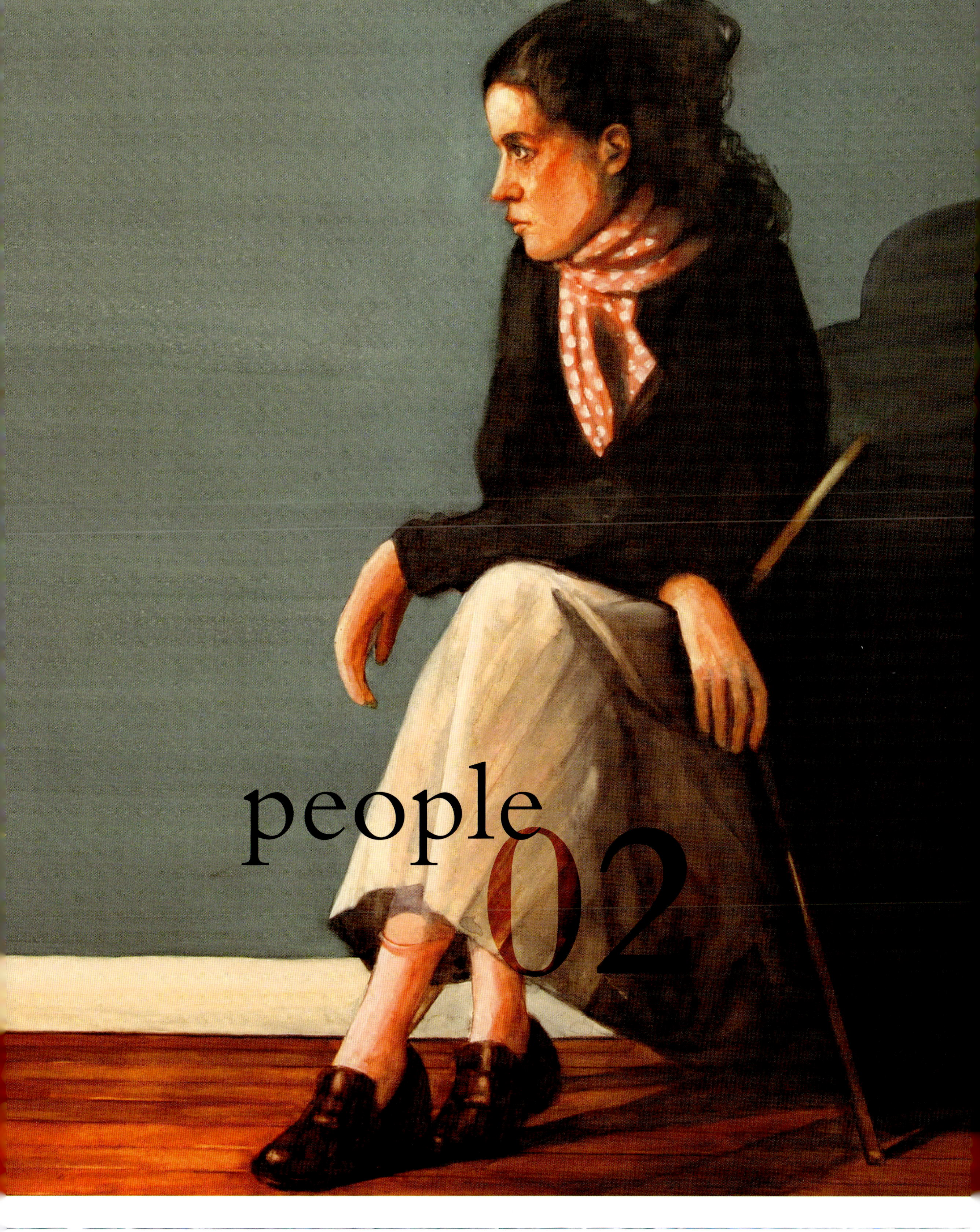

people 02

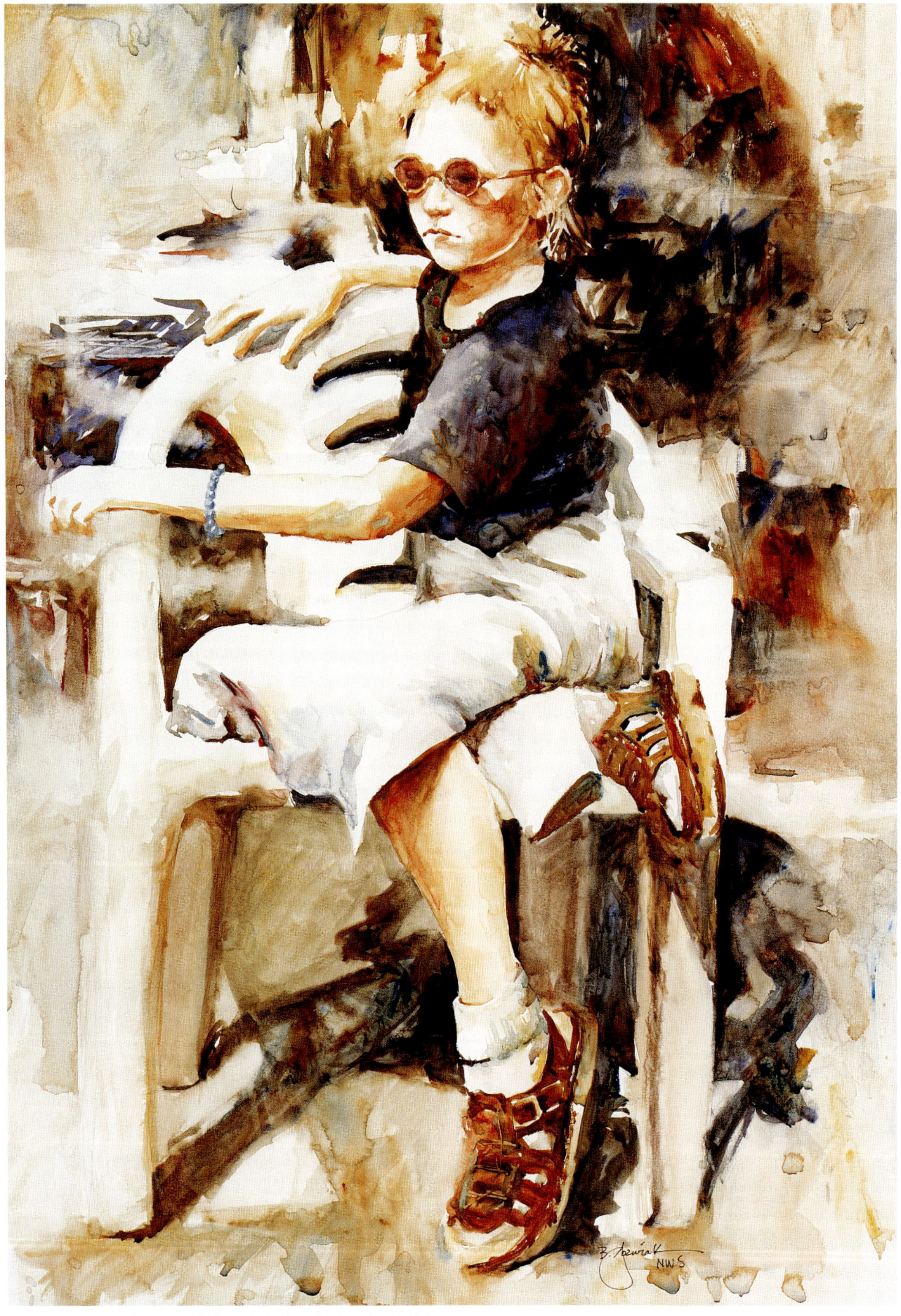

SHADES, SHAPES, AND SHADOWS

Bev Jozwiak • transparent watercolor • 24" × 17" (61cm × 43cm)

Shades, Shapes, and Shadows was painted from photographs. They are a great tool, but don't be a slave to them, because they are usually lifeless and flat. You have to make your own magic happen. Pissarro said, "Blessed are they who can see beautiful things in humble places, where other people see nothing." Art is about finding your own personal beauty in everyday things. Brushwork is a key element in all my work. I want the viewer to be aware of the fact that this is a painting, not a photograph. Painterly strokes and varied color let the viewer feel the energy, excitement and pure joy that this artist feels while painting!

Seventeen years ago, I left what for me was the sterile field of dentistry to follow my heart into the lush and vibrant world of watercolor. Now my instruments are a palette and brushes. And I use them to paint sonnets and love songs to the artist in all of us.

FEALING LIN

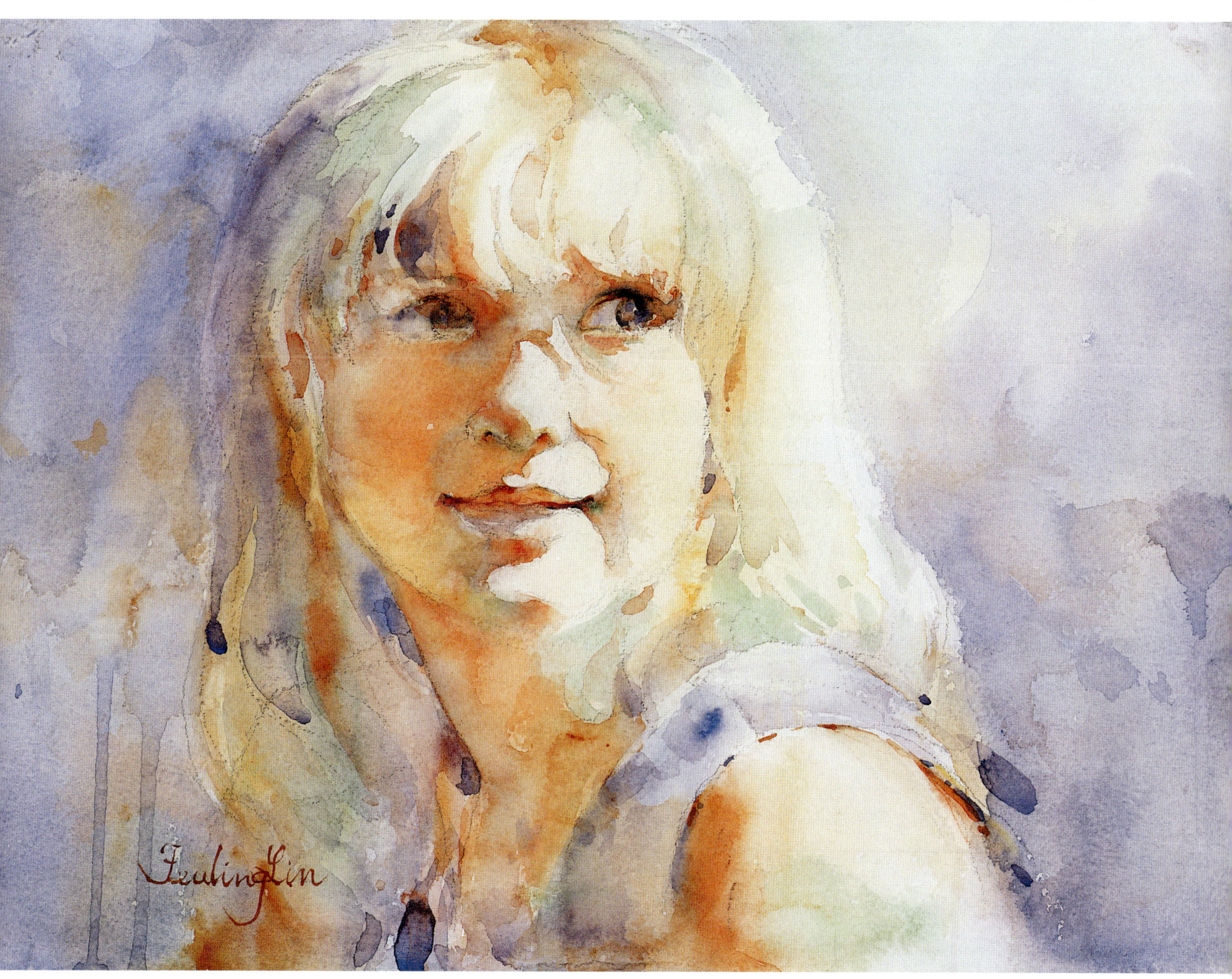

HER SMILE

Fealing Lin • transparent watercolor on paper • 11" x 15" (28cm x 38cm)

My passion is for painting people of all ages. Light and dark patterns give people bathed in sunshine a magical quality. Both *Her Smile* and *Afternoon Walk* (page 2) were finished in the studio, using photos and sketches. After a careful pencil drawing, local colors are applied wet-into-wet. I make sure to save some generous white and light areas. After the paper dries, I create the features and shapes using a medium value. In the last stage, I add the details with darker values. I find that free, loose brushstrokes express the mood and life of my human subjects.

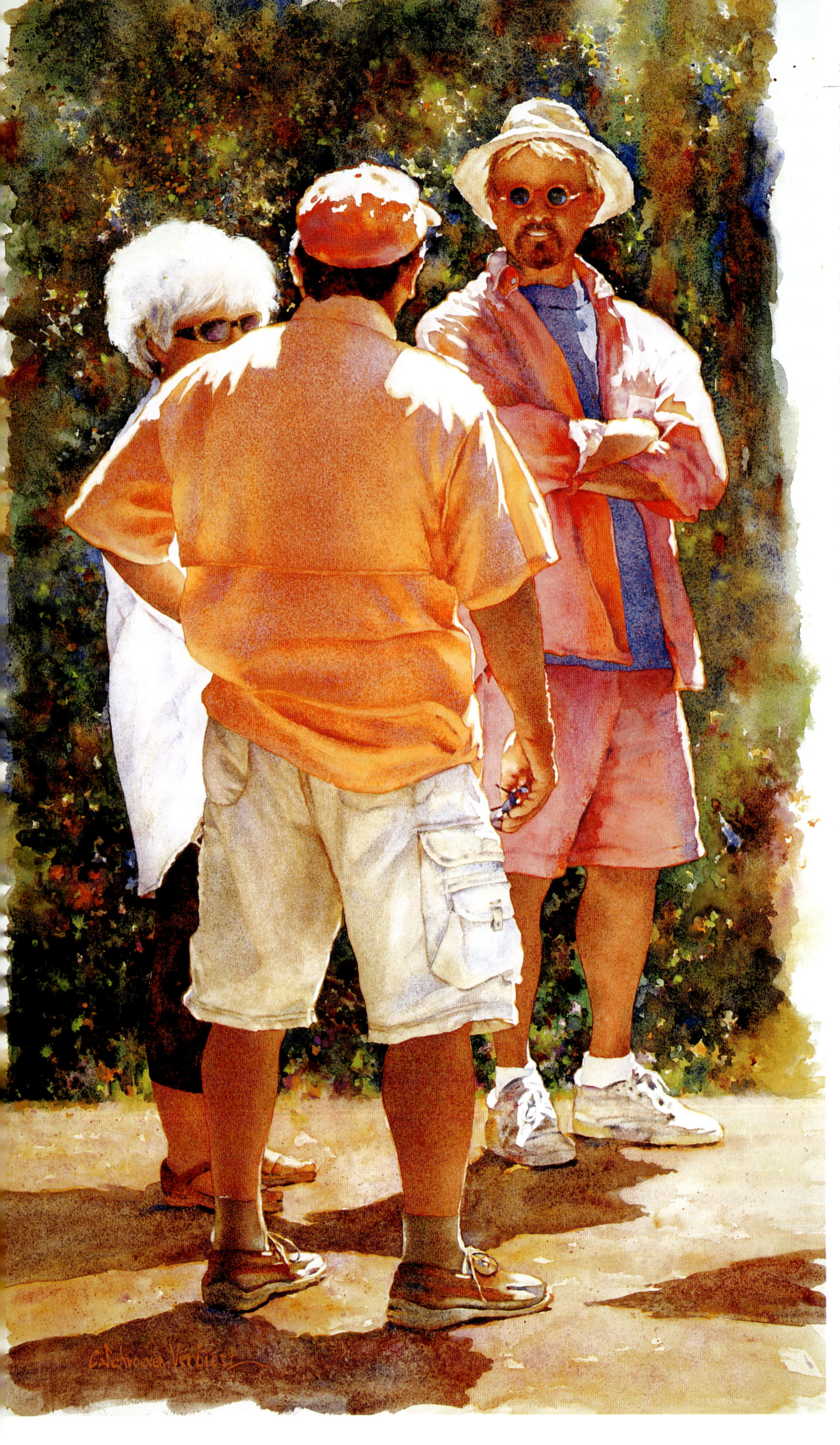

SUMMER

Claire Schroeven Verbiest • transparent watercolor with white gouache accents • 24" × 12½" (61cm × 32cm)

I turned the corner and there they were—standing and chatting, the glorious, saturated color of their outfits virtually pulsating in the warm August sunlight. Back in the studio, my task was to translate the photo I had taken into a painting drenched in contrast and chromatic drama. As a result, the painting process was quite captivating; I did not want to take a break, and, when I had to, I couldn't wait to get back. Intuition and experience were called upon to paint the wet-into-wet background. Stippling and a little white gouache were put to good use in rendering the smooth garments.

KISSED BY THE SUN

Marci Boone • transparent watercolor • 20" × 15" (51cm × 38cm)

Kissed by the Sun was painted in my studio from a photograph and an on-site sketch. I try to shoot pictures in the early morning or late afternoon when the light casts long, beautiful shadows. The most important brushstrokes were those used in applying the mask that saved the bright light of the sun on the truck farmer and his cantaloupe. I poured the transparent, luminous washes that filled the cast shadows with a triad of Hansa Yellow, Permanent Rose and Phthalo Blue. This painting is a story of light—the light of the strong Texas sun that scorches the earth but allows the growth of the Pecos cantaloupe, the sweetest cantaloupe found anywhere.

It is more than a passion—it is an obsession. Being able to capture light and shadow with luminous color is beyond words . . . it is magic.

MARCI BOONE

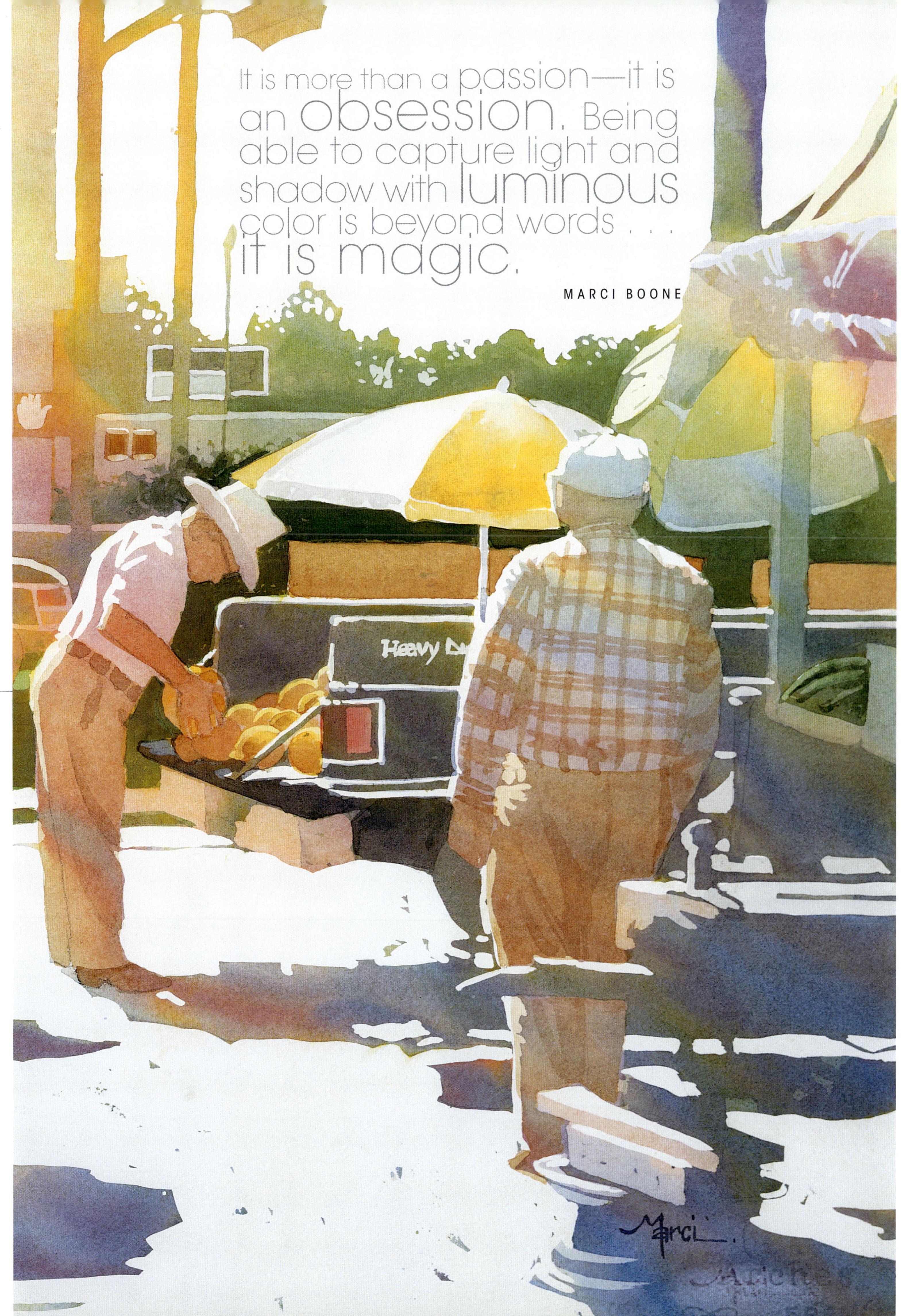

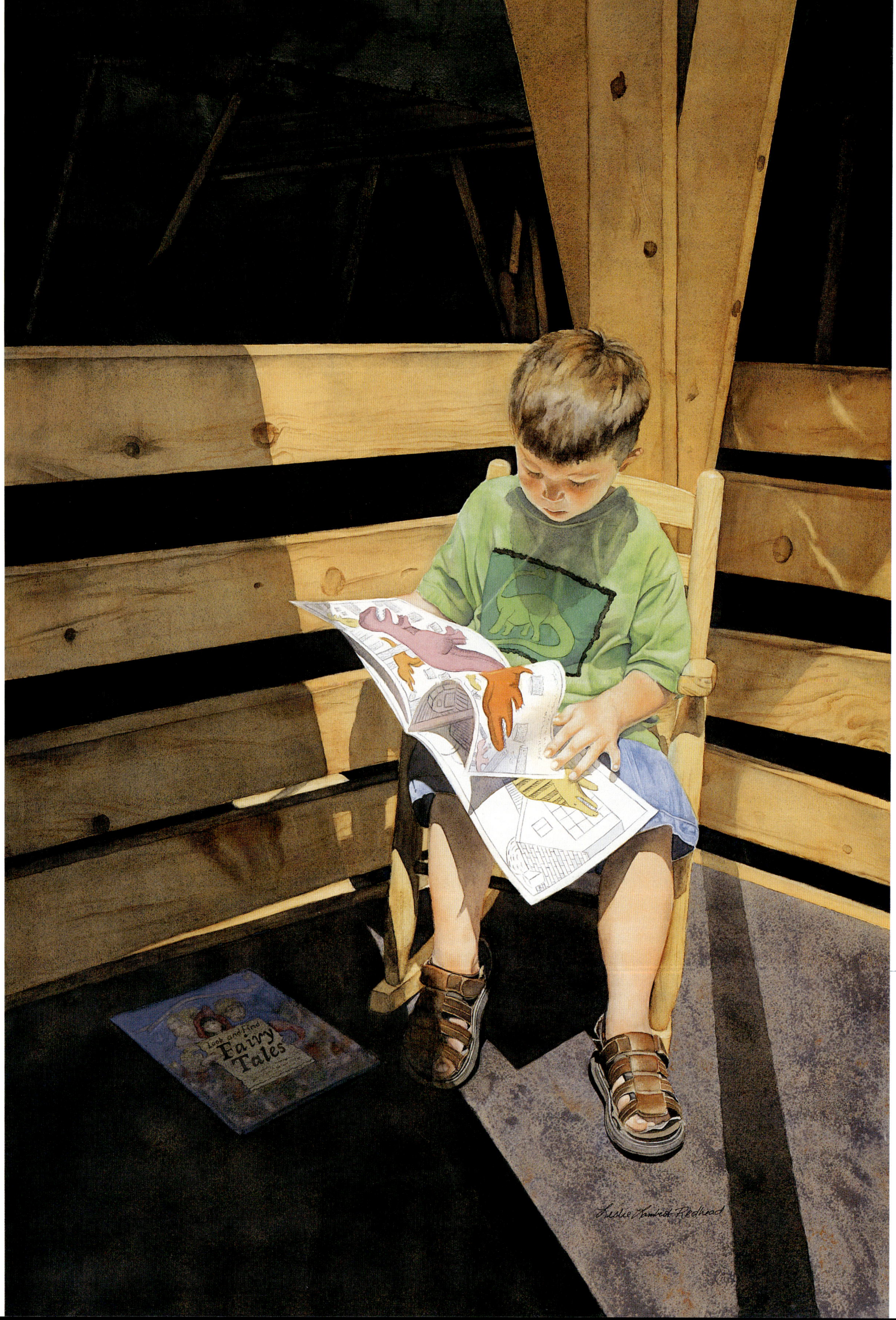
Fairy
Tales

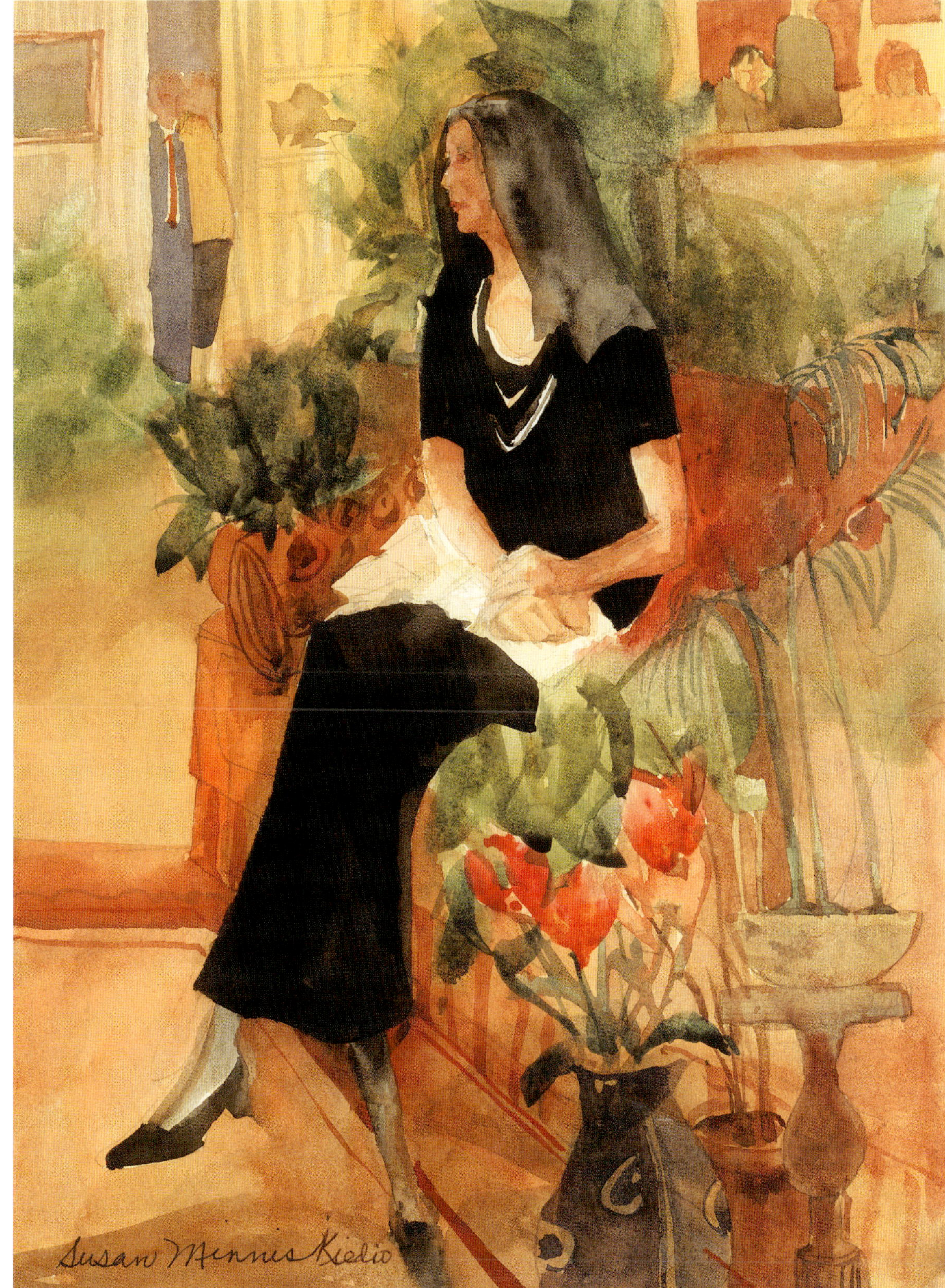

HOTEL LOBBY

Susan J. Kiedio • watercolor on hot-pressed paper • 14" × 10" (36cm × 25cm)

I love taking a figure study painted from life and placing it in an imagined environment, as in *Hotel Lobby*. My first teacher encouraged us to work with the best materials one could afford. I am still using my first brush, a no. 23 Royal & Langnickel. With this I can concentrate on big shapes first. For the same reason, I do not wear my reading glasses until I need them for the small details at the end.

THE ATTIC ROOM

Leslie Lambert Redhead • transparent watercolor • 40" × 25" (102cm × 64cm)

I love to capture my children forever in life's fleeting moments. We were visiting the Salt Lake City Public Library when my son ran ahead and discovered an area called the Attic Room. As I entered, he was quietly sitting in a chair reading a book. A beam of light surrounded him perfectly. Back in the studio, I did a careful drawing using my reference photos. Glazes of transparent colors created the bright hues of children's books. Burnt Sienna and Ultramarine Blue formed the blacks, which easily lifted out to create the ceiling beams behind him.

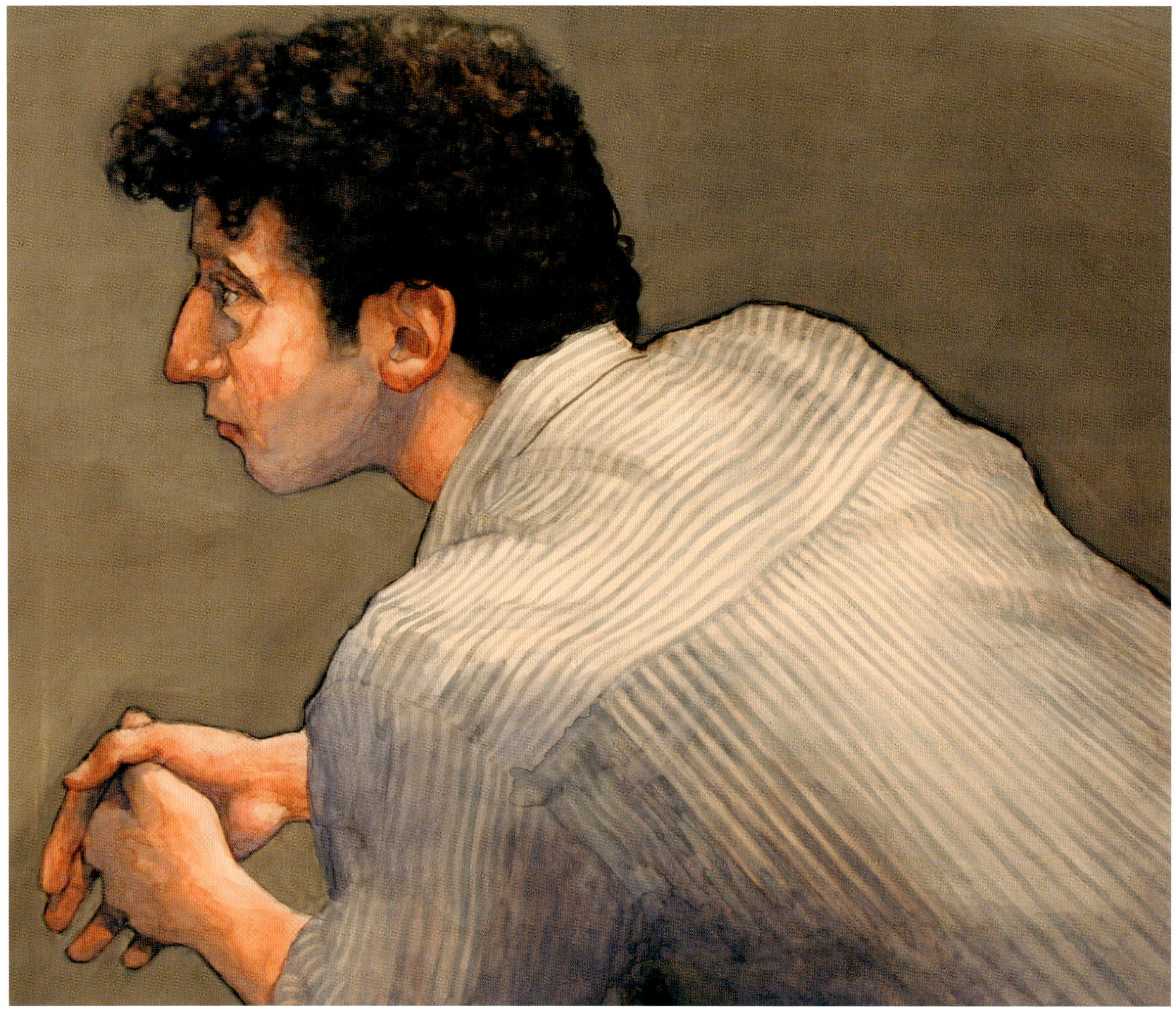

DECISION

Al Zerries • transparent watercolor • 22" × 28" (56cm × 71cm)

My paintings begin with a very detailed pencil sketch from life. I then take photos of the model from all directions. Thumbnails in pencil follow, then a loose value sketch in color. This is followed by a detailed, full-size charcoal drawing on vellum, laid over the watercolor paper. This is done for the size and location of the figure. I start my painting on an untouched sheet of paper. I do light washes first, delineating value areas covering the entire paper. The mood I try to achieve is usually linked to the design. The personality of the sitter is a strong influence, as well as the pose itself (body language) and the original lighting. Whatever I pick up on my radar as the psyche of the sitter is the single most important factor. But I'm constantly evaluating the design aspect of the entire piece. I'm a relatively quick painter, but my paintings take a long time to complete because I take more time looking at the painting than using a brush. Capturing the myriad secrets of the human face in a given moment is my quest.

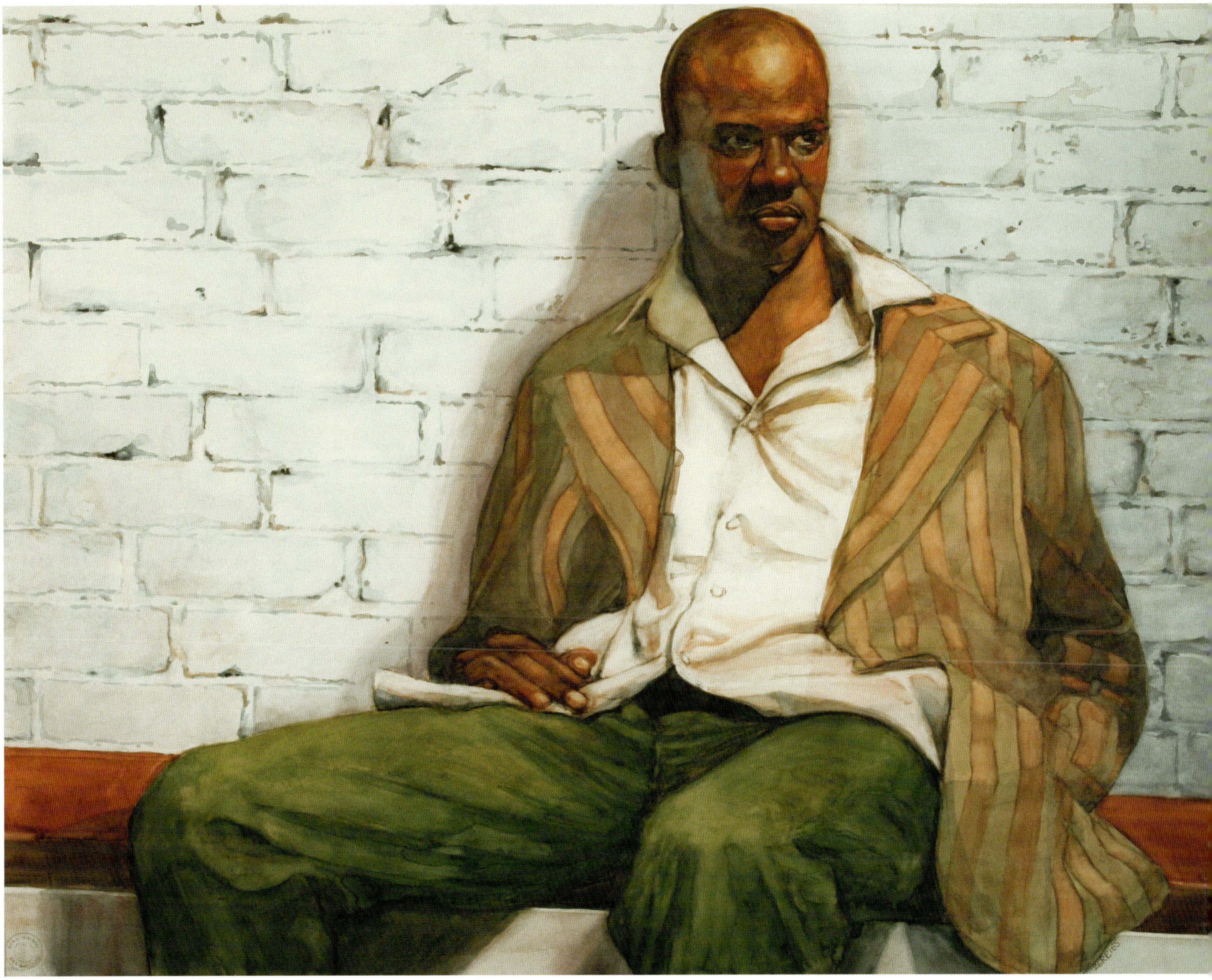

THE LONG WAIT

Al Zerries • transparent watercolor • 23" × 29 " (58cm × 74cm)

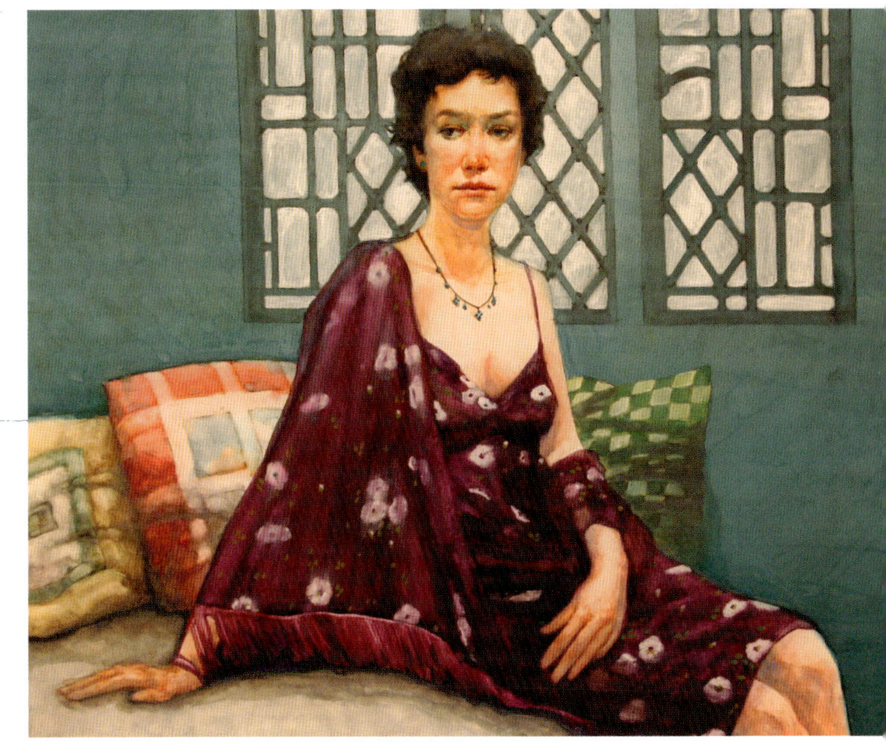

THE WEDDING GUEST

Al Zerries • transparent watercolor • 23" × 28" (58cm × 71cm)

I love to take circumstances that excite me and then communicate my feelings through my painting.

DON HARVIE

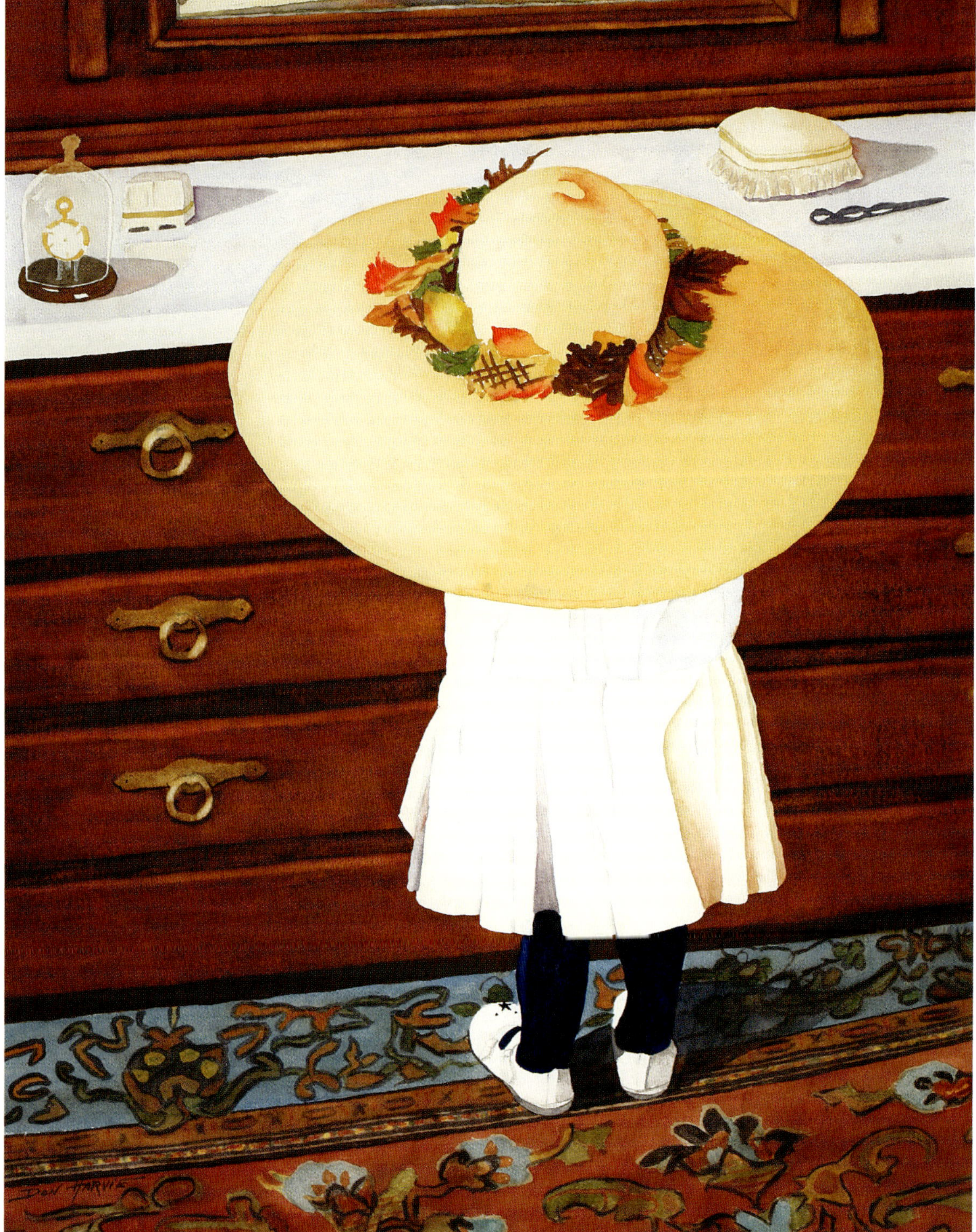

MOMMY'S HAT

Don Harvie • transparent watercolor • 36" × 28" (91cm × 71cm)

I snapped a photo of my grandniece trying on her mommy's hat, and I knew I would someday paint this appealing image. It was a magic moment, but the photograph was not a good design. What would effectively show her off with that big hat on? In my mind, I saw her playing "dress-up" with our old family dresser as a backdrop. I knew I would want warm colors to dominate, evoking a nostalgic mood. Even the blue carpet is a warm blue.

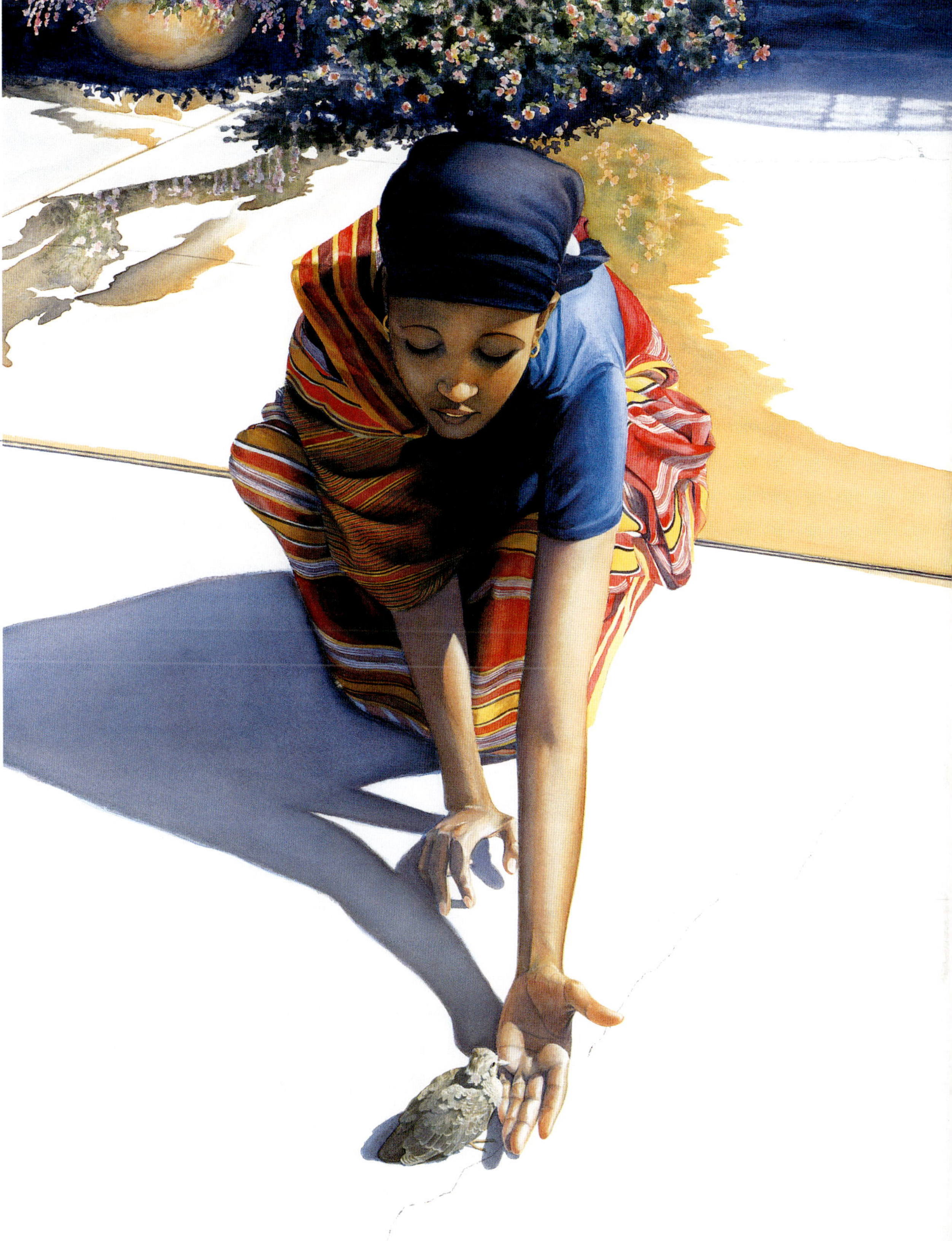

POOR BABY

Alan Rogerson • transparent watercolor on 300-lb. (640gsm) paper • 28½" × 21½" (72cm × 52cm)

When I was a youngster, it seemed I could paint with any medium I tried—except watercolor. It completely eluded me. After years of trying, one night, lying awake, I had an epiphany! "I finally know how to do watercolors!" I was ecstatic, like a hopeless romantic who finally holds his elusive dreamgirl. While photographing my neighbor, we startled a baby Inca dove. It ran and then froze. Layla and I knelt in toward it as I fumbled with the manual focus and an adjustable wide-angle lens. Watching her hand get so close, I feared the chance would flee. Click, and it was gone. My art, like my breath, is a gift that I strive to appreciate before it's gone.

You can't see my brushstrokes. They're hidden like lovers behind closed doors.

ALAN ROGERSON

My passion to paint is sparked by something I see. If I am struck by something beautiful, I'll spend time staring and thinking, "How would I paint that?"

BARBARA FOX

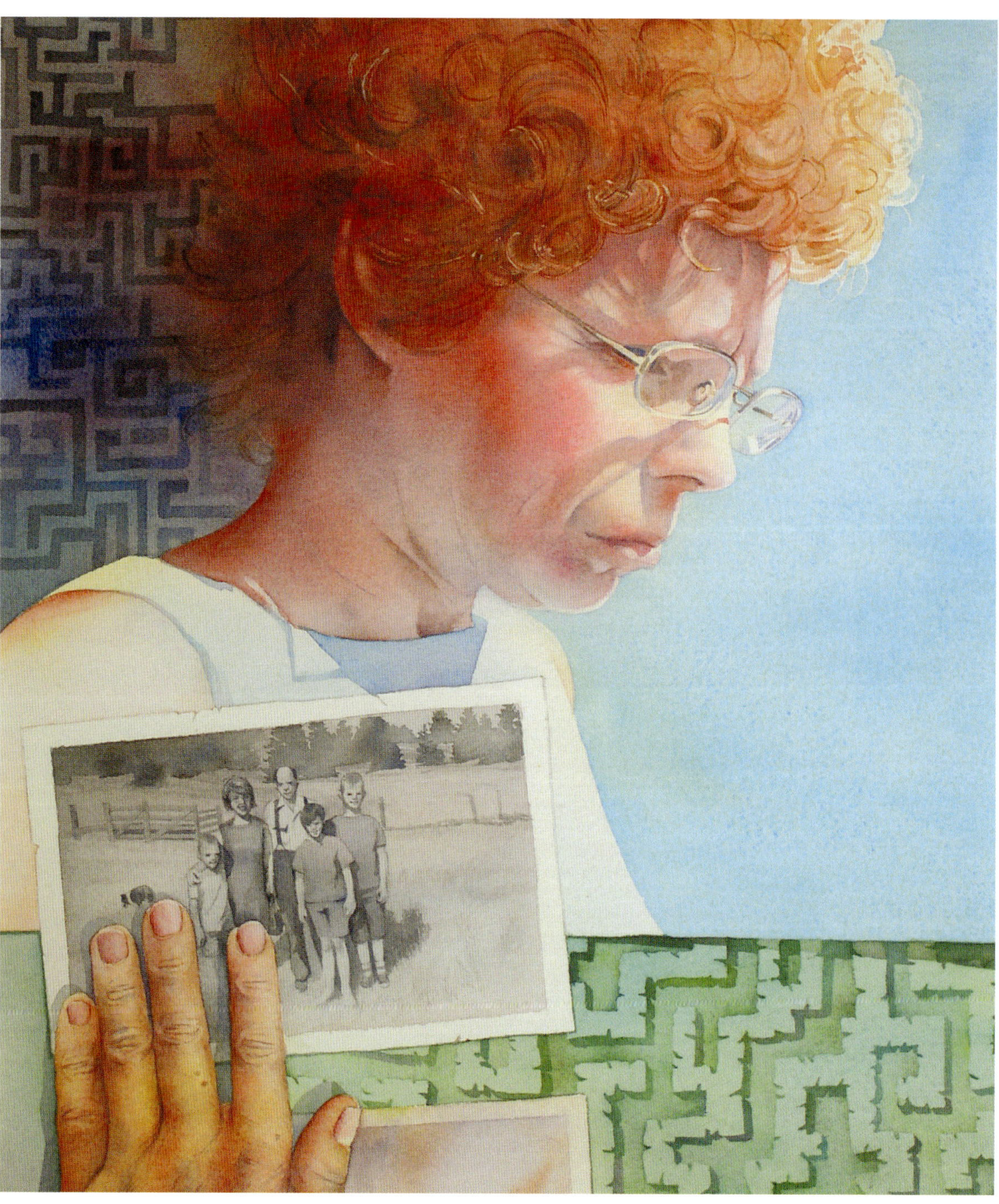

ARRANGEMENT

Barbara Fox • transparent watercolor • 19" × 16" (48cm × 41cm)

I painted this self-portrait in a trompe l'oeil fashion. My goal was to portray myself in an interesting and personal way, a composite of experiences and memories. I used several photographs as reference, some symbolic imagery, and added my hand, painted from life. I work in a traditional watercolor method—from light to dark—applying many transparent glazes to achieve luminous color. I don't mix my paints on the palette, but apply almost all the glazes wet-into-wet. The pigments flowing and settling in the water create the beautiful transitions of color and value.

ELLA, SAN GIMIGNANO

Ted Nuttall • watercolor on 300-lb. (640gsm) cold-pressed paper • 15" × 11" (38cm × 28cm)

I am a fascinated observer of human behavior—the quintessential people-watcher. Sometimes I am rewarded with a moment when the play of light and shadow combines with a gesture or expression, and I see a painting. I photographed Ella on the piazza in San Gimignano, where she would appear every morning to visit with her friends and family. Her dress, expression and bearing tell the story of a life full and well-lived. The painting was rendered with a single no. 16 round, kolinsky sable, a brush flexible enough to allow me to paint in broad, loose shapes, as well as add the details and definition that are critical to creating contrast and interest in the painting.

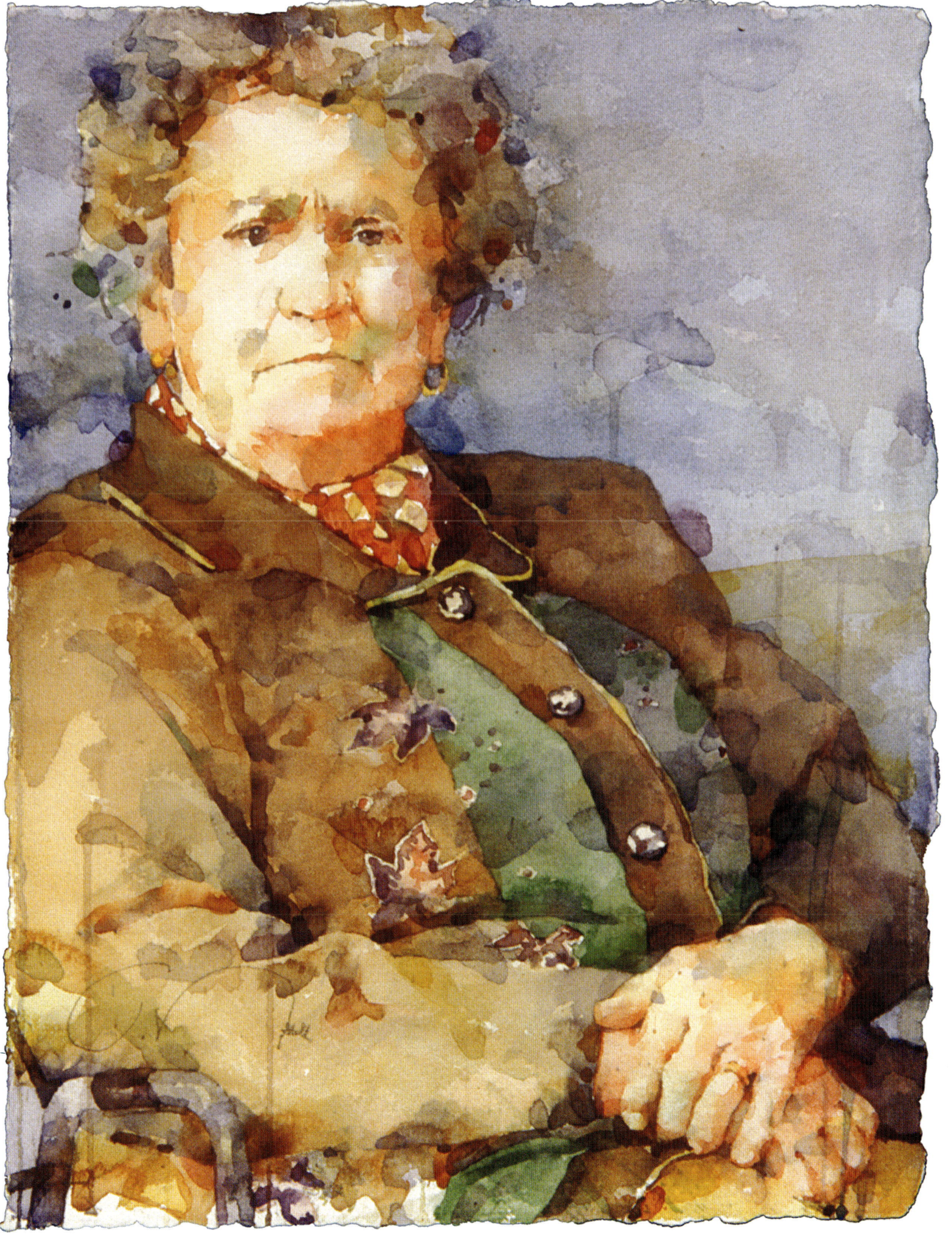

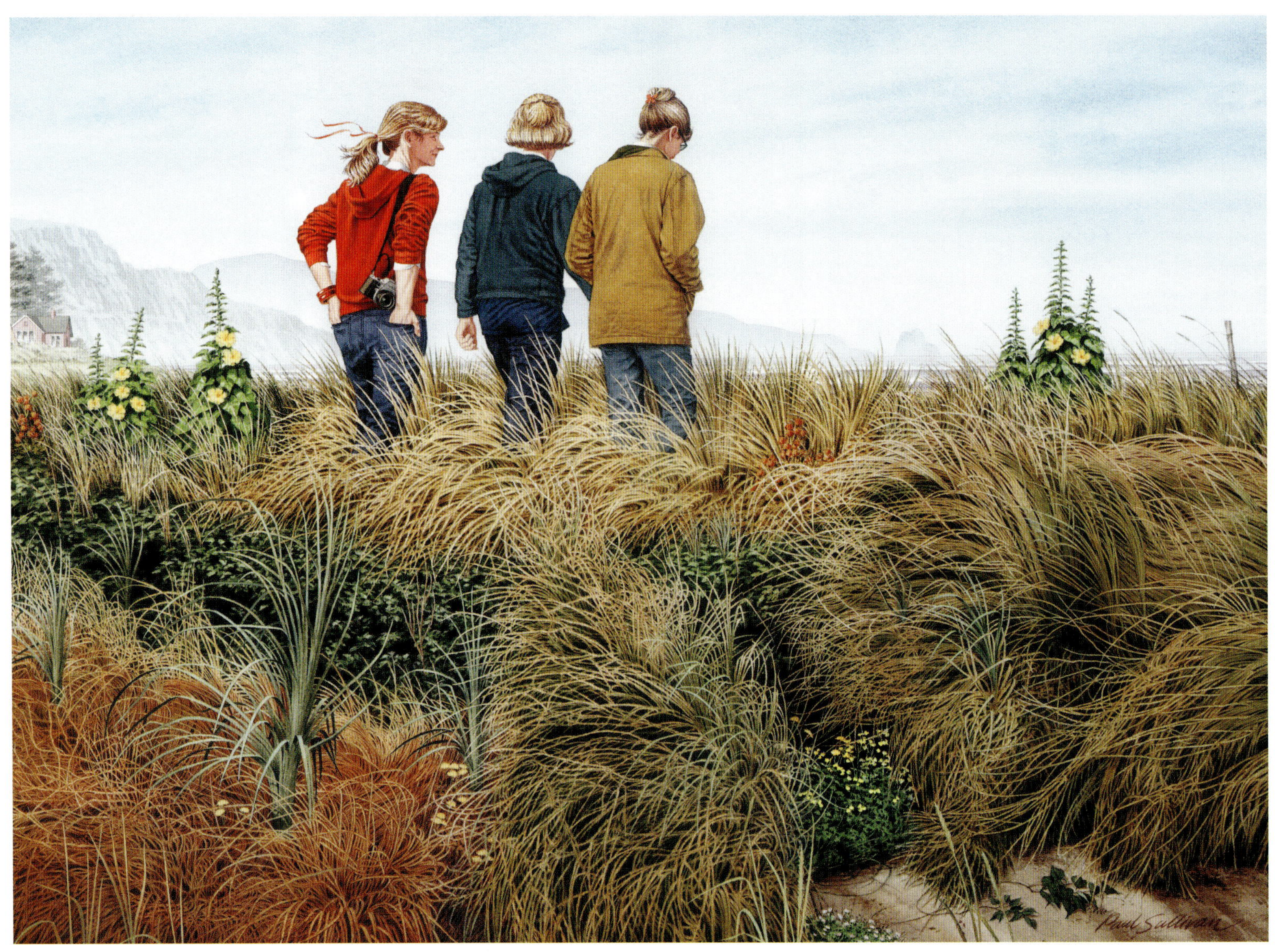

MANZANITA MORNING

Paul Sullivan • watercolor with some transparent acrylic • 18½" × 25½" (47cm × 65cm)

The preliminary phase of a watercolor is the most important part of the process. *Manzanita Morning* went through a lot of changes during the preparatory work. After the first round of composition sketches and color roughs, I threw everything out and started over. I had met and photographed the three girls as they walked along a sandy beach. However, I decided to place them in a field of old beach grass and weeds, silhouetting them against the sky. This meant I could raise the horizon line, making a better overall design. Also, I made changes in the key figure at the far left, using my niece as a model, and created new color sketches. Not only did this preliminary work solve a lot of problems, but it resulted in having a picture that I truly wanted to paint—with passion.

Most early societies thought that a picture captured the spirit of its subject. Actually, that is what I try to do each day. It is my passion to capture the spirit—the soul of the subject I am painting.

PAUL SULLIVAN

CONTEMPT

Bill James • watercolor with transparent gouache • 27" × 19" (69cm × 48cm)

All of my watercolors are painted on gesso-coated illustration board from my own reference photos. I loosely draw in the subject with a graphite pencil, and then apply strokes of color, one over the other, until the desired effect is achieved. I also use glazing and scumbling. I am a storyteller. In *Cuban Grandmother* (page 5) the placement of the woman's hands around the little boy's head expresses deep love and protectiveness. In *Contempt*, I'm interested by the look the girl in the front of the group makes to another girl. It seems as though anger is expressed toward that person for some unknown reason.

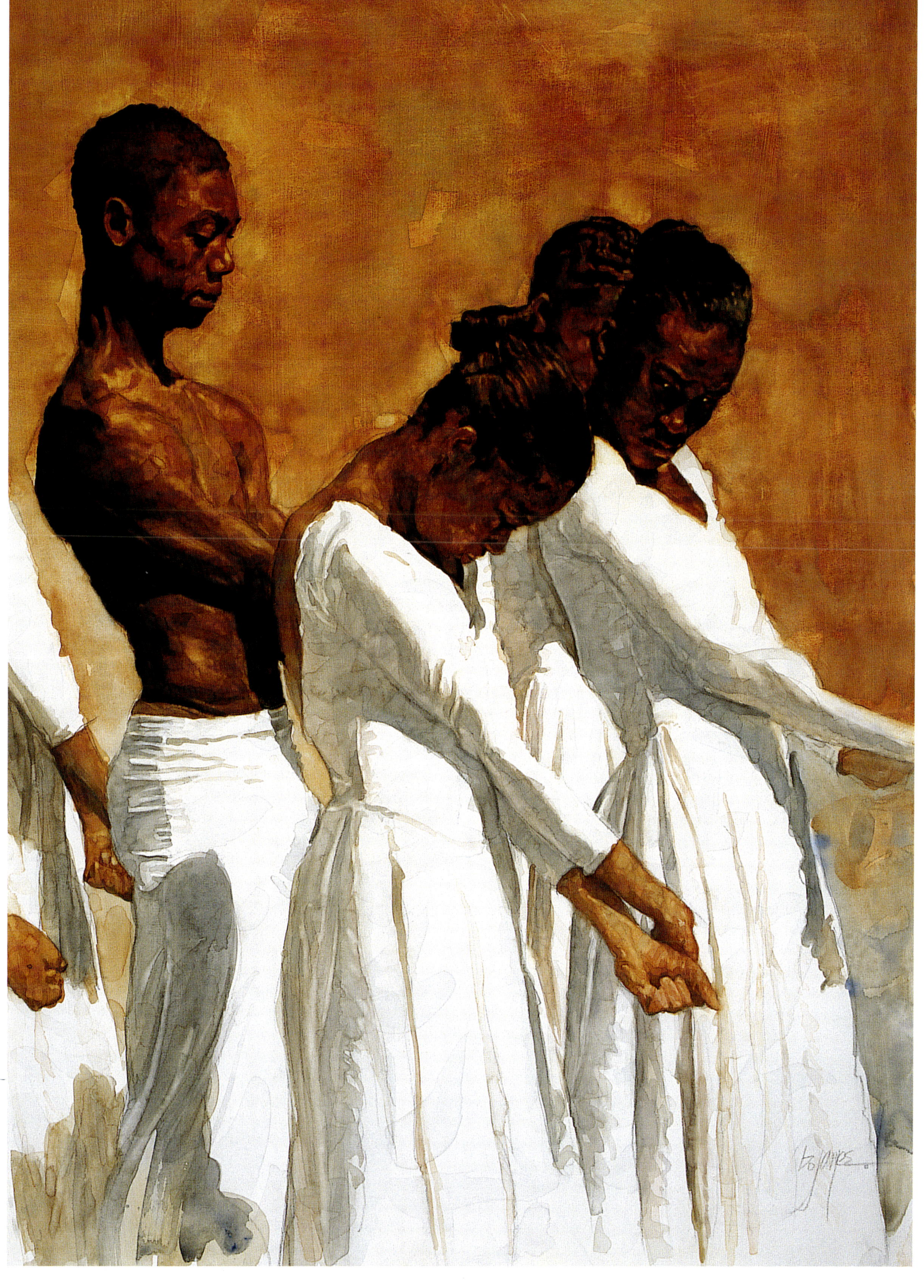

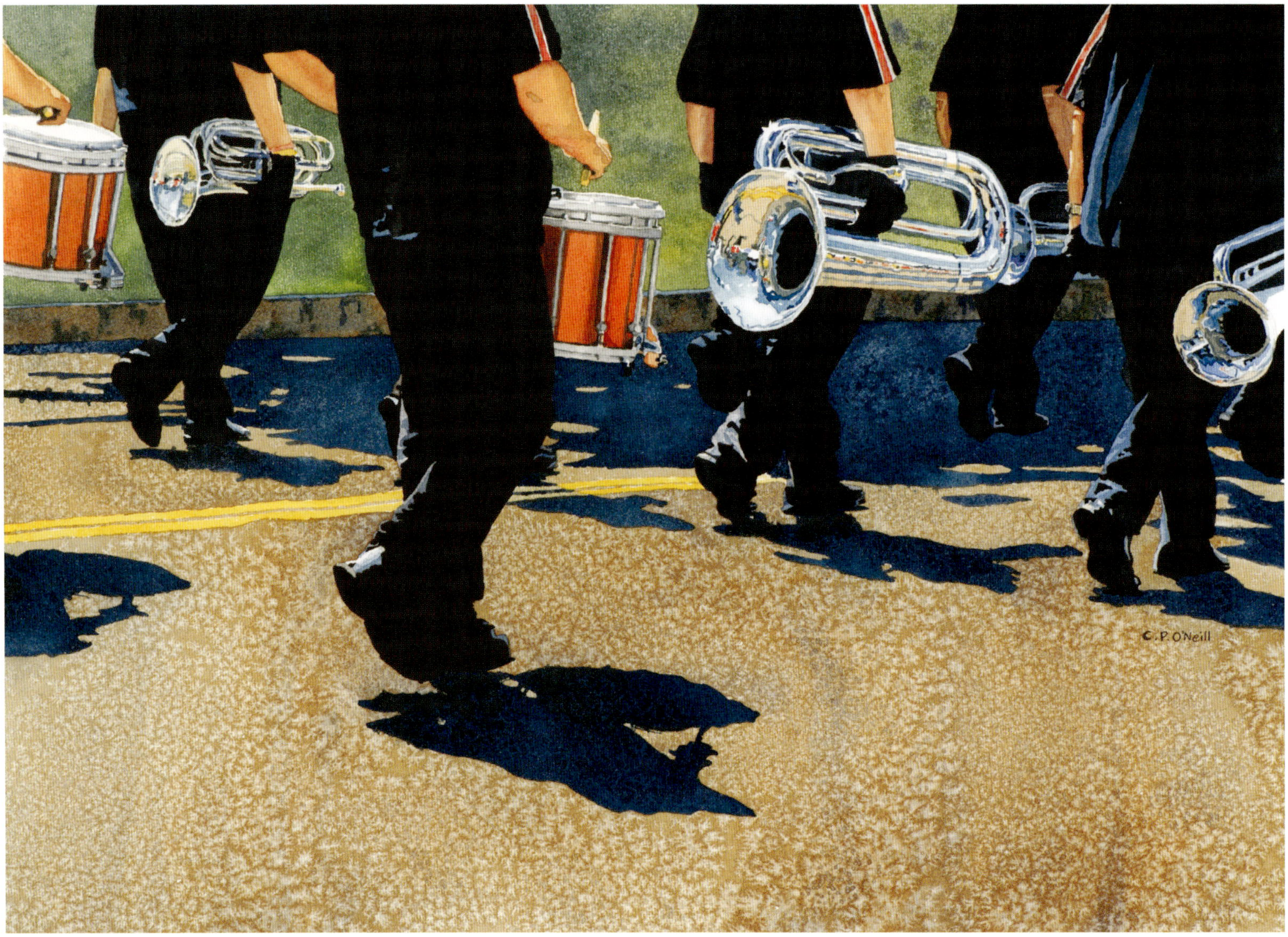

MARCHING HOME AGAIN

Catherine P. O'Neill • transparent watercolor • 13" x 20" (33cm x 51cm)

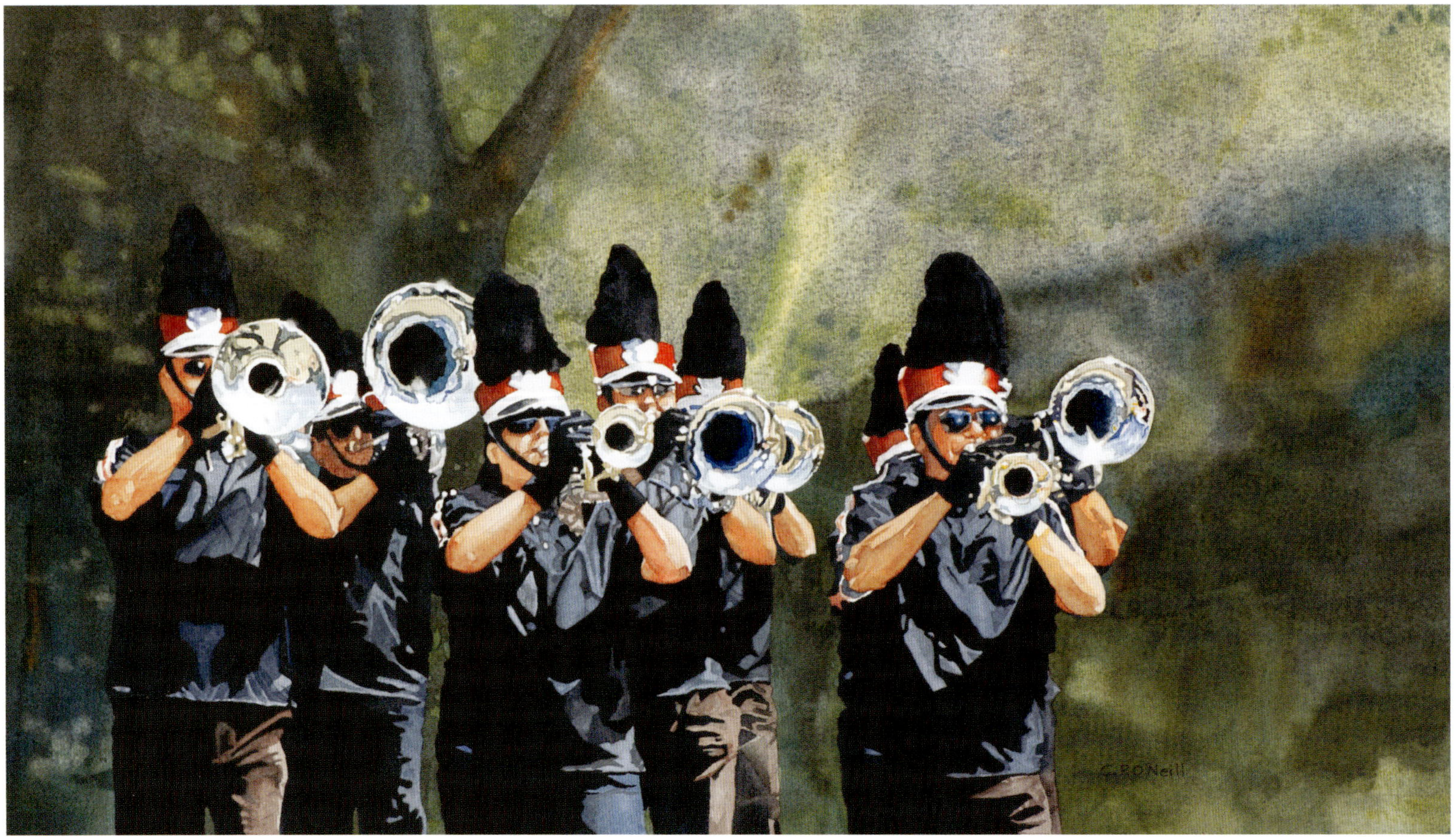

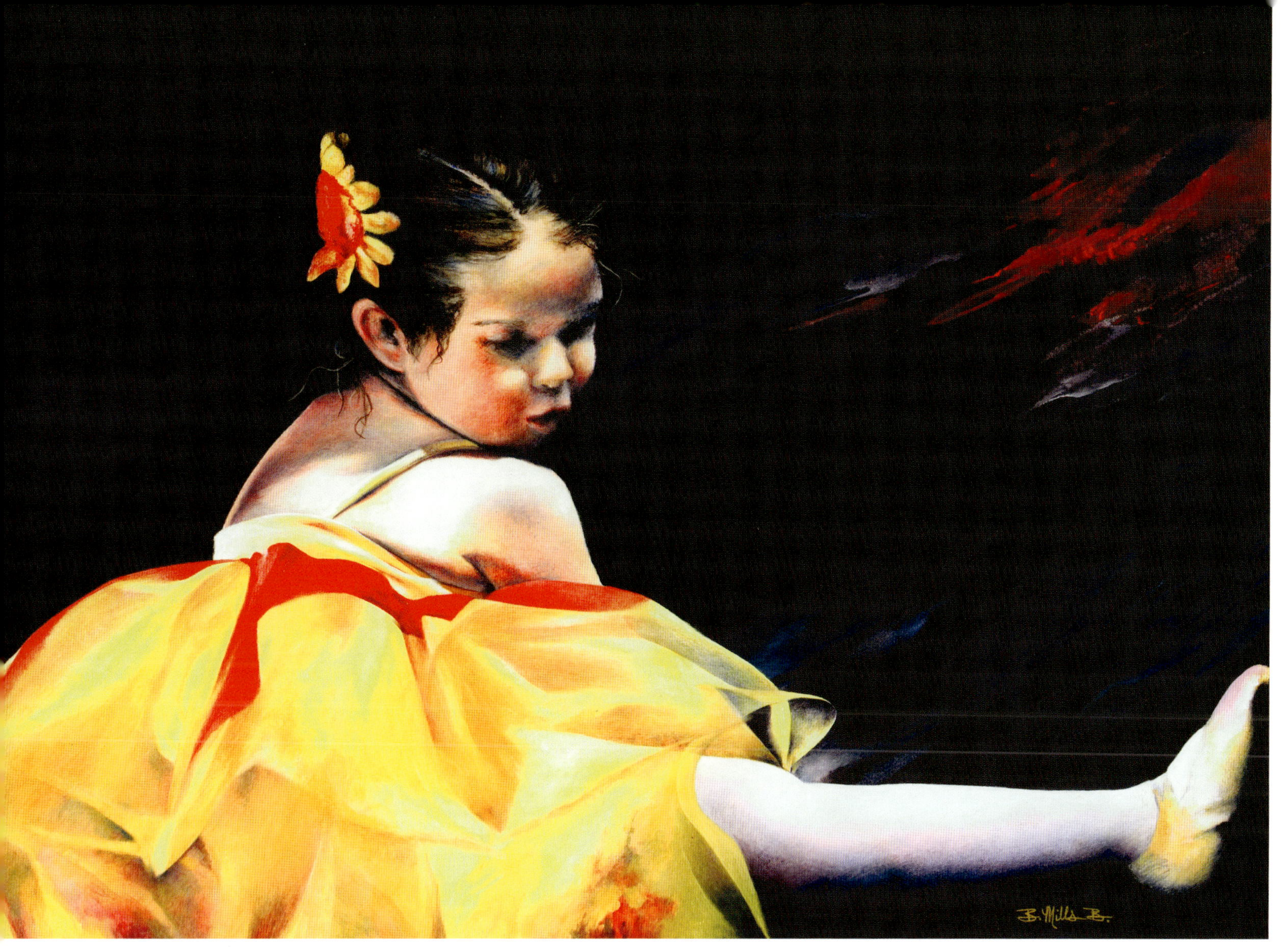

DREAMER

Brenda Mills Brannan • acrylic on watercolor paper • 20" × 28" (51cm × 71cm)

I love people's stories. We all have stories of our growth and our passions. This painting is a tender narrative of a young girl discovering herself and her budding passion for dance. The versatility of acrylic allowed me to vary my technique. The heavier opaque background anchored the lighter transparent figure. Paint was layered quickly but with thorough planning. The goal for this painting, as for most of my work, is to create drama and elicit emotion.

COMES MARCHING HOME

Catherine P. O'Neill • transparent watercolor • 15" × 24" (38cm × 61cm)

My hometown of Rome, New York, commemorates "Honor America Days" with a big parade that passes my childhood home. Each summer my family gathers from far and wide to attend the celebration. Watching my eager children with their cousins and relatives line up on the curb year after year makes this event a precious and exciting occasion. As the marching bands passed, I was struck by their reflections and shadows and took lots of photographs for reference. I had been experimenting with salt techniques after attending a demonstration by Judy Morris, and I was pleased with the texture effect achieved by the salt in the foreground of *Marching Home Again*. I tried it again in the background of *Comes Marching Home*, but didn't like the results. I washed the paint out by holding the painting under the faucet. This is the first time that I liked what was left after I finished rinsing an entire painting.

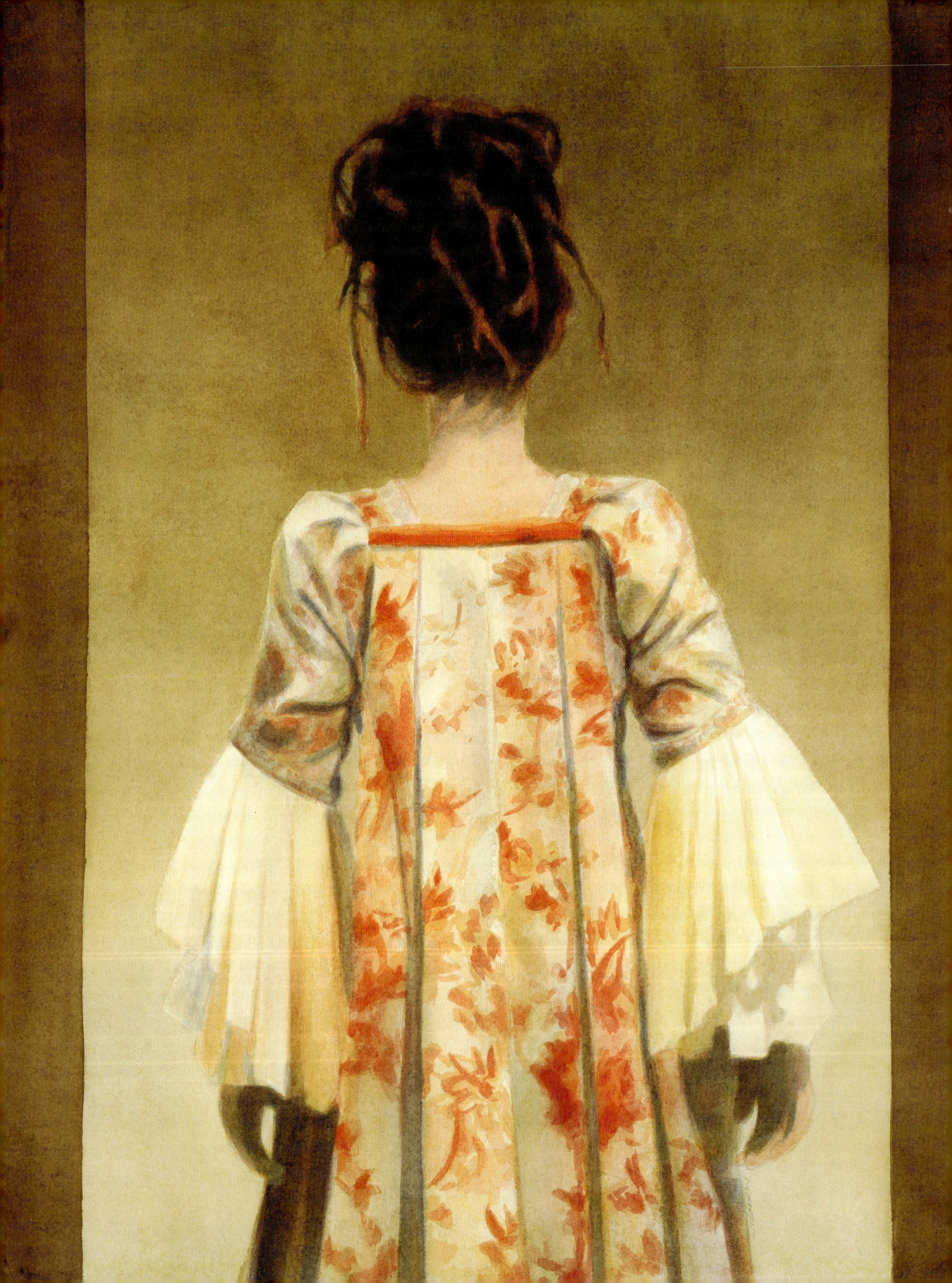

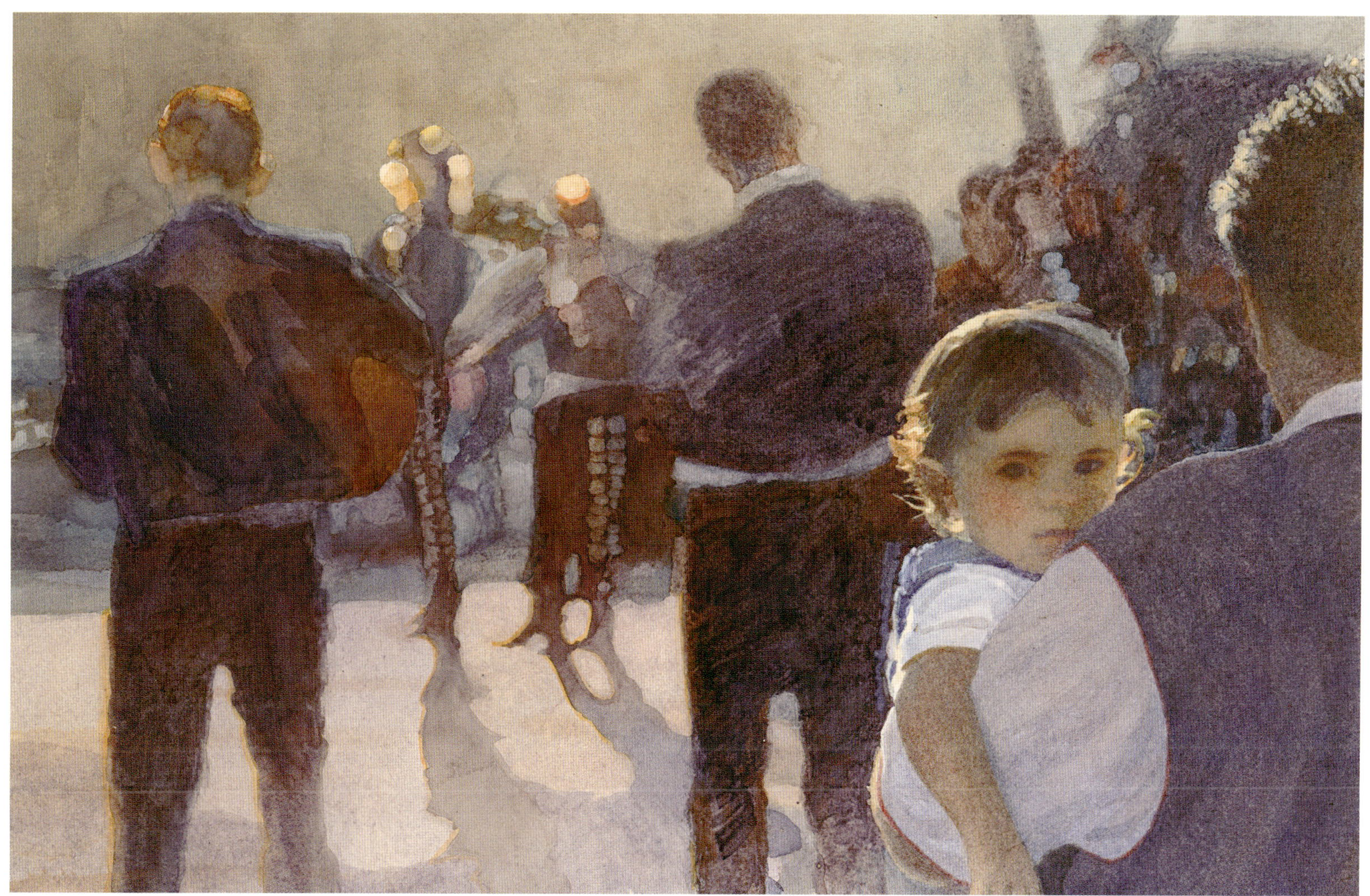

NIGHT OF THE GYPSIES

Fred Chilton • watercolor on 140-lb. (300gsm) cold-pressed paper • 16" × 24" (41cm × 61cm)

Night of The Gypsies was painted in my studio using photographic references. This painting contains everything I always strive for. It represents the fragile expression of innocence supported by love and strength. The atmosphere reflects the mystery and romance of mariachi music. The contrast between the child's face, presented so clearly and directly, and the musicians, presented so indistinctly, creates a powerful visual mystery. I used a Winsor & Newton blending medium on the child's face to soften the features, and in areas that are in immediate proximity to the child. This sets off the crispness of the child's backlit hair. The extensive use of purple (the color of passion), along with its warm complement, enhances the drama and romance.

BEYOND THE BORDERS

Jean Pederson • transparent watercolor on 140-lb. (300gsm) cold-pressed paper • 30" × 22" (76cm × 56cm)

I had the pleasure of working with this naturally gifted model in a period costume. We worked on several poses both indoors and outdoors, and I sketched and photographed her throughout the session. I used these references as inspiration, moving beyond what "was" to create a fresh composition. Several layers of wet glazes were applied first. The embellished floral pattern would have overwhelmed me had I not used quick gestural brush marks with thick, heavily pigmented paint. This model was so convincing in her mood and gesture that it made me think about how things have changed for women due to the strength and determination of those who dared to go beyond the traditional borders of their society.

I am a line and edge fanatic. A great brushstroke can offer interesting variety of edge and line, especially with the final strokes of a painting.

JEAN PEDERSON

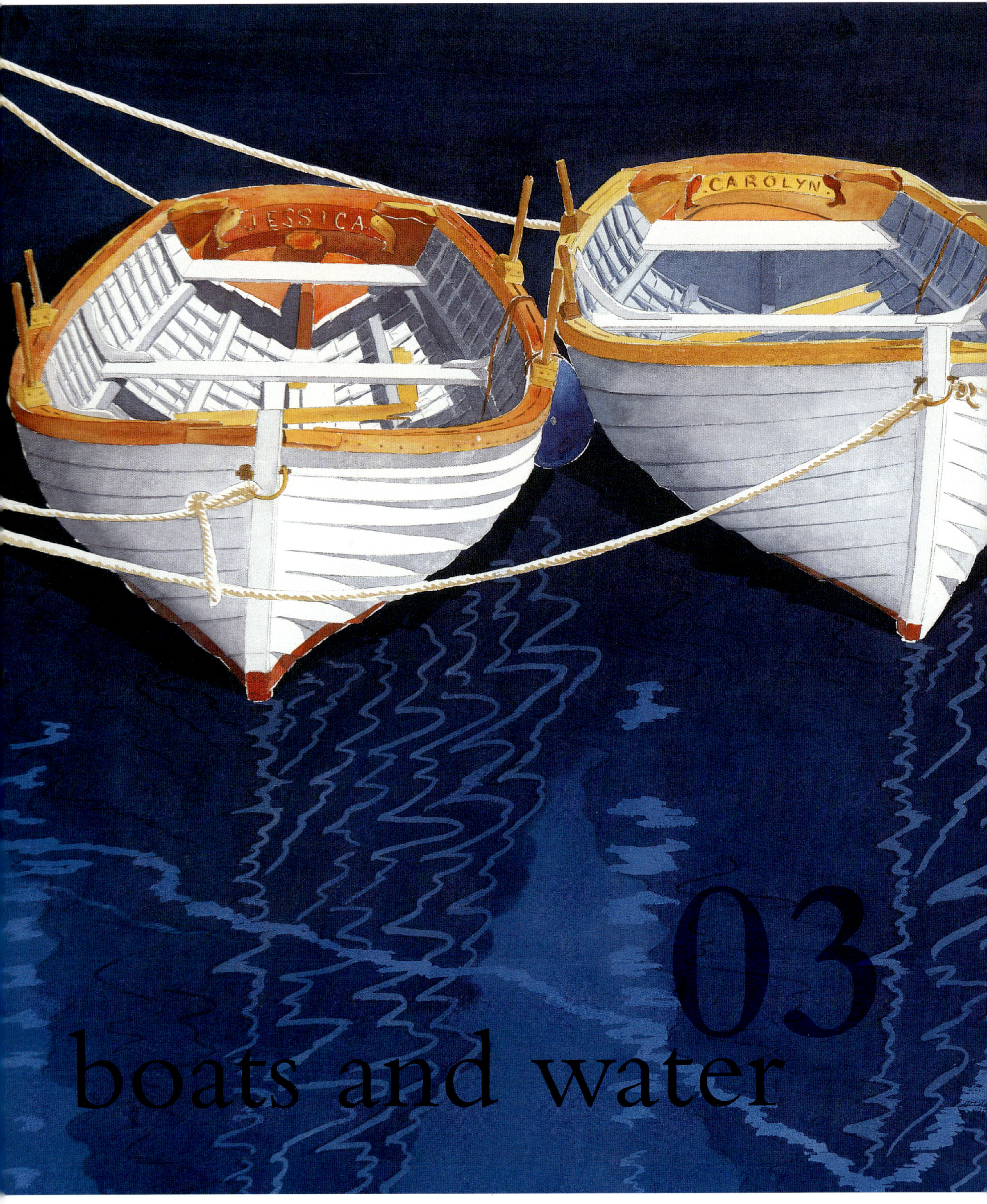

03 boats and water

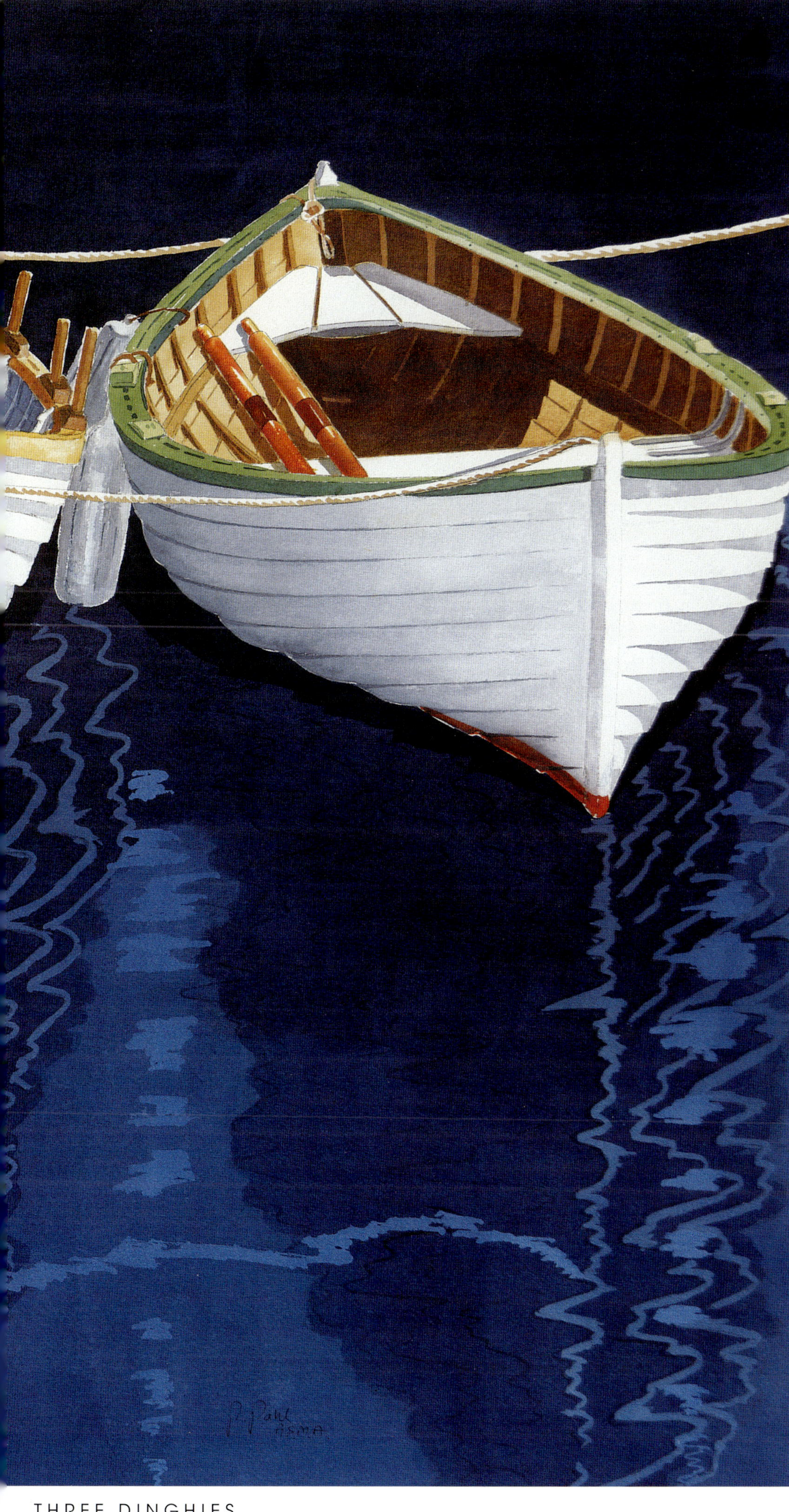

I love using vivid colors, and, although my boats are real, I take a lot of liberty. I can barely wait to finish my drawing so I can layer on the colors!

PAM PAHL

THREE DINGHIES

Pam Pahl • transparent watercolor • 30" × 42" (76cm × 107cm)

Painting from within arouses a passion that gives me the freedom to apply brushstrokes with conviction.

MIKE MAZER

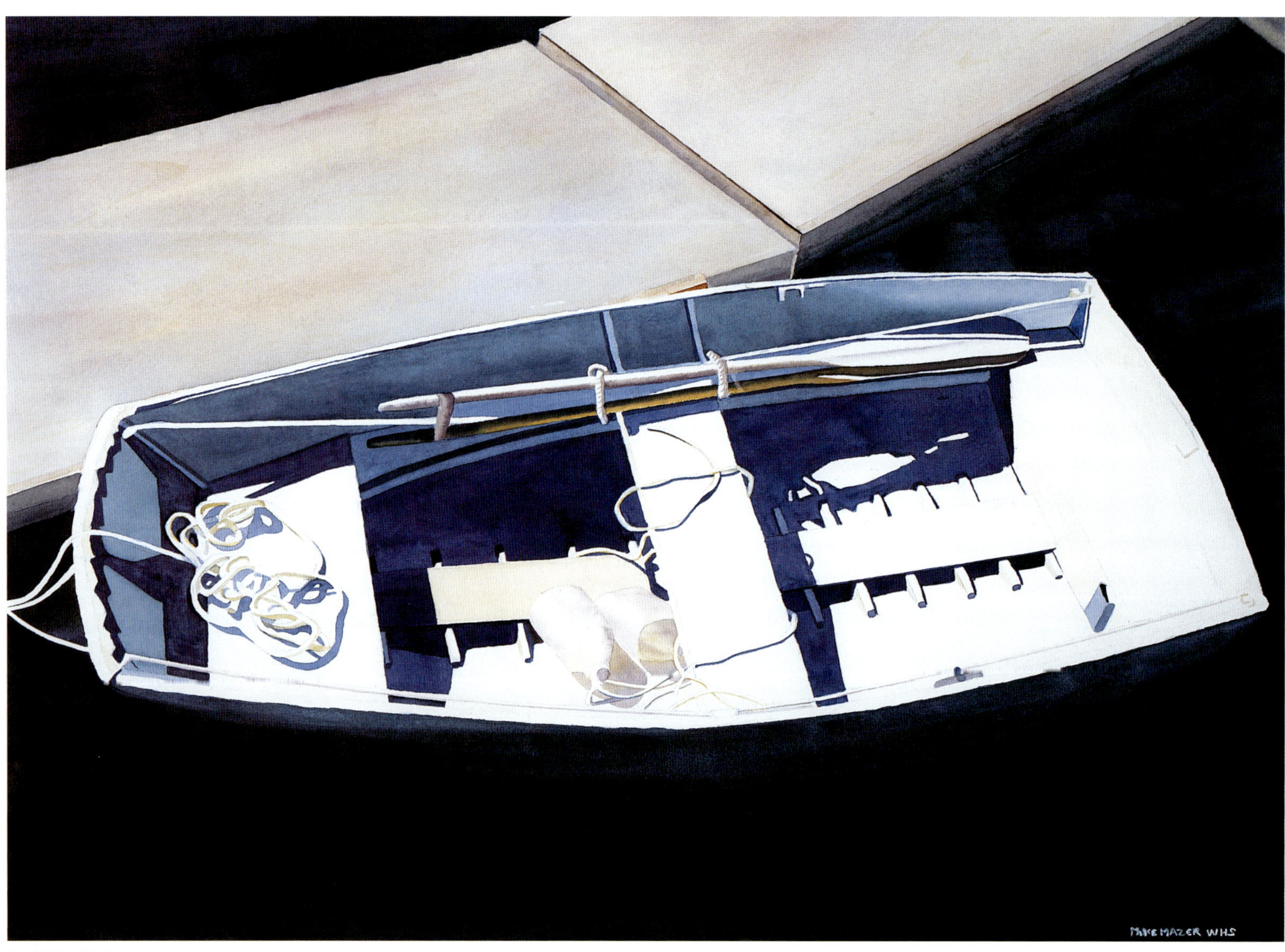

TIED UP

Mike Mazer • transparent watercolor • 22" × 30" (56cm × 76cm)

The many ways atmosphere and light affect value and color are what excite me about watercolor. The facts of a scene are not as important as this immediate impression. Prior to sketching and photographing a scene, an image has already been formed in my mind that expresses my feelings about the scene. With a limited palette of a warm and cool version of three primary colors along with a 1½-inch Robert Wade flat and a no. 38 Golden Fleece round, I commit myself to presenting only the image set in my mind. Fresh colors are generally applied wet-into-wet or removed with a damp brush. One of these paintings expresses the essence of the scene almost monochromatically, while the other relies on rich colors. But both are dependent upon a simple design of three to five triangular shapes.

IT AIN'T EASY

Mike Mazer • transparent watercolor • 24" × 18" (61cm × 46cm)

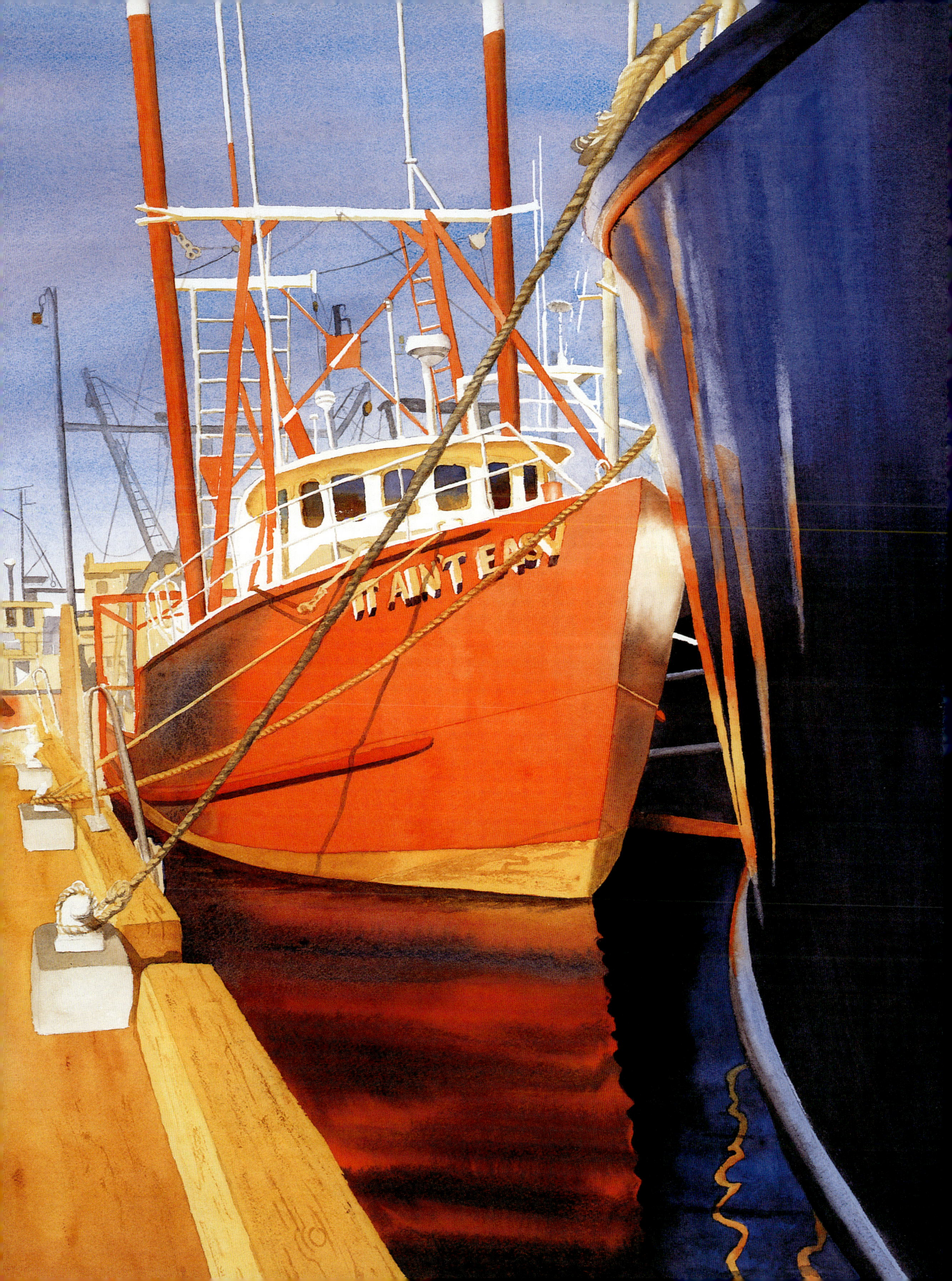
IT AIN'T EASY

For me, art is about quietly looking, digesting and visualizing the world around me and finding a meaningful spark of excitement.

MARGARET M. MARTIN

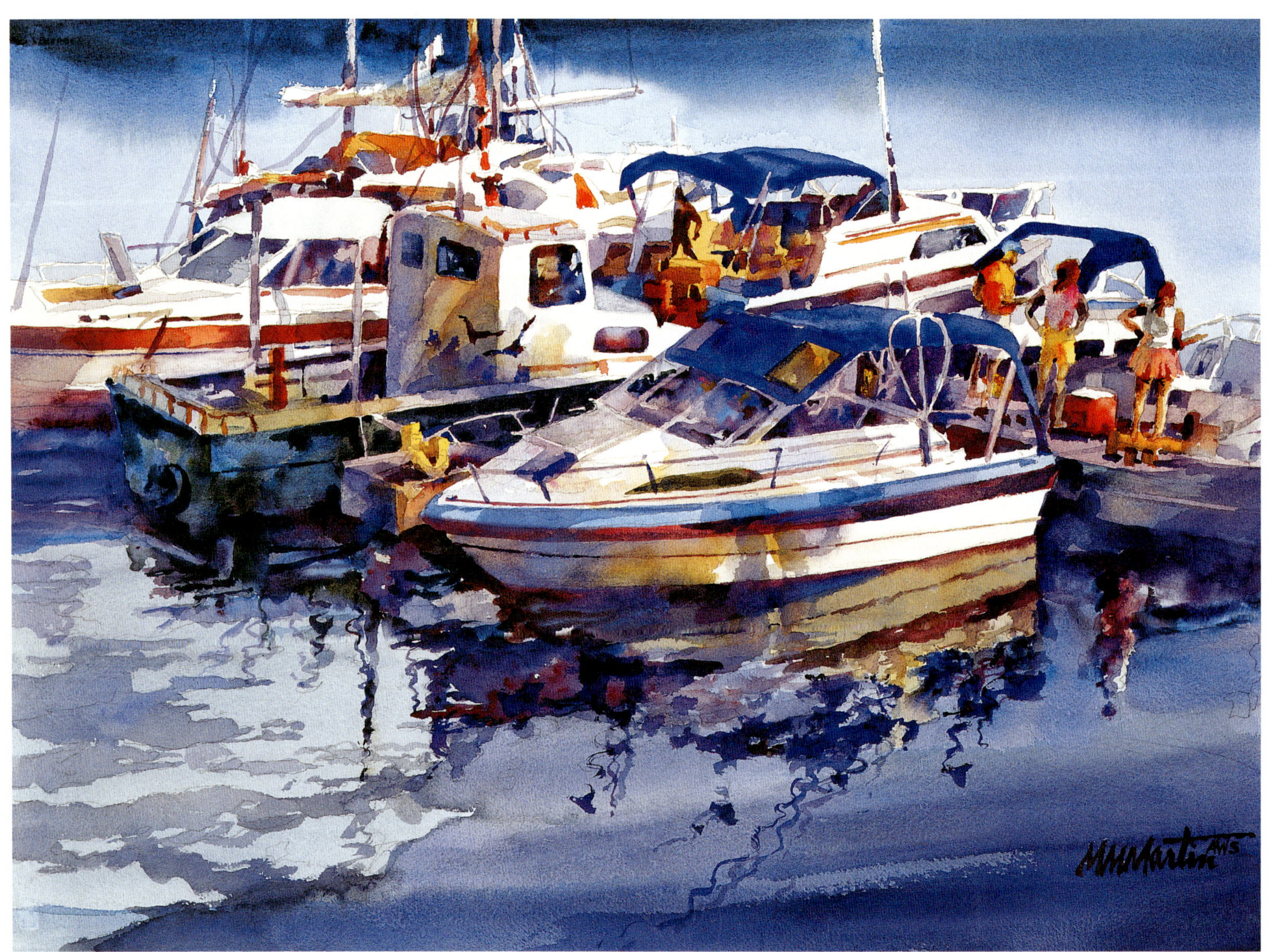

DOCKSIDE DESIGN

Margaret M. Martin • transparent watercolor • 22" x 30" (56cm x 76cm)

The staging of water and boats often presents dramatic visual opportunities. I like the shapes, the rhythms, the pulse, as well as the chance to utilize the purity of white paper. A superb full day was spent creating many quarter-sheet-size, black-and-gray value sketches on location at this scene. This quiet time allowed my passions to stretch. It was a time of intensity with subject and self. The sketches were organized and designed another day in my studio, but I will never forget the immediate feelings and celebration of on-site research. Wow! One needs time to digest the personal meaning of passion. A 3-inch (8cm) brush was used to stroke in the foreground and background to indicate gesture and action.

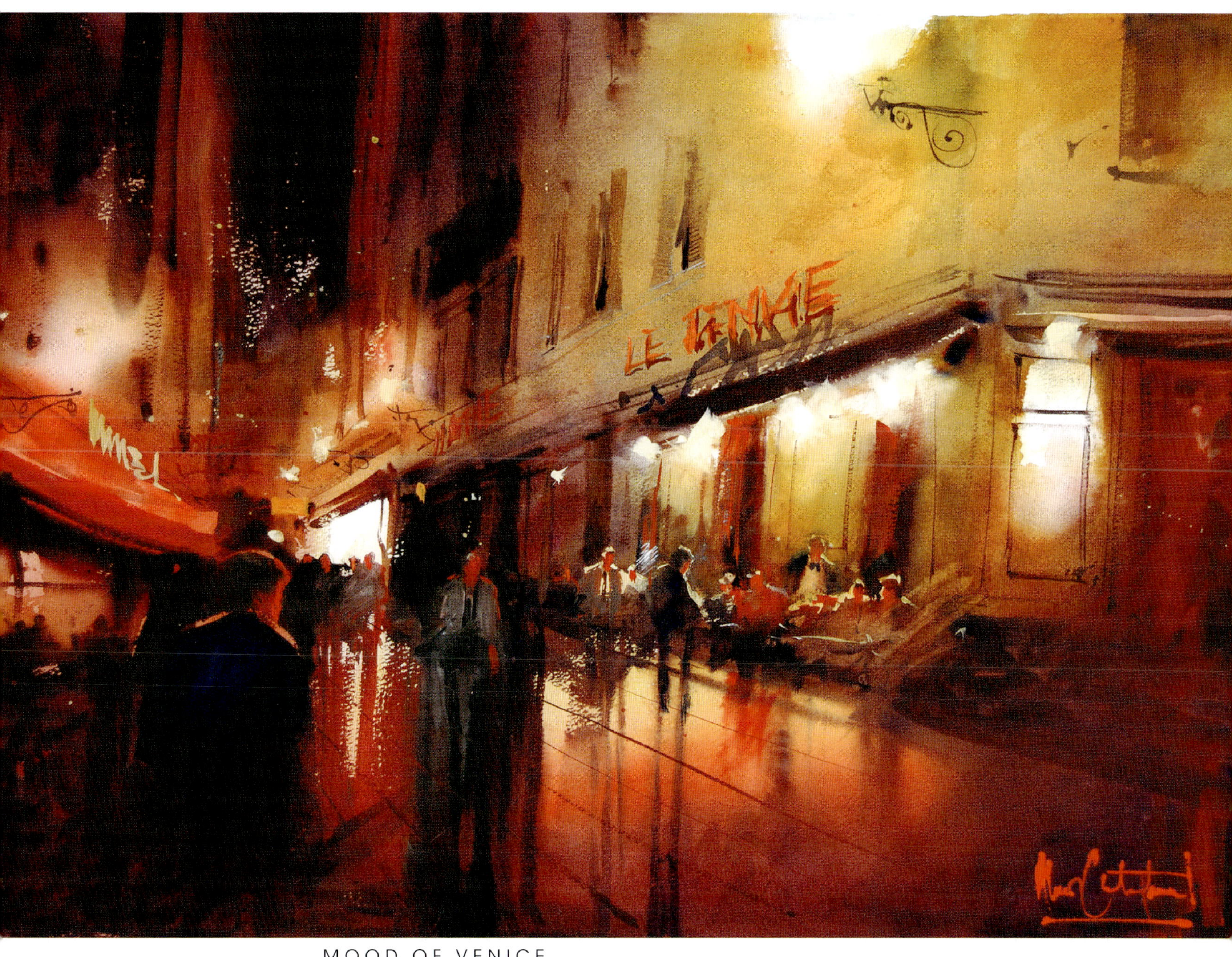

MOOD OF VENICE

Alvaro Castagnet • transparent watercolor • 22" × 30" (56cm × 76cm)

This painting is based on a sketch I did on a warm, summery evening, wandering around Venice. It was painted almost entirely with one wash, going from light to dark, simultaneously creating a sense of depth. The drama and mystery of twilight has always inspired me. I was attracted to the yellow corner, nicely lit against the dark, ambiguous light of the night.

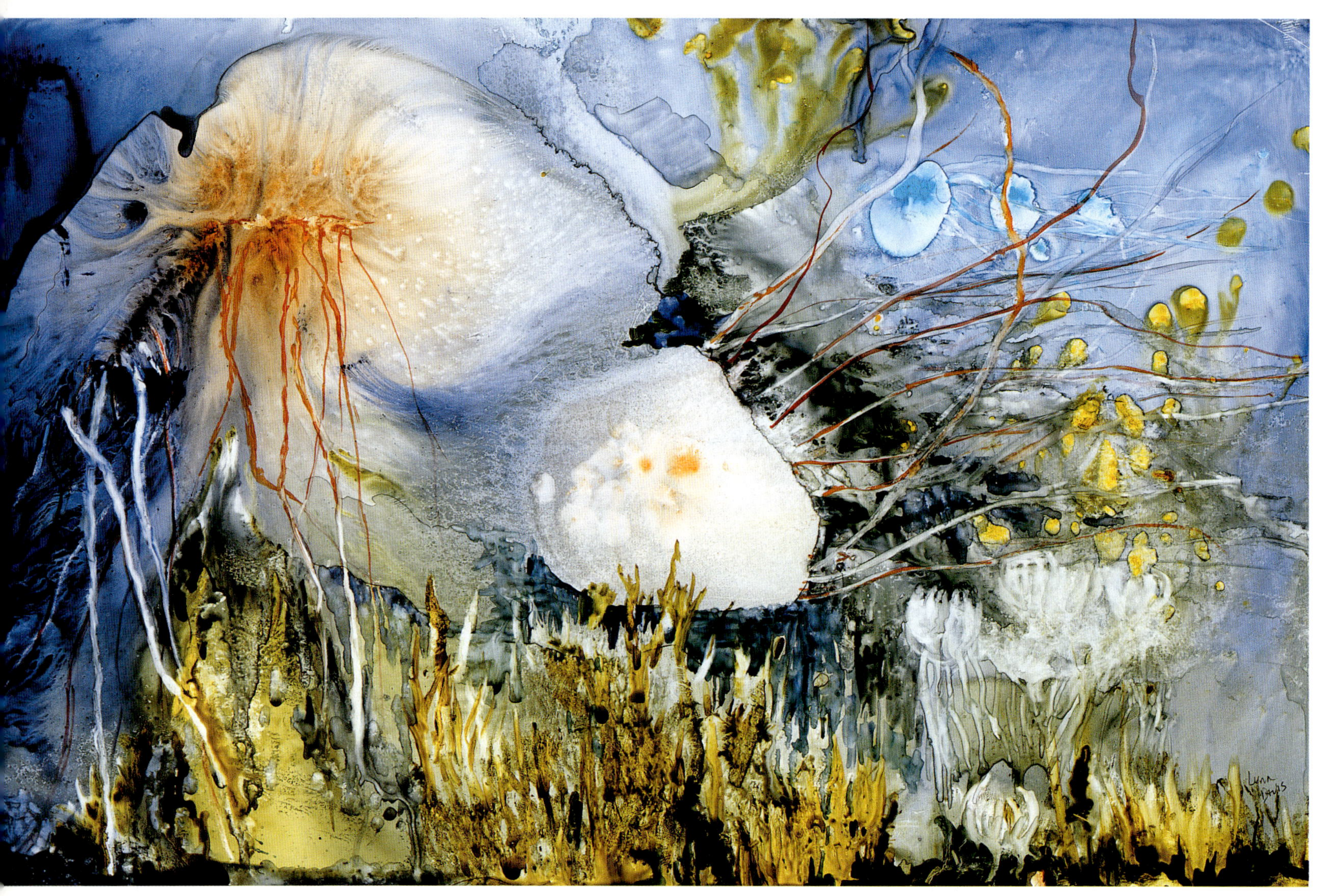

SEA JELLIES

Lynn C. Davis • watercolor on synthetic paper • 13" × 20" (33cm × 51cm)

I love painting on plasticized Yupo paper because of the element of surprise. In *Sea Jellies*, I started with blues, very wet and thick. Then I dropped in different colors, some liquid acrylic, some watercolor, and drew with a bit of alcohol, letting it swirl. As the picture set up, the jellyfish forms emerged. I imagined a beautiful underwater ocean scene such as I had seen while snorkeling in Baja. I then dropped in thick dark greens to create the environment and to accentuate the jellies. When the painting dried, I painted on the jellies' tentacles.

GONDOLA BASIN II

Laurel Covington-Vogl • transparent watercolor • 29" × 21" (74cm × 53cm)

Venice, wherever one looks, is an inspiring subject that allows me to indulge my passion for glowing color. Artfully decorated windows, masks, canal bridges, gondolas and luminous light can be experienced from dawn through dusk. The rich colors and distorted abstractions of reflected images particularly intrigued me. This painting was developed from several of my photographs taken of the Hotel Orseolo and its reflection in the basin next to it. My preferred method of painting is to place my watercolor board on a tilted surface, flood the selected area with water and quickly flow a rich color down over the surface. A large amount of paint must be prepared in advance to be successful.

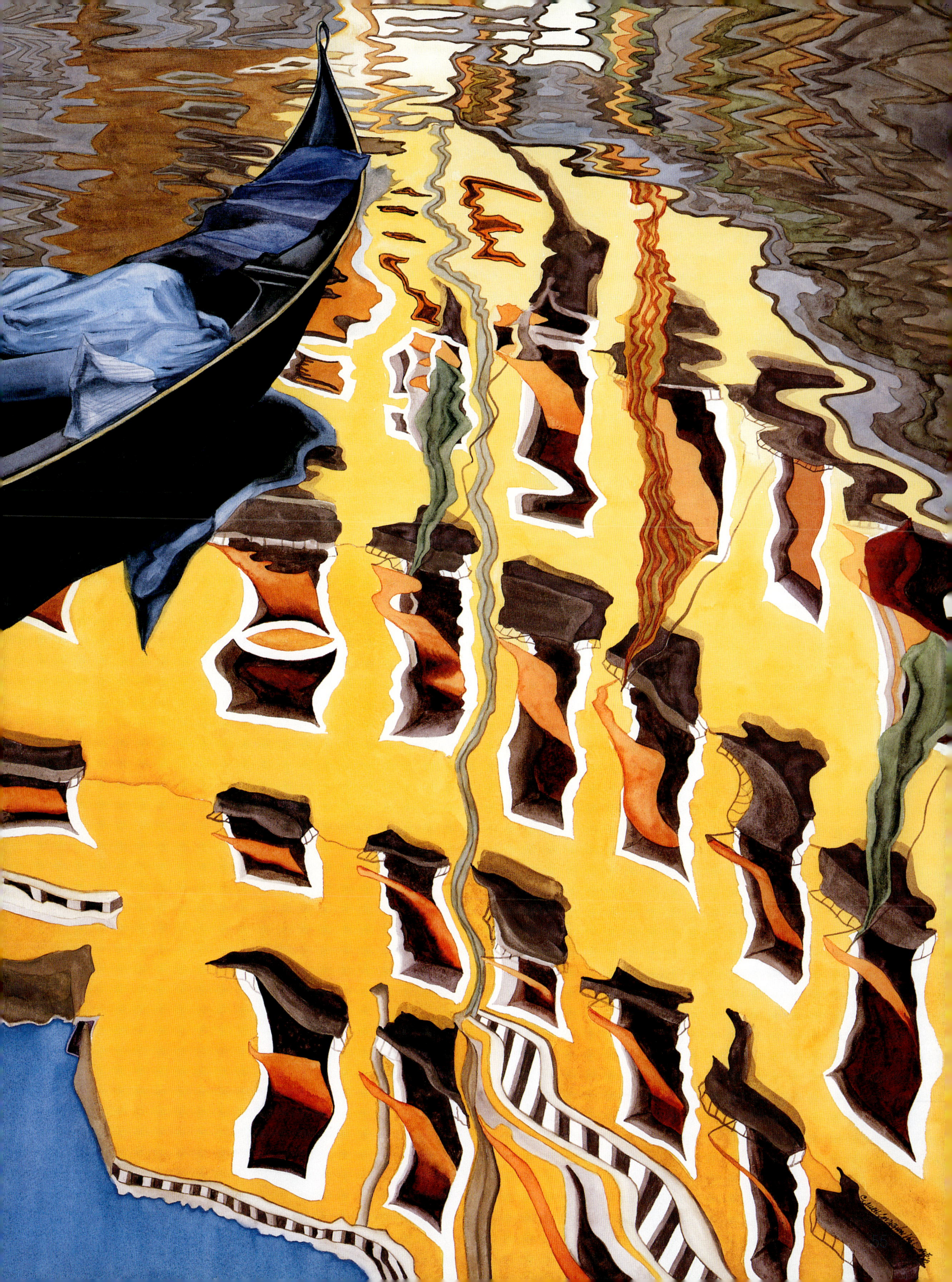

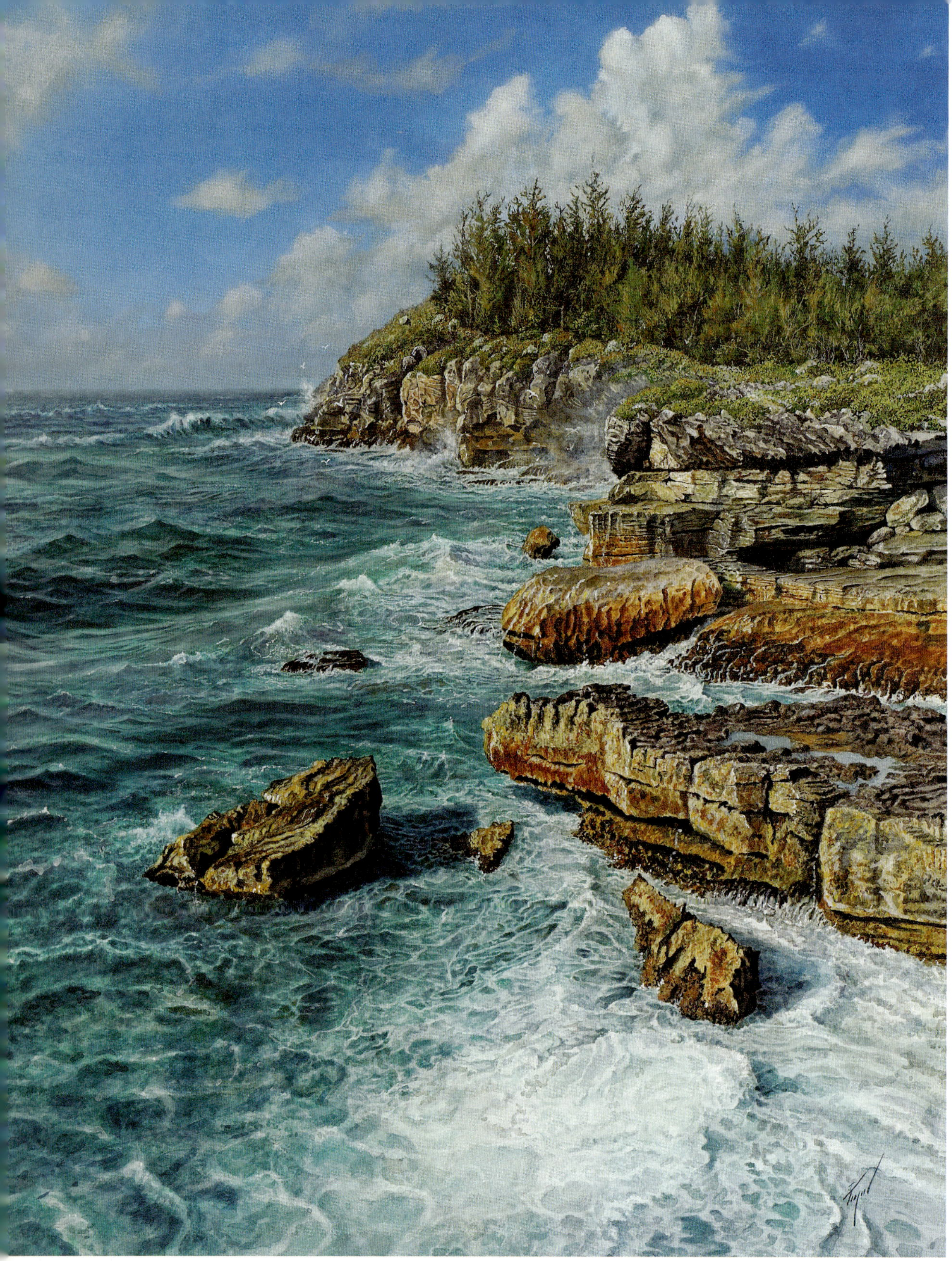

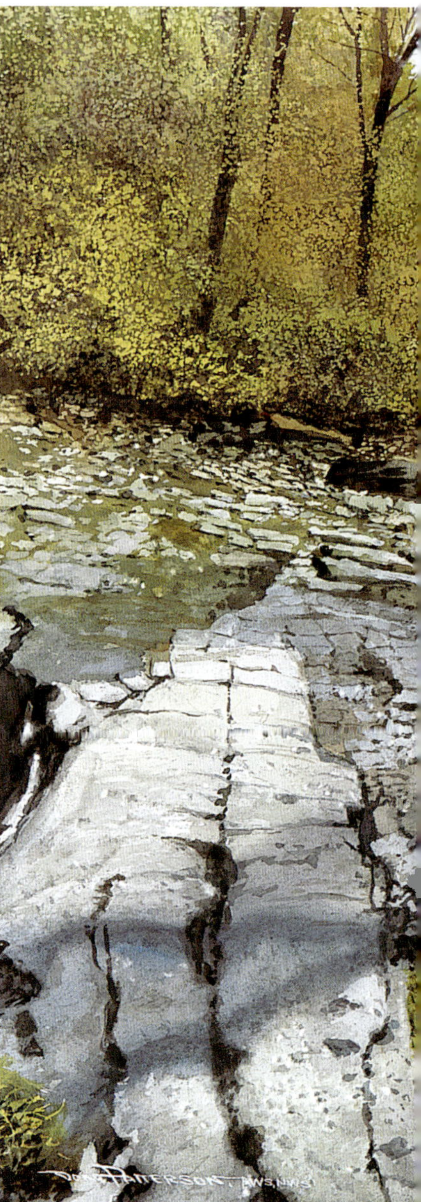

BREAKERS ON A ROCKY COAST

James Toogood • transparent watercolor • 23½" × 17½" (60cm × 44cm)

This painting was done in the studio from a series of on-site studies and photographs. To make the rocks, I applied the paint rather wet, almost dripping it onto the surface. When these brushstrokes dried, they formed dark, jagged edges that help convey the rocks' rough texture. To paint the kinetic energy of the water, I made a series of brushstrokes that were themselves fluid, often using my whole arm. I backed off on the amount of water used in each stroke to prevent dark edges from forming around these marks. This is the second painting I did of this location along the south shore of Bermuda. Unlike the first painting, which depicts a placid sea at low tide, this painting depicts the violence and danger of an angry sea. For me, it is at once thrilling and terrifying.

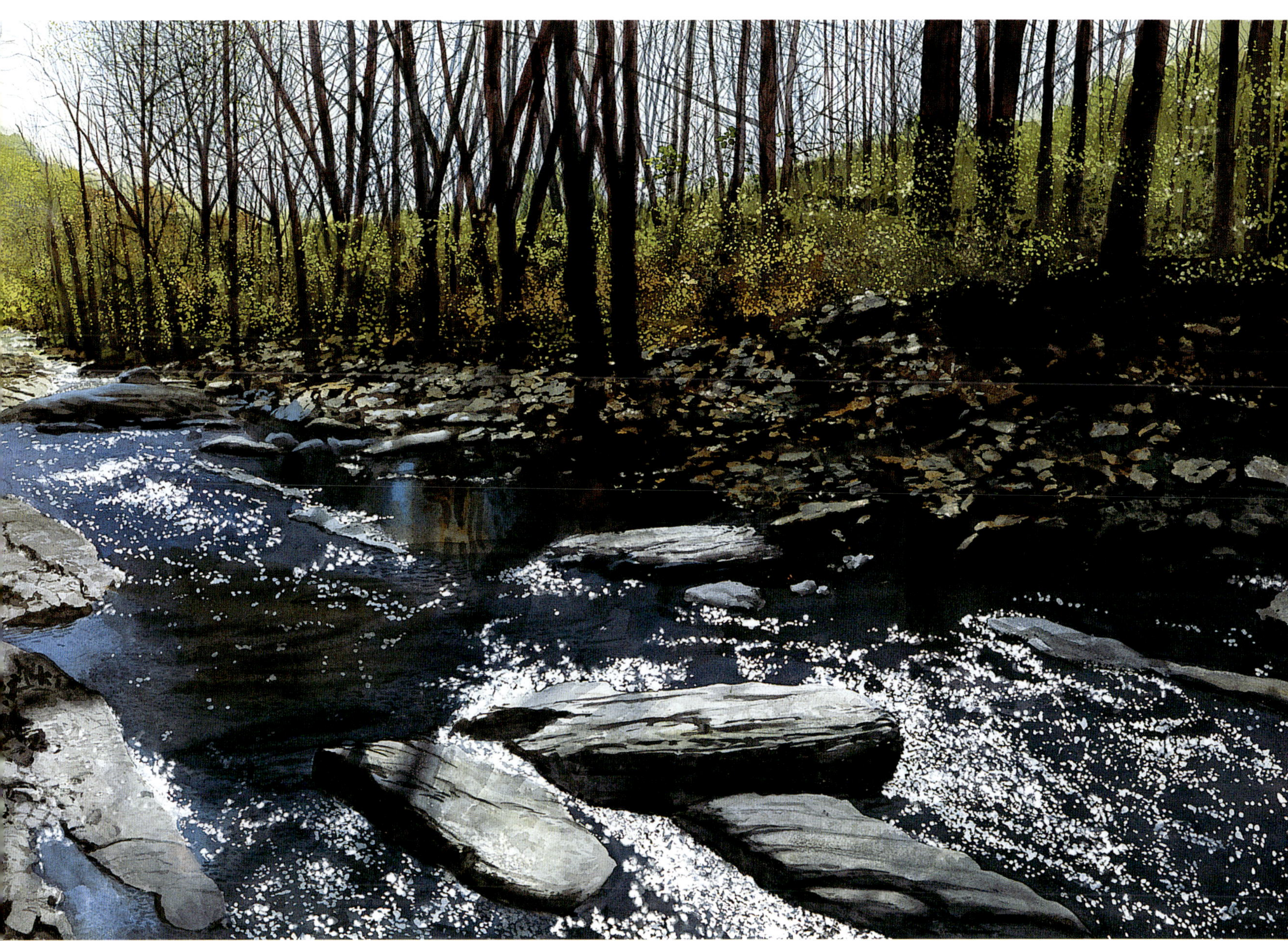

SHIMMERING WATERS

Donald W. Patterson • transparent watercolor • 19¾" × 36¾" (50cm × 93cm)

I came upon this scene while on a field trip with my camera and was immediately struck by the backlit water. Here was a challenge I could not resist. My passion for painting is fueled by two things: the difficulty of painting the subject and my fervent hope that viewers of my works will internally *feel* the subject as I do. Before any color was brushed onto the paper, it was necessary to preserve all of the hundreds of sparkles. I applied masking fluid with a tapping motion using an old-fashioned ruling pen. Before removing the masking, I completed the entire work with transparent watercolor. The last step was to use an electric eraser; keeping it sharpened to a point, I proceeded to soften the sparkles where necessary.

I like to make people smile when they see my work. I want to create a painting that tells a story—evoking a memory or unleashing the imagination.

STEPHEN BATES

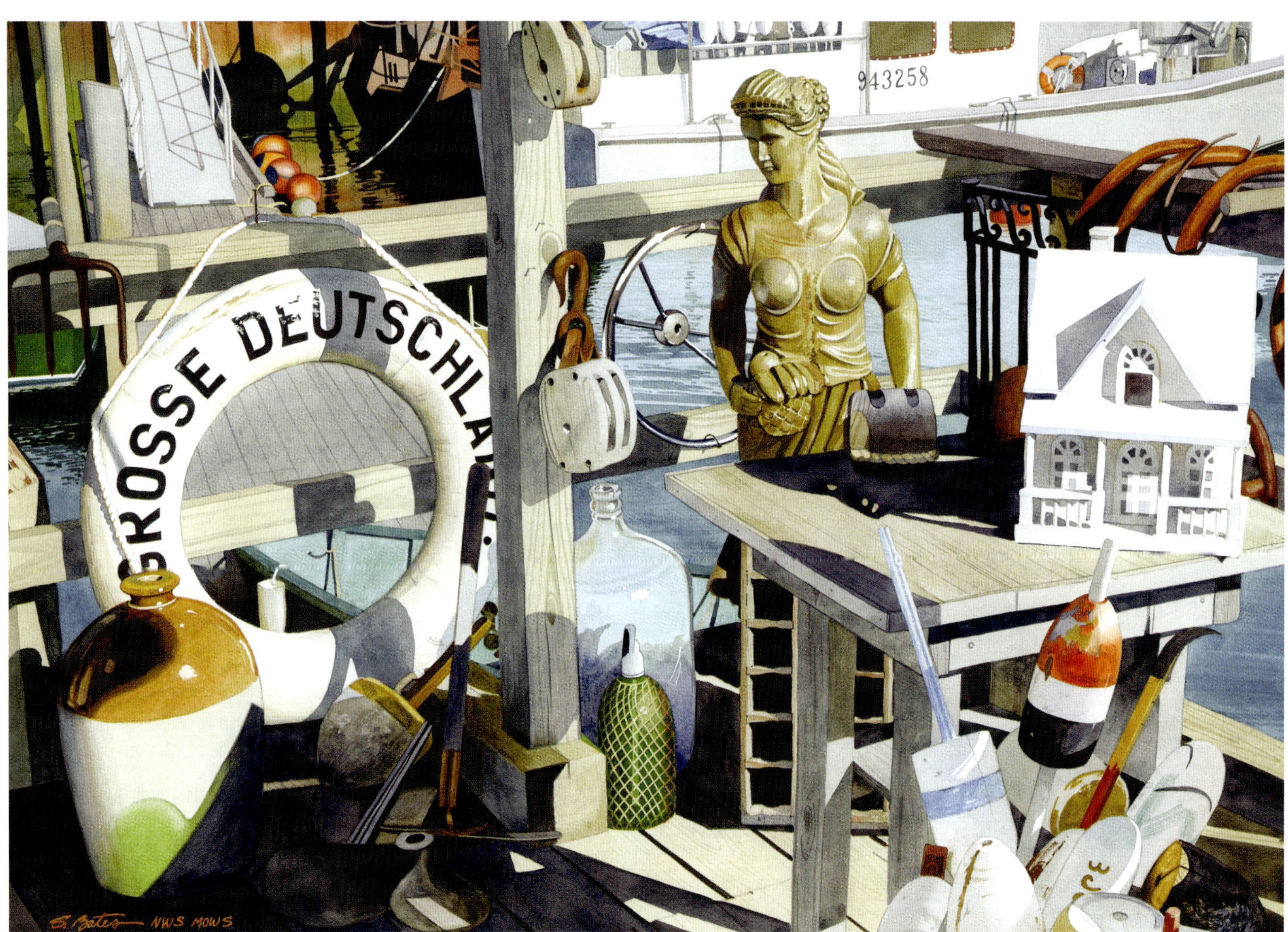

THE LADY OF SCITUATE

Stephen Bates • transparent watercolor • 16" × 22" (41cm × 56cm)

We were traveling from Boston to Cape Cod and stopped in the village of Scituate. I stepped out on the deck of a waterfront shop and knew I had a painting! All the interesting objects and shapes, lights, shadows and textures created an enticing challenge. I took several reference photos and decided to make the statue the focal point. Its metallic sheen would be especially fun to paint. To keep the painting totally transparent, I applied Pebeo liquid frisket where needed with a quill pen before using glazes of rich Winsor & Newton colors.

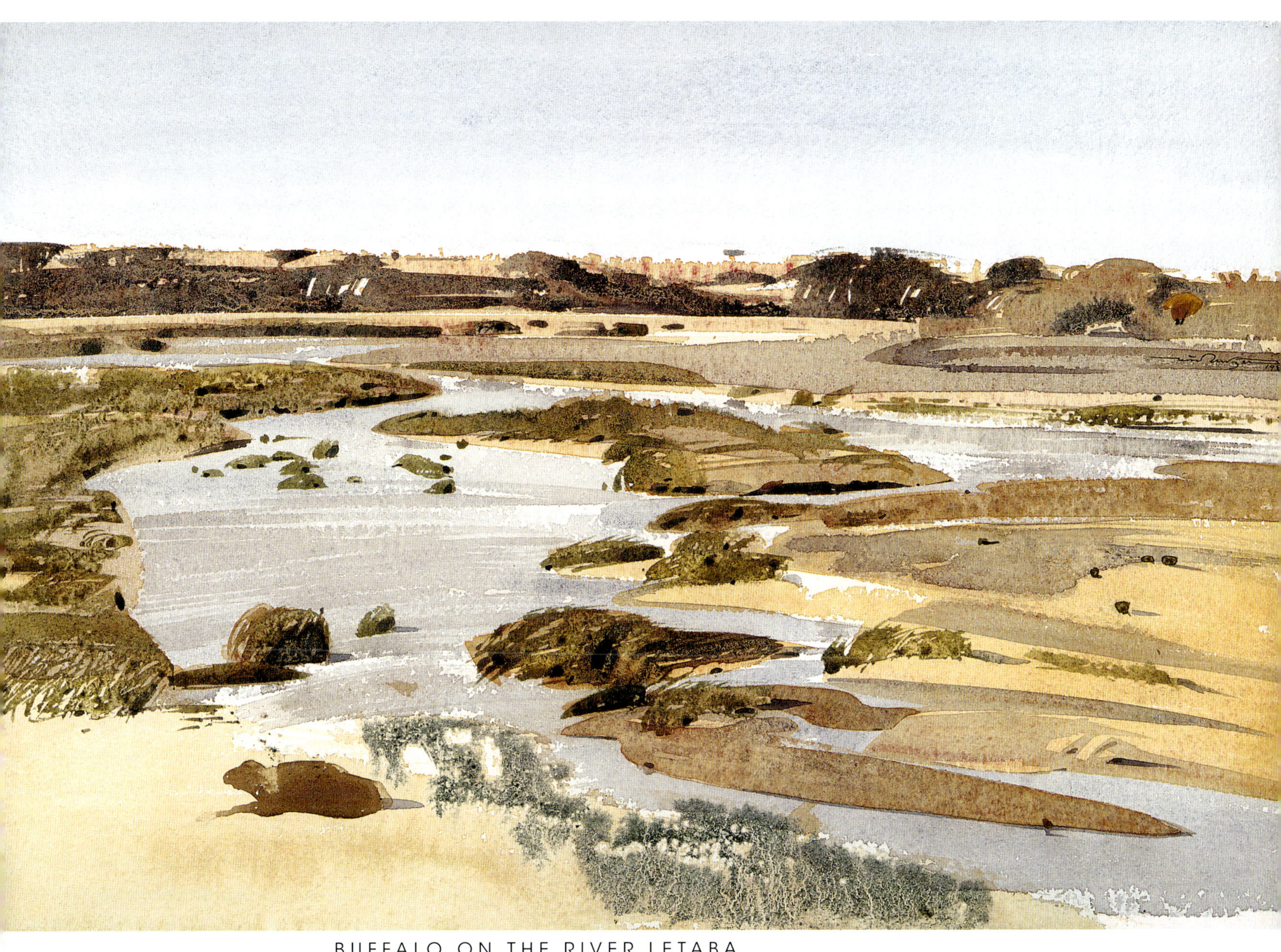

BUFFALO ON THE RIVER LETABA

Charles Timothy Prutzer • transparent watercolor • 15" × 22" (38cm × 56cm)

For two years I lived in Africa, working on a mural, but took every free moment to paint on location in the bushveldt. There is something about rivers and the stacking of landscape elements that I find alluring, particularly when the watercourse in Africa is frequented by dangerous game. In this case, I spent three late afternoons painting this plein air life study in South Africa. No photography was used. Some of the passages appear as though they were quickly struck; however, each stroke required a good deal of thought in the heat of the moment.

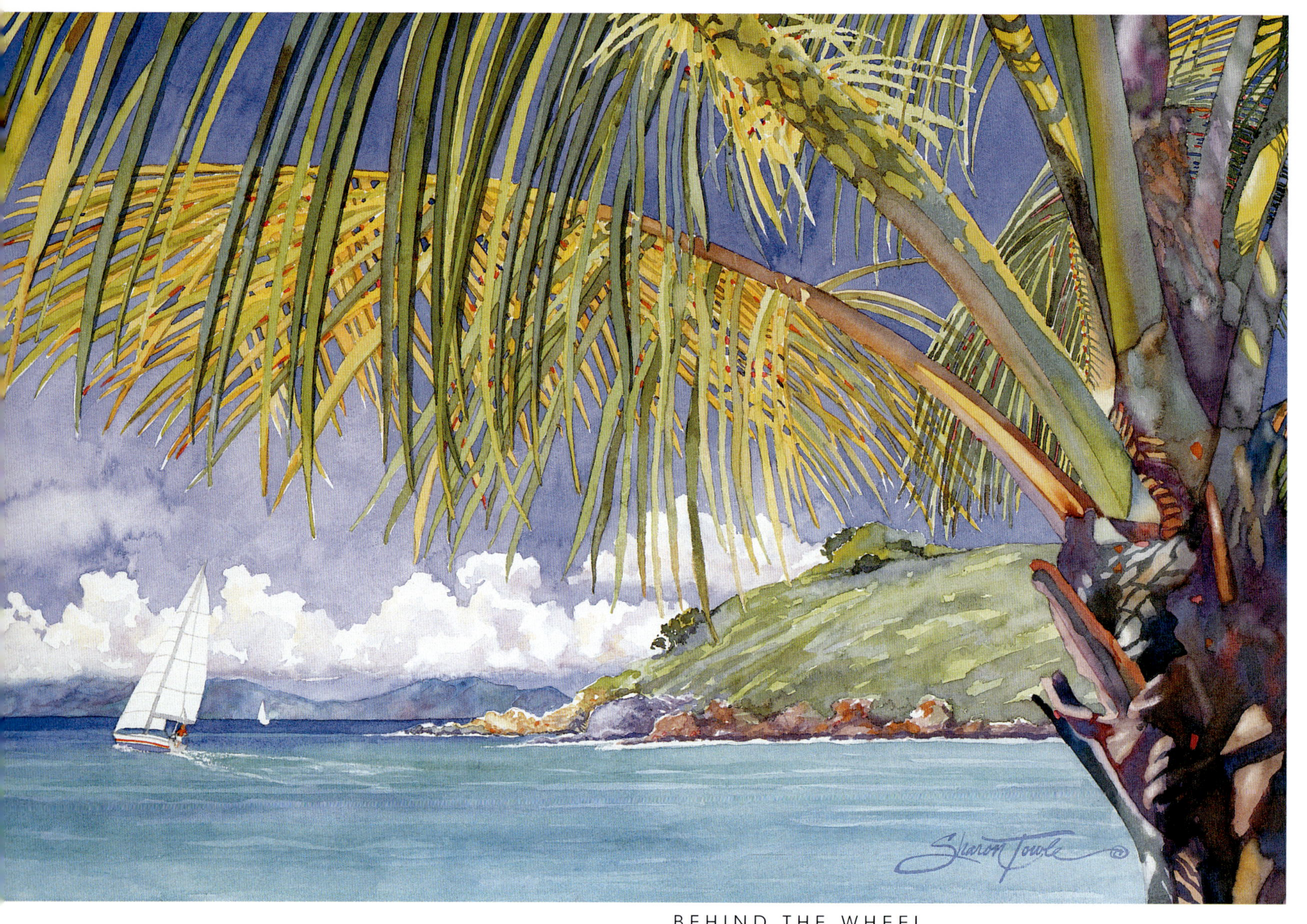

BEHIND THE WHEEL

Sharon Towle • transparent watercolor • 15" × 22" (38cm × 56cm)

Other than painting, my greatest passions are sailboats, islands and the tropics. So what would be better than to combine them all—the sun, the clatter of wind in the palms, the Windex-blue water and the breeze blowing across the sails? I take lots of photos—I'm much too busy having fun to stop and paint. It's also usually too humid for my style of painting. I use wet-into-wet for the softness of the distant hills and the underpainting of the sea and closer hills. I then use a hard-edge technique to define wave action and the hillside. There are color variations in each crisp-edged palm frond. The clouds are a combination of crisp edges on top and softness on the bottom. The finishing touches are the small spots of bright, colorful sunlight.

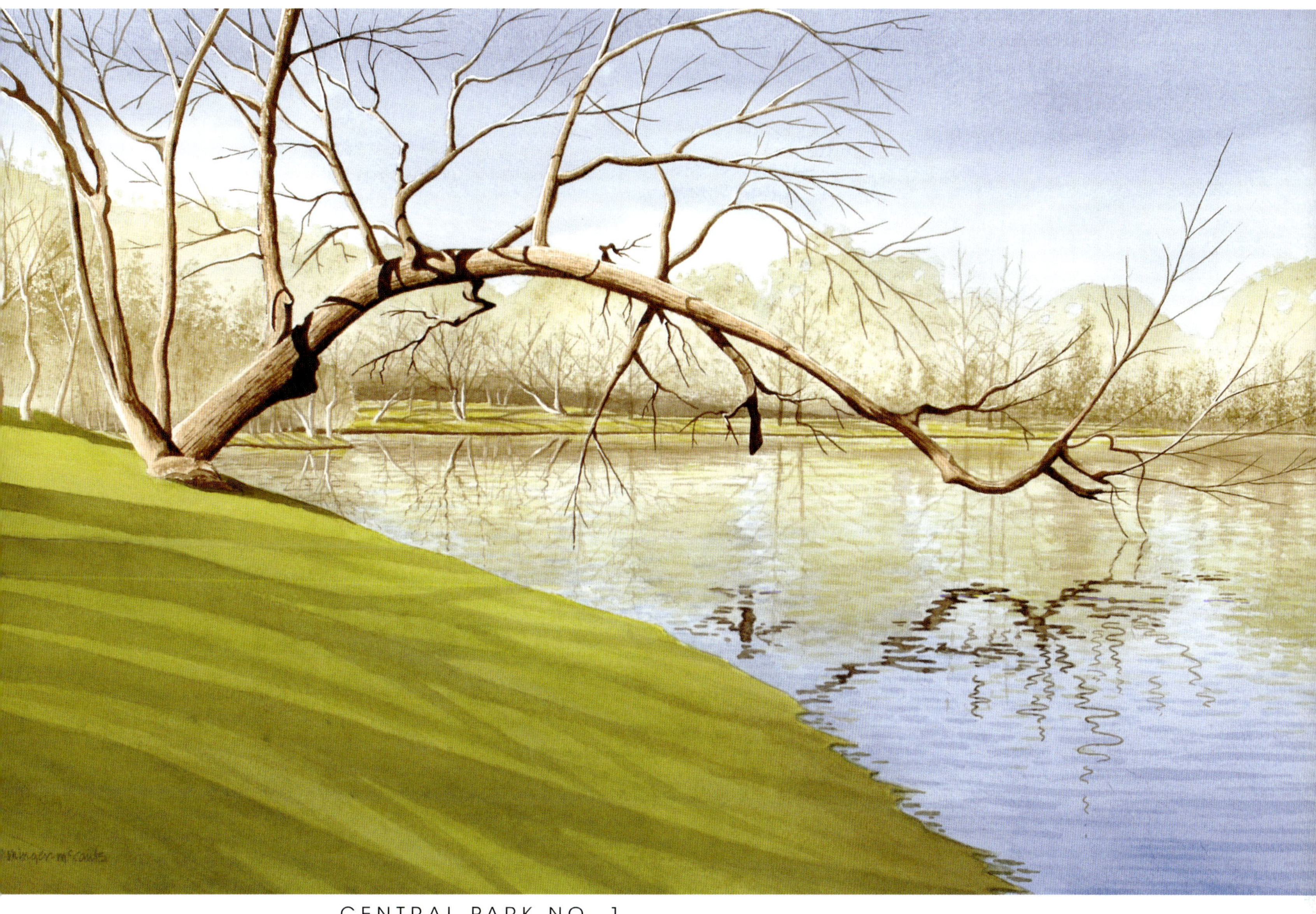

CENTRAL PARK NO. 1

Peggy Minger-McCants • transparent watercolor on 140-lb. (300gsm) cold-pressed paper • 17½" × 28" (44cm × 71cm)

This is a winter scene near my home in California where I often walk in the morning. I was especially inspired by this gnarled old tree bent low to the sparkling water where one or two tiny branches connected the tree to its reflected self. I spent more time doing sketches, value studies and a small watercolor study than I did painting the final picture. But, by the time I put brush to paper, I knew my subject intimately and could relax. After I established the color zones with the initial washes, I applied the paint to the grass and water using large brushstrokes, one layer over the next, until the desired color and value were achieved. I textured the tree bark by lightly dragging the dry brush in the direction of the tree's growth. The crystal water (mostly Cobalt Blue) was enhanced by the vibrating adjacent green (Winsor Green plus Aureolin Yellow). This unusual color combination captured the essence of that morning as the long shadows swept over the velvetlike grass, contrasting the sparkling reflections in the water.

I am entranced by the spectacular moments created when the warm late-afternoon sun partners with rich, cool cast shadows.

SANDRA BRAY

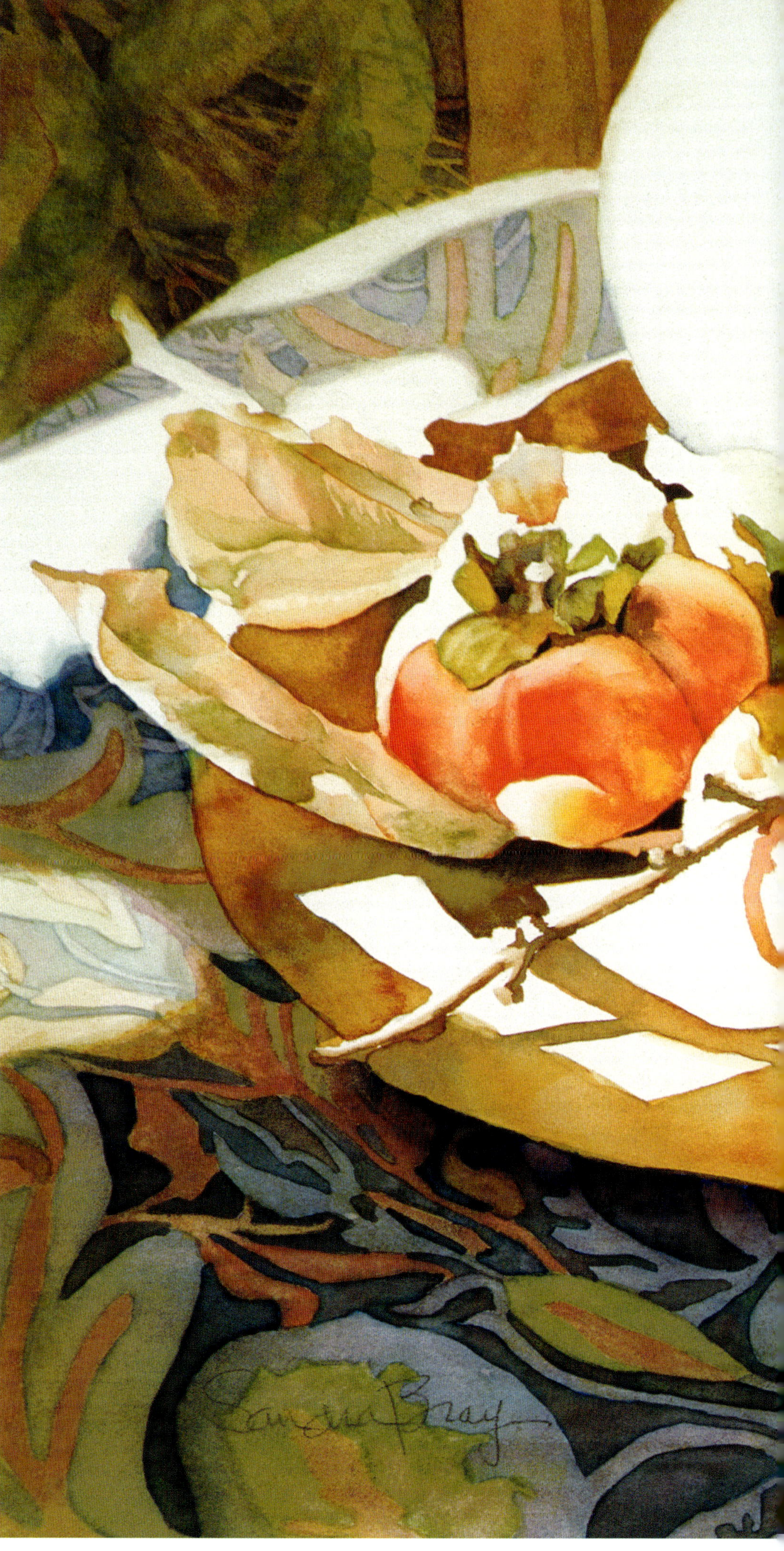

BLUE VASE

Sandra Bray • transparent watercolor • 22" × 30" (56cm × 76cm)

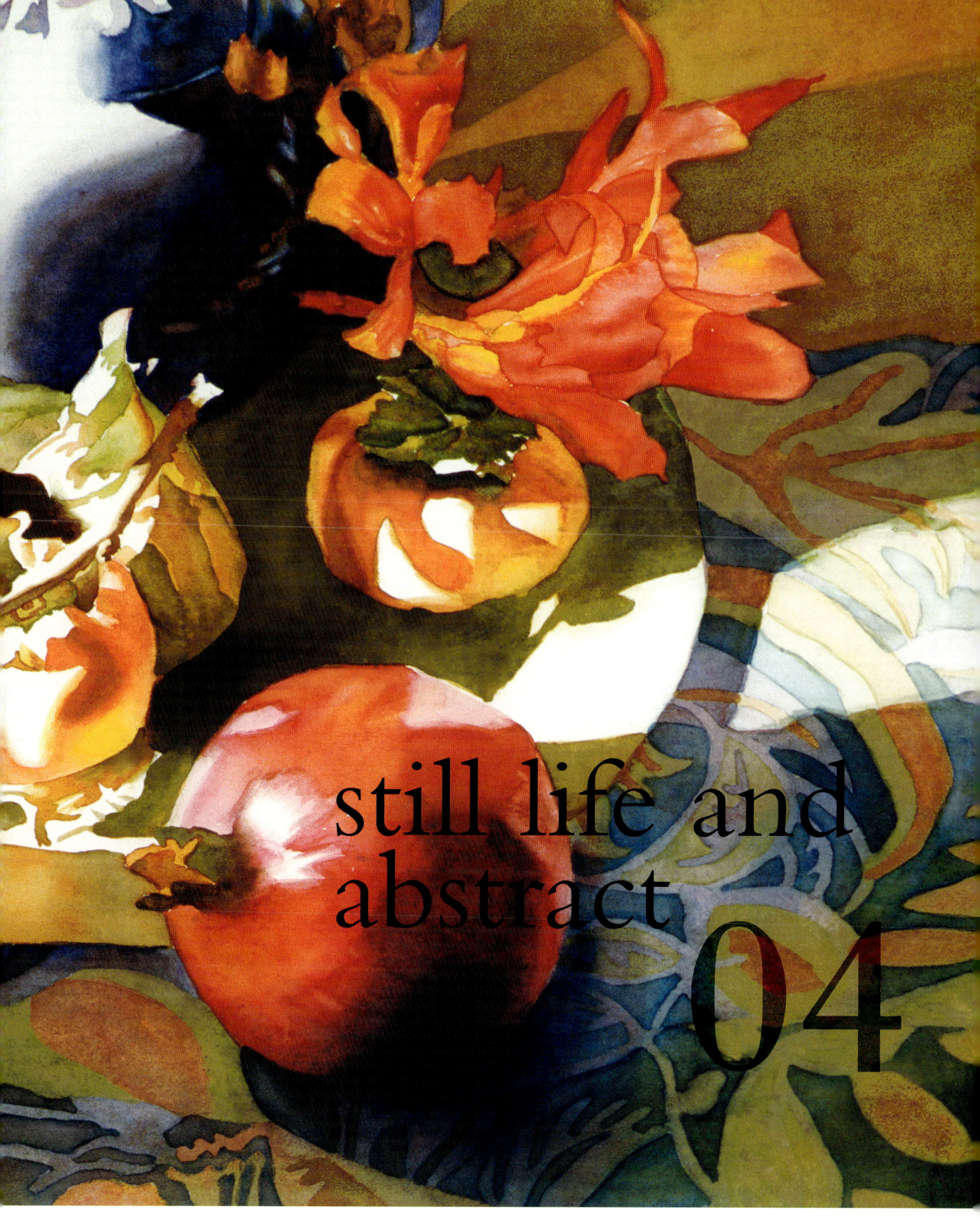

still life and abstract 04

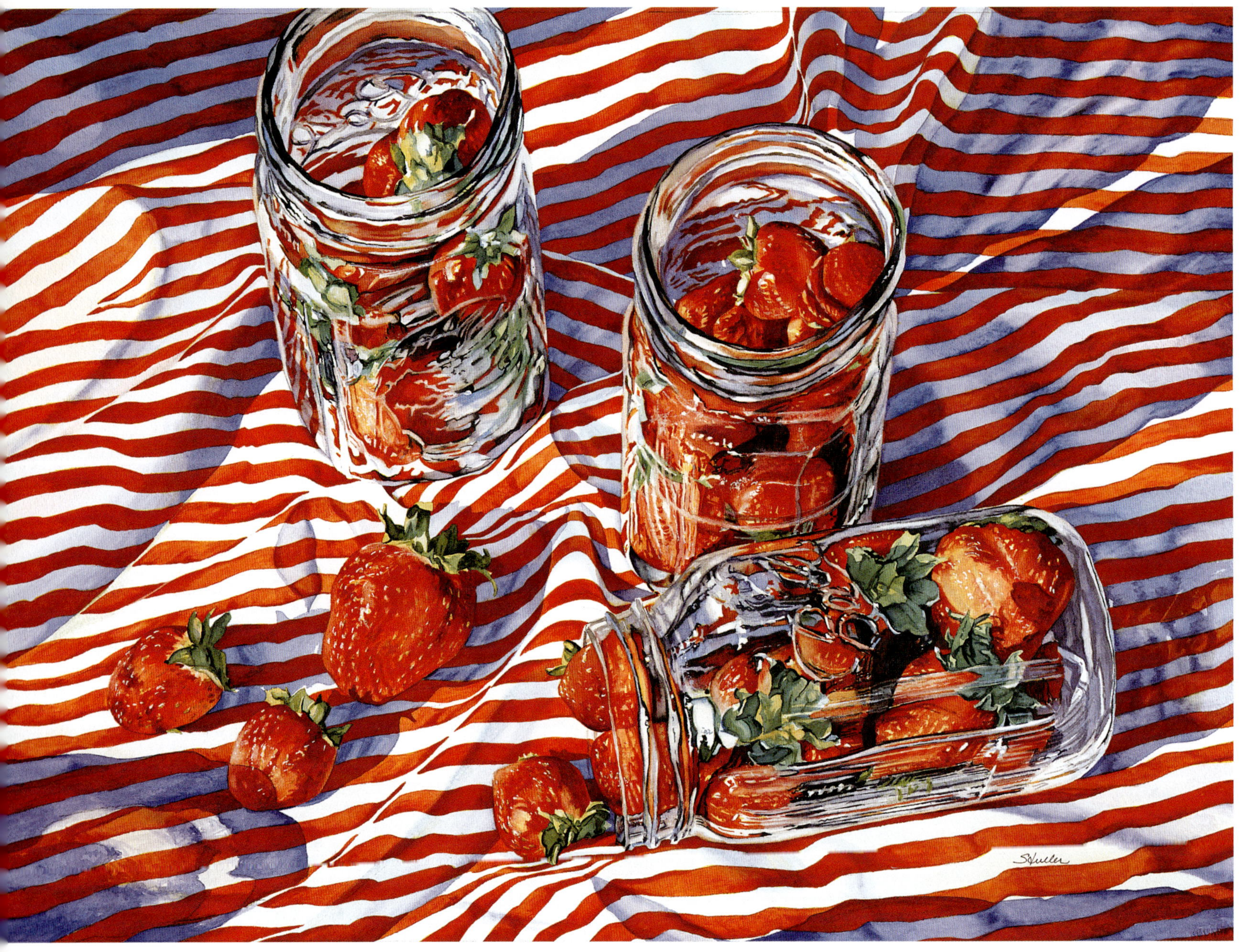

STRAWBERRY JAMMING

Susan M. Stuller • transparent watercolor • 21" × 29" (53cm × 74cm)

I approach painting with one main goal: "to kick it up a notch." I set up my still lifes with an eye toward value and contrast—capturing light is crucial. I love the drawing process and believe that a great painting starts with a good foundation. I work from original photographs, often combining several to achieve the composition I desire. Color is built up using glazes of transparent watercolor. The paint should be rich enough to swirl across the palettelike cream. I push the color intensity past realism using Dr. Ph. Martin's (Hydrus) Watercolors. After painting for many years, I still strive to find new methods and mediums to intensify realism.

Many of life's trials and celebrations are worked through with a paintbrush in hand; painting is both my passion and my therapy.

SUSAN M. STULLER

> The slow building of strong contrasts creates the appearance of visual depth that I crave.
>
> LAURIE HUMBLE

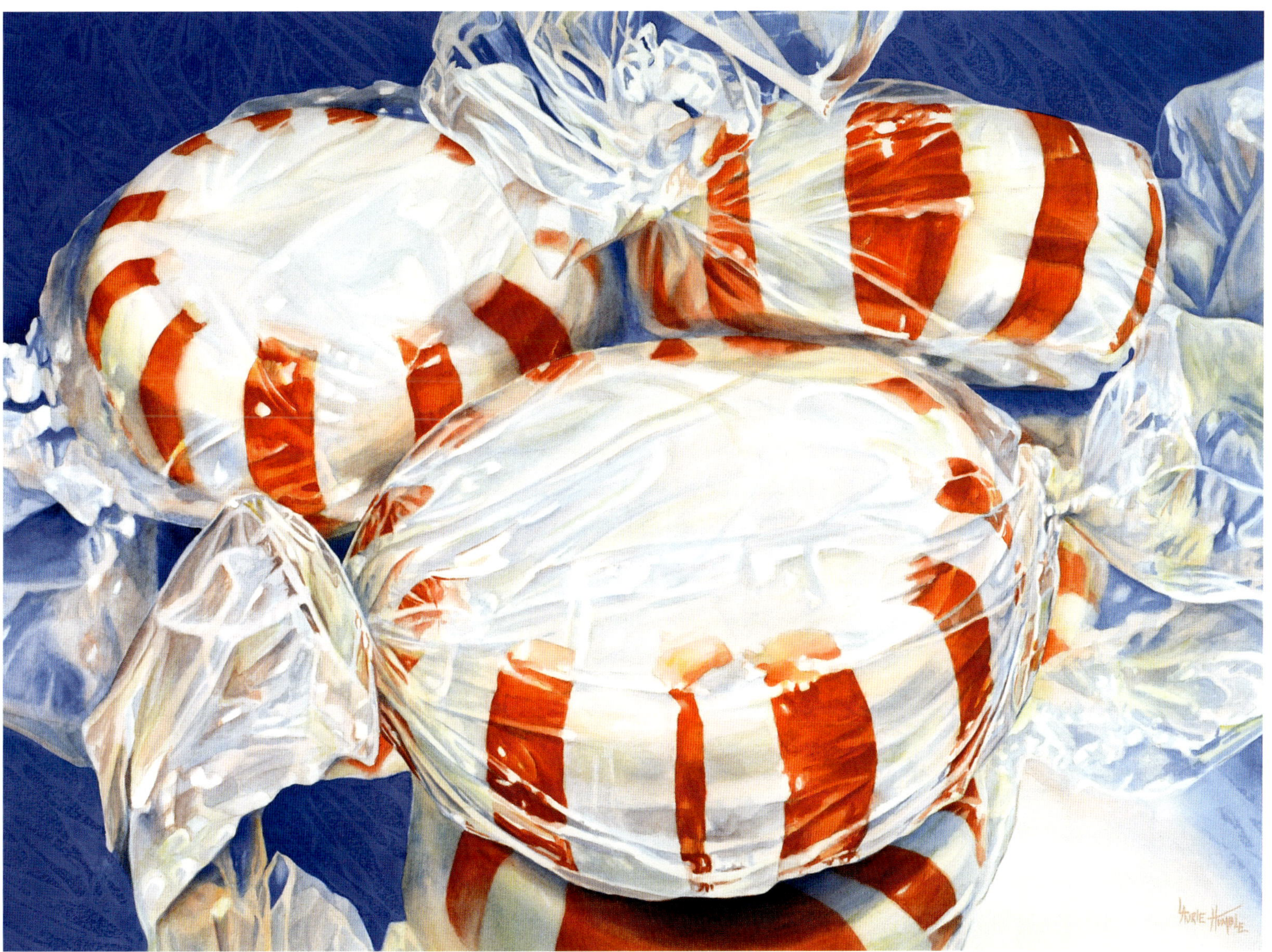

AFTER DINNER

Laurie Humble • transparent watercolor • 22" × 30" (56cm × 76cm)

I initially set up the after-dinner mints as an assignment for my students. As I explained that they would need to think of the mint as "background" to the cellophane in order to capture it, I couldn't wait to paint it myself. The cellophane was both reflective and transparent, presenting just the kind of challenge I enjoy most. I worked from both the live setup and photographs, because I was interested in capturing specific light conditions. I began by painting carefully around my white and lighter spaces using very pale washes. I save my whites from the beginning because I find masking fluid too messy to work with, and I don't like the look of opaque white paint. Rich, vibrant colors and darks were then built up slowly through many layers of transparent color.

Painting impacts how I see and experience the world, and I try to capture that visual abundance in my paintings.

LAURIN MCCRACKEN

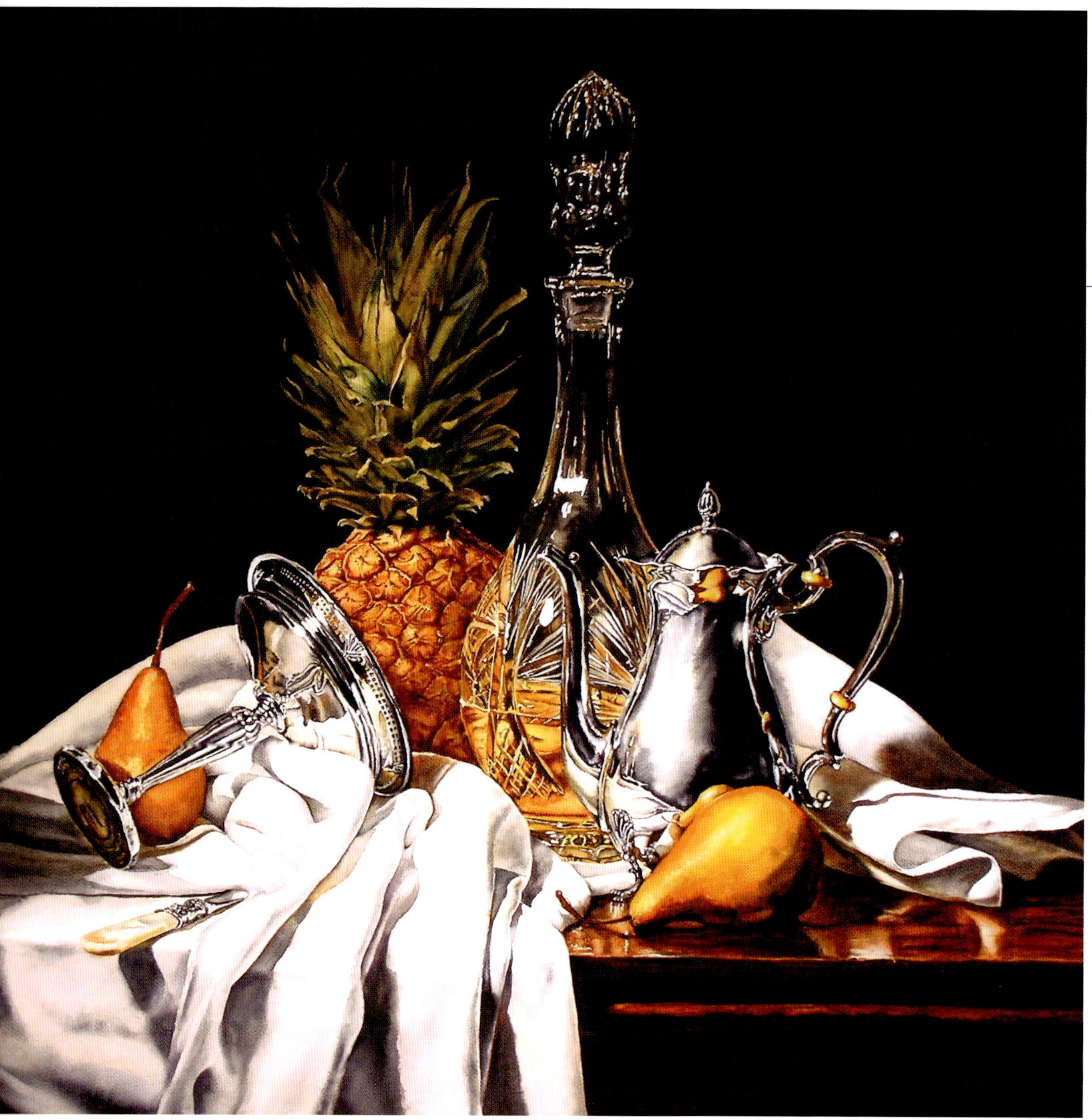

HOSPITALITY

Laurin McCracken • watercolor • 20" × 20" (51cm × 51cm)

I was in search of an image that reflected the Dutch still lifes of the seventeenth century, an image of abundance. I set up a still life in a friend's house, using her cut glass and silver. Over the next two days I added items and subtracted them. From the over two hundred images I shot, I have produced four paintings. This painting shows just a portion of the elaborate still-life setup. I used very conventional transparent techniques. Almost everything, including the smallest details, was painted in a two-brush method with one brush for color and the other charged with water to soften edges. The pineapple, a universal symbol of hospitality, gives the painting its name.

NAPA MERLOT

Cindy Agan • watercolor and gouache • 26½" × 18¼" (67cm × 46cm)

Napa Merlot was set up next to a window in my studio, and the closer I moved in with the camera lens, the more excited I became. I left the props in place as reference for the details, but I relied on my photographs for consistent lighting. High concentrates of watercolor pigment, applied in multiple glazes, were used to build up the deepest colors, while the white of the paper was preserved for the brightest highlights. White gouache was used sparingly to clean up the edges of the glass reflections.

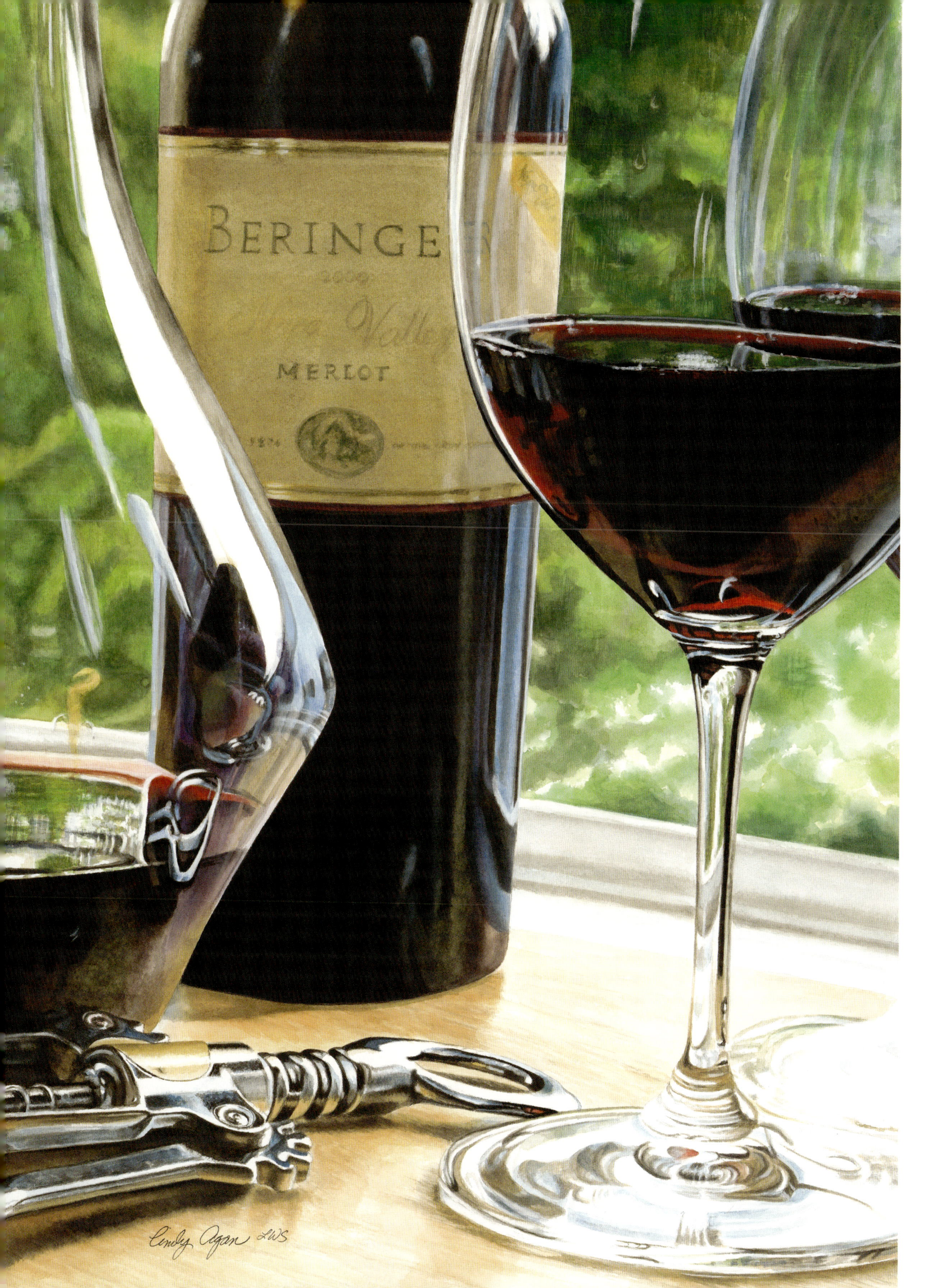
BERINGE
MERLOT
Cindy Agan LWS

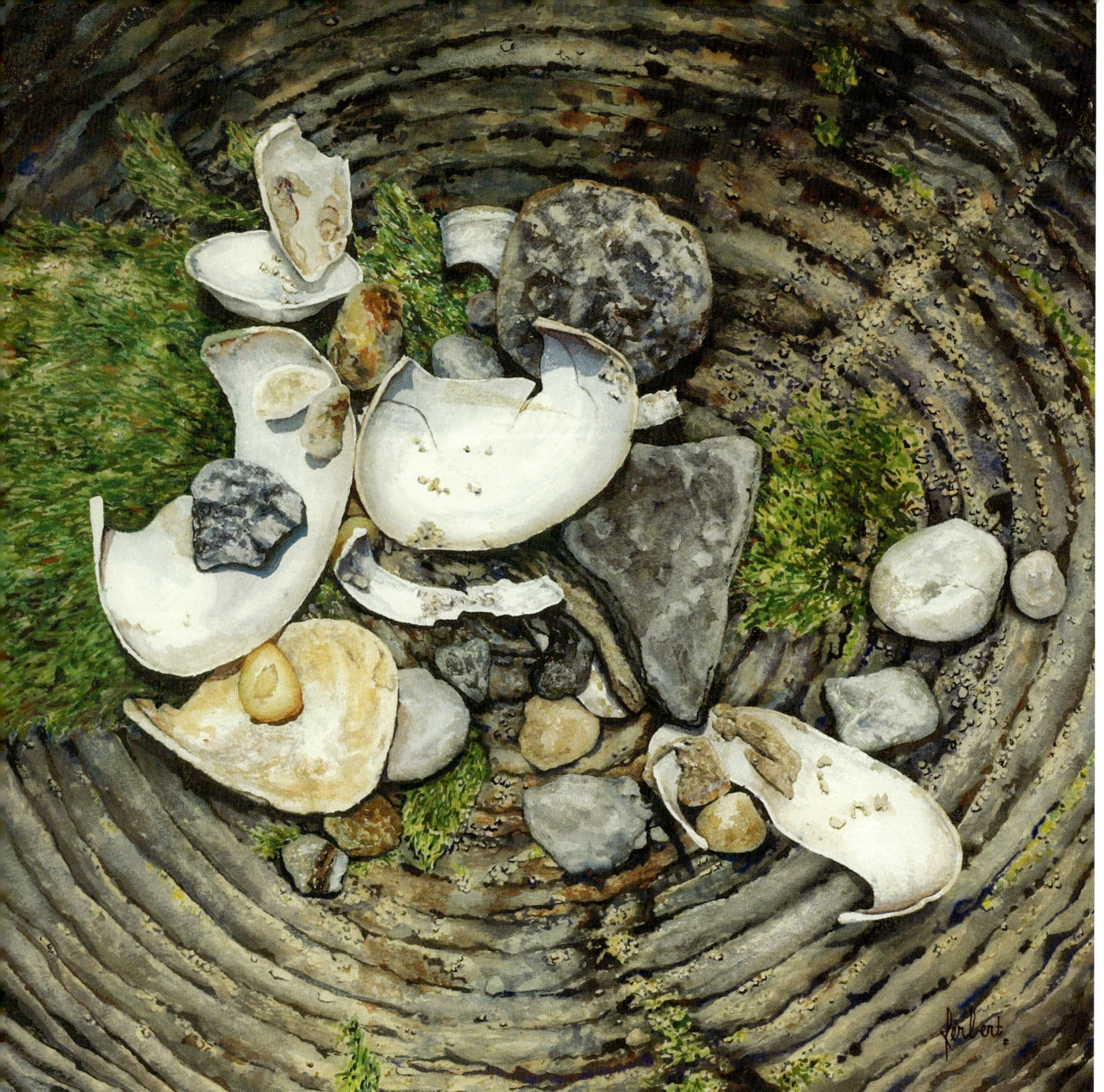

SEA/SHORE V

Mary Lou Ferbert • transparent watercolor on fiber-based mounting panel • 16¾" x 16⅞" (43cm x 43cm)

Passion is the requisite in all of my subjects, and this series is perhaps the most ardent in any of my work. My *Sea/Shore* series celebrates the timeless renewal of the tidal zone with its infinite variations. The paintings are quiet statements that intend to slow perception, permitting time for reflection. I came upon these shells during my summer of 2004 annual sojourn in southern Delaware. Not one of the imperfect, ordinary shells would typically intrigue an adult. My scenario for the shells on the jetty is that they are the gatherings of a child with an untainted eye, attracted only by the wonder and inherent beauty of residue deposited on the sand by the last wave. Perhaps a parent called to say they were leaving, and the young person dropped the shells and ran. I recorded the still life with my camera, bent to the eye level of a child.

When I am home, I paint at every opportunity. When I am traveling, I carry my camera with me at all times. When I am not painting, I am planning future paintings. Even if I live to be one hundred, I will never have enough time to paint all my ideas.

GLORIA AINSWORTH MOUT

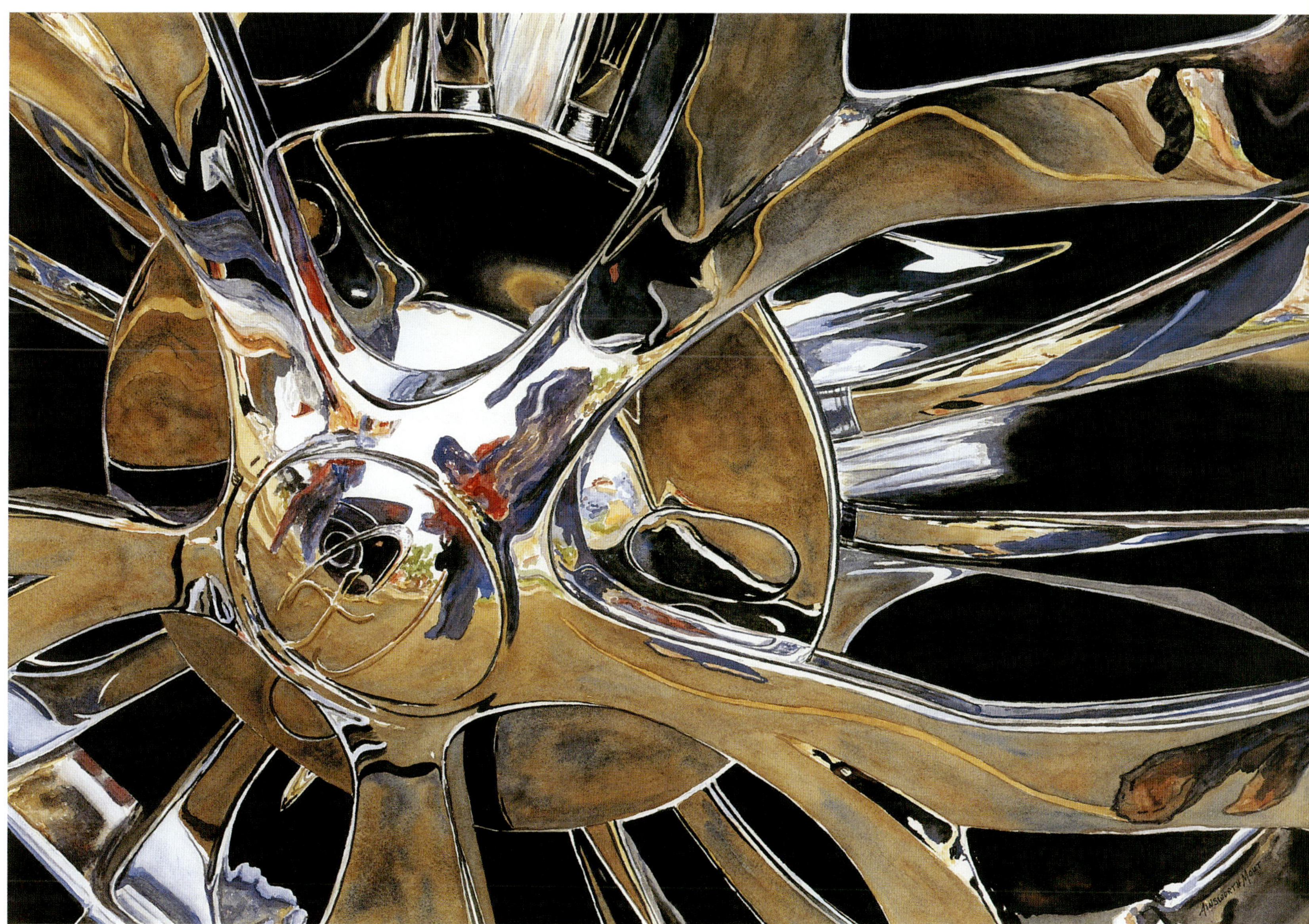

SPINNER

Gloria Ainsworth Mout • transparent watercolor • 17½" × 25½" (44cm × 65cm)

This painting was done from photographs taken at an antique car show that I attended with my brothers. I was very intrigued with the images and colors that I saw reflected in the shiny surfaces on the vehicles, particularly the wheels and hubcaps. The abstract designs in this spinner hubcap got me very excited about using them for a series. While completing a fairly detailed drawing in my studio on stretched 140-lb. (300gsm) Arches paper, I changed some of the lines to make a better design and omitted some things, such as a reflection of me holding my camera. I painted wet-on-dry, except for some of the larger areas where I used wet-into-wet, floating in colors. I enhanced the darks, gradually establishing values. I did not want the brushstrokes visible, because I wanted to show the smoothness of the chrome spinner.

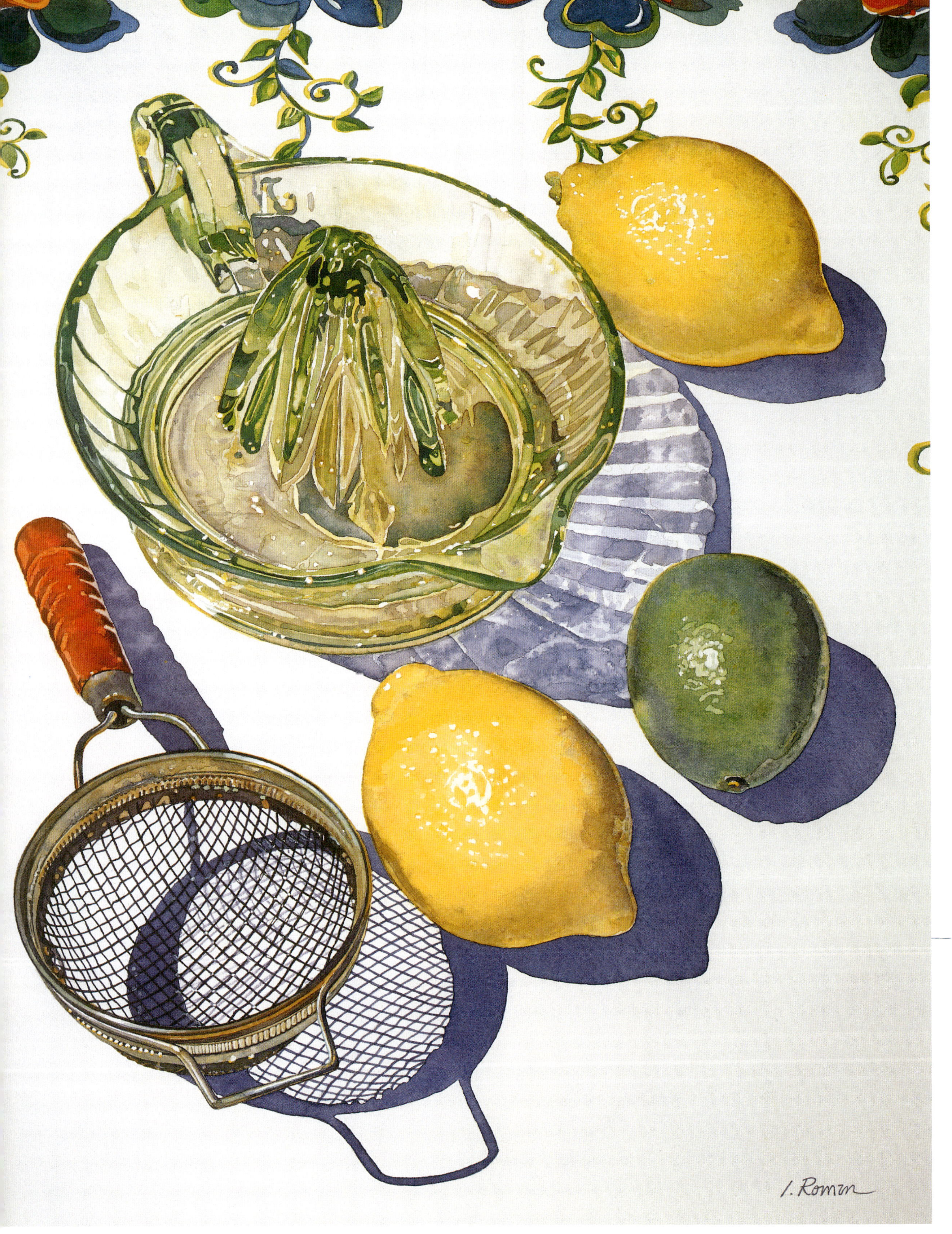

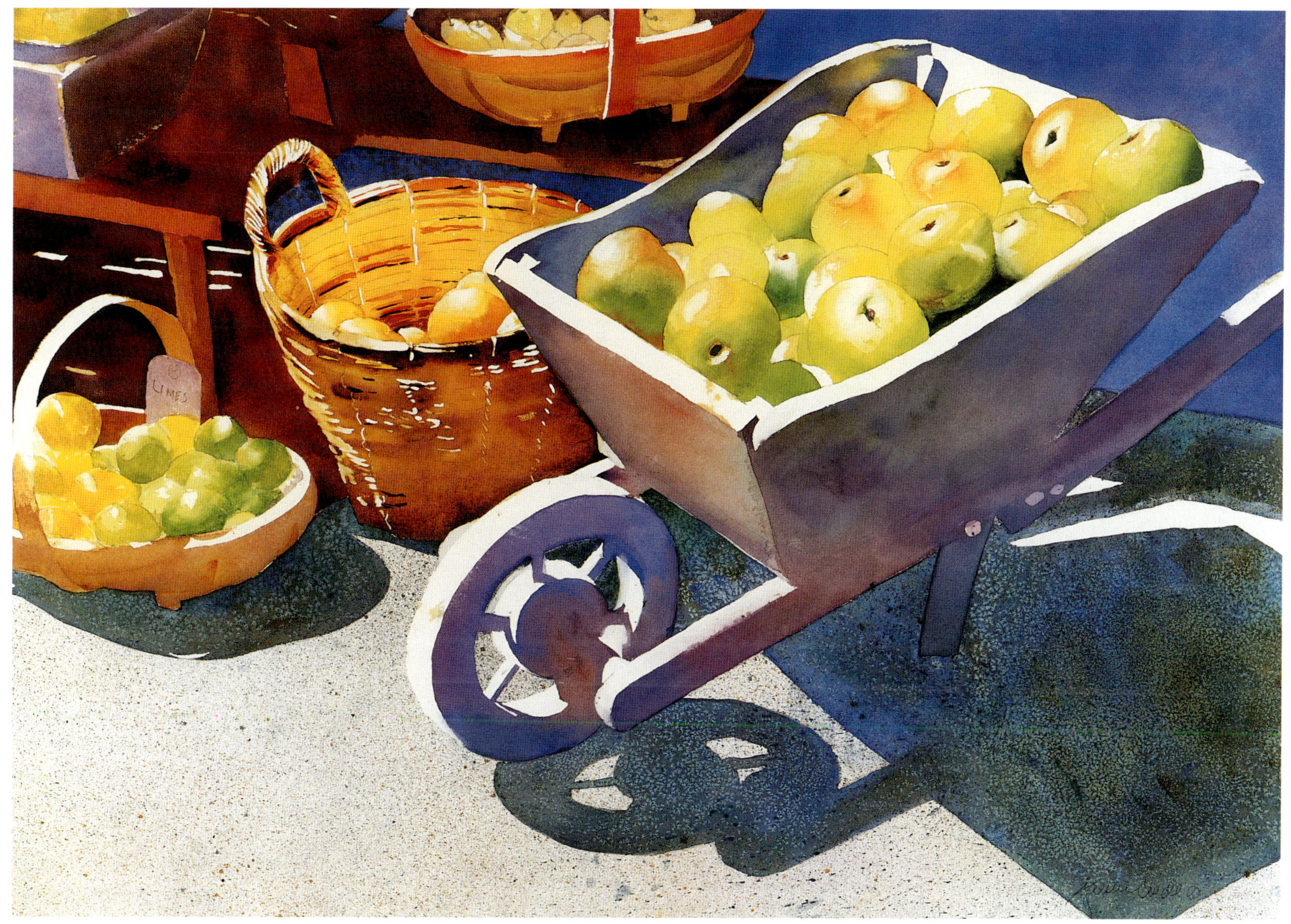

SUNRISE WALK IN GREENWICH

Jaimie Cordero • transparent watercolor • 22" × 30" (56cm × 76cm)

Two of my greatest passions in life feed each other. First, I love to get up at sunrise, walk outdoors and inhale the fresh dawn air, absorbing the sights and sounds of nature awakening. My second great passion is recalling those sensations and expressing them in paint. I chanced upon this scene one brilliant, sunny morning in Greenwich, England. As I turned to look at the flower market, I glanced down and saw the sunlight bursting through the wooden wheel of an apple cart, and my heart stood still upon seeing the wonderful shadow that it cast. Using my sketches and photographs, I first masked a large portion of the design with contact paper, then spattered it with a toothbrush. After removing the mask, I applied two or three glazes of transparent watercolor using a limited palette of warm and cool primary colors, large brushes and as few brushstrokes as possible.

FRESH SQUEEZED

Irena Roman • transparent watercolor • 26" × 18" (66cm × 46cm)

Fresh Squeezed is from an ongoing series of tabletop still-life paintings I began after my mother passed away. Focusing on objects that belonged to her enables me to enjoy their soul and personality while celebrating her life. I loved setting up this arrangement outdoors in direct sunlight, looking to maximize cast shadows and brilliant highlights. I sketched a few studies as well as shot photos. The cast shadows are the heart of the image, and, while they hold the painting together, I felt they shouldn't be overly dominant. So with a less-is-more philosophy, I chose to downplay any brushstrokes and let the water do the work. Using masking fluid to save the lightest areas, the pigment was applied wet-into-wet directly onto the paper, which allowed for tonal variation. Working this way is like using brushstrokes in reverse. It creates shadows with a quiet presence.

Observing how light and shadow transform the ordinary into the extraordinary fuels my passion to paint.

IRENA ROMAN

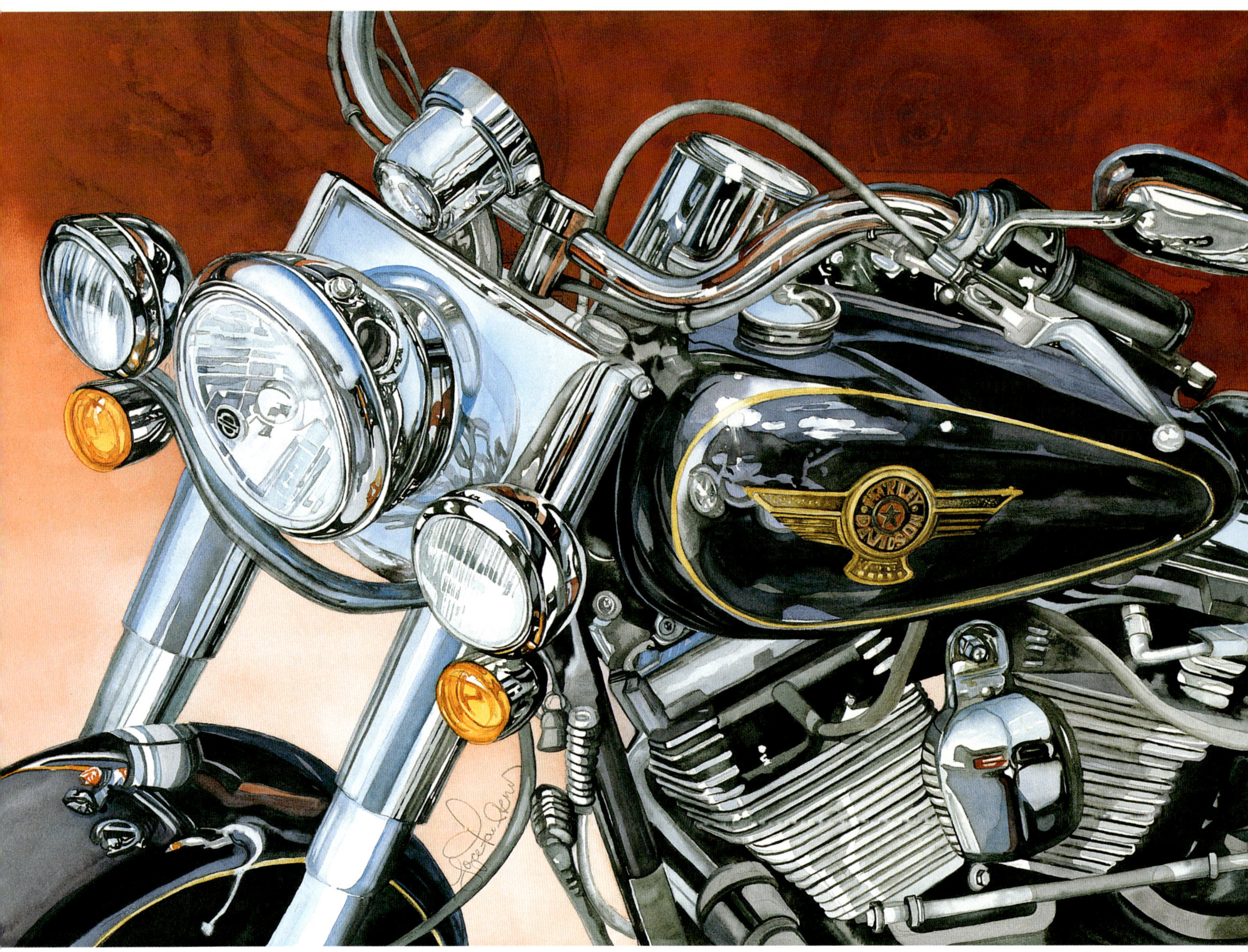

ROAD KING

Joyce Roletto Faulknor • watercolor on 140-lb. (300gsm) cold-pressed paper • 22" × 30" (56cm × 76cm)

The reflective surface of chrome began to fascinate me shortly after finishing my book, *Stunning Crystal and Glass*. I found that chrome and cut crystal are similar in approach yet vastly different in results. Working from a photo, I paint all the darkest values first to lay an excellent foundation for the playful portion of the painting. This allows me to both paint the shapes I see, and let my imagination explode in the abstract shapes of the chrome. Seeing a hint of a reflection of a motorcycle gives me a shape to bend and stretch to enhance the turning of the chrome. Placing the highlights next to the darkest value is a key for reflective surfaces. Although I never ride motorcycles, I am fascinated by their chrome.

Brushstrokes come from two sources: one, technical skill, and two, that inner voice that tells me to paint a certain way. I am not sure why, but trusting that voice is right.

JOYCE ROLETTO FAULKNOR

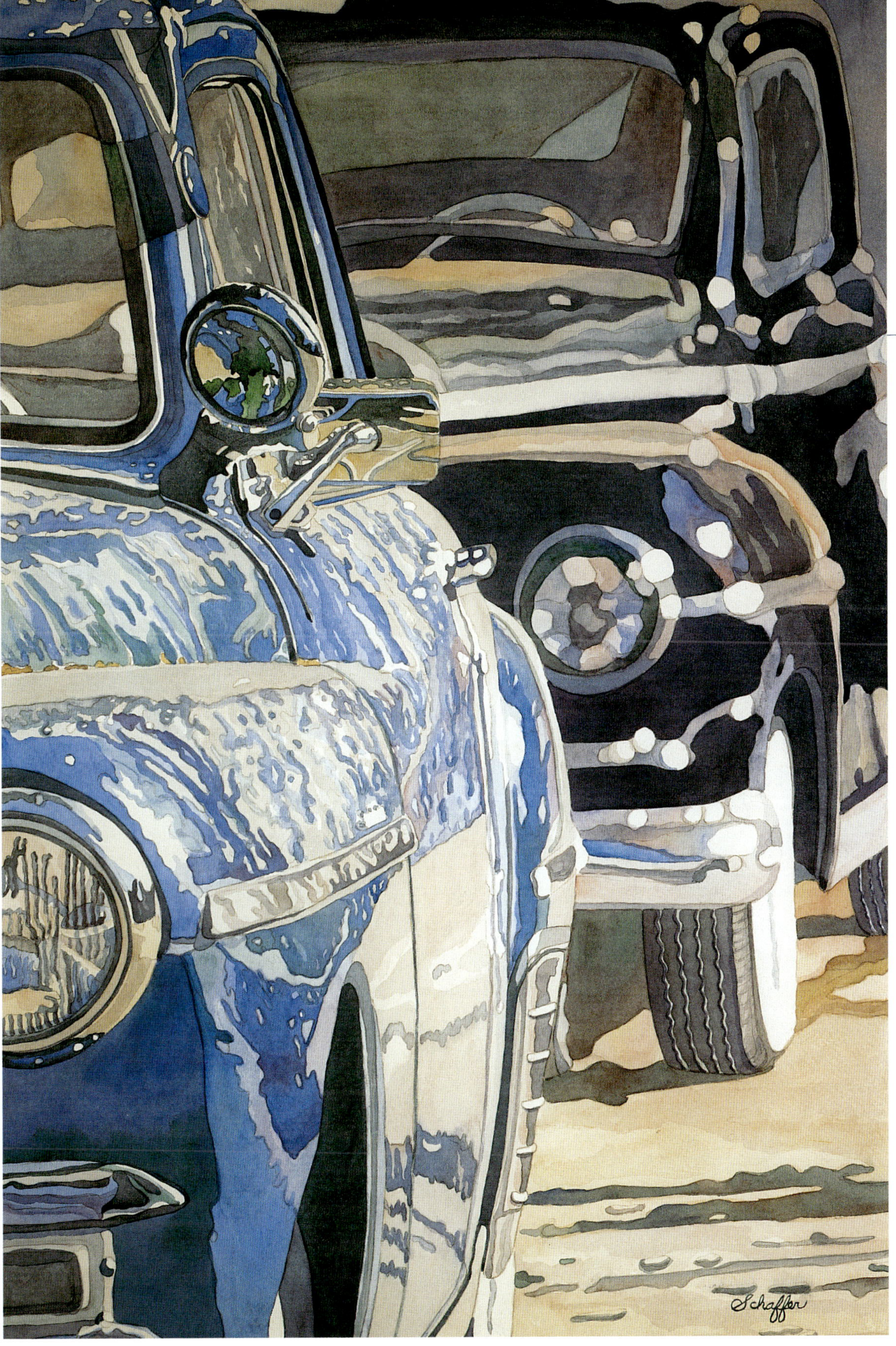

BLACK AND BLUE

Sandra Schaffer • transparent watercolor • 26" × 17" (66cm × 43cm)

My recent passion for painting classic cars stems from an appreciation of their uniquely rounded lines and solid feel. Most are pampered and loved like children, spruced up and put on display for the world to admire. The dust on these classic Plymouths made them more a part of their natural surroundings than the glistening models usually seen at classic car shows. Although the cars appear somewhat abstract, the brushstrokes I used were extremely methodical and calculated in an attempt to bring the dusty surface forward from the body of each car. The title of the piece has a double meaning, denoting both the actual colors of the cars and their dusty condition.

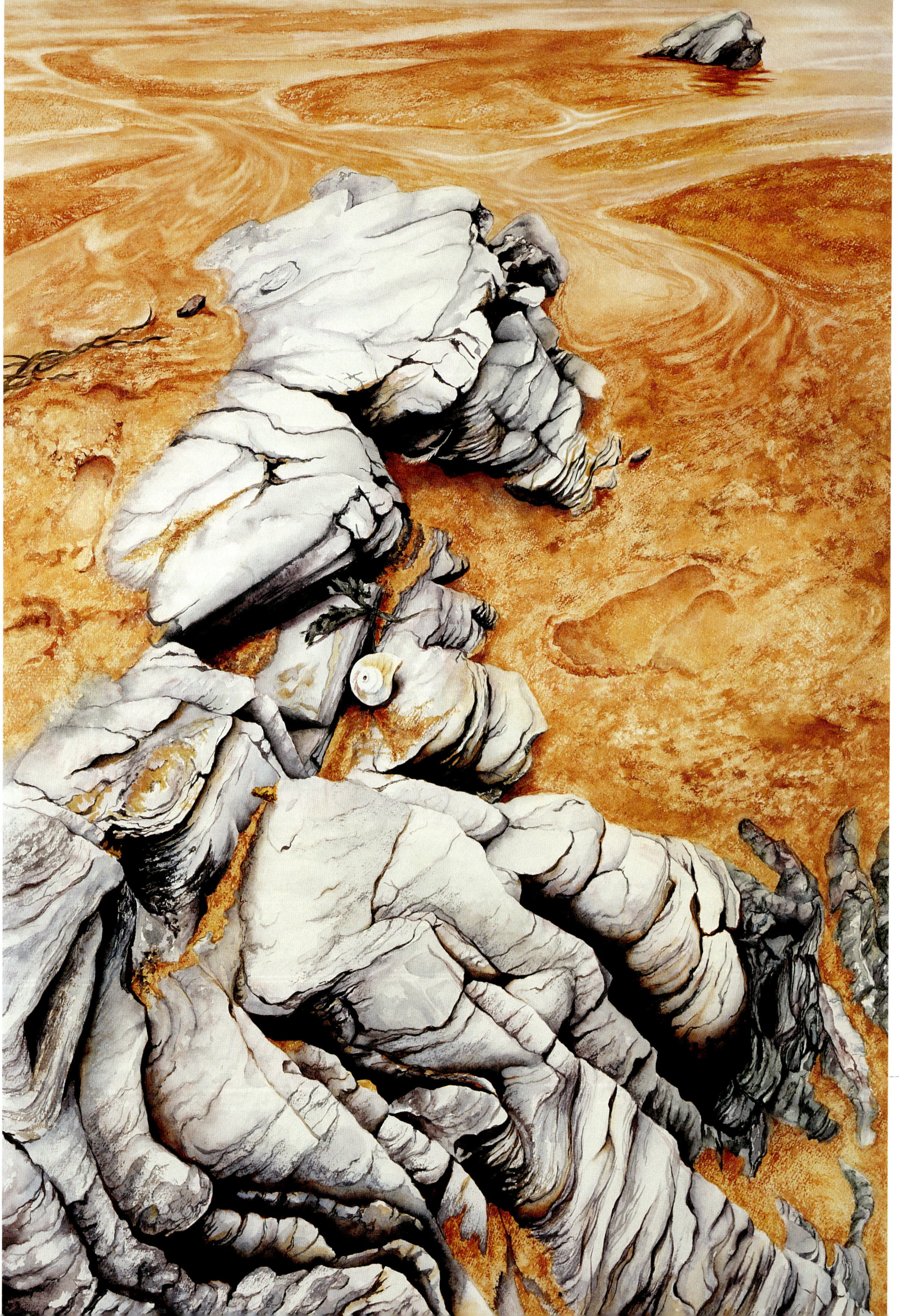

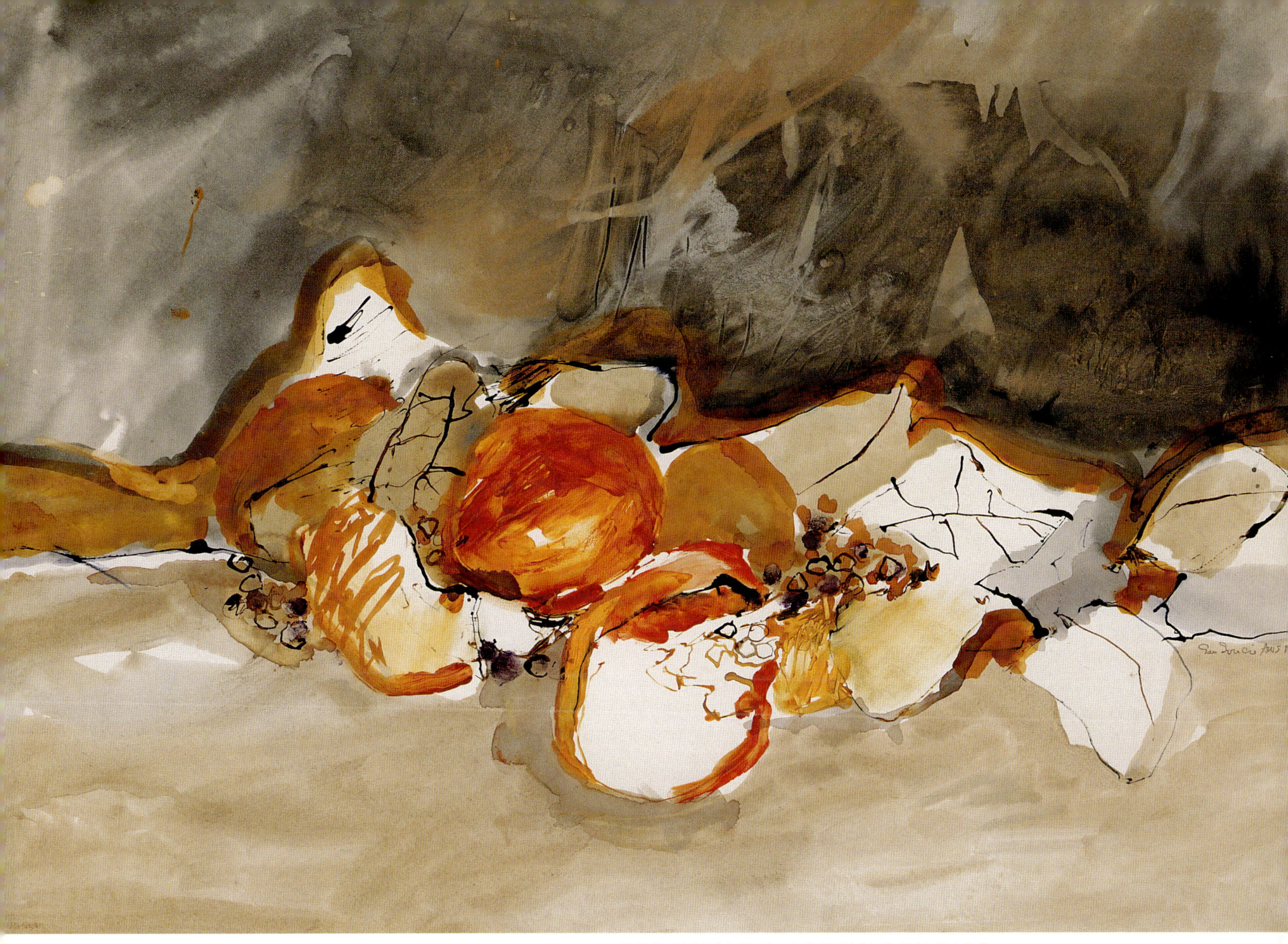

PERSIMMON ASTRINGENCIES

Pat San Soucie • transparent watercolor with gouache, dyes, ink, pencil, bleach and persimmon juice • 22" × 30" (56cm × 76cm)

The work began with watercolor pigment, ink applied with a stick and washes of gray-greens to delineate the leaves of the persimmon. Actual pulp and juices of the persimmon flesh were painted on the unstretched 140-lb. (300gsm) hot-pressed paper, augmenting the other varied media to suggest a more rounded fruit. Seeds from the rich pulp were laid onto the drawing. When the surface was totally dry, the seeds were brushed off, and Quinacridone Red and deeper purples enhanced the seed areas. Two strips of two-ply rice paper were laid on the page, a light color at the bottom and dark gray at the top, each bleached with suggestions of Oriental calligraphy to round out the design.

DRAMATIC ENCOUNTER

Gretchen Krause Holesovsky • watercolor on 300-lb. (640gsm) cold-pressed paper • 31½" × 20½" (80cm × 52cm)

From a photograph of Old Orchard Beach in Maine, I was drawn to the surreal landscape of curves and color sculpted by the ever-moving ocean tides. By working my scrub brush, pushing and dragging the almost dry washes of Raw Sienna, Burnt Sienna, Permanent Rose and French Ultramarine Blue to expose textures in the stained paper, I created the illusions of water and sand. Pushing, lifting, scrubbing … a lot like the sea.

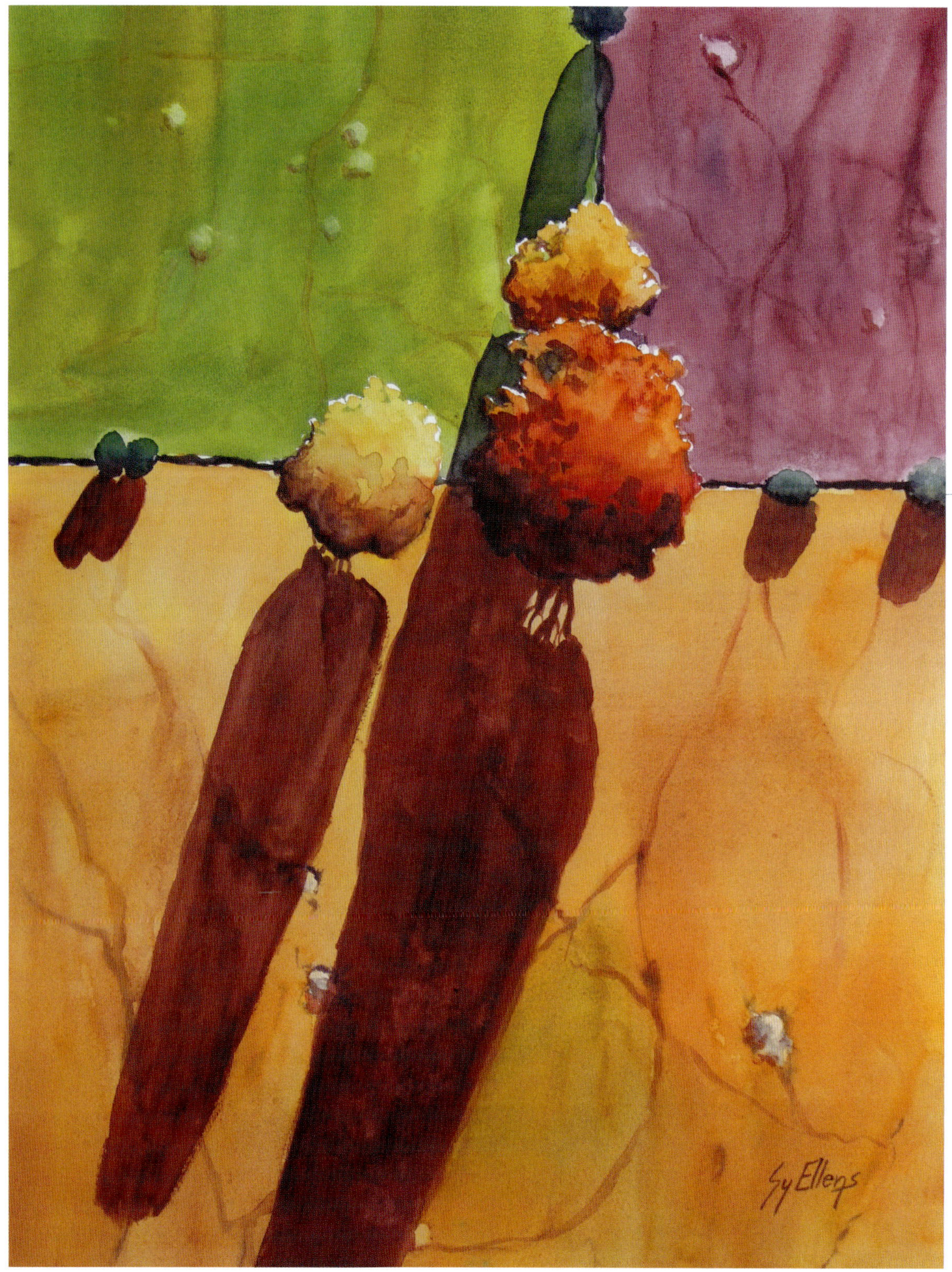

HEAT OF THE DAY

Sy Ellens • transparent watercolor • 24" × 18" (61cm × 46cm)

I did this painting in my studio from memory after riding in an airplane late one autumn afternoon. The abstract patterns of the fields meeting with a few trees at the corner stuck with me, and I knew I had to paint it. I used the wet-into-wet method, doing some of the detail when the field areas were almost dry so that I could achieve soft edges. I then painted other details after it was dry, which created some hard edges where needed. The shadows tell the story of the tree shapes, and the colors reflect the heat of the day. This all combines to form the abstract design in this painting.

KINGDOM CAMP

Robert J. O'Brien • watercolor with gouache • 21" × 14" (53cm × 36cm)

The close focus of *Kingdom Camp* gives it an abstract quality. The diagonal of the door dominates the piece. The circular shape of the window serves as a focal point, and the red color sets the mood. *Kingdom Camp* was painted in the studio using photo and sketchbook references. The painting was built up with transparent watercolor, and then I introduced gouache at the end to render the tattered screen, resulting in a semi-opaque appearance. This subject is so ordinary that most would not even acknowledge it when passing by. When focusing in on an ordinary subject, a mysterious transformation can take place in the treatment.

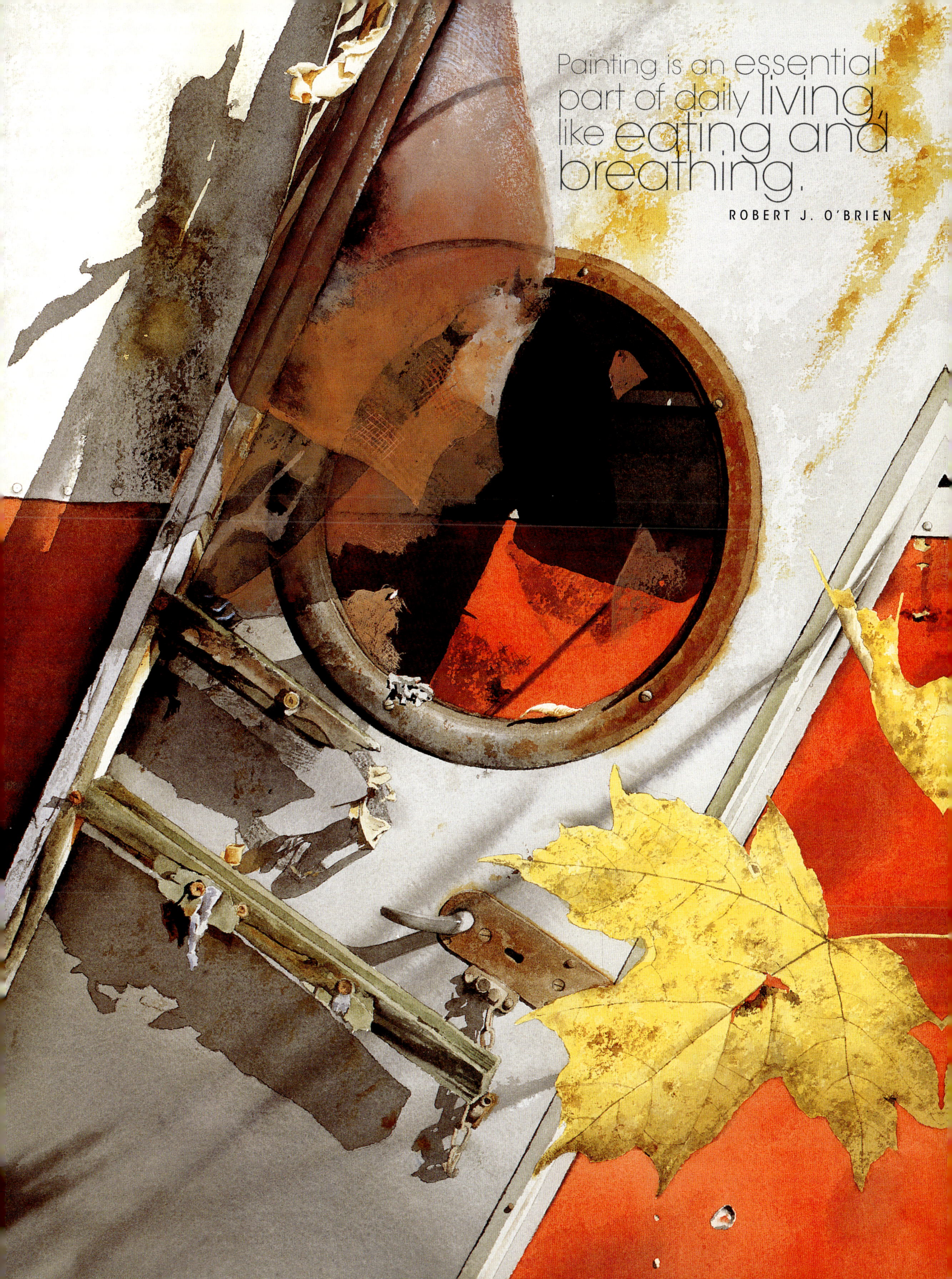

Painting is an essential part of daily living, like eating and breathing.

ROBERT J. O'BRIEN

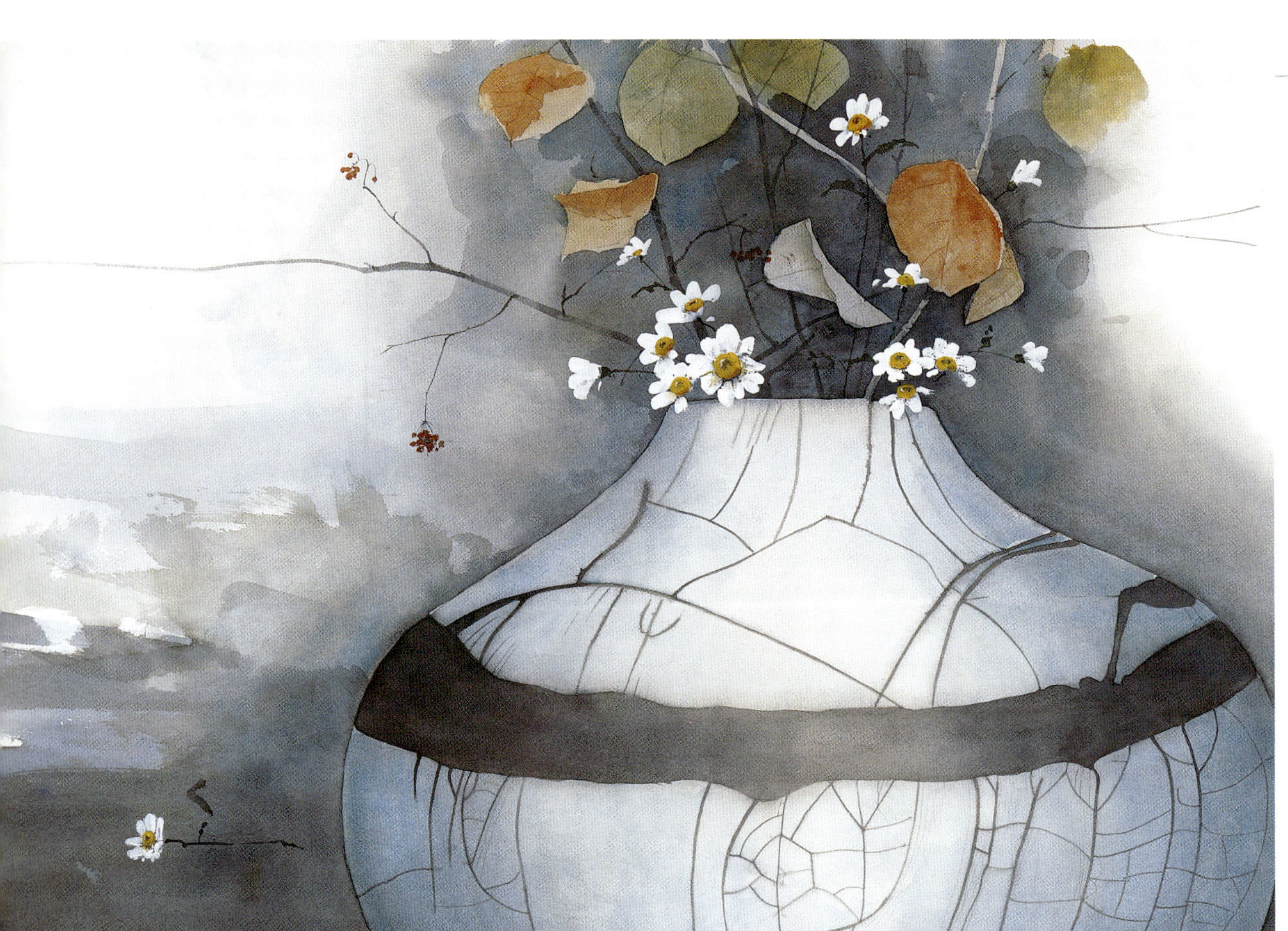

POTTER'S TRIBUTE

Mel Grunau • transparent watercolor with gouache on 140-lb. (300gsm) cold-pressed paper • 22" × 30" (56cm × 76cm)

Potter's Tribute resulted from a casual conversation with the passenger seated next to me on a domestic flight; it turned out he was a ceramic artist. Following my trip, I visited his studio and borrowed several of his pieces as subjects for paintings. Having this piece in the studio allowed me to see it in varying light and from different angles. With a single pot as the subject, I exaggerated its proportions to nearly fill the frame of the painting. I began with a light pencil sketch of the pot and the branches, then added transparent watercolor washes, built up using several layers. The stylized fall branches are rendered with a long, narrow rigger using sepia and dark blues, while the daisies are white gouache.

I apply broad, sweeping brushstrokes layered with fine detail. I experiment using not only brushes, but pencil, charcoal, graphite, collage, palette knife and even my fingers and hands.

MEL GRUNAU

THREE LONG STORIES

Elisa Khachian • pencil, transparent watercolor on two sheets of transparent paper • 25" × 16" (64cm × 41cm)

In my studio, I set down two long sheets of Mylar, one on top of the other. My materials are photos of my sister, my father and myself. The supporting characters are pieces of Oriental carpets, tags, and drawings and paintings from my memory. Marigolds were my dad's favorite flower—I painted some and printed others from a seed catalog. Then I transferred them onto small pieces of acetate and layered them between the Mylar. I wove the stories and designs throughout, using a suitable color code and my own symbolism. My father was a talented weaver and a respected Oriental rug dealer. He taught me many lessons about survival, love, creativity and humorous curiosity. In his desk at his store, the drawers were filled with small pencil stubs just waiting to be used. I carefully selected six and arranged them into a small box. The box is attached to the outside glass on the painting. I feel as if we created the piece together, with joy, love and shared memories.

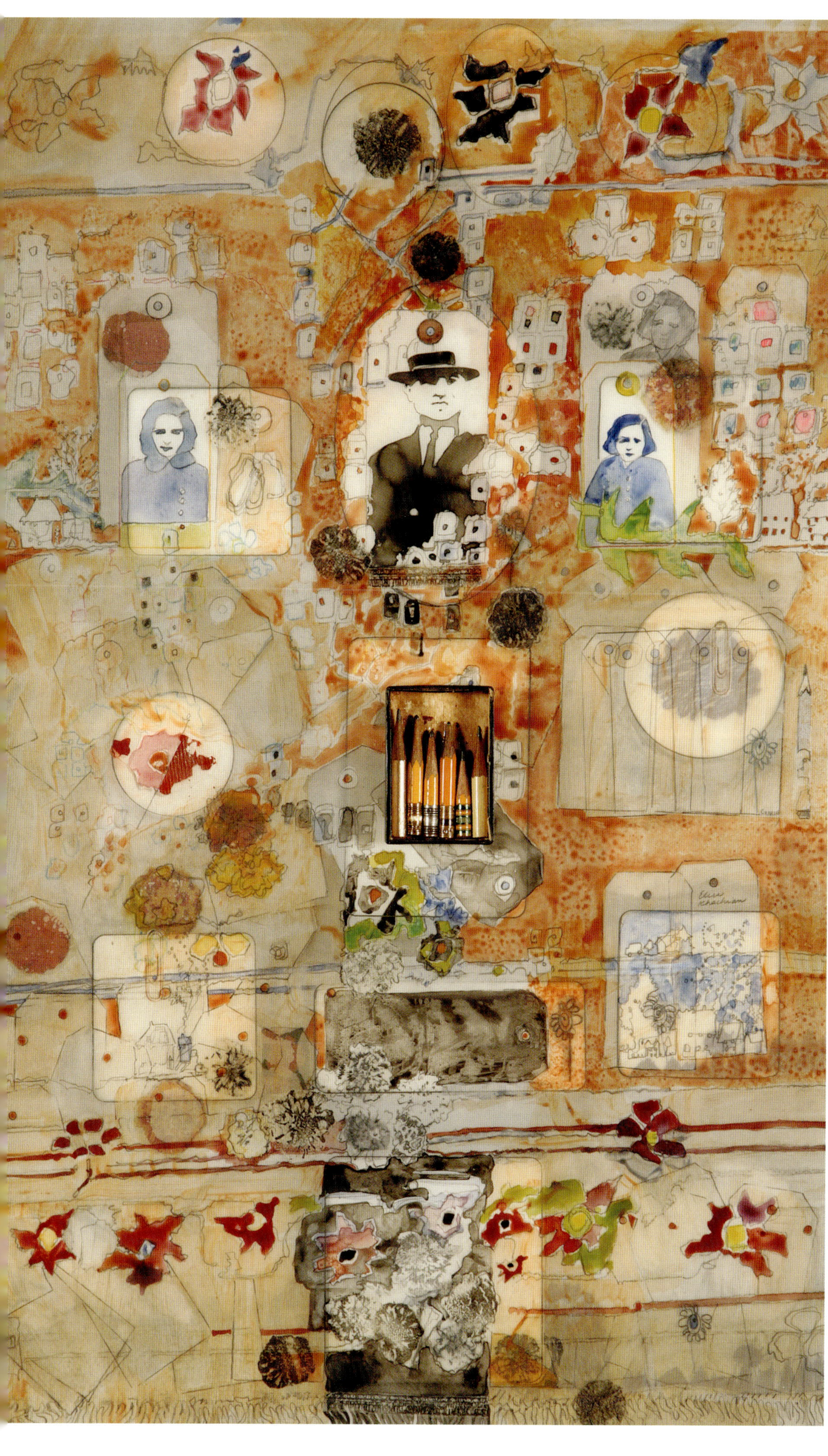

Don't paint through a **dollar** bill.

ELISA KHACHIAN

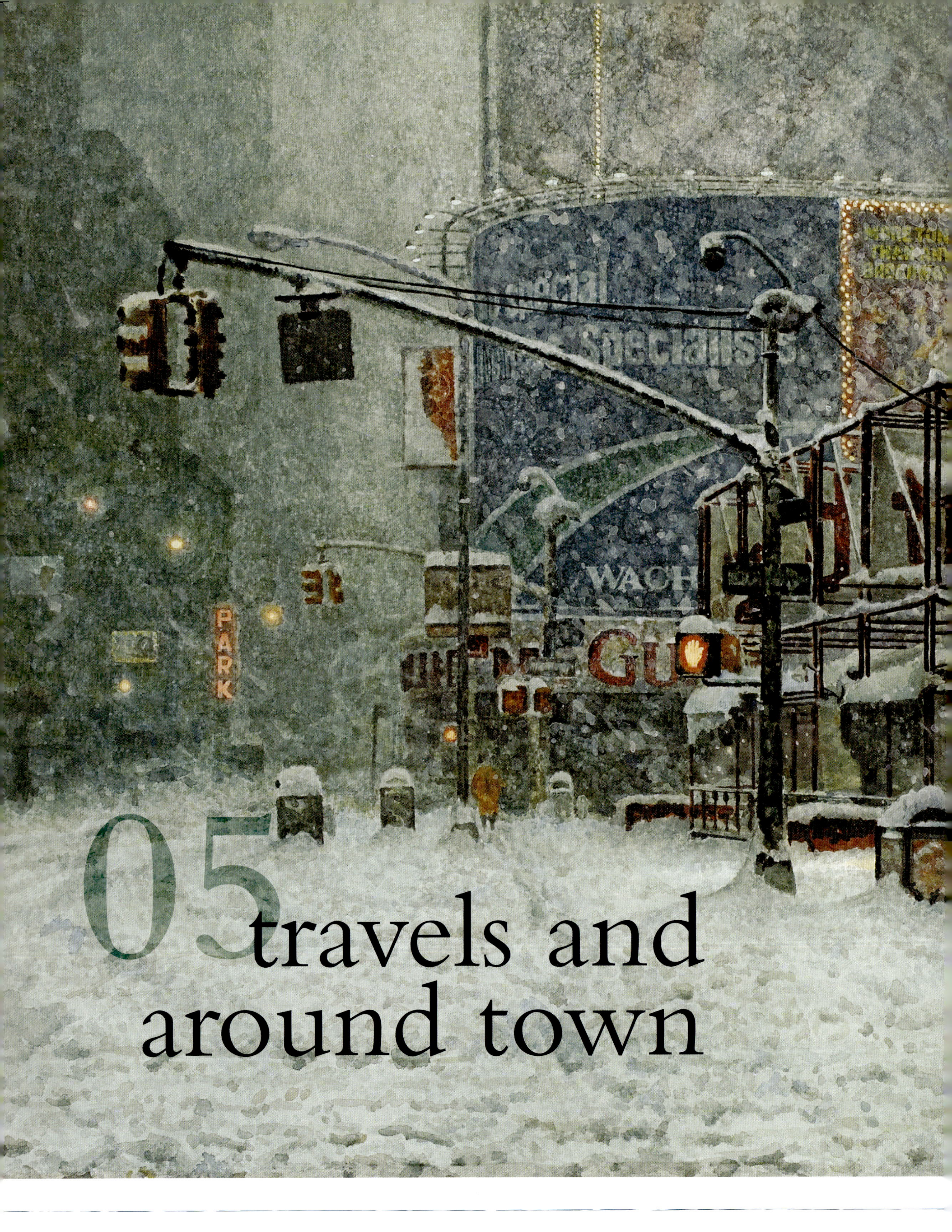

05 travels and around town

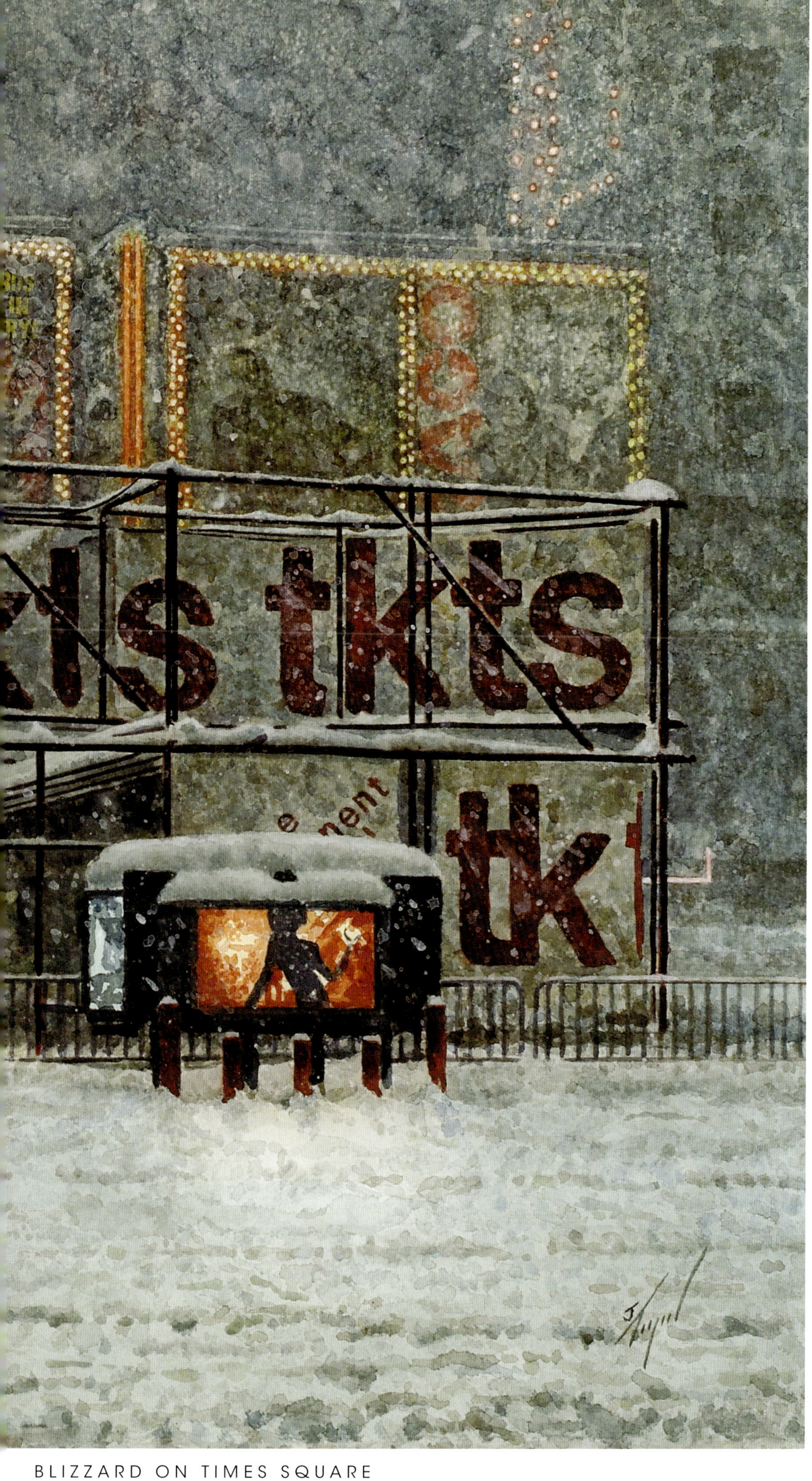

I am fascinated by the delicate and mysterious qualities of cold, snowy days. The bustling city gets strangely quiet and empty; solid shapes seem to dissolve like apparitions into a dense, frozen shroud.

JAMES TOOGOOD

BLIZZARD ON TIMES SQUARE

James Toogood • watercolor on paper • 15½" × 22" (39cm × 56cm)

PONT AU CHANGE

Michael Reardon • transparent watercolor • 21" × 10" (53cm × 25cm)

Just as the Pont au Change connects one bank of the Seine to the other, the bridge in this painting leads the eye from the foreground buttresses to the midground opposing bank. Once across the river, the viewer perceives the soft, backlit building silhouettes which evoke the tranquility of a late afternoon turning into evening. This calmness is reinforced by the muted characteristics of a limited palette. It is, however, the strong diagonal of the bridge, together with the lively brushstrokes of the rippling water, that activates an otherwise quiet, four-part composition.

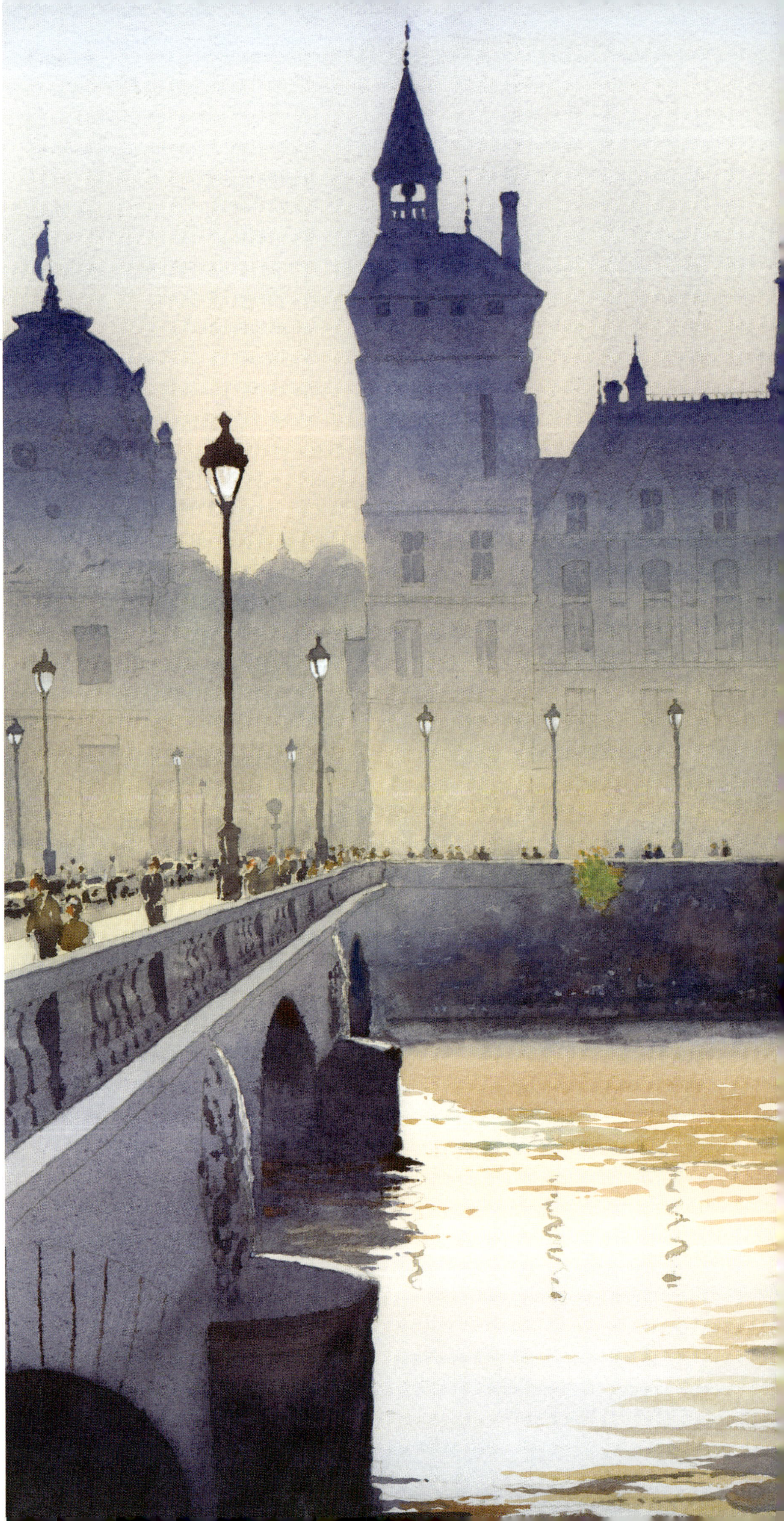

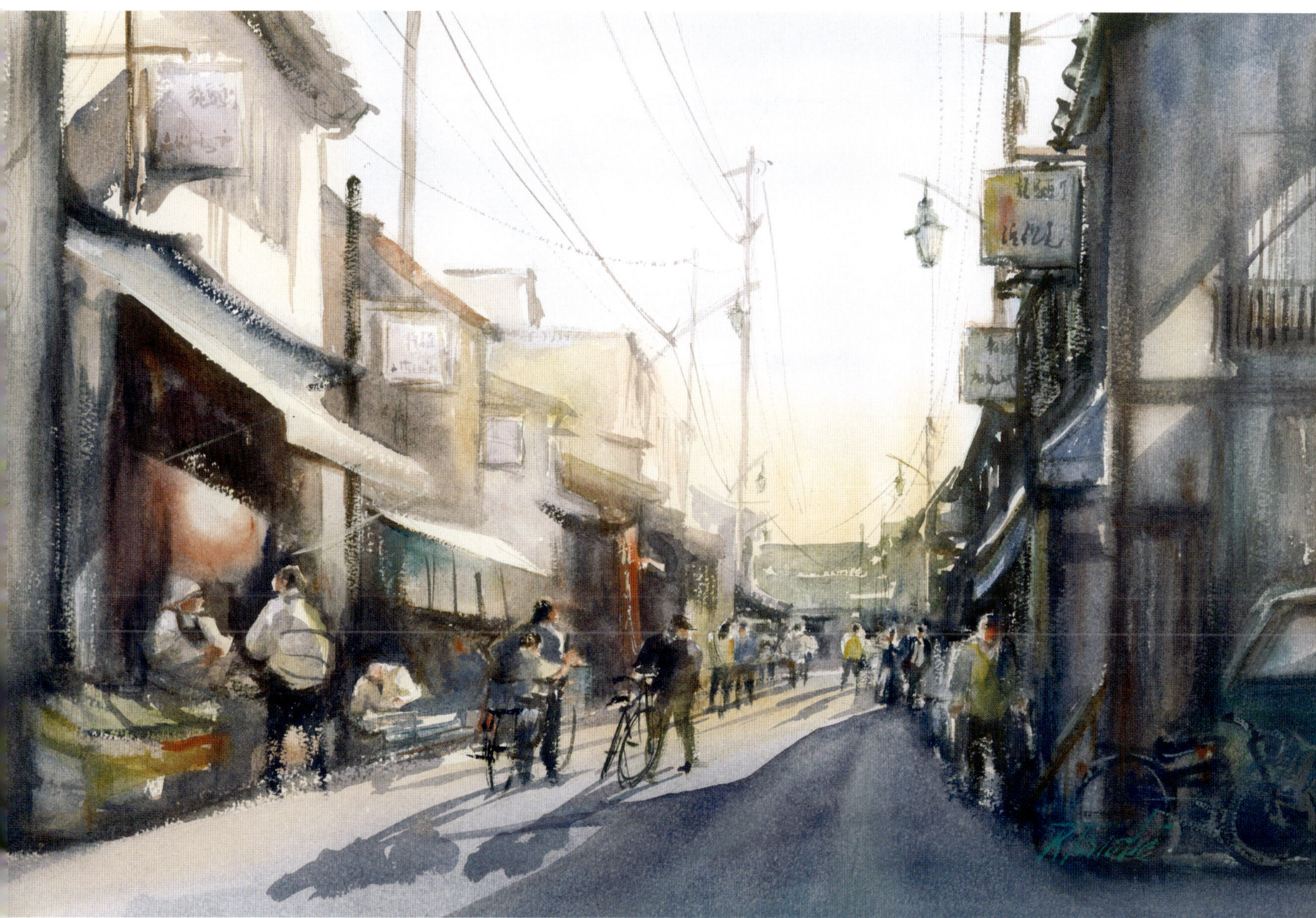

JOURNEY HOME

Keiko Tanabe • watercolor on paper • 14" × 21" (36cm × 53cm)

Living thousands of miles away from home, I sometimes find myself consumed by an overwhelming yearning to go back. I am fortunate that painting is one way to cope with these strong emotions. *Journey Home* is based on my photos from a recent trip to my hometown, Kyoto, Japan. I often use my travel photos, but they are mere aids to the design. My interpretation of the subject is the most important element in all of my successful work. Because I paint quickly, squirrel-hair mop brushes work well both in wet-into-wet and wet-on-dry. Their absorbent nature allows me to dance across the paper much longer than the other types. When I can sing in unison with my brushes, I see my feelings honestly reflected in all of the brushstrokes in my painting, such as this one.

When I am true to my inspiration, my brushstrokes sometimes surprise me by exposing something of my inner spirit I was not even aware of.

KEIKO TANABE

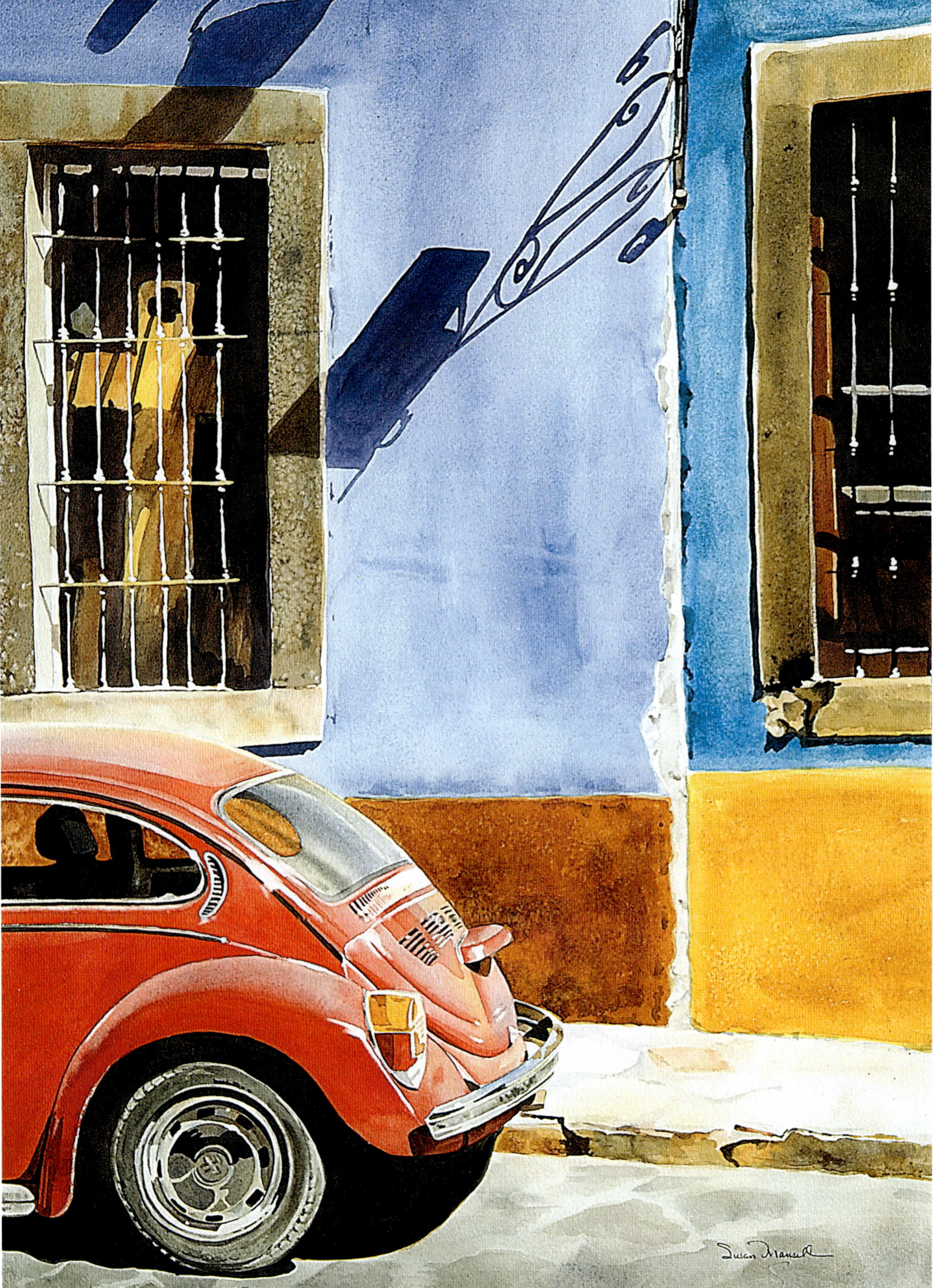

I love color, and I love texture!

SUSAN MANSELL

COLORS OF MEXICO

Susan Mansell • watercolor on paper • 28" × 20" (71cm × 51cm)

My daughter lived in San Miguel de Allende for three years, providing ample opportunities to visit and enjoy the Mexican community. What strikes me most about the area are the ever-present rich, vibrant colors. Even the walls have personality. For this painting, I worked from a photograph, moving the car around until I arrived at a pleasing composition. The shadows play an important role in directing the eye around the painting. I applied some salt to resemble the texture of plaster on the walls. A fun, happy painting!

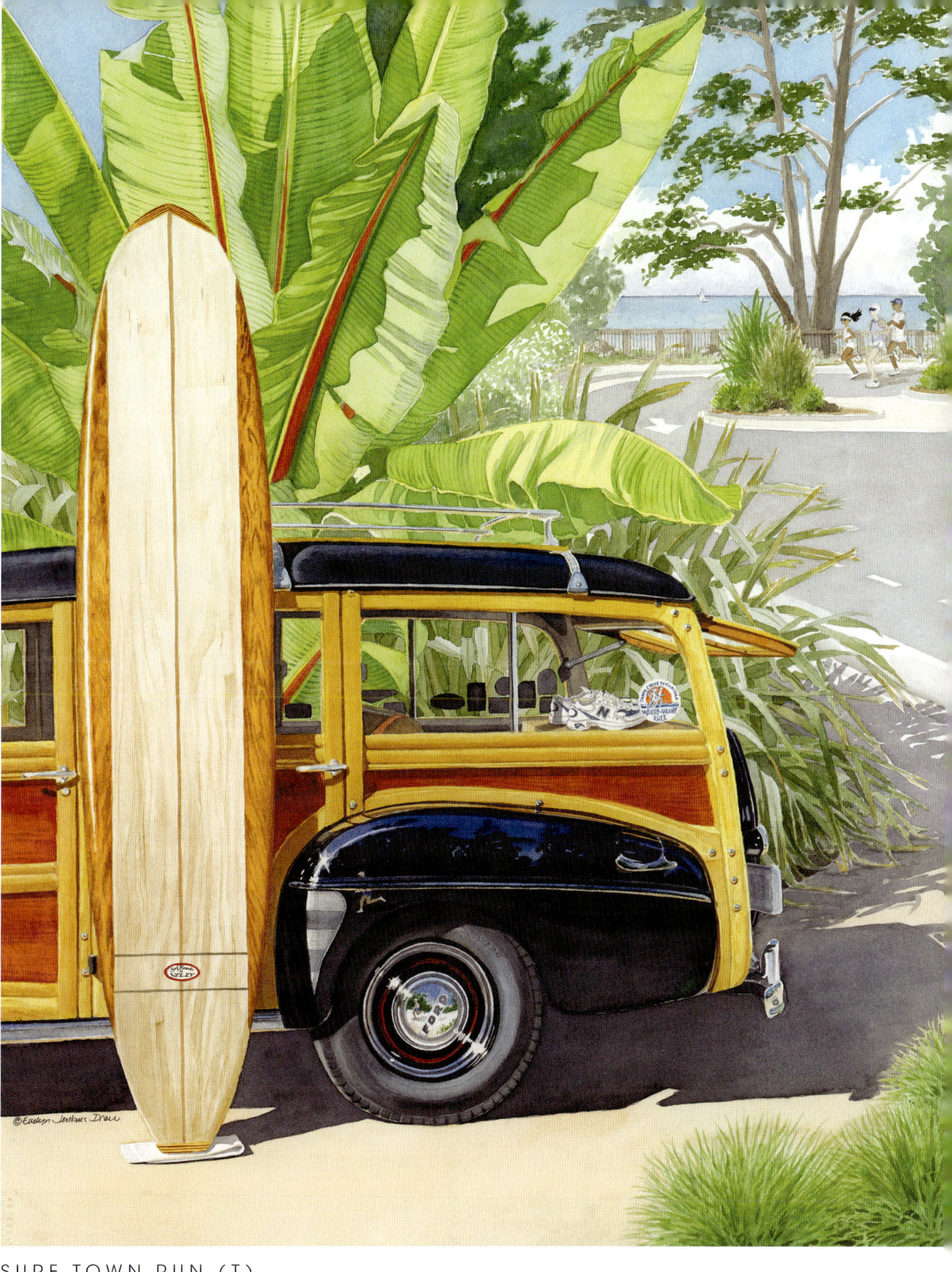

SURF TOWN RUN (T)

Evelyn Jenkins Drew • transparent watercolor on 300-lb. (640gsm) cold-pressed paper • 30" × 22" (76cm × 56cm)

I live near Santa Cruz, California, where surfing and running and beautiful old cars are ingredients in the special coastal quality of life. I aspire to bring a sense of pleasure, a memory of good times and places, to my viewers. I arranged to photograph the black "woody" from a specific angle of light, and I photographed the location and a separate banana tree all at the same light angle. My technique is to pre-wet small areas and then to use many layers of smooth transparent washes to achieve a rich color saturation. I love painting little details in the chrome reflections that come as delayed surprises, such as the runner reflected in the hubcap and the black fender. I save these delicious details until the end of the painting as a sort of artistic dessert!

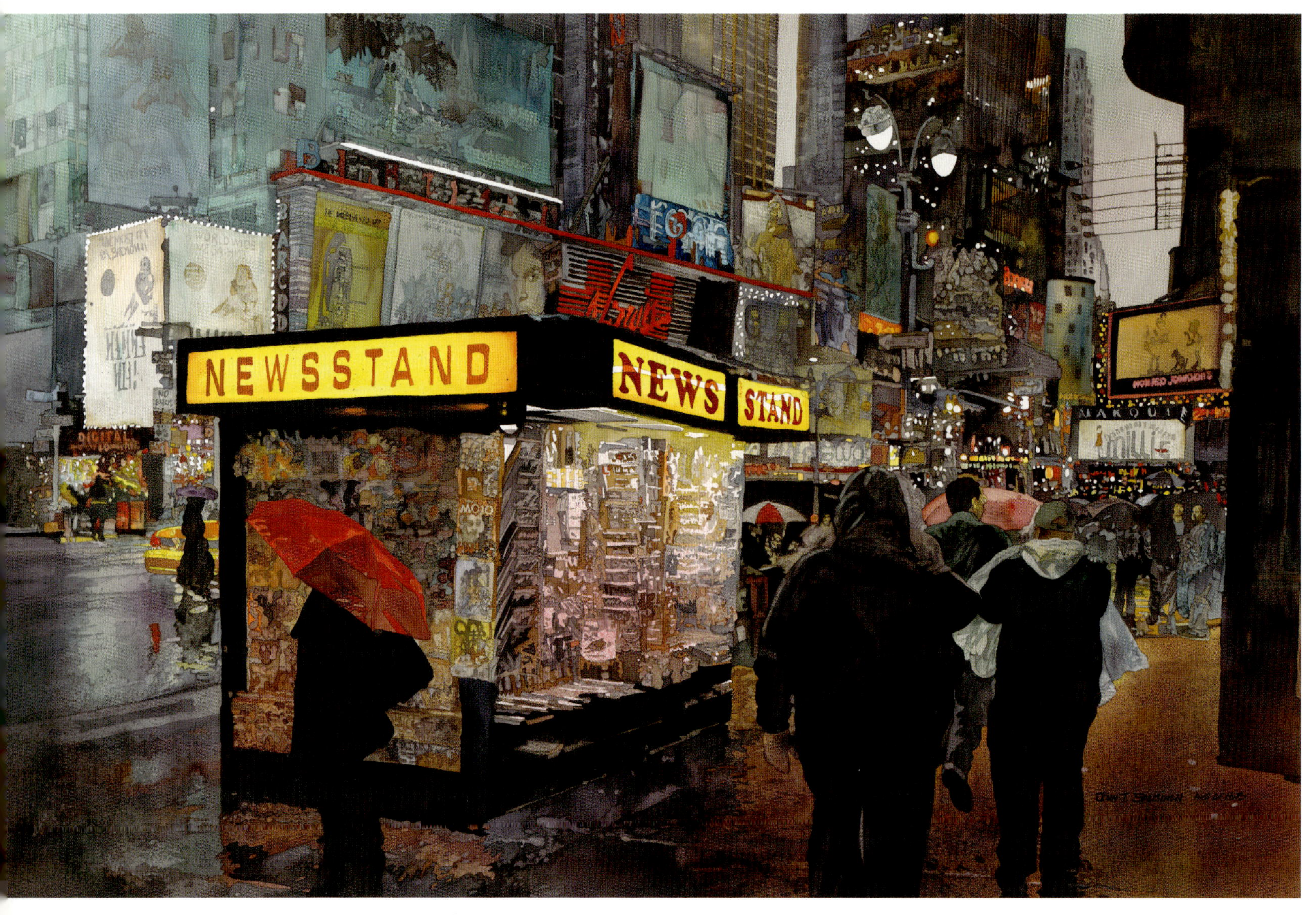

NEWS STAND

John Salminen • transparent watercolor • 25" × 35" (64cm × 89cm)

I'm fascinated by the details of life in a big city, in part because I live in the quiet solitude of the northern Minnesota woods. Intrigued by the energy and visual complexity of the urban scene, I use my 35mm camera with a zoom telephoto lens to help me create ordered compositions out of visual chaos. My next challenge is to translate that image into a convincing painting. Photographs record detail, but they often lack the emotional impact of the original experience, so I have to breathe life back into the work, suggesting sounds and smells as well as sights. To this end, I often change colors, add or eliminate figures and details, and dramatically alter the light quality and mood. My ultimate goal is to impart some of the excitement I experienced as I discovered the wealth of images generated by daily life in the city.

Once I begin a painting, the process becomes all-consuming. I am passionate about both the physical act of painting (the tactile sensation of making marks on the paper) and the intellectual challenge of organizing a cohesive visual statement.

JOHN SALMINEN

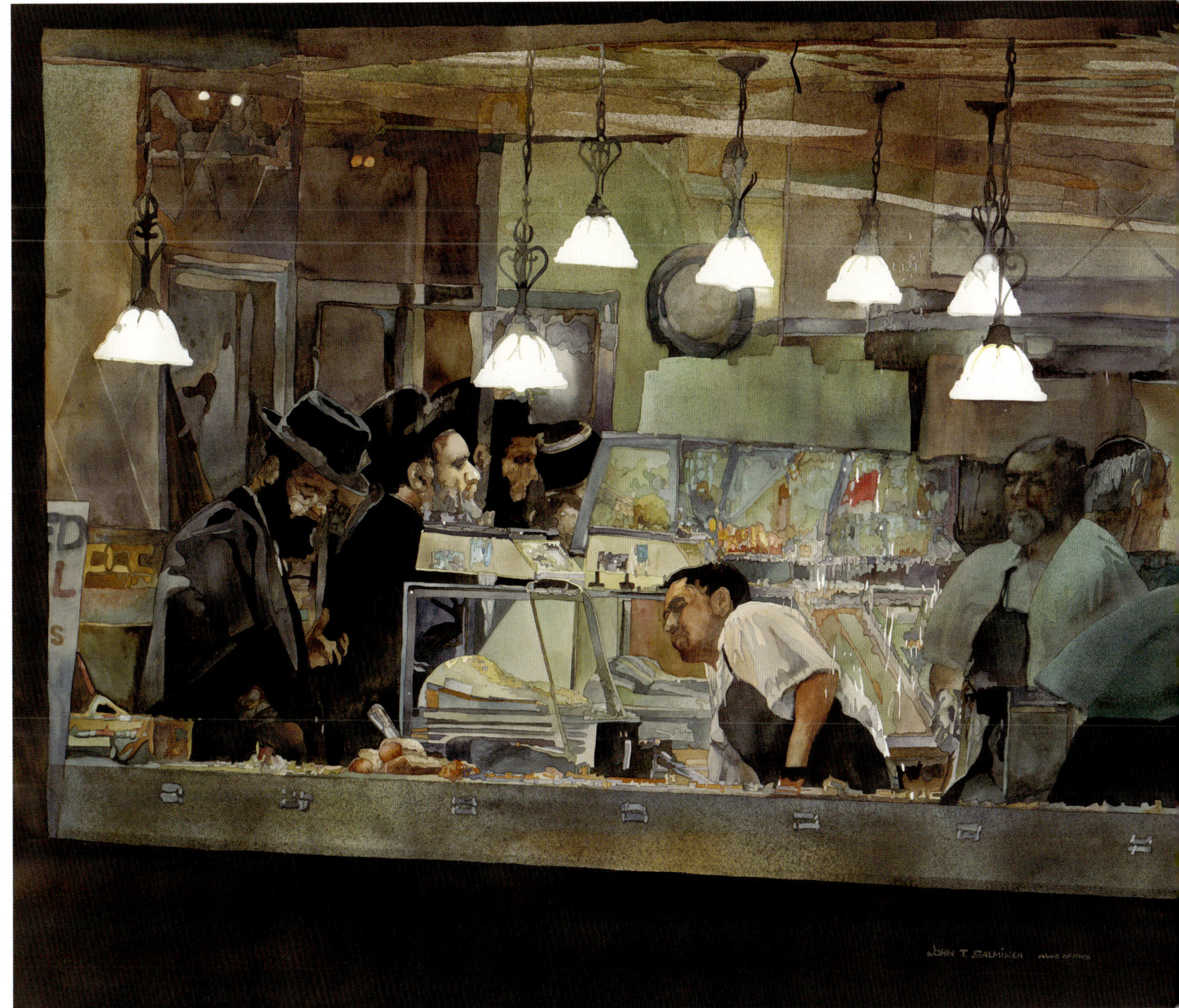

BROOKLYN BUTCHER SHOP

John Salminen • transparent watercolor • 32" × 37" (81cm × 94cm)

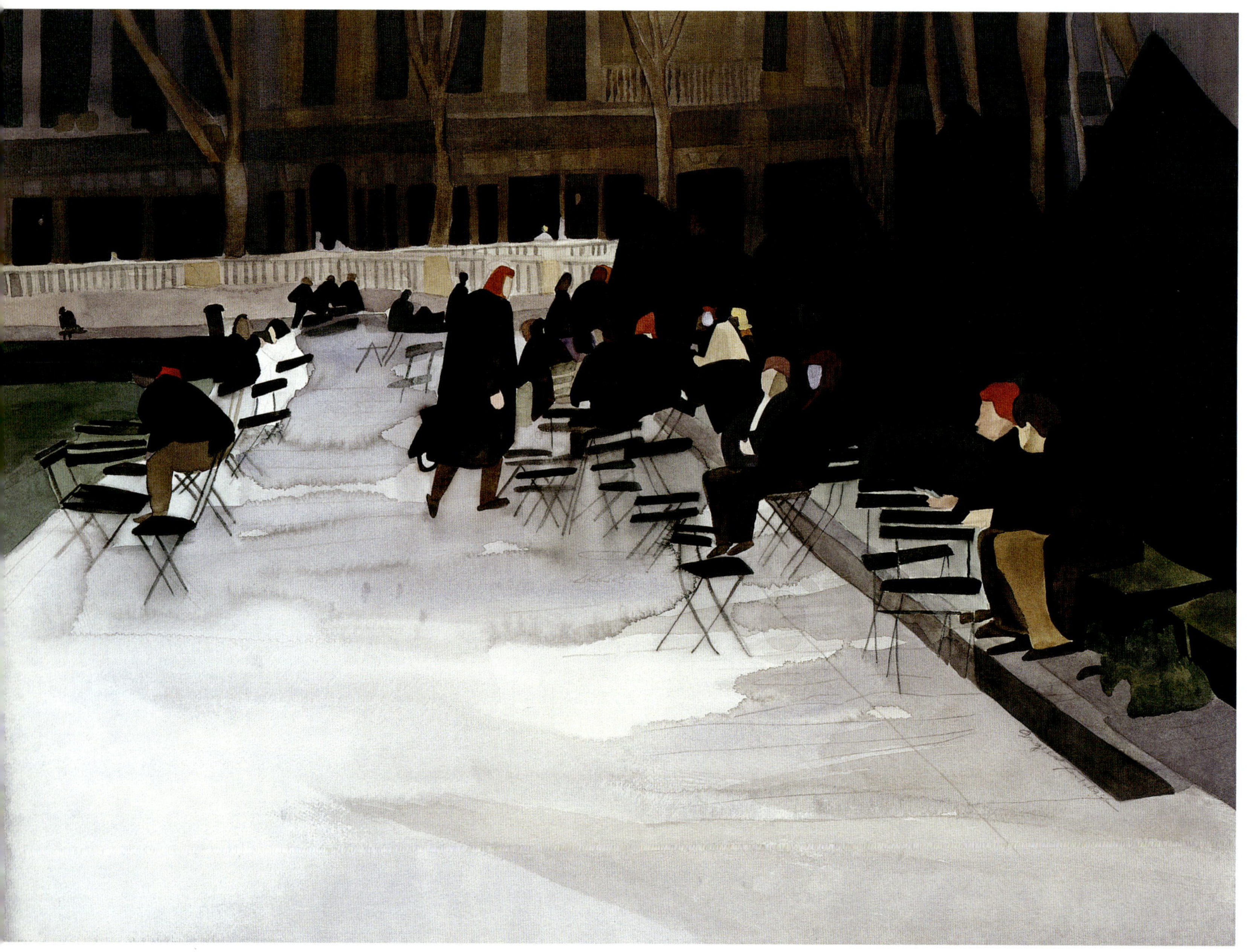

THE WHITE COAT

Angela A. Barbalace • transparent watercolor • 22" x 30" (56cm x 76cm)

When painting *The White Coat,* I was having fun with perspective using a small palette to create different values. Even though I try not to show brushstrokes when using watercolors, I feel the passion comes from the liveliness of the piece. I love doing rain scenes, and this piece was drawn after a rainy morning, when the sunlight was peeking out of the clouds and reflecting into the puddles. I did the painting in my studio from an on-site study and other reference material. My street scenes are very perspective-oriented. One color is the prima donna, and the others are muted values.

SAN MARCO

Daryl Bryant • transparent watercolor • 15" x 11" (38cm x 28cm)

Early training taught me to follow the old adage, "less is more." A favorite teacher reminded me to "not paint the fleas before the dog." With this in mind, my first consideration is to lay out the large areas of color with a 1½-inch (37mm) or 2-inch (51mm) brush. Small brushes are reserved for the final details. While living in Italy as a young art student, I fell in love with the architecture, the art and the people. I have returned many times to sketch and paint Italy's splendor and beauty. San Marco in Venice is a focal point of the area; with a backpack of pencils, brushes, paints and paper, I quickly captured the image of the moment.

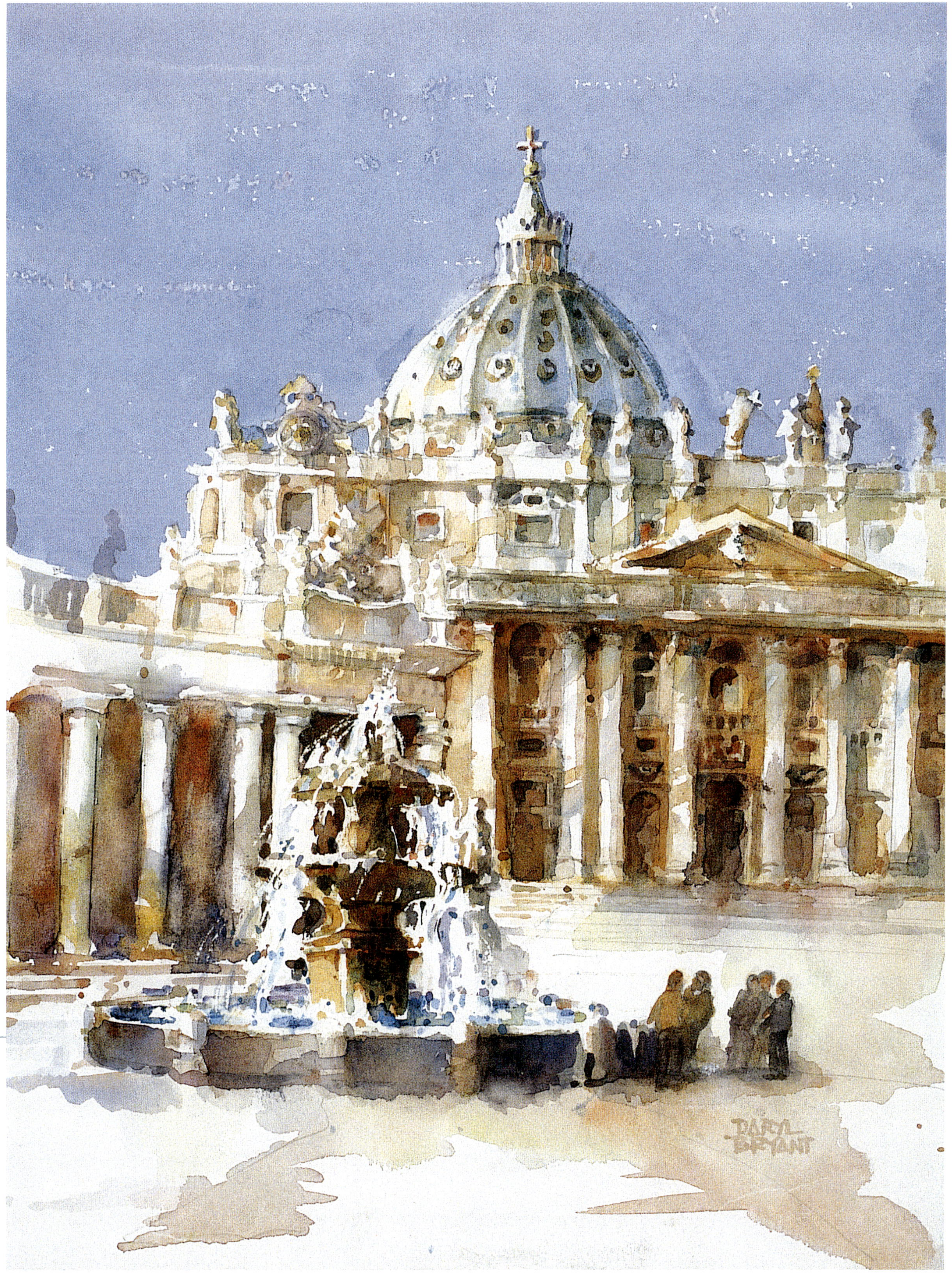
DARYL
BRYANT

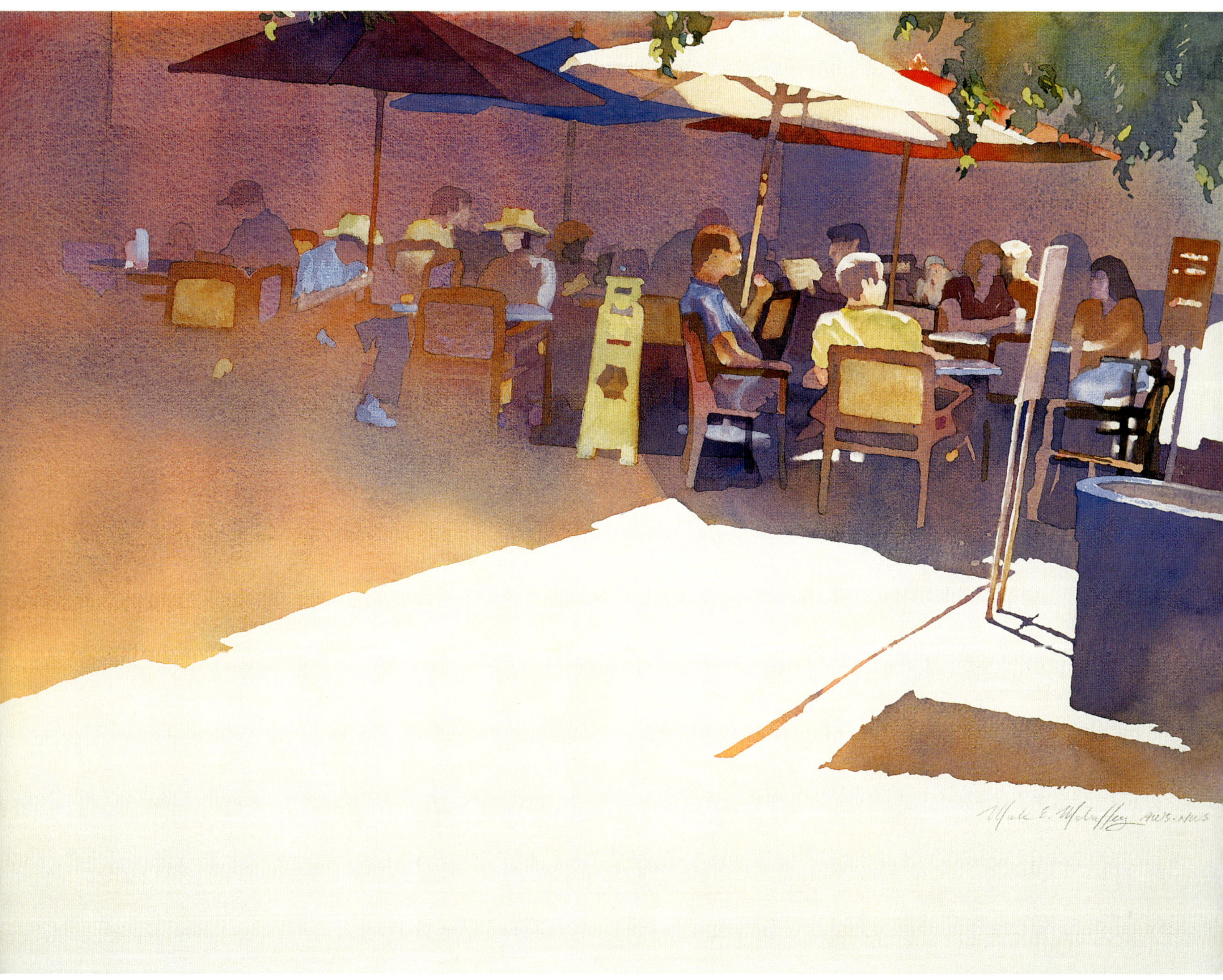

LUNCH TIME LIGHT

Mark E. Mehaffey • transparent watercolor • 22" × 30" (56cm × 76cm)

Different approaches toward different intentions were used for each of these two paintings. The sketch for *Lunch Time Light* was done on-site during my stay as a workshop instructor for the San Diego Watercolor Society. It is a small café located in Balboa Park above the city. The light was strong and the shadows were deep. By simplifying the shapes and concentrating on light and shadow, I could get to the essence of the pictorial space. Later, I worked from my sketch and further simplified the shapes of the people having lunch, the umbrellas and all the shadows. Most of the lights were masked, then the whole painting was brushed with water. After the shine had just disappeared, I dropped in my colors (New Gamboge, Quinacridone Rose and Cobalt Blue) and allowed them to blend together to form the large shadow that acts as the glue to hold everything together. The smaller shapes were masked and then worked on in stages after the largest shapes were defined.

There is no other activity that is as hard, mentally engaging, frustrating, maddening or time-consuming—or as exciting, uplifting, joyous and wonderful—as when I have a paint brush in hand.

MARK E. MEHAFFEY

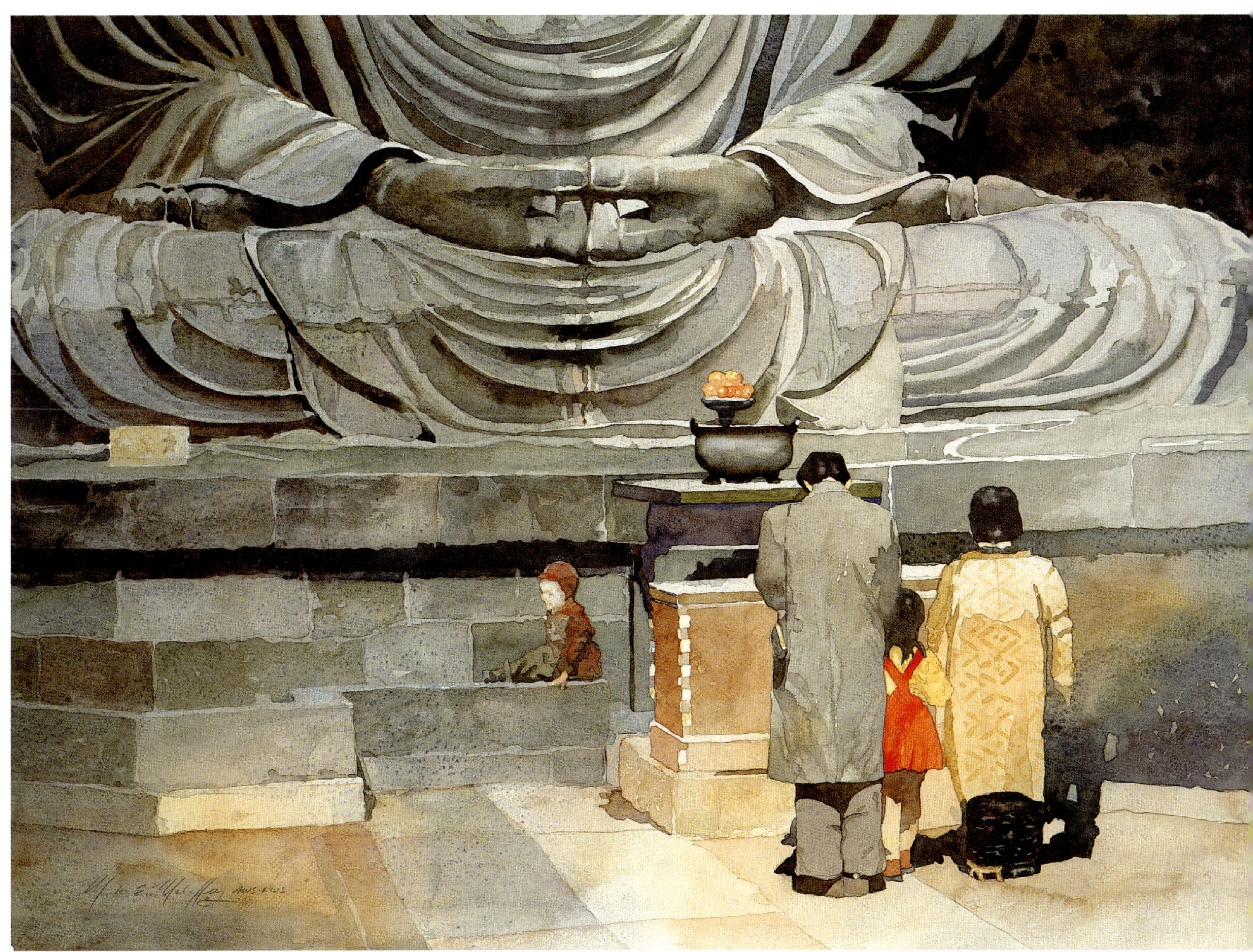

THE OFFERING

Mark E. Mehaffey • transparent watercolor on rough paper • 22" × 30" (56cm × 76cm)

The Offering is from one of three hundred slides I inherited after my mother passed away. We had spent a year in Japan when I was five years old. To honor my parents and that wonderful time, I took the best of those slides and did drawings based on the slide record. Most of the slides were of the tourist variety, so a major redesigning had to be done in my sketchbook. The painting was executed from that sketch. First, I did a detailed drawing directly on Fabriano Artistico rough watercolor paper (a hard-surfaced paper that allows the paint to sit up on the surface). The paint was applied in many layers with an evaluation of the value pattern between every layer. A cool dominance was established, with accents of red in the little girl's jumper, the bowl of apples (the offering), and the neutralized red in the little boy's coat. The little boy on the stone fence before the Buddha—that is me at the age of five! An honor to my parents, a lesson in design and a self-portrait all in one!

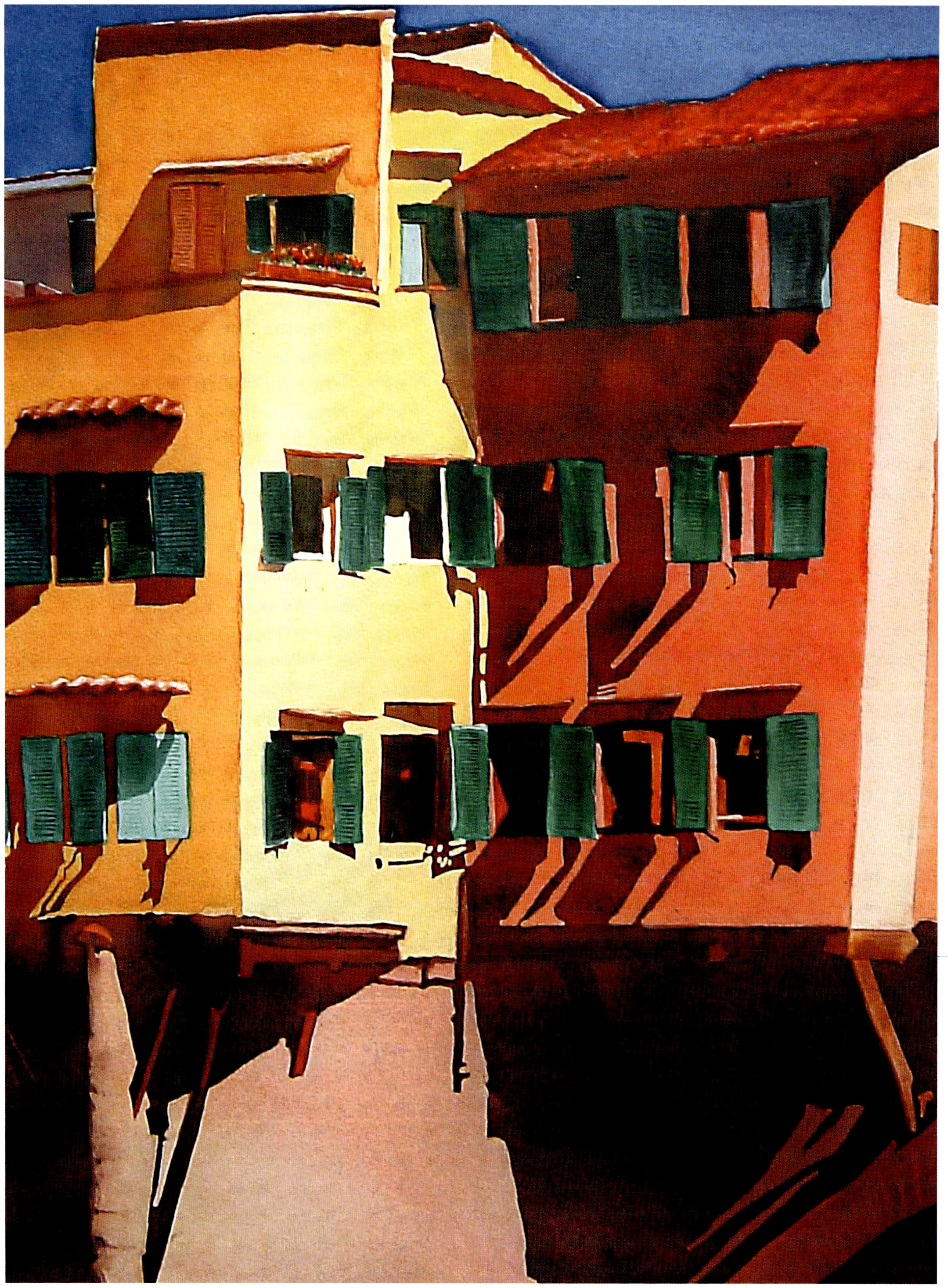

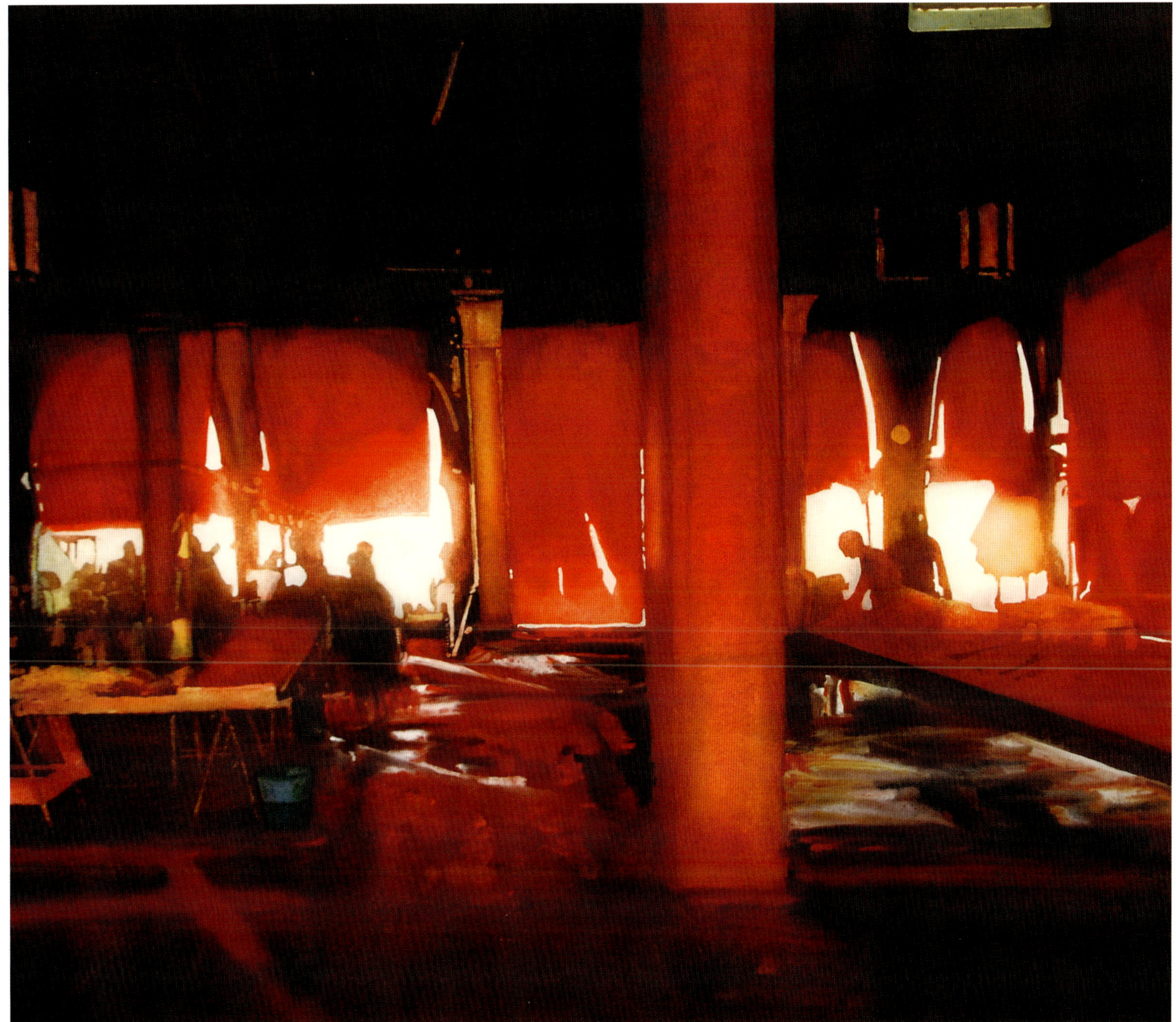

RIALTO MARKET (VENEZIA)

Donna Jill Witty • transparent watercolor on rag paper • 22" × 26" (56cm × 66cm)

PONTE VECCHIO (FIRENZE)

Donna Jill Witty • transparent watercolor on rag paper • 30" × 22" (76cm × 56cm)

Both *Rialto Market* and *Ponte Vecchio* reflect my love for dynamic color, dramatic light and strong value patterns. Derived from frequent travels covering the length and breadth of Italy, the subject matter is a passionate expression of the culture and sense of place of my heritage. Whatever your motivation, passion is what drives the creative spirit. My paintings are carefully planned, utilizing photographs, journaling and on-site color sketches. Because each painting can take two weeks or more to complete, the actual painting is done in my studio. For me, the true beauty of a watercolor is expressed in the washes—in the way the paint explodes with color, transparency and texture when suspended in the vehicle of water. To accomplish this, I "save" the places where I don't want the wash to go. This allows me the freedom to use water and paint in large areas that make the painting seem to stand up and shout, "Look at me! Aren't my washes beautiful?"

My brushstrokes are filled with paint to suggest the strength and emotion of the subject. No sneaking up here; rather, punch in all of the energy possible right from the start!

DONNA JILL WITTY

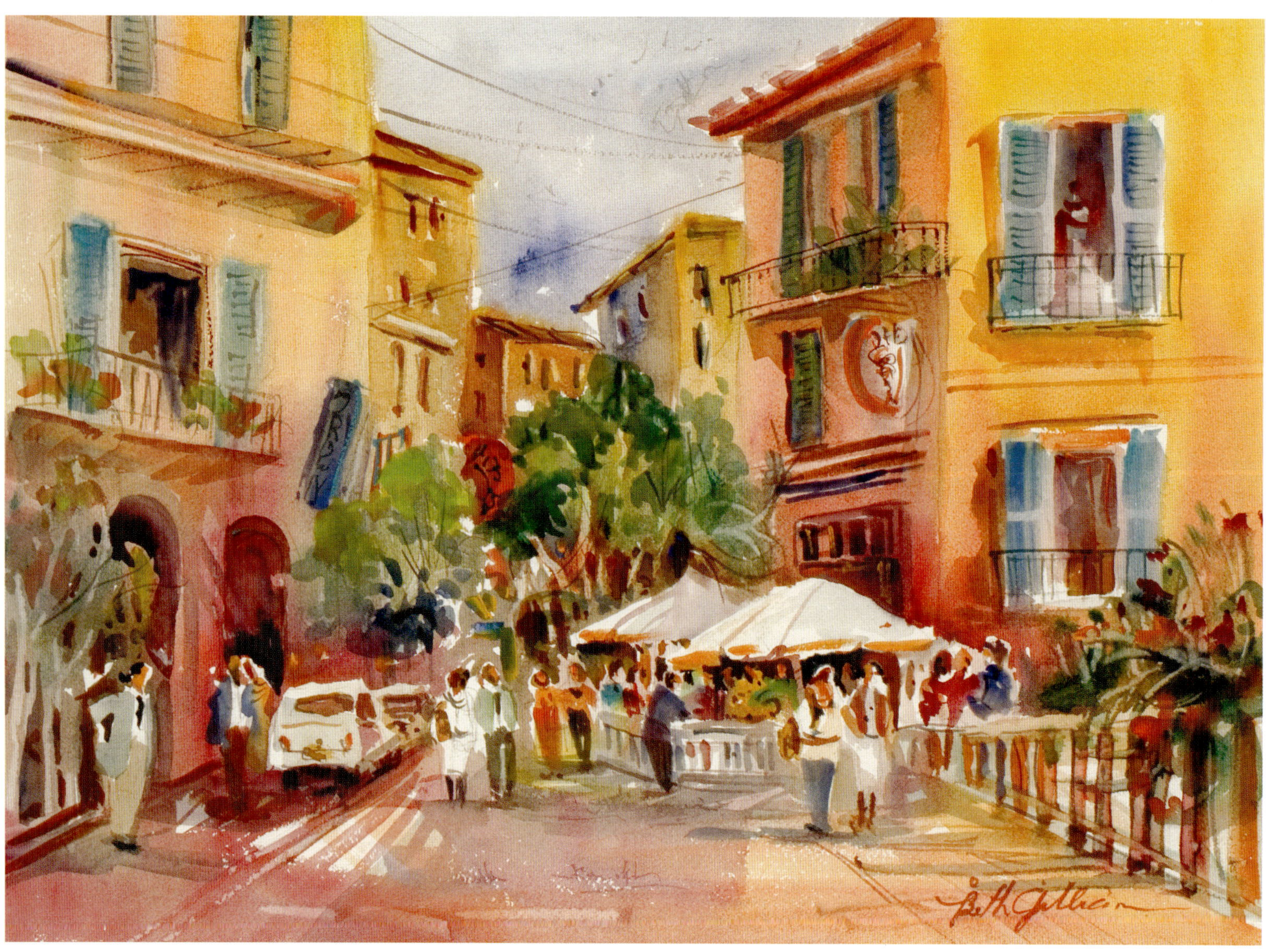

SANTA FE MORNING

Jo Beth Gilliam • transparent watercolor • 15" × 22" (38cm × 56cm)

A rich mix of people, architecture and history surrounds Santa Fe any time of the year. But on this fall morning, as in every fall, the yellow, gold and amber of the cottonwood trees reflect their warm glow on the whole town. You cannot see the actual cottonwoods in this image, but you see the glow they produce on the buildings and surroundings. I double- or triple-load a large flat brush and apply quick, loose strokes to damp paper. This technique allows variation and contrast while developing unity within the painting.

Two or more colors on the tip of a flat brush making colorful shapes or intuitive marks is my recipe for passionate brushstrokes.

JO BETH GILLIAM

MEDIEVAL CITY

Dan Burt • transparent watercolor • 30" × 22" (76cm × 56cm)

Medieval City was born out of staying in a farmhouse within sight of Trevi and Montefalco, two medieval Umbrian hill towns in central Italy. The inspiration came from an on-location watercolor in Trevi. I couldn't resist the big antique shapes, value contrasts and direction contrasts. I painted light to dark in stages with pure colors and sable brushes on dry paper, painting around saved whites and high chroma colors. The darkest dark was saved until last, which pushed out the prima donna at the top of the stairs.

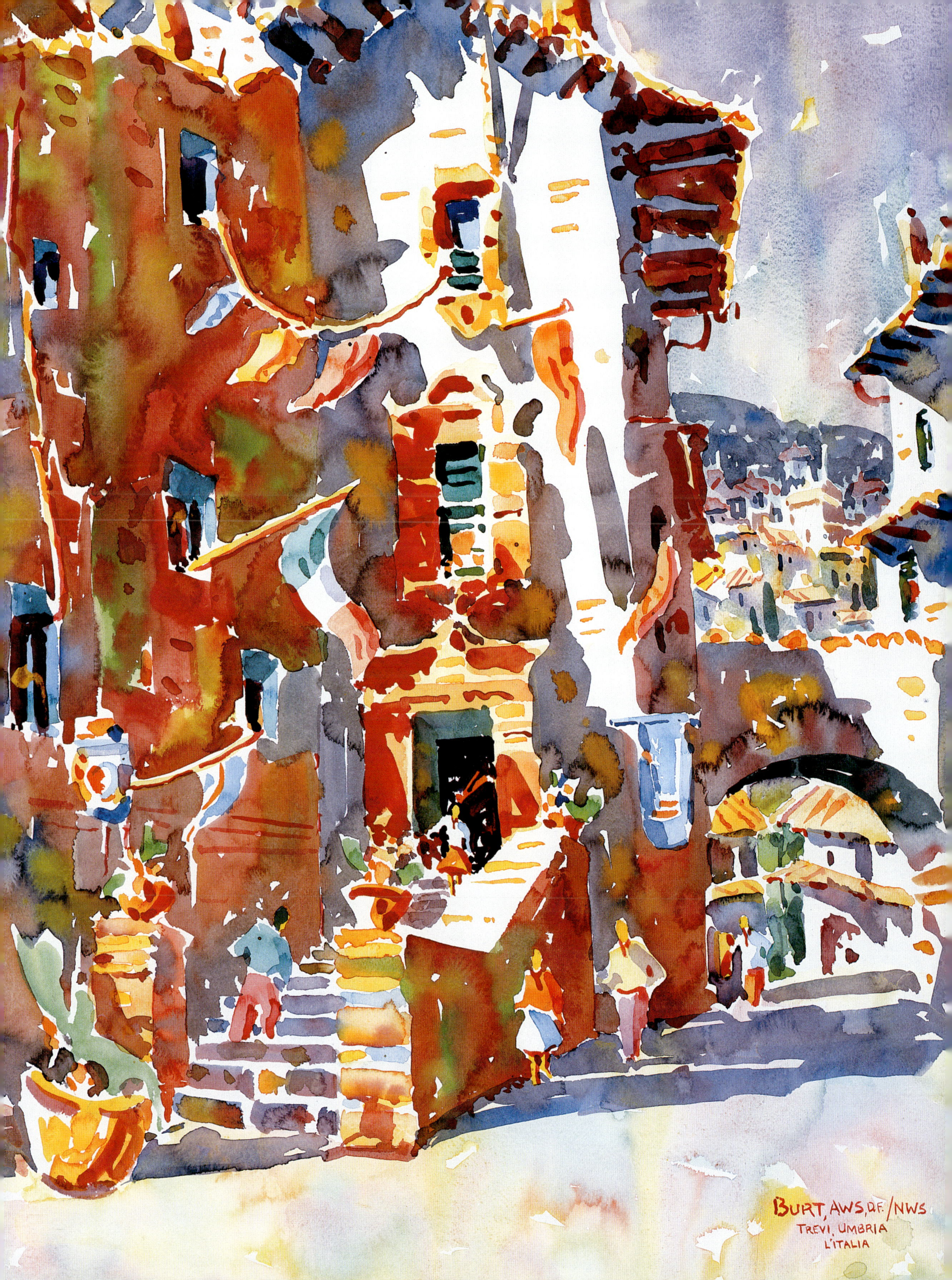
BURT, AWS, D.F. /NWS
TREVI, UMBRIA
L'ITALIA

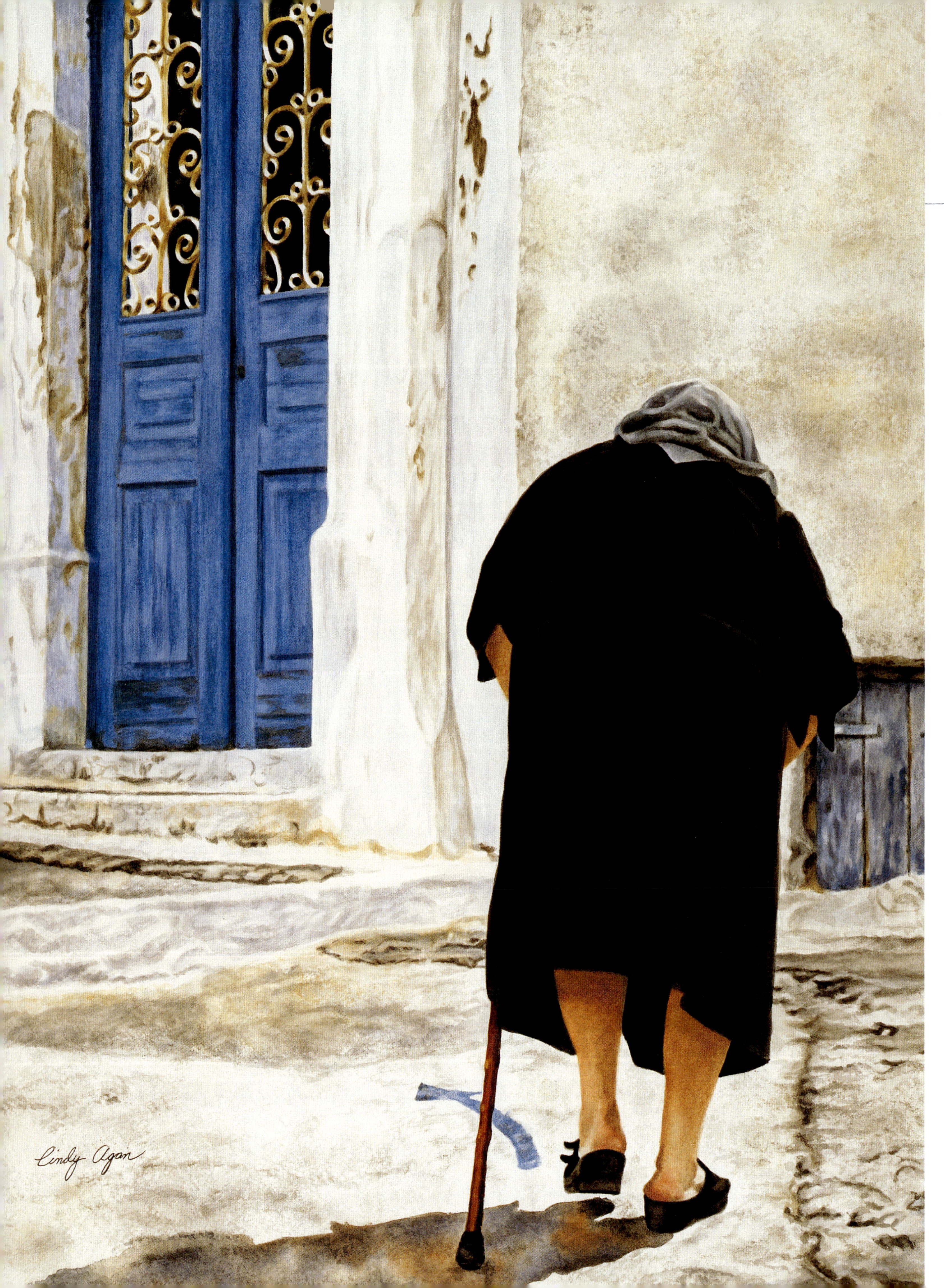
Cindy Agan

LONG ROAD HOME

Cindy Agan • watercolor and fluid acrylic • 26½" × 18¼" (67cm × 46cm)

This dear, old woman, a round fragile figure, reminded me so much of my great-grandmother (down to her dress and sensible shoes!) that she brought tears to my eyes. You can feel her fatigue as she navigates the narrow streets with her walking cane. Working from a photograph in my studio, I began *Long Road Home* with a detailed drawing. Focusing the attention on the Greek woman and striking blue doors, I subdued the background with wet-into-wet washes. A sponge dipped in diluted watercolor pigment was used to create the stucco wall. I painted multiple transparent glazes of fluid acrylic to intensify the blue in the door and the black in the dress.

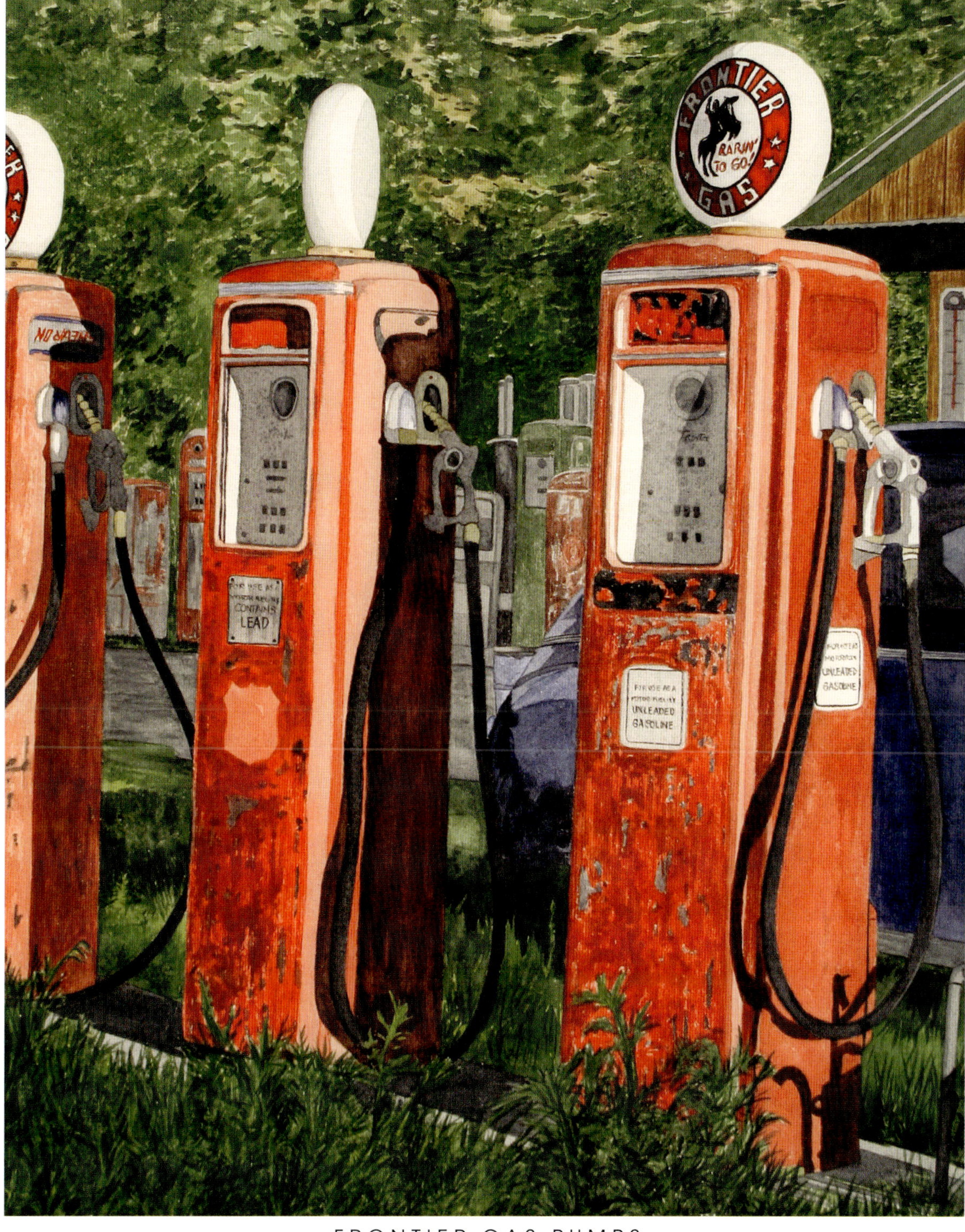

FRONTIER GAS PUMPS

David Milton • transparent watercolor on 300-lb. (640gsm) paper • 15" × 11" (38cm × 28cm)

I discovered this wonderful subject near Taos, New Mexico, several years ago on an old country road. My technique involved building up many layers of washes to achieve depth of color. Patience is the key. Finding a fresh scene like this in its natural setting is a quest I have been on for more than thirty years. So, having found it, I don't mind spending as much time as required to achieve the result. This small painting took about two months of work.

> My passion for painting is a lot like making love—the better the preparation, the better the result. Of course, some spontaneity can't hurt either.
>
> DAVID MILTON

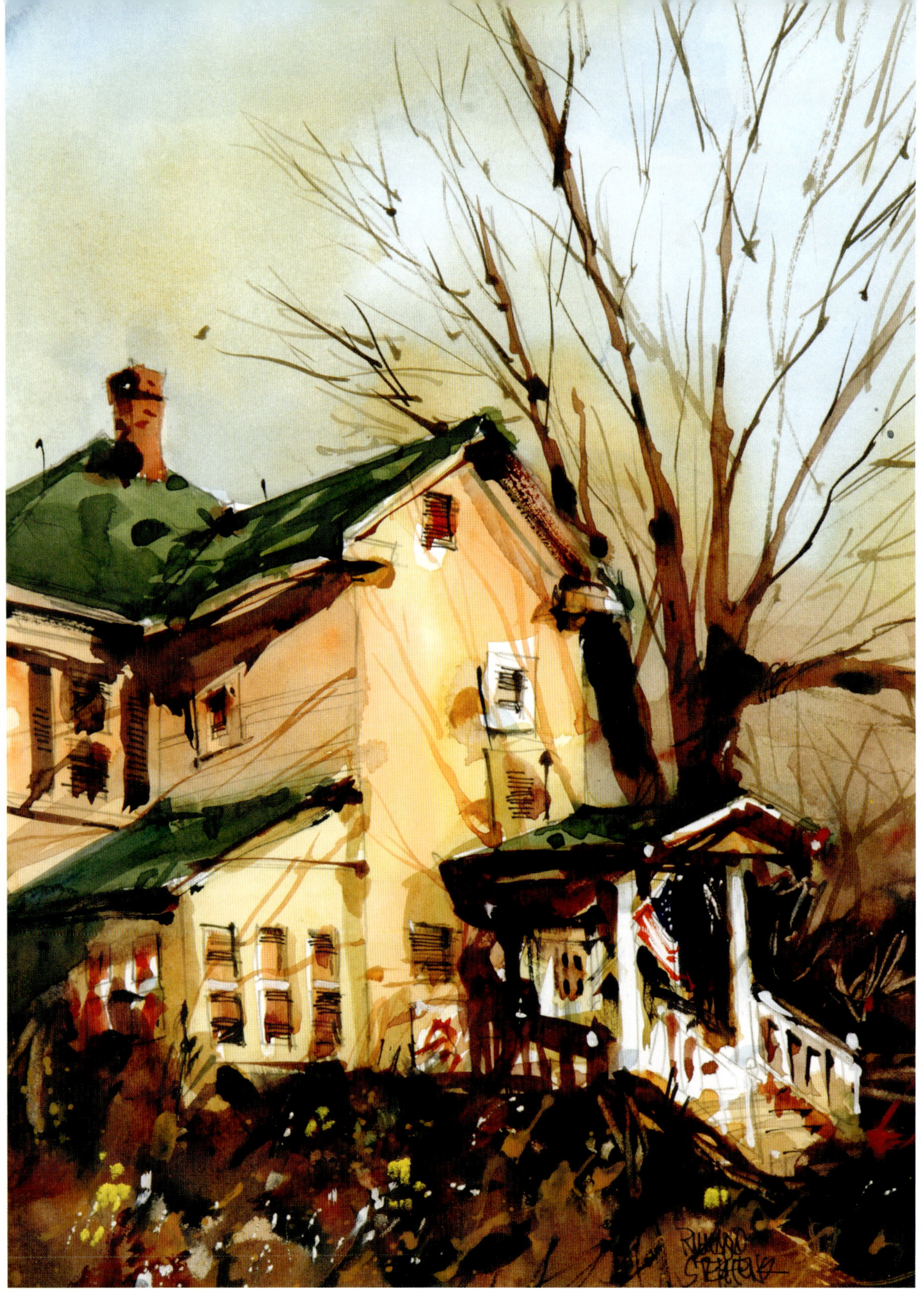

BACK PORCH AMERICA

Richard Stephens • watercolor on 300-lb. (640gsm) cold-pressed paper • 15" × 11" (38cm × 28cm)

Painting is the most important thing I do. When I am gone, more than anything else, it will represent my life.

RICHARD STEPHENS

ROYAL STREET IN NEW ORLEANS

Richard Stephens • watercolor on 300-lb. (640gsm) cold-pressed paper • 15" × 11" (38cm × 28cm)

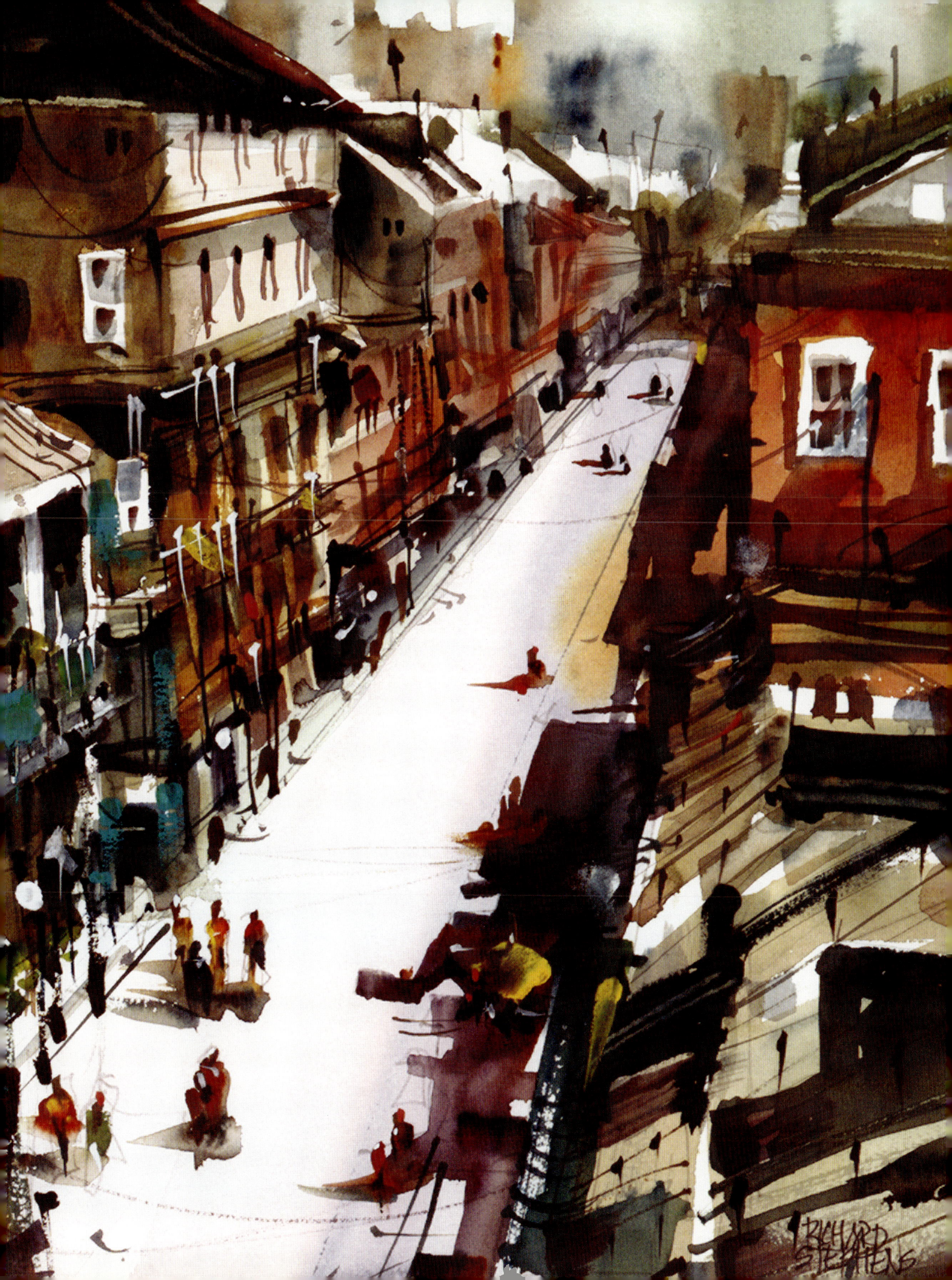
RICHARD
STEPHENS

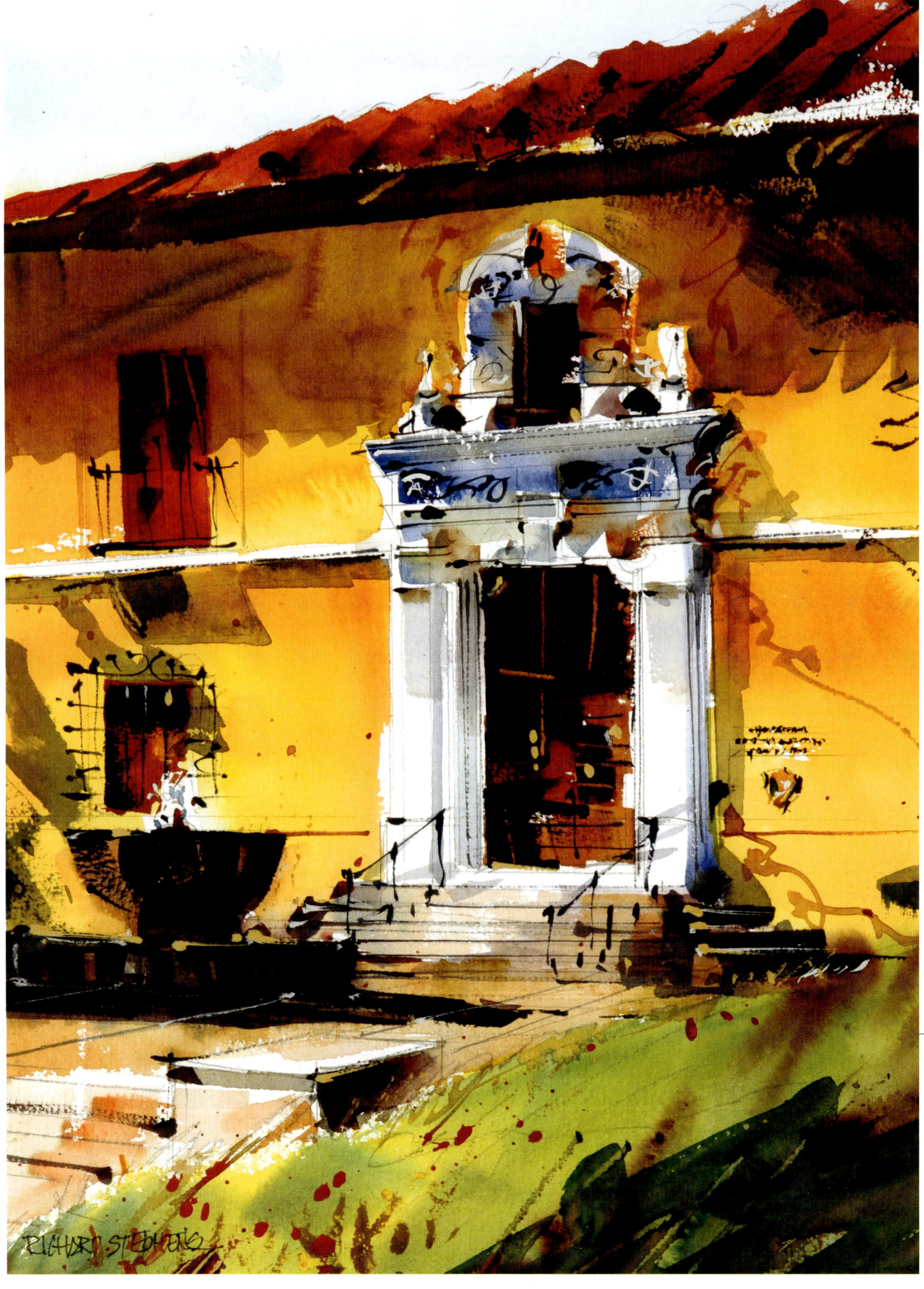
RICHARD STEPHENS

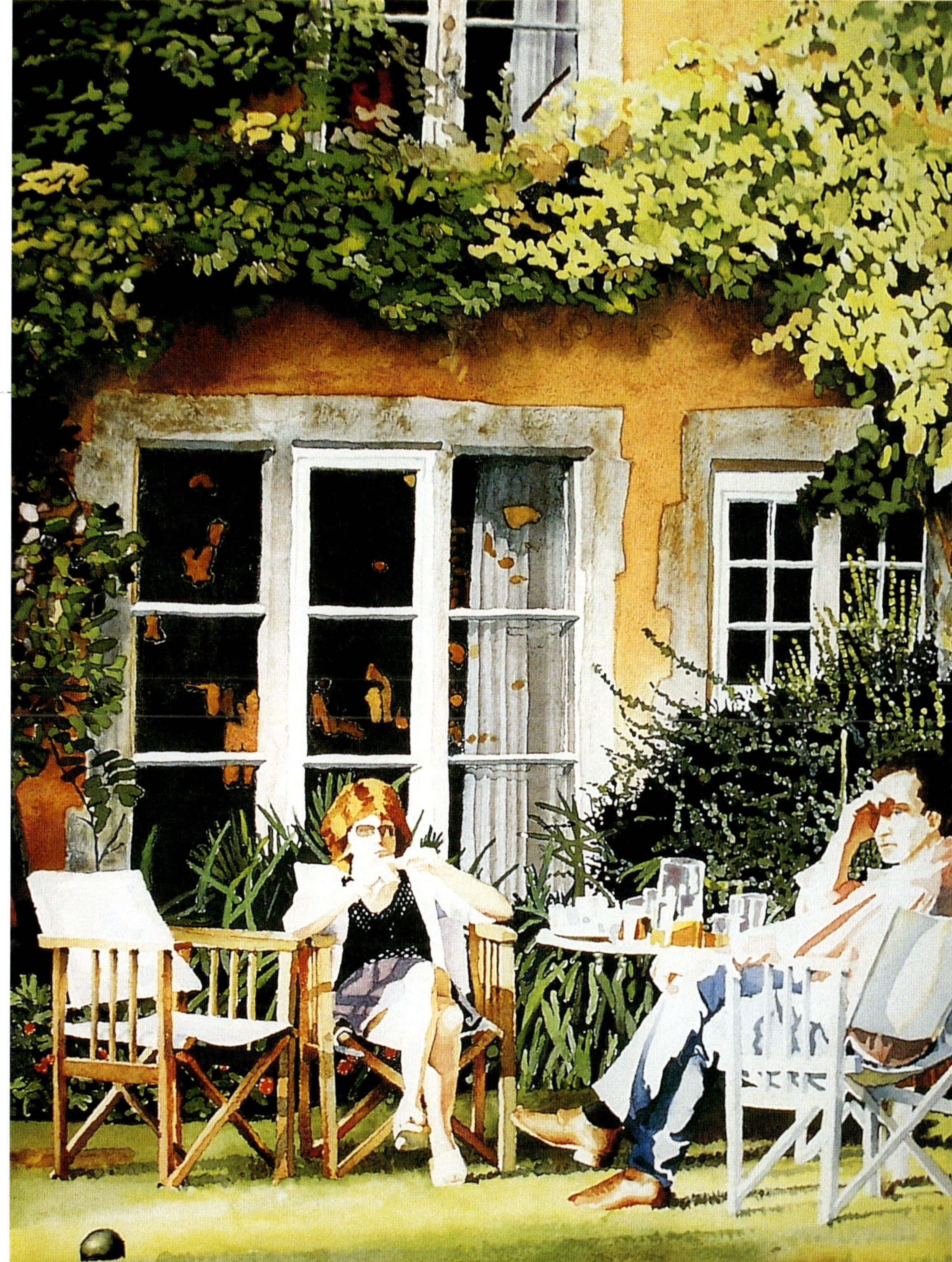

CROQUET SUNDAY

William McAllister • transparent watercolor • 20" × 14" (51cm × 36cm)

Country living in England is epitomized by many things, among them relaxing afternoons with good friends, pitchers of Pimm's and croquet mallets within easy reach. When played properly, croquet could be a cut-throat, take-no-prisoners game were it not for all the laughter. As a painter who celebrates the best environments that man is capable of producing, the English country home took me a very long time to plumb to a depth of understanding.

FOUNTAIN OF LIGHT

Richard Stephens • watercolor on 300-lb. (640gsm) cold-pressed paper • 21" × 14" (53cm × 36cm)

Back Porch America (page 98), *Royal Street in New Orleans* (page 99) and *Fountain of Light* were produced in the studio working with location sketches and photographs. I first do a simplified value sketch, then begin painting by washing in larger shapes with a no. 12 squirrel-hair mop brush. I paint with the largest brush I can for as long as I can. Working quickly, I am much more concerned about creating an interesting stroke than an accurate one. The paintings were done with various sizes of mops. I find rounds make a more organic stroke than flats, although there are certainly times when a flat is the right tool. All the subjects represent a special history or experience for me.

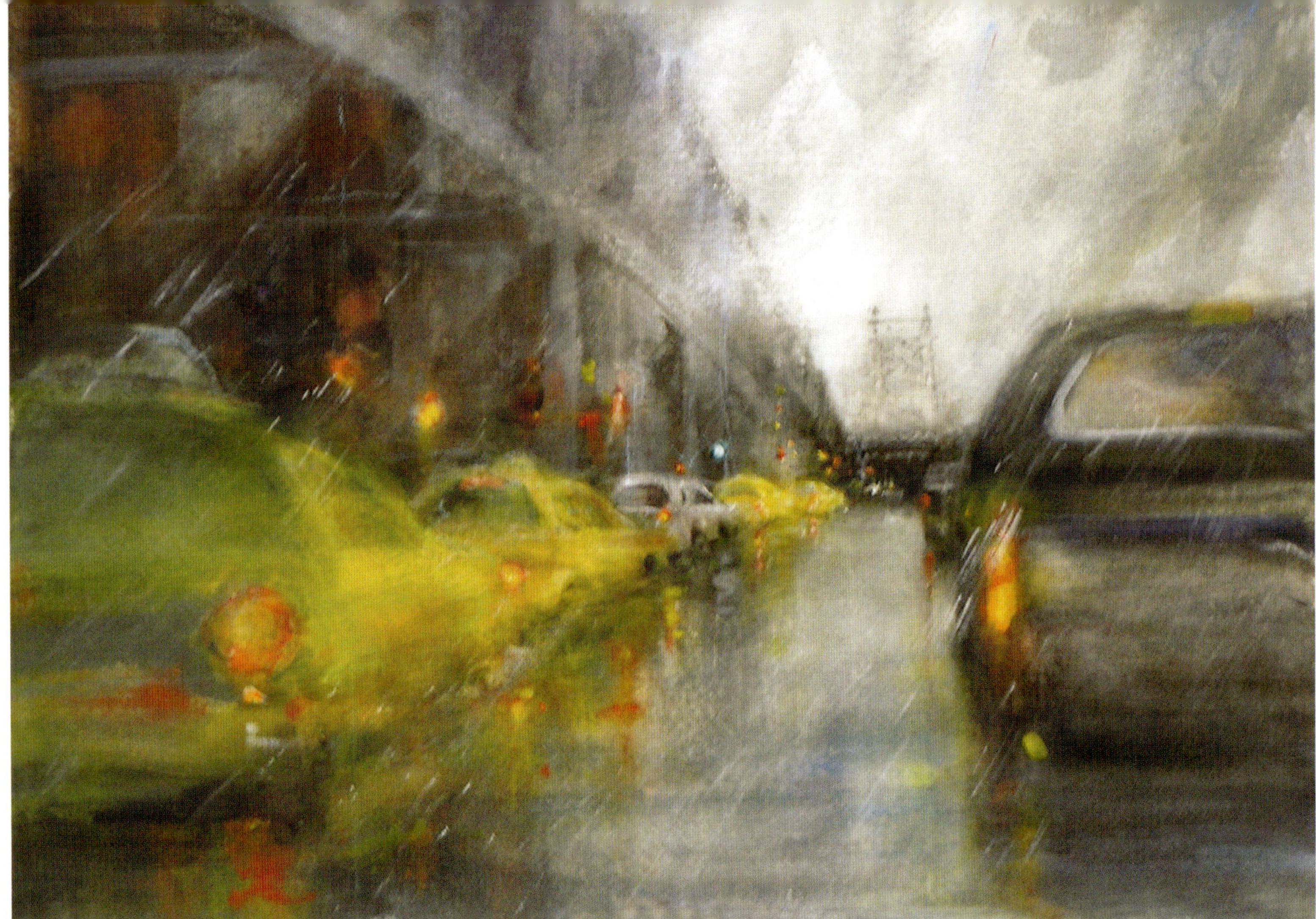

DOWNPOUR

Ruth Baderian • watercolor with body color • 22" × 30" (56cm × 76cm)

Downpour was born on a rainy, foggy, humid morning during a time of limited visibility and unlimited frustration. There were construction delays driving into New York City, and I snapped many digital photos from my car, sitting in traffic. I later worked many sketches directly from the LED, then combined the most expressive ones into a final composition. The 300-lb. (640gsm) rough surface creates broken marks that express splashing rain. I rarely use Ivory Black, but here it sets off the mood of this oppressive situation, and contrasts the brilliant Gamboge Yellow glow of taxis and gleaming Cadmium Red leaking from taillights, suggesting the city's energy. Delicate wisps of body color were used to suggest driving rain. Downward brush marks imply wet pavement. One-point perspective was used to exaggerate the claustrophobic feeling of driving into the city tunnel. Even the churning emotions of traffic-bound frustration can give way to the passion for painting.

BLIZZARD ON FIFTH AVENUE

James Toogood • watercolor on 300-lb. (640gsm) cold-pressed paper • 30" × 22" (76cm × 56cm)

This and the paintings on pages 8 and 80–81 are part of a series of winter paintings I did of New York City. Rough compositional ideas were developed on location, but the final composition was done in the studio using numerous photographs and sketches. In each case, I first executed a precise drawing of the major compositional elements on the back of the sheet. I then applied a series of washes followed by ever-smaller brushstrokes. These brushstrokes were applied rather wet and with a long riggerlike brush. The paint was allowed to run ever so slightly, softening some edges. Areas that would become the snowflakes were reserved.

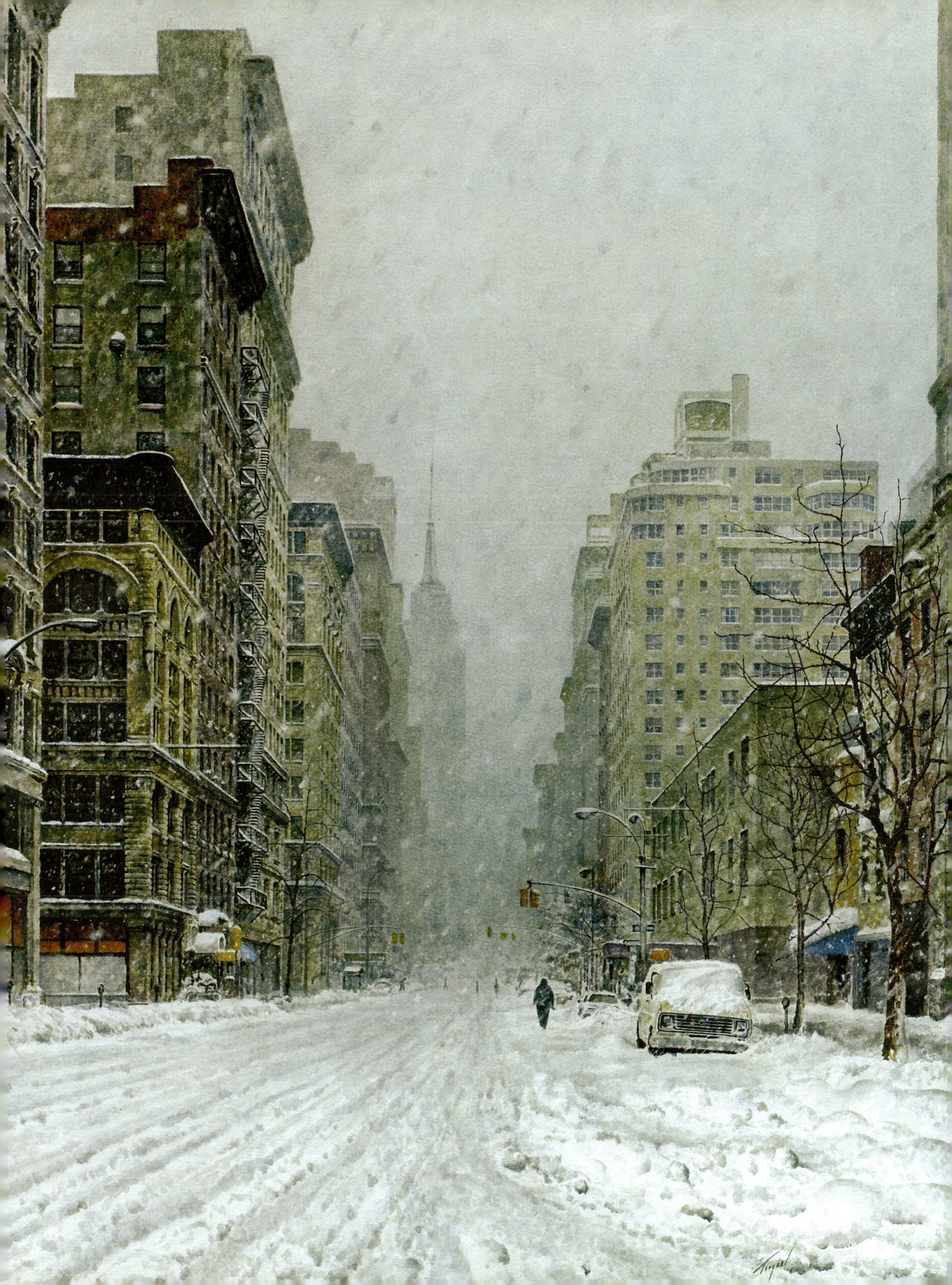

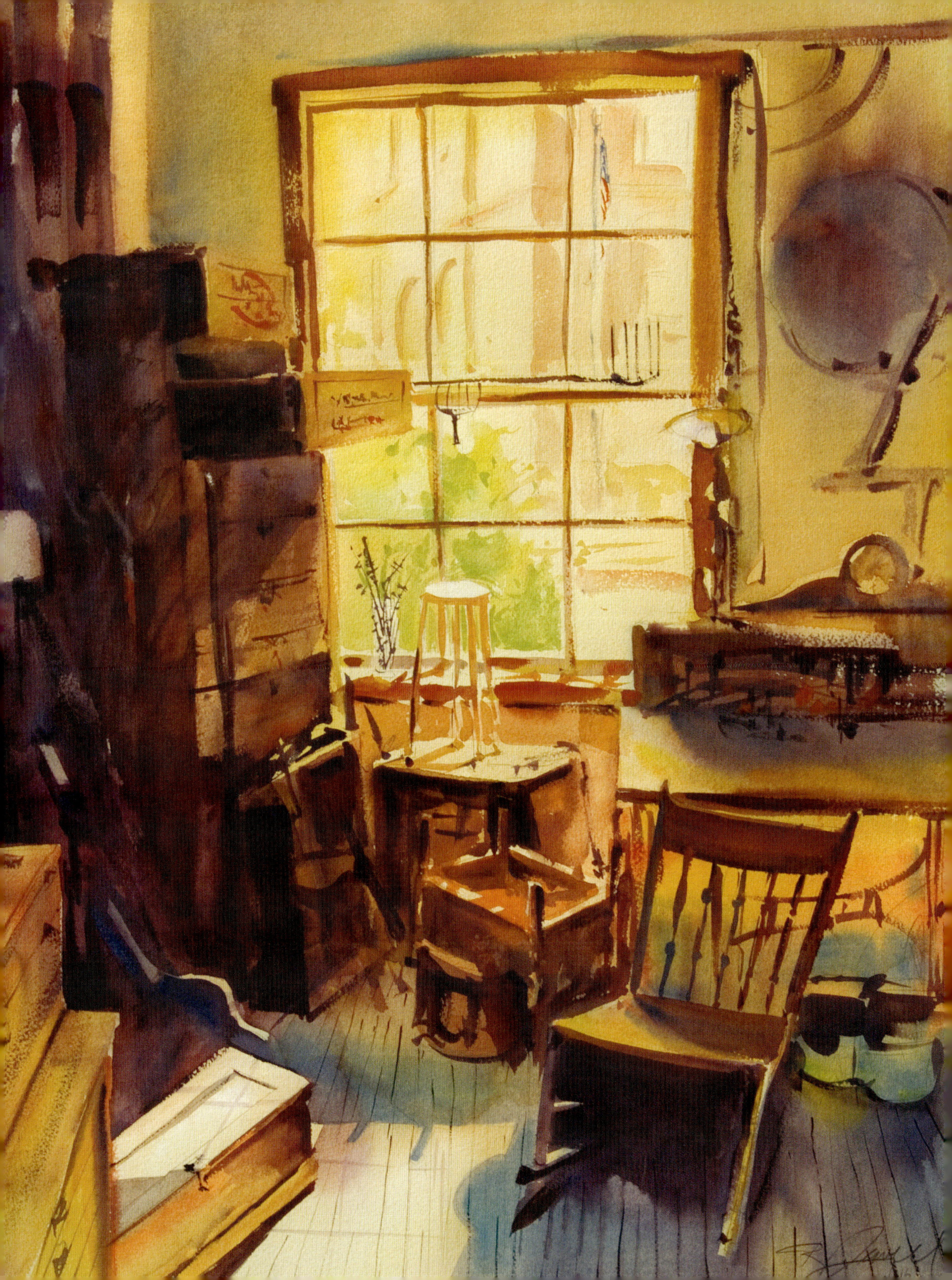

BURFORD LAMB

William McAllister • transparent watercolor • 7½" × 5½" (19cm × 14cm)

British public houses are unique in so many ways, yet they encompass much of the common humanity that I find in public spaces worldwide. The Lamb in Burford, in the heart of the wool-producing Cotswolds, may be numbered as one of the best examples of an old, traditional pub that has evolved over the centuries to serve the needs of patrons of all ages and backgrounds. This very small sketch reflects my thoughts about an older couple, alone in their private corner for the moment, whom I have isolated from others by placing an empty table between them and the rest of the room. I think that later they will join a few good friends at the bar. Cheers!

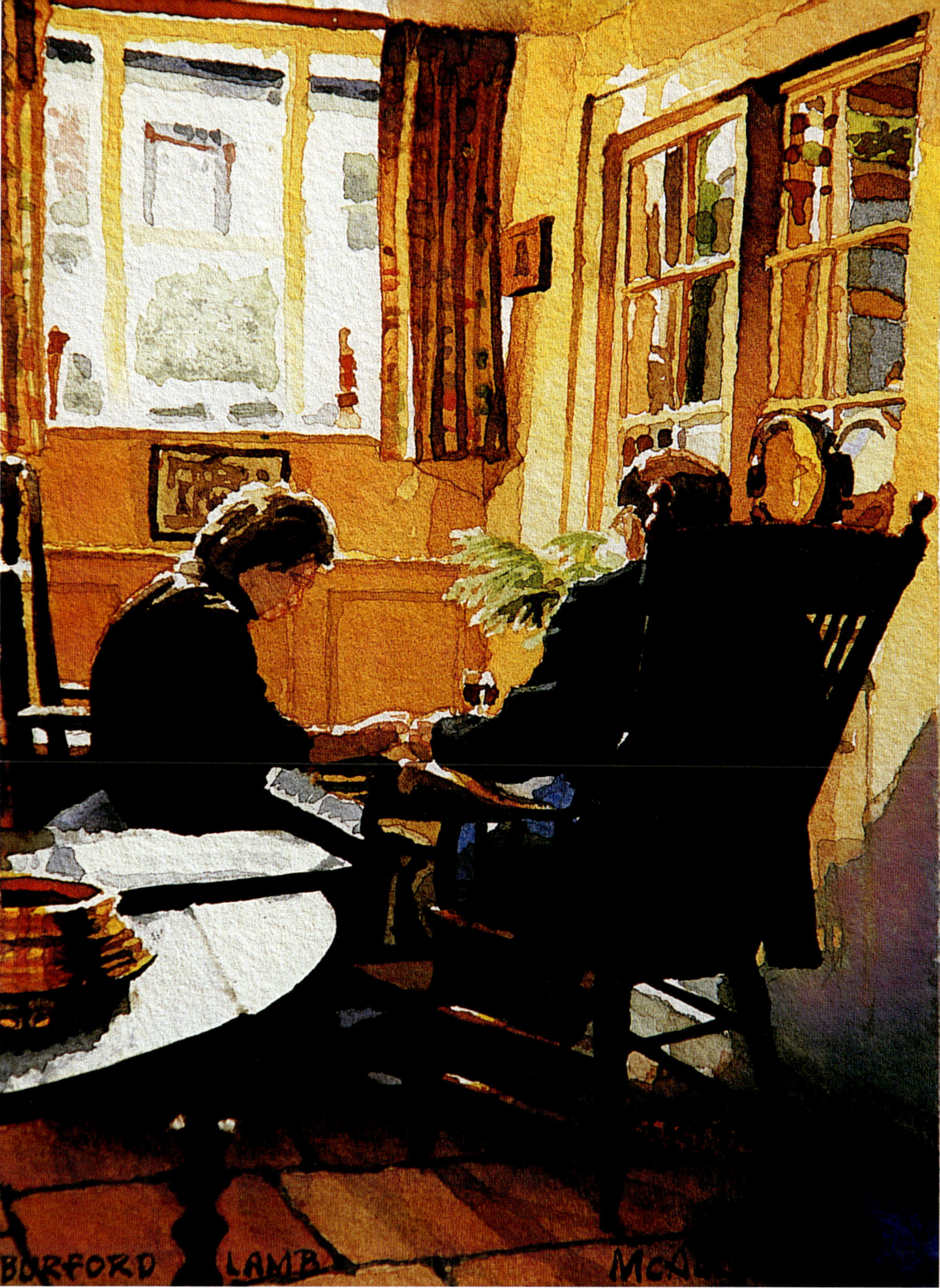

HOT SEAT

Rusty Jewell • transparent watercolor • 30" × 22" (76cm × 56cm)

My passion is to combine the spontaneity of watercolor with the effects of light illuminating objects. *Hot Seat* was inspired while antique shopping in Rockland, Maine. To avoid directly reproducing the photograph back in the studio, I view it through a viewfinder and make changes to develop a stronger composition. I also apply initial values to the painting with diffused wet-into-wet brushstrokes. As the paper dries, I use juicy, more direct brushstrokes to focus areas of interest. In the original photo, every object is in focus, but, with this contrasting brushstroke approach, I can express my passion for the subject.

When painting in oil, I am fishing in a pond—I know the exact brushstroke I am fishing for. When painting in watercolor, I'm fishing in the ocean. I'm never quite sure what I might catch.

RUSTY JEWELL

> I enjoy making broad strokes, twisting the brush to variegate shapes and using the edges of flat brushes for great results. Detail is always my passion.
>
> CINDY BRABEC-KING

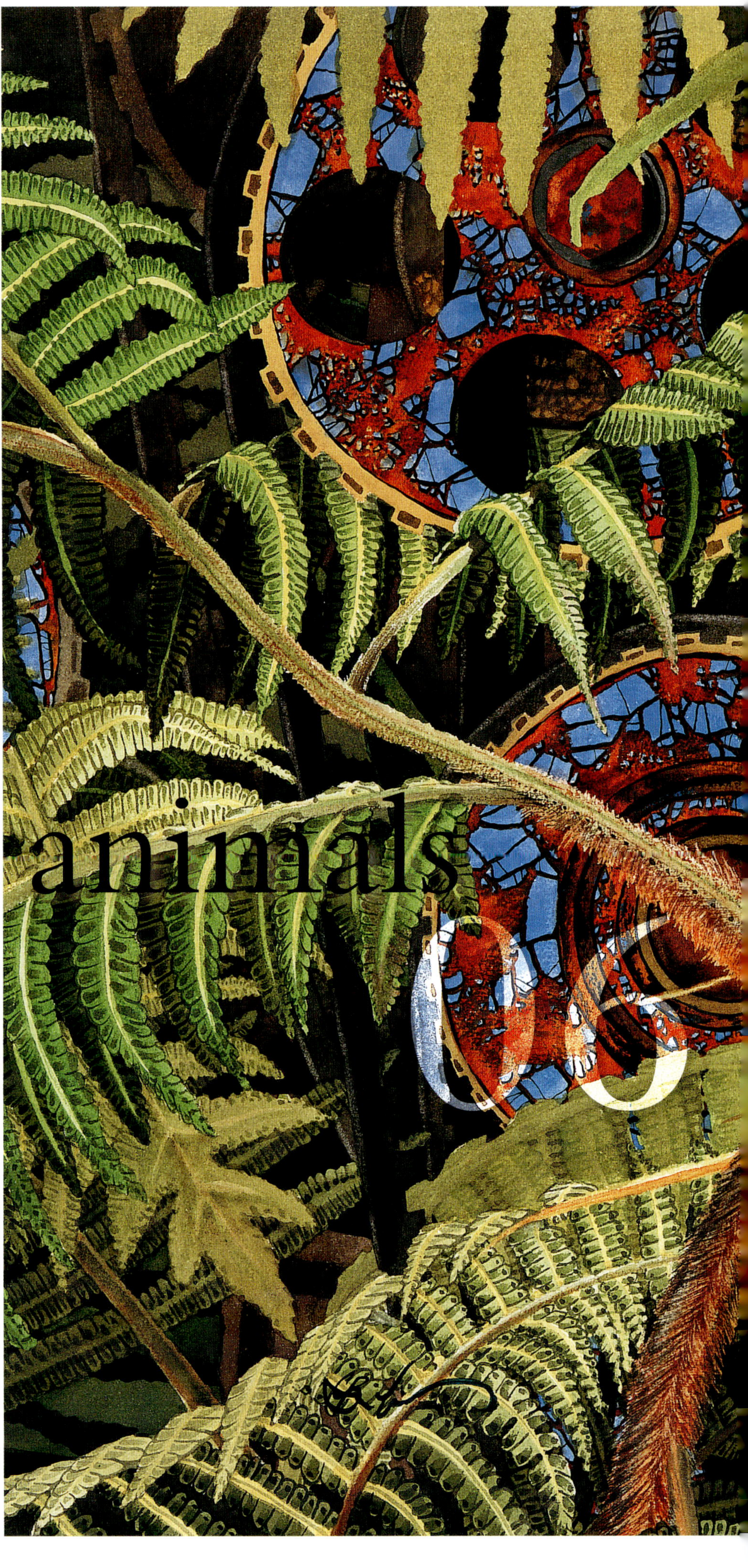

animals

06

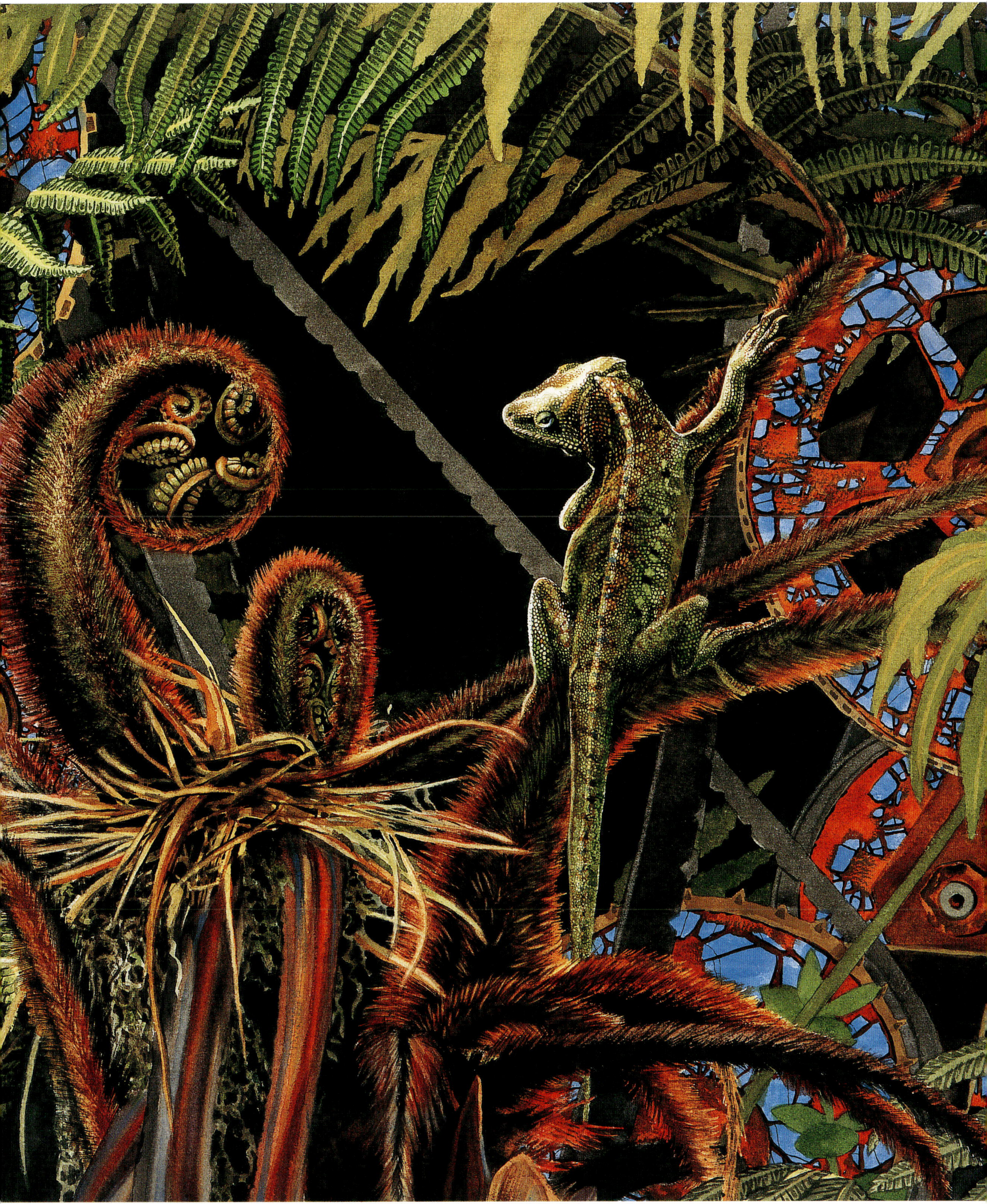

HAWAIIAN BLEND

Cindy Brabec-King • transparent watercolor • 22" × 30" (56cm × 76cm)

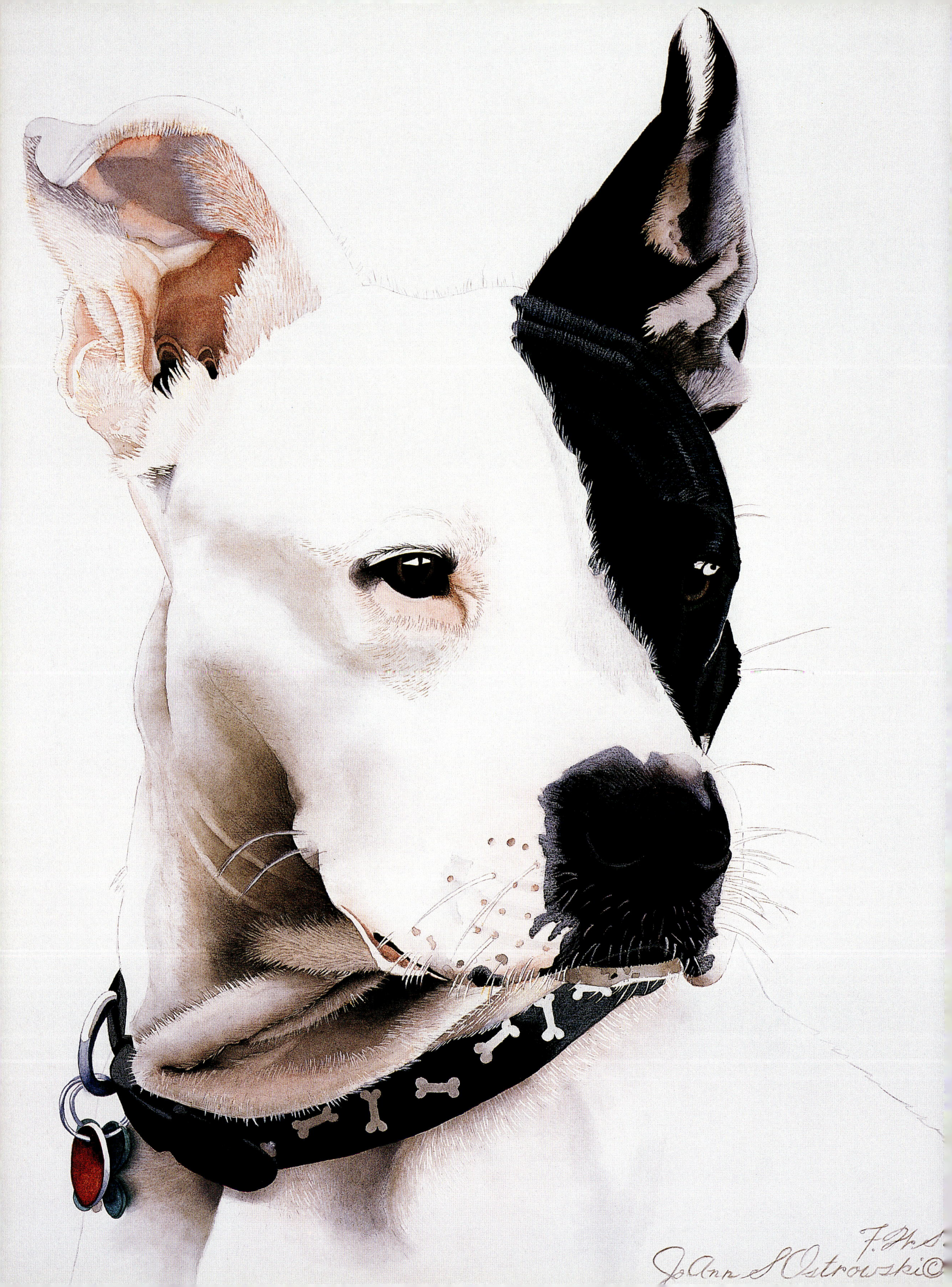
F.Ph.S.
JoAnn S Ostrowski©

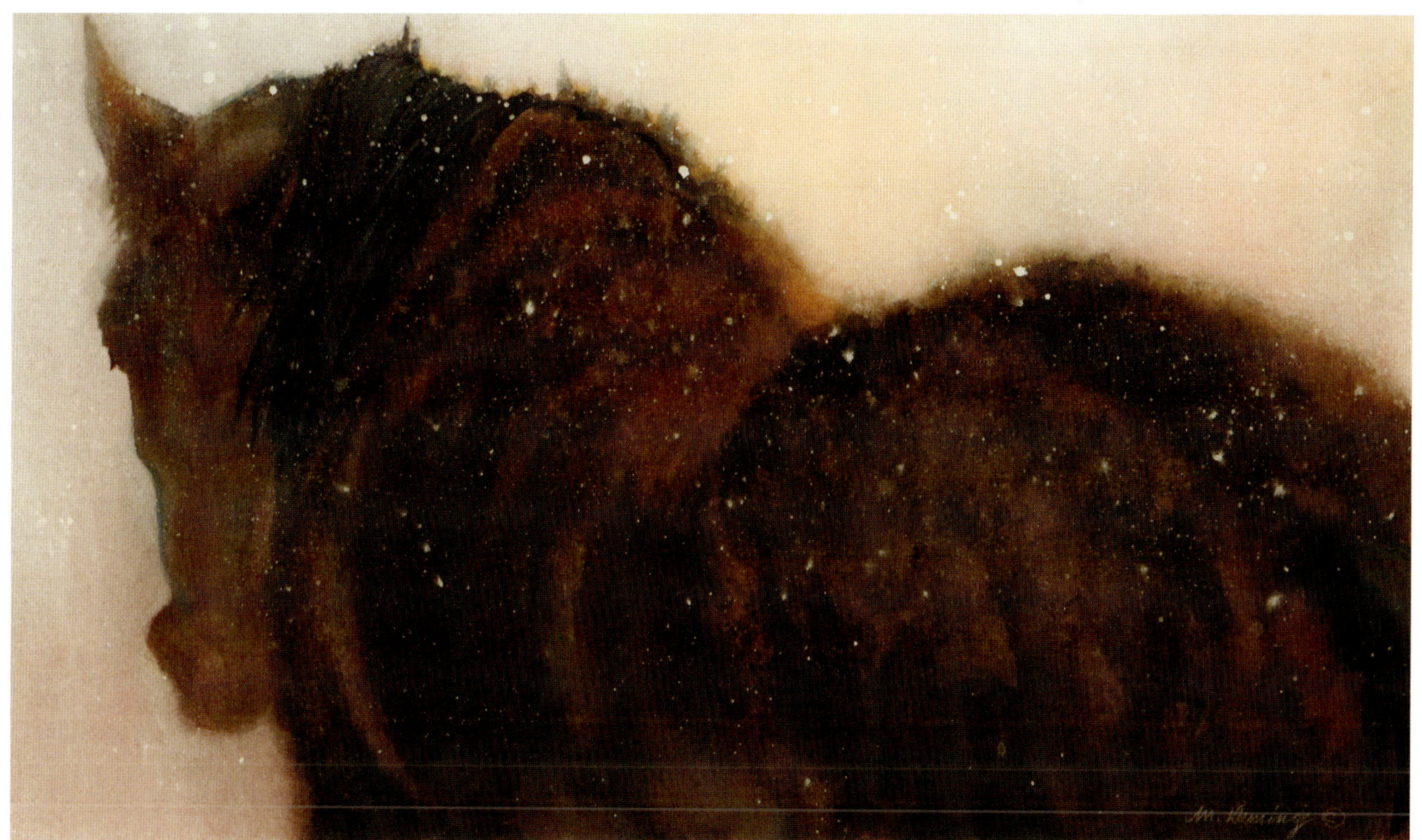

WOODSY NAPPING

Martha M. Deming • transparent watercolor with white gouache • 10" × 16¾" (25cm × 43cm)

I was standing in my studio one winter day, looking out at my beloved horse, so graceful and beautiful, dozing on his feet in a gentle snowfall. He was old and frail; I wondered if he'd make it through that winter (he did) or the next (he didn't). The painting was a way for me to capture memories of this horse, this moment. Using a piece of 140-lb. (300gsm) cold-pressed paper that I had tinted earlier, I re-soaked it to saturation, the underpainting undisturbed, and began creating the image of Woodsy as he stood there in the snow, working from life and photographs. The pigments ran and blurred as I first brushed them onto the saturated surface. As the paper slowly dried, refinements were developed. Finishing touches were added after complete natural drying. A thin glaze of white gouache was added last around the horse to further soften the remaining underpainting colors. Light spatters of white were done at various stages of drying. The moment and the memory of my old pal were captured.

TUGBOAT

JoAnn S. Ostrowski • semi-transparent watercolor and India ink • 22" × 15" (56cm × 38cm)

This Staffordshire Bull Terrier, named Tugboat by my dentist, had been rescued but was destined to be euthanized due to malnutrition and heartworm infection. With some expert veterinary care and TLC, he is thriving and has gone on to be one of the top agility dogs in the country. My dentist was amiable to the idea of me painting her new true love, so we set up a photo shoot. I decided to use the white of the paper as a background to enhance the black and white contrast. A masking technique isolated individual white and shaded gray hairs in the folds of the neck and ears. Dimensional shades of black were created by utilizing semi-transparent black watercolor and India ink.

I love the challenge of getting it right. That means utilizing all of the techniques at my disposal to express what I want to say.

JOANN S. OSTROWSKI

KEEP LOOKING FOR A BLUEBIRD

Tom Yacovella • transparent watercolor with acrylic accents • 18" × 24" (46cm × 61cm)

I love bluebirds because they represent spring, happiness, beauty and love. My idea for *Keep Looking for a Bluebird* evolved from a photograph I saw in the June 1977 issue of *National Geographic* of eleven bluebirds clustered to conserve body heat in the hollow of a tree. I expanded on this theme by creating sixty-eight bluebirds, each representing one year of my life. I roughly cut out sixty-eight similarly sized paper shapes in hues of blue (Peacock Blue for males and teal for females). Next I arranged the paper shapes so that the males formed a spiral design flow. From this abstraction, I developed the painting. I hope my painting inspires people to become educated about the vulnerability of bluebirds, whose nesting cavities and habitats are at high risk from competition with house sparrows and starlings, both introduced species.

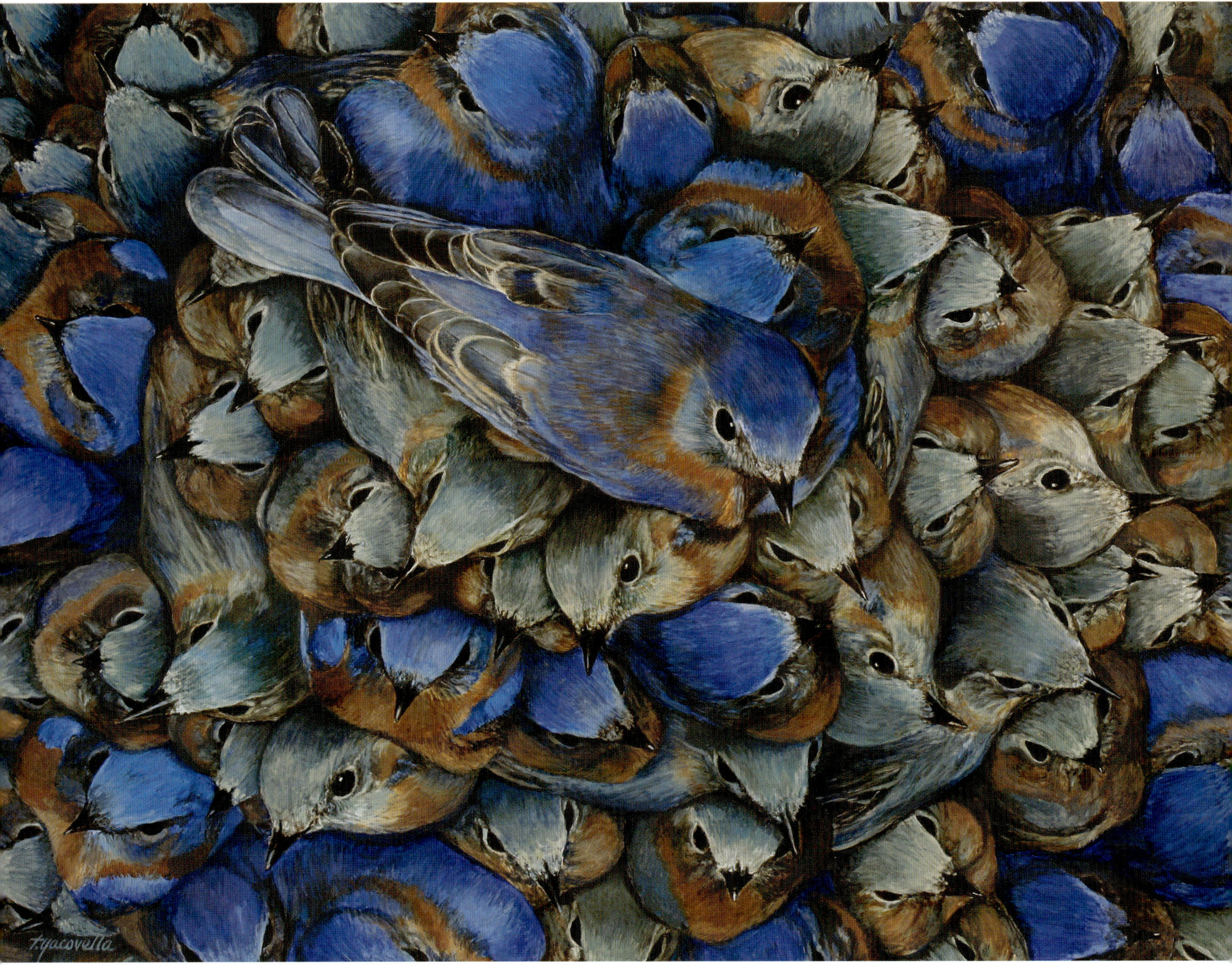

THAT RADIANT GLOW

Fran Mangino • transparent watercolor on 140-lb. (300gsm) paper • 30" × 22" (76cm × 56cm)

The water and flamingos literally glowed in the hot sun. I was able to capture this effect with my camera, but my challenge was how to convey the radiant glow in watercolor. I knew that the birds had to sparkle, but the background water had to glow also. I wanted to finish in one sitting, so I mixed enough heavily saturated colors to cover the paper. I masked the outline of the birds and laid down the first wet brushload for the water's color. I dropped the subsequent colors in wet to avoid brushstrokes, pulling them together lightly with a brush, letting the colors mix on the paper. I used the same technique to show the reflected glow in the shadow areas of the birds' necks, leaving the backlit outline of their silhouettes paper-white.

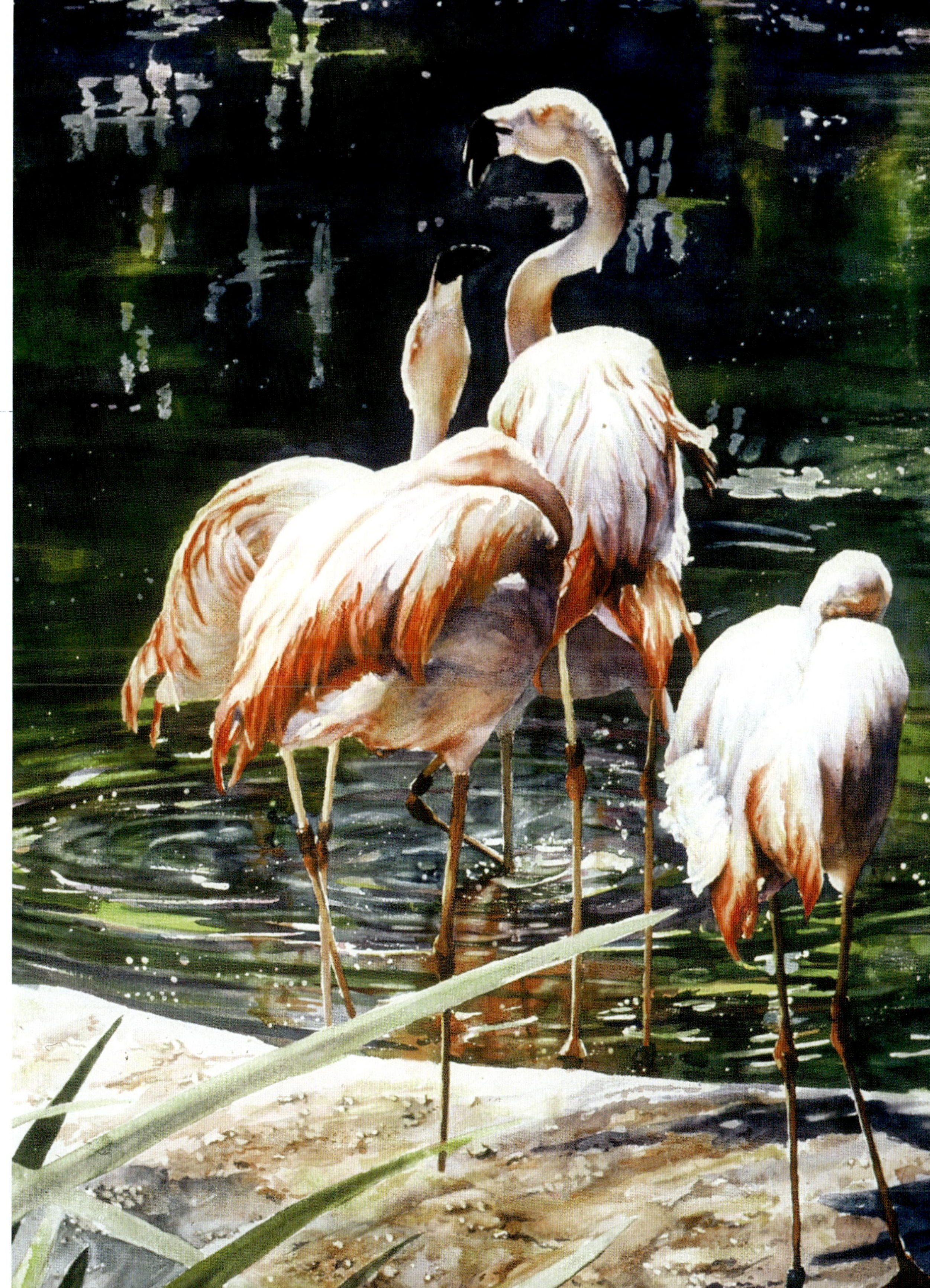

Art is electrifying. What a God-given privilege to create and to be among friends who feel this same passion!

FRAN MANGINO

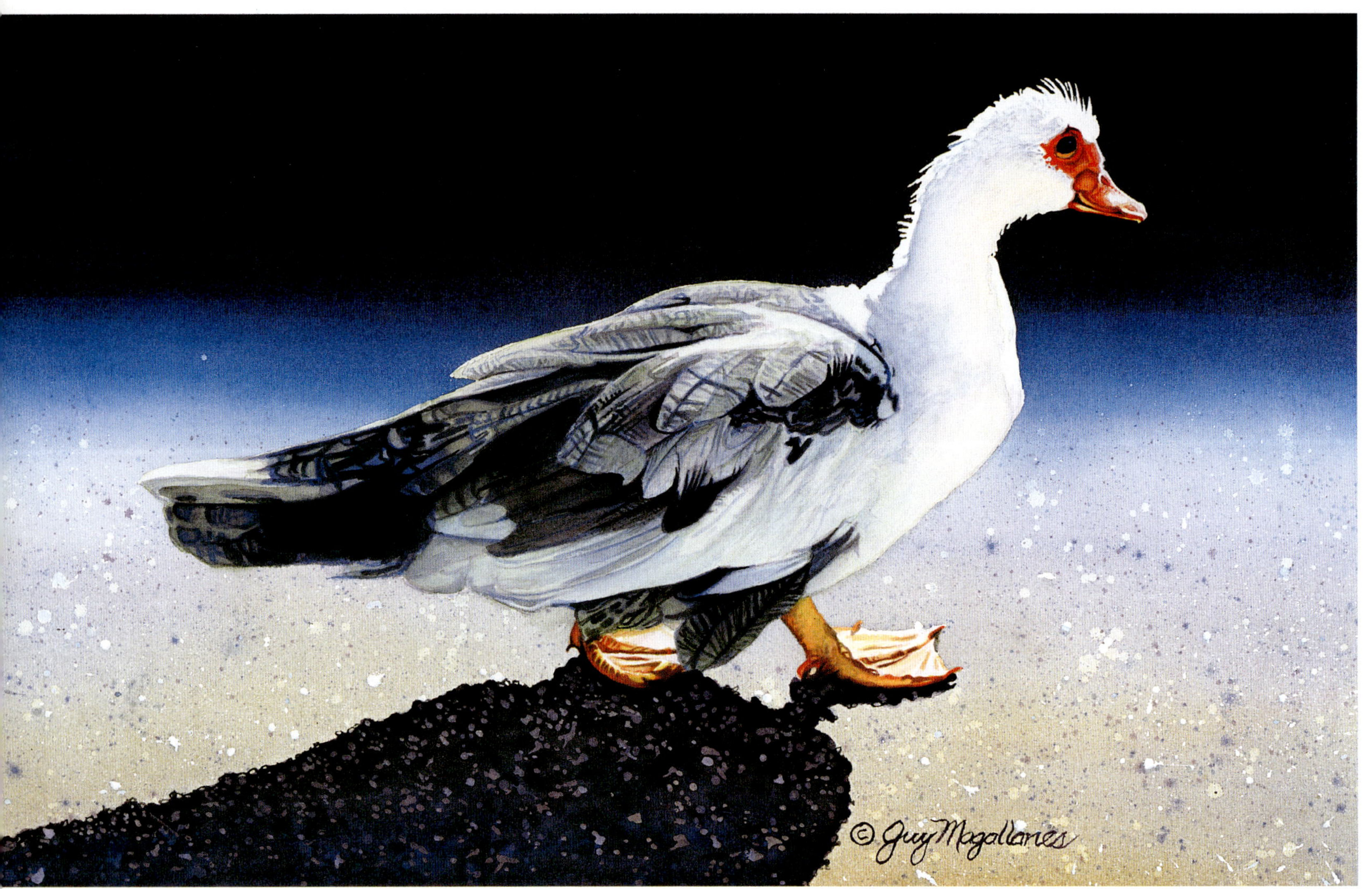

DUCK, DUCK, GOOSE!

Guy Magallanes • watercolor • 13½" × 21½" (34cm × 55cm)

I spent an afternoon feeding ducks at a park and fell in love with this Muscovy duck. This hen was so ugly with her red face and big tooth at the end of her duck bill that I ended up spending most of the afternoon feeding and taking pictures of her. I loved her aloof attitude—just pick up the food and move on. One photograph captured her attitude, but the background was not strong. So I masked off the duck and went to work, wet-into-wet, creating a different background. At the bottom edge, I spattered paint and masking between glazes to get a gravel texture. At the top, I worked wet-into-wet for the gradation of colors, moving, tilting and adjusting quickly because the darks wanted to travel down the painting. Once satisfied with the background, I removed the masking and began working on the duck with a limited color palette. I wanted to really show the light hitting the white of her crown and the glow of light shining through her little legs.

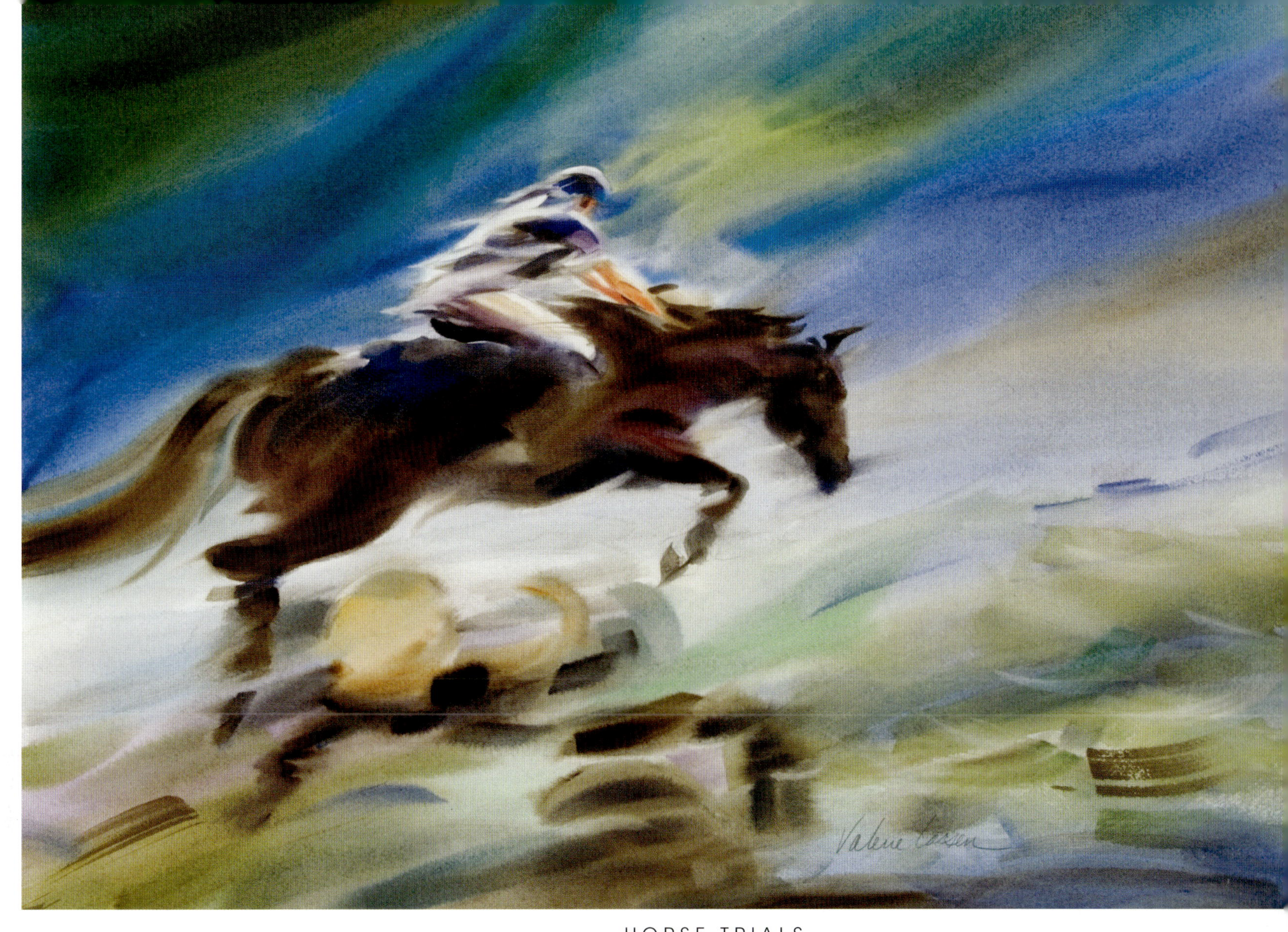

HORSE TRIALS

Valerie Larsen • transparent watercolor • 19" × 26" (48cm × 66cm)

Rider and horse in rhythm, pounding through a cross-country course, is the culmination of endless hours of practice and a nurtured relationship between man and animal. The painting was inspired by a photographic expedition to the Stuart Horse Trials in upstate New York. From a safe viewpoint, horse and rider can be seen working through a grueling course of hazards, this one a jump over a massive log down into a shallow pond. To imitate the perception of movement, the painting was done in a wet-into-wet approach, adding glycerin to the water to slow drying. Soft edges of the first aggressively placed brushstrokes create the out-of-focus movement that is the major theme of the painting. The addition of a few crisp, dry strokes brings key elements back into focus.

An artist is somehow wired differently, sees differently and is driven by that which can only be expressed in a manner other than language.

VALERIE LARSEN

Since retirement, my passion for painting has lifted off like a rocket ship. I may never come back to earth!

ROBIN SEVESTER AVERY

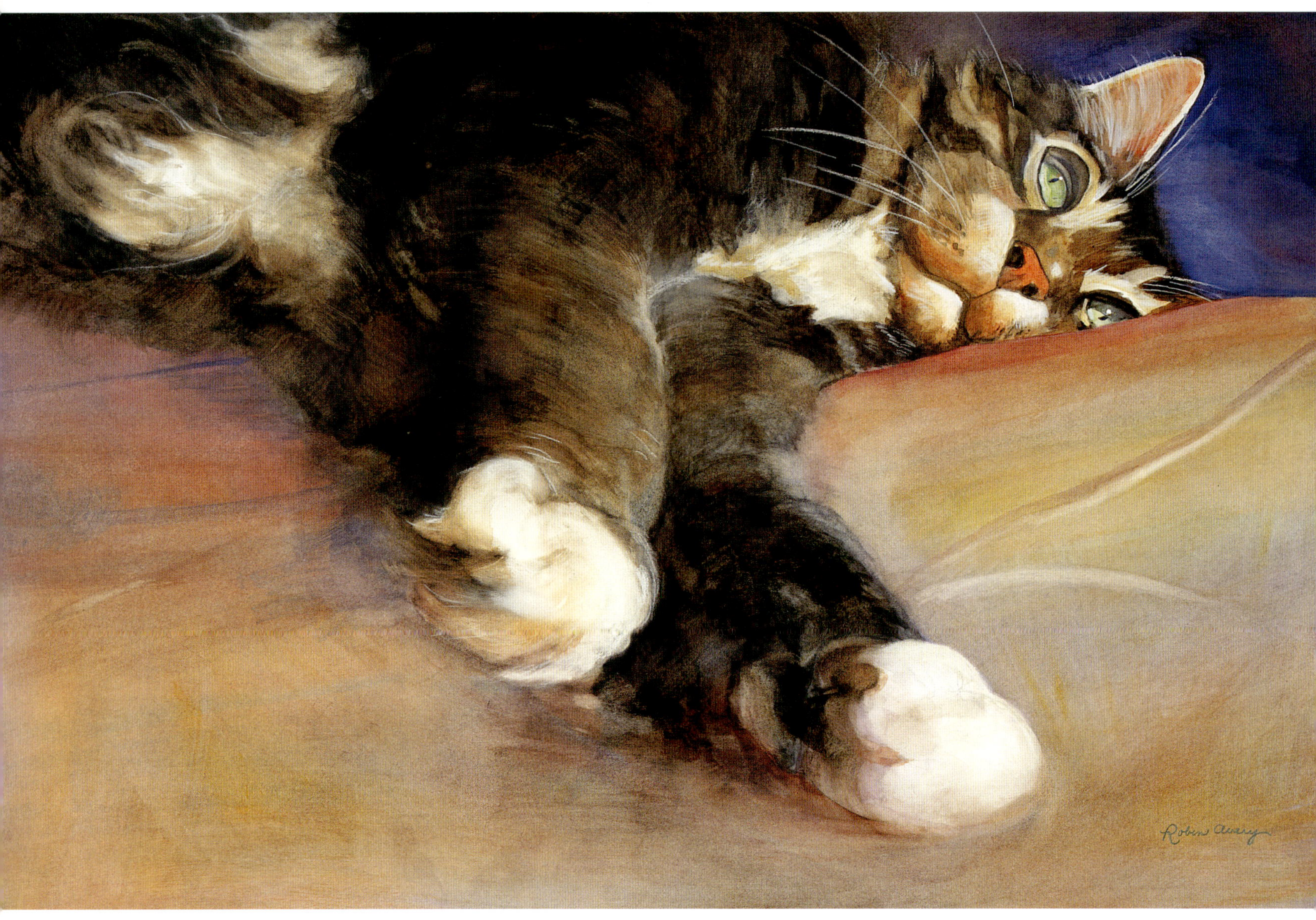

JUST CHILLIN' BABY

Robin Sevester Avery • transparent watercolor with watercolor pencil accents • 20" × 30" (51cm × 76cm)

I know my subject well. He is my studio friend, Jerry, a Maine Coon cat. Each morning, he saunters into my studio, springs onto my drawing table, inspects my materials, then regally takes center stage, assuming he is my model of choice. Using photos, I sketched him with a mechanical pencil, then mixed enough paint to cover large areas. I moistened my paper, but I am not particular about application. Using large strokes, I apply the colors I know to be in his fur. The essence of my technique is not in the application, but in the removal. With a damp tissue or a brush, I make strokes in the dry paint as though I am combing him or petting his fur. My strokes are in the direction his fur grows. His modeling fee? A can of tuna!

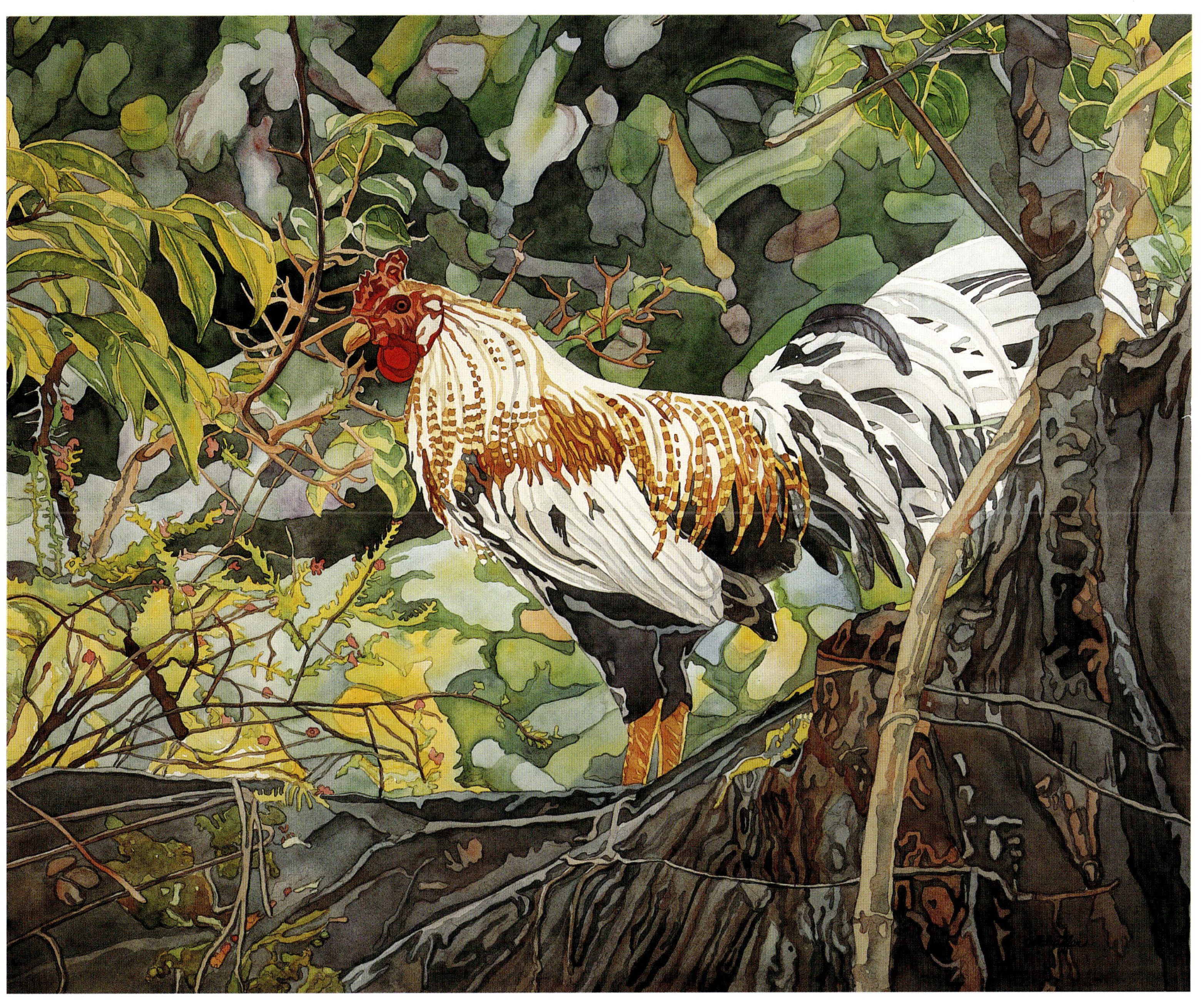

REGAL BEARING

Sandra Schaffer • transparent watercolor • 21" × 24" (53cm × 61cm)

Regal Bearing was based on a photograph taken in Indonesia. Much of my work is focused around images from Asia and South America. My passion for these images stems from my love for the natural beauty and vibrant cultural history of the more rural areas of these continents. There is a feeling of stepping back in time, to a more idyllic and perhaps idealized way of life. In this idealized world, roosters run free, and communities are more closely knit. Crafts and fabrics are created by individuals, not factories. As an artist, I strive to project this kind of world through my work. My technique involved precision in rendering and the use of multiple glazes, thus making the work very labor-intensive. The brushstrokes were either precise or broad, a combination of calculation and spontaneity.

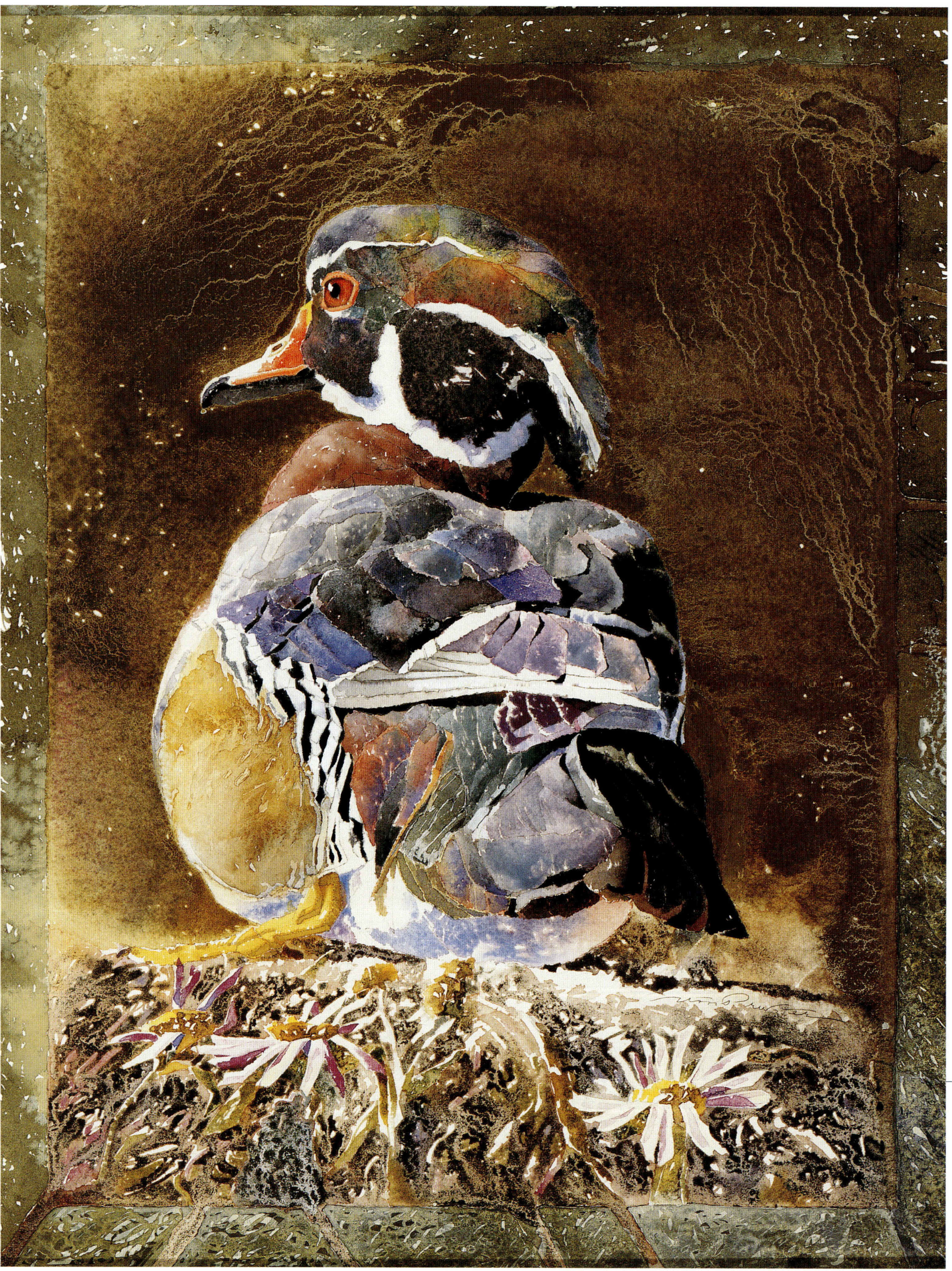

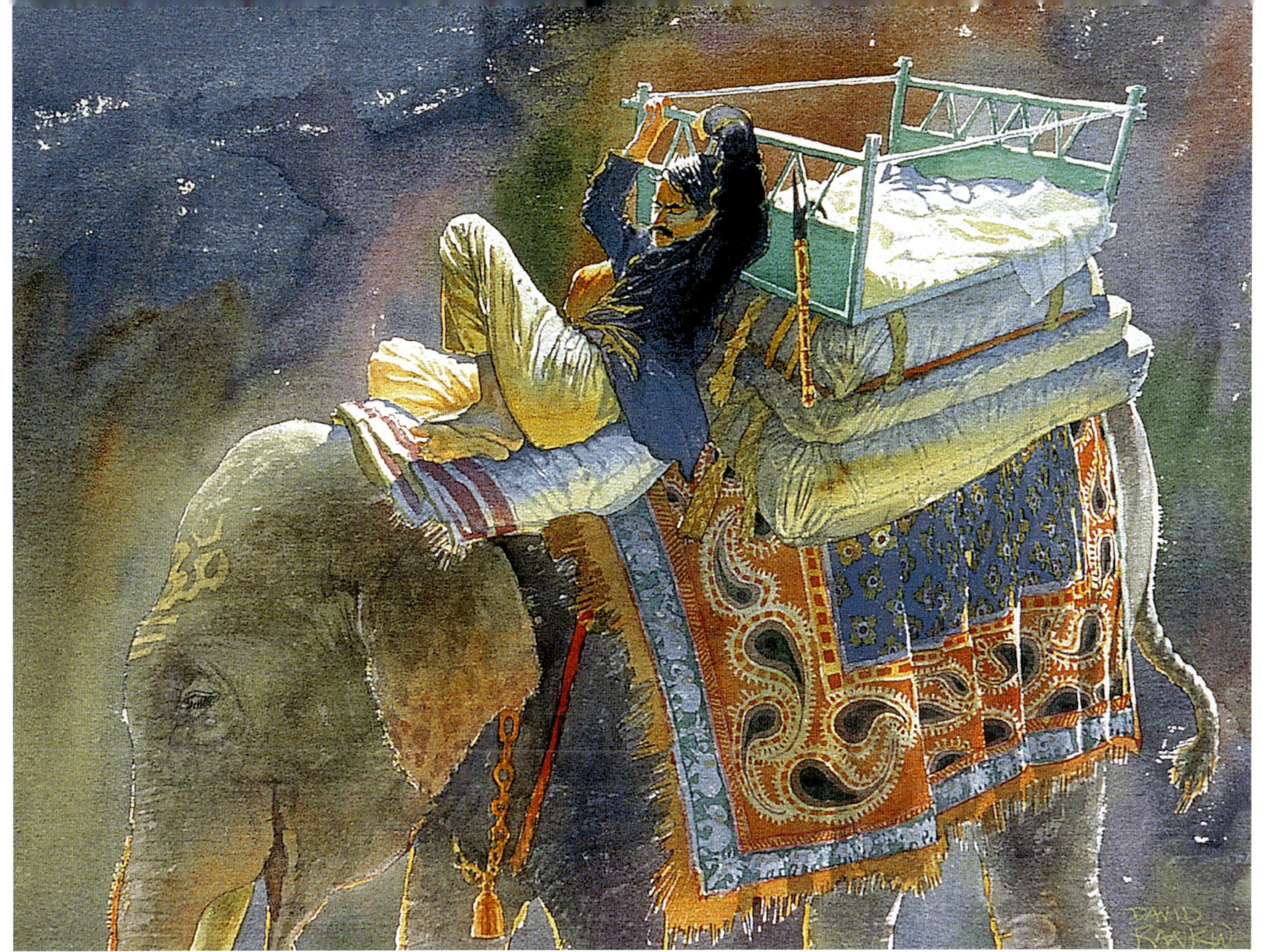

NAPTIME

David Rankin • transparent watercolor on 300-lb. (640gsm) rough paper • 21" × 26" (53cm × 66cm)

I saw this mahout (elephant handler) asleep in the midday sun at the famous Amber Fort Palace in Jaipur, India. I perceive the world with what I refer to as "watercolor vision." I oftentimes gravitate toward a particular subject simply because of how I see it painted in my mind's eye. That's how this subject evolved, from my initial sketches and photographs to my full-scale studio painting. One might think that it was the intense midday light illuminating the mahout that attracted and inspired me. But, in fact, what attracted my eye was the delicious quality of the middle-valued colors that defined the highlights. For me, the powerful magical charm of transparent watercolor lies in the artist's ability to see and paint the full range of middle-valued colors in any subject.

PORTRAIT OF A WOOD DUCK

Charles Timothy Prutzer • watercolor and transparent acrylic • 12" × 9" (30cm × 23cm)

The beauty of watercolor paint is enthralling in itself, and this wood duck was an excellent subject on which to hang as much pure pigment as possible. The abstract elements of the plumage attracted me. I laid clear water on high-quality paper, then dropped in concentrated pigment and let the color explode. Watching the settling and granulation of color particles is humbling and therapeutic. It quiets the soul.

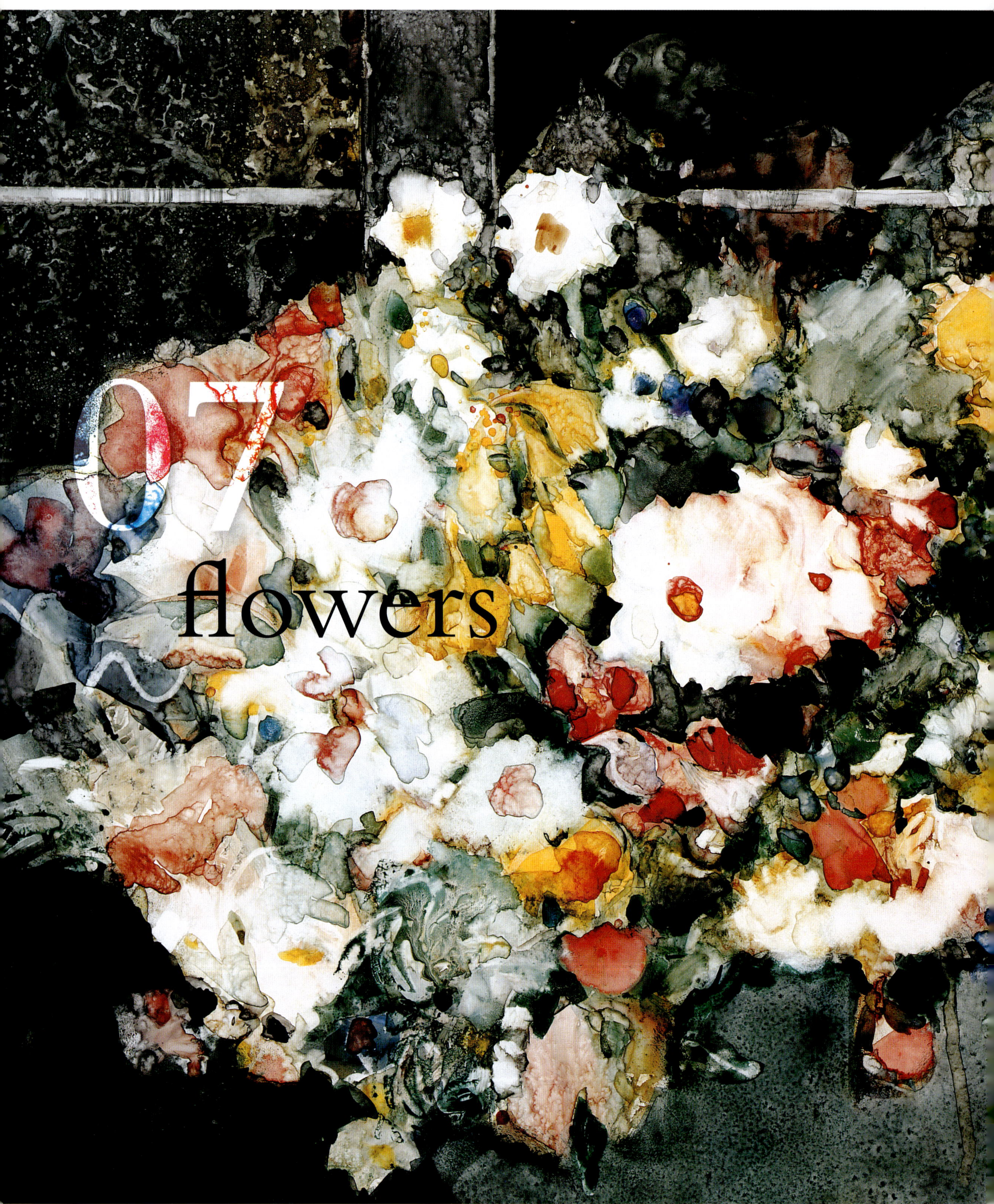

NIGHT BLOOMS II

Chica Brunsvold • transparent watercolor on synthetic paper • 21" × 30" (53cm × 76cm)

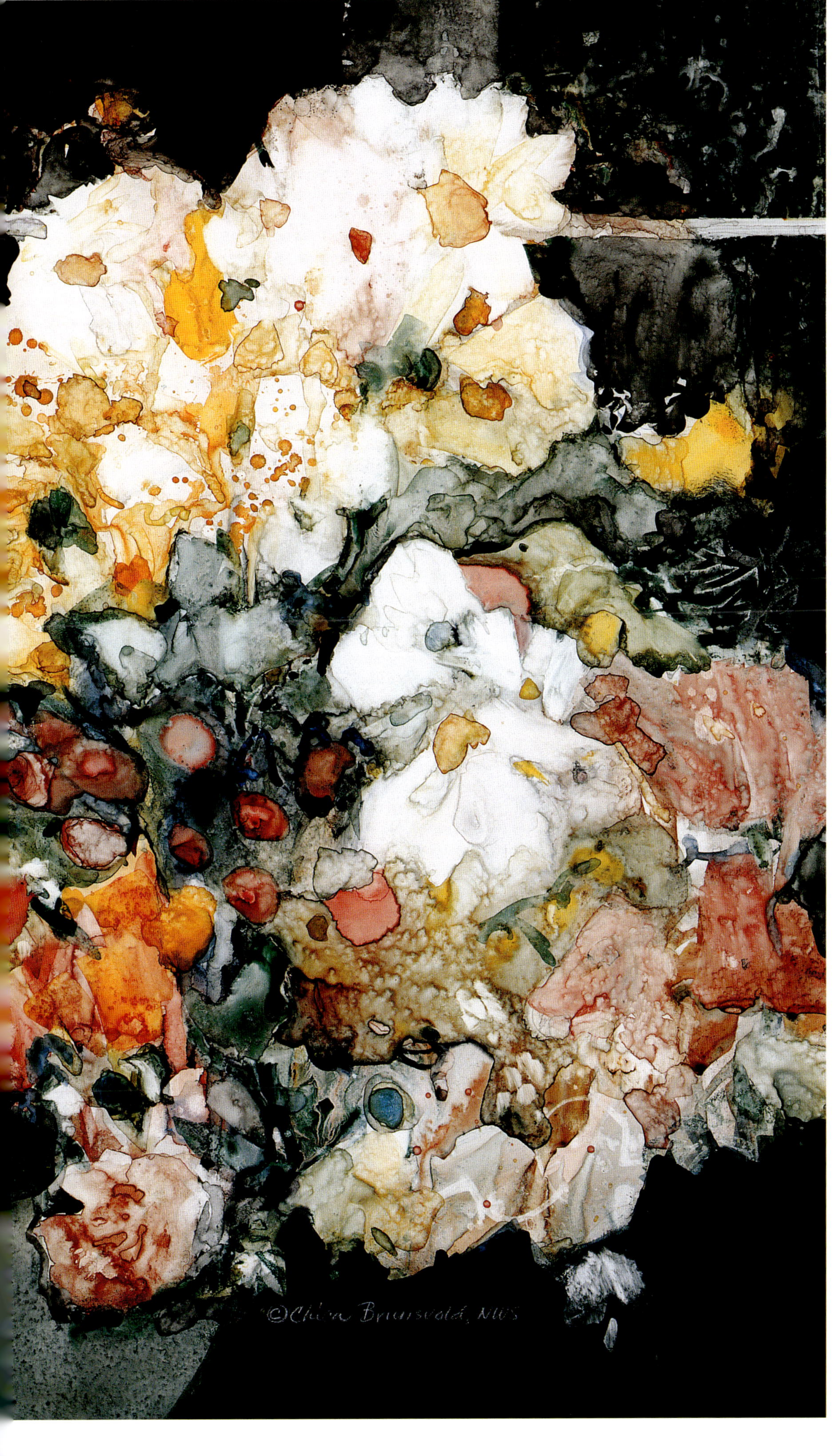

I find Yupo paper very exciting because it allows me to follow my passion and "go with the flow" to continually add and subtract forms and incorporate lots of texture.

CHICA BRUNSVOLD

I'm passionate about not having my brushstrokes show.

JUDY MORRIS

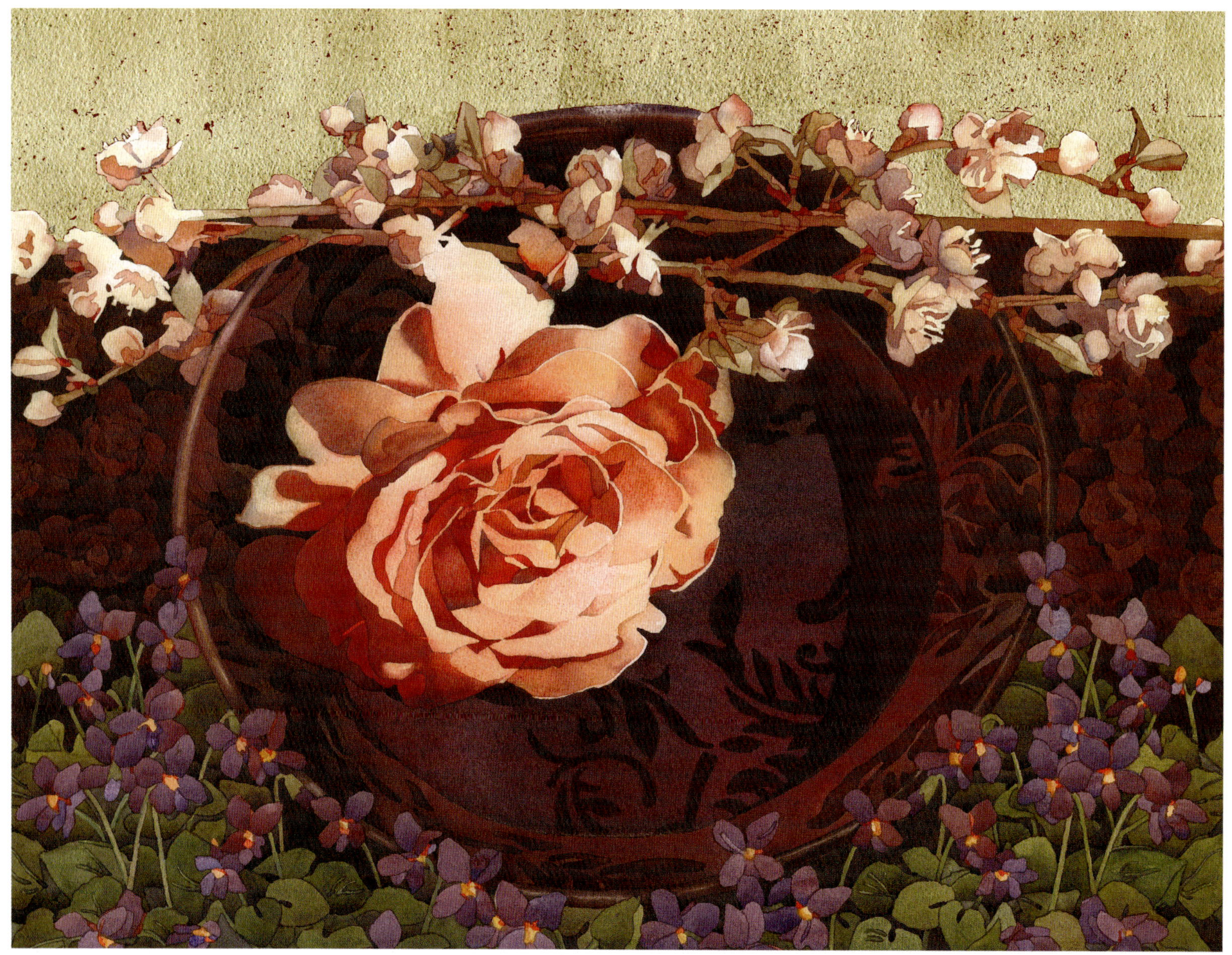

BLOSSOM, ROSE, & VIOLET

Judy Morris • transparent watercolor with gold leaf • 20" × 26" (51cm × 66cm)

I am a shape painter. When I plan a painting from my reference photographs, I draw individual shapes, much like the pieces of a puzzle. The placement of these pieces determines an interesting composition. I paint subjects I want to share with the world. *Blossom, Rose, & Violet* is a tribute to my mother and her two sisters and was painted with loving memories of "my flowers." As I painted the blossoms and the rose, my mind was filled with precious memories of the times I spent with Aunt Blossom and Aunt Rose. The violets represent the sweetest flower of all, my mother, Violet. If you look closely, you will see the violets on the left are a mirror image of the violets on the right. That is because I am an identical, mirror-image twin. When you paint meaningful subject matter with techniques you love, your paintings will be a success.

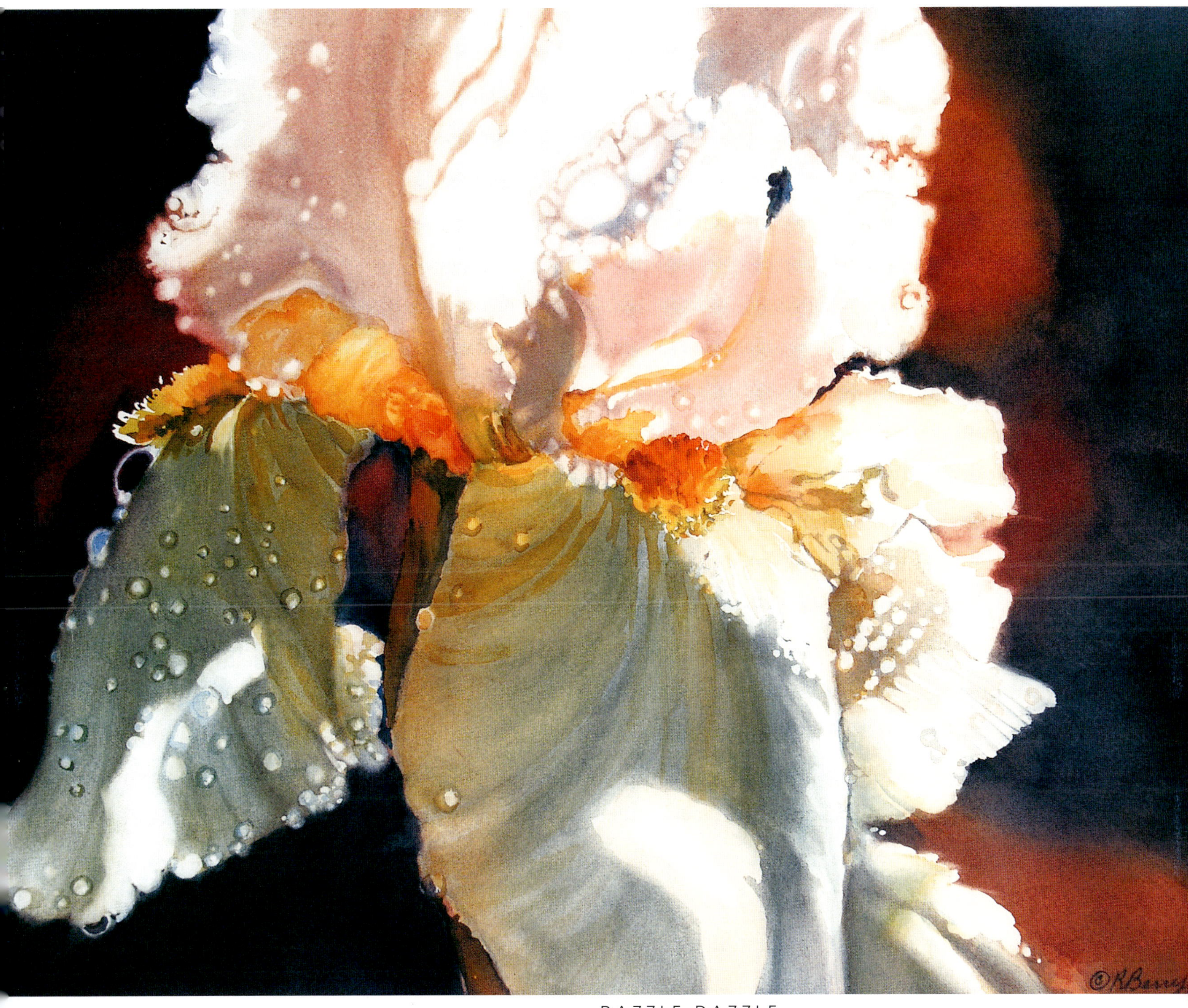

RAZZLE DAZZLE

Robin Berry • transparent watercolor on 140-lb. (300gsm) cold- pressed paper • 19½" × 29½" (50cm × 75cm)

How do brushstrokes express my passion? Broad, wet, saturated strokes of pure color with big brushes and arm-swinging application.

ROBIN BERRY

Working from a wonderful photo I took more than a decade ago, I stretched my paper over plywood and masked out the whites and lights. Then with a palette of fresh paint beside me, I used a 3-inch (77mm) wash brush to begin, but often had three or more brushes in my hand. It is always exciting to "dance" with the brushes, applying strokes of pure color to wet paper, alternately turning and tilting the board to let the color move and blend. The energy seems to run right from my shoulder and arm into the brush. At this stage, I've captured the immediacy of watercolor in an underpainting that eventually holds all the finishing details together.

Learning from the master, nature, brings forth awe and creative energy with sincere appreciation. Incorporating my love of vibrant color and extensive detail drives my mind into a timeless world where I am forever young and happy, painting.

SOON Y. WARREN

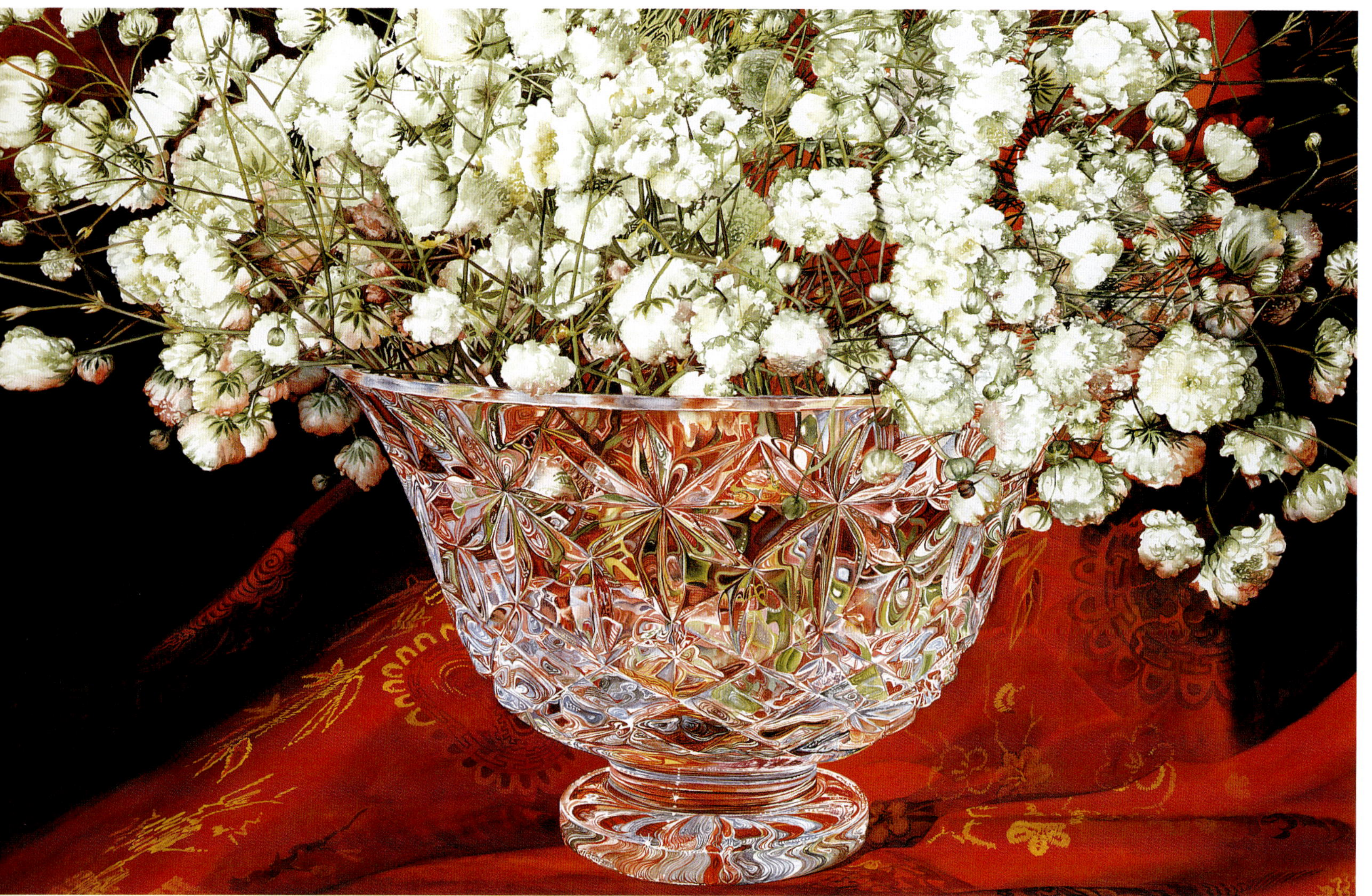

BABY'S BREATH

Soon Y. Warren • watercolor on cold-pressed paper • 26" × 40" (66cm × 102cm)

Great art is born when you follow your passionate intuition to make the extraordinary out of the ordinary. I see my watercolor paintings as beautiful lush fabrics I am creating, using various brushstrokes to dye, weave and design the fabric of my work on a two-dimensional surface. The watercolor medium enables an artist to create art as delicate as a string of silk out of cocoon, or as lush and rich as a Persian rug. I usually set up my subject matter and then take photos with interesting combinations of light, color and composition. Because my representational paintings usually take from a few weeks to a few months to complete, it is essential that I have a lasting reference to work from. I usually start with a detailed drawing and wash the surface of the paper with a hake brush for quick and clean application. Then I start to develop details, continuing until I am satisfied with the result. These two paintings have the common theme of complementary color harmony within a simple composition. *Baby's Breath* uses green/red complements, while *Yellow Daisy* uses yellow-orange/blue complements.

YELLOW DAISY

Soon Y. Warren • watercolor on cold-pressed paper • 30" × 22" (76cm × 56cm)

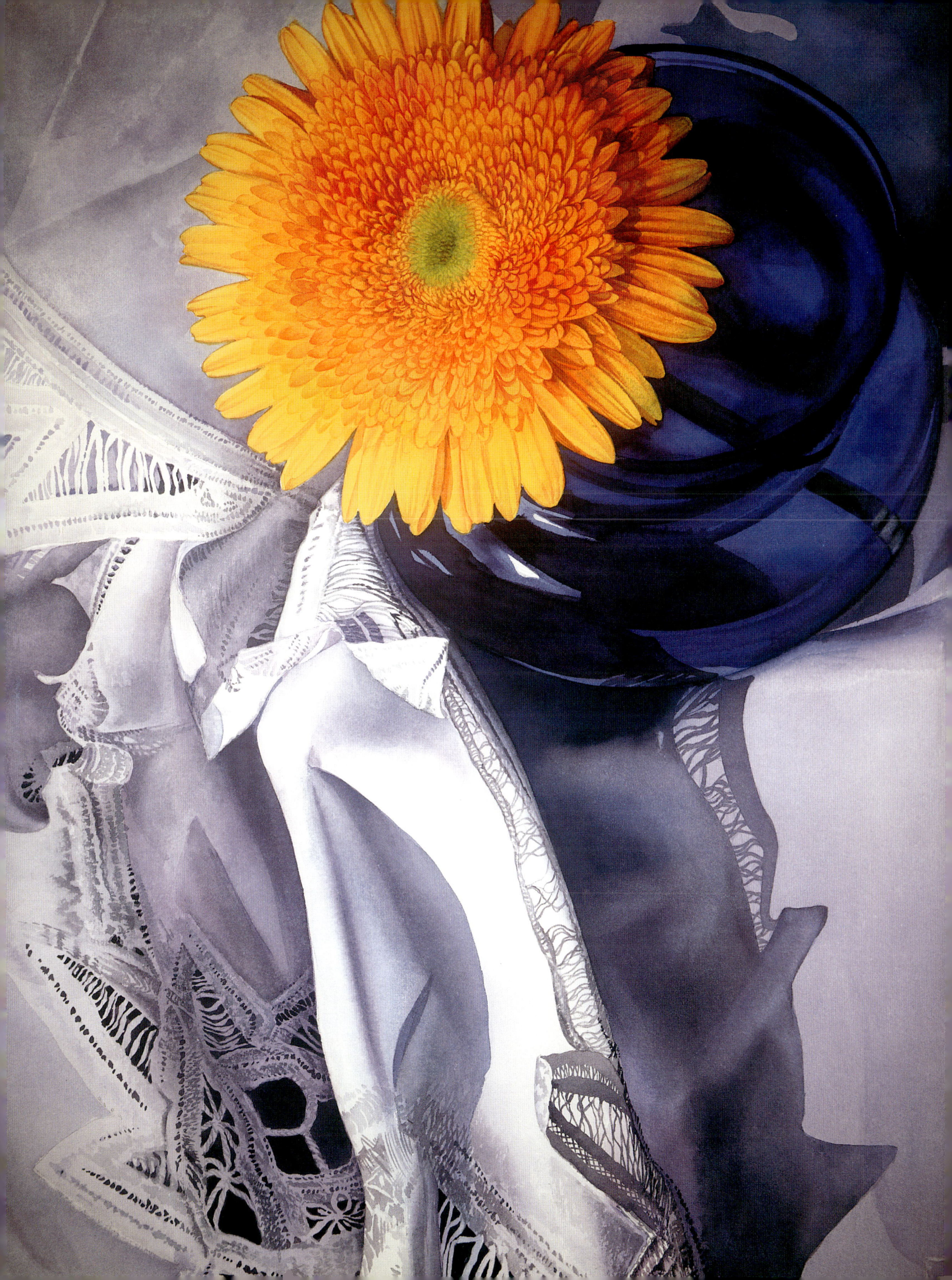

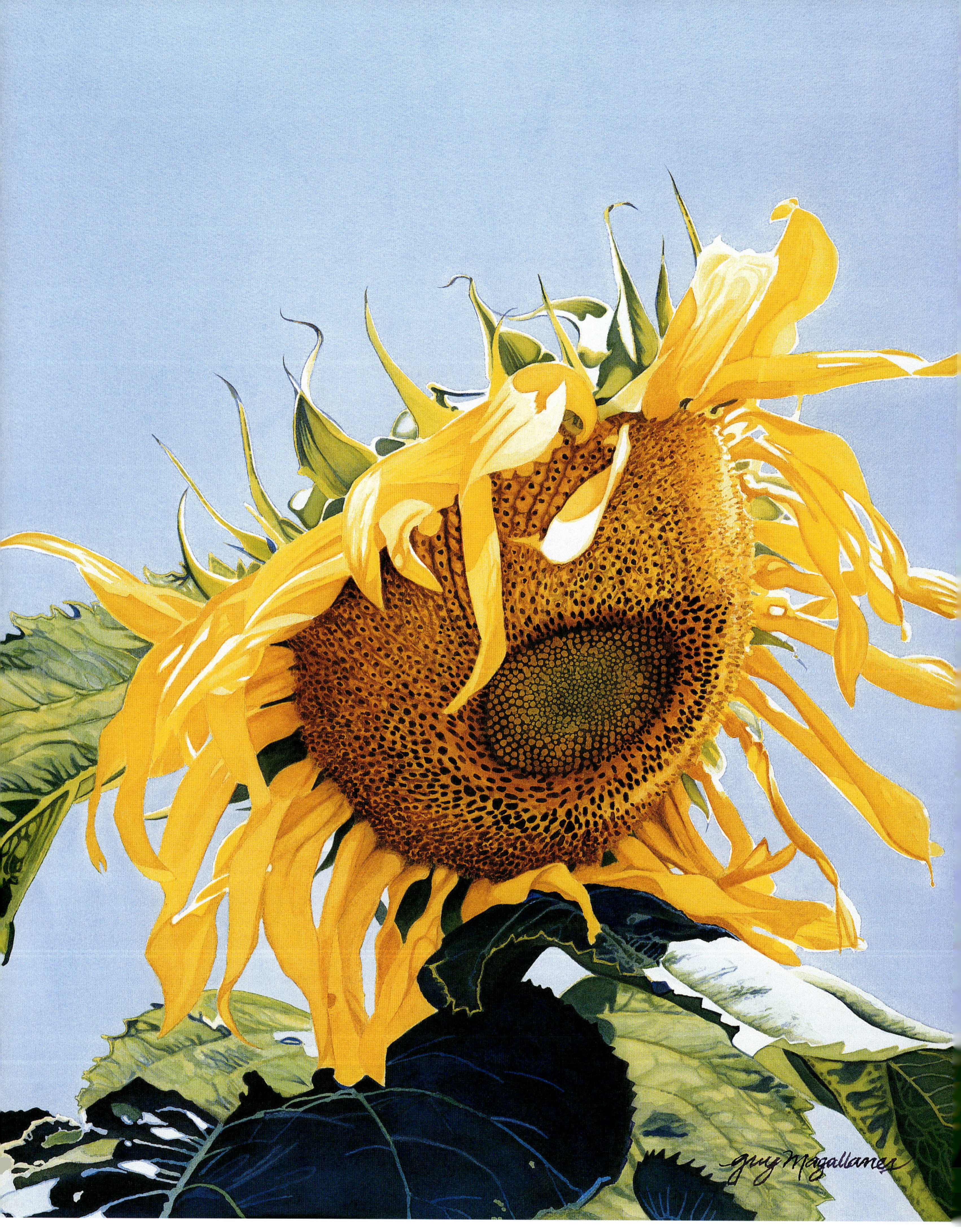
guy Magallanes

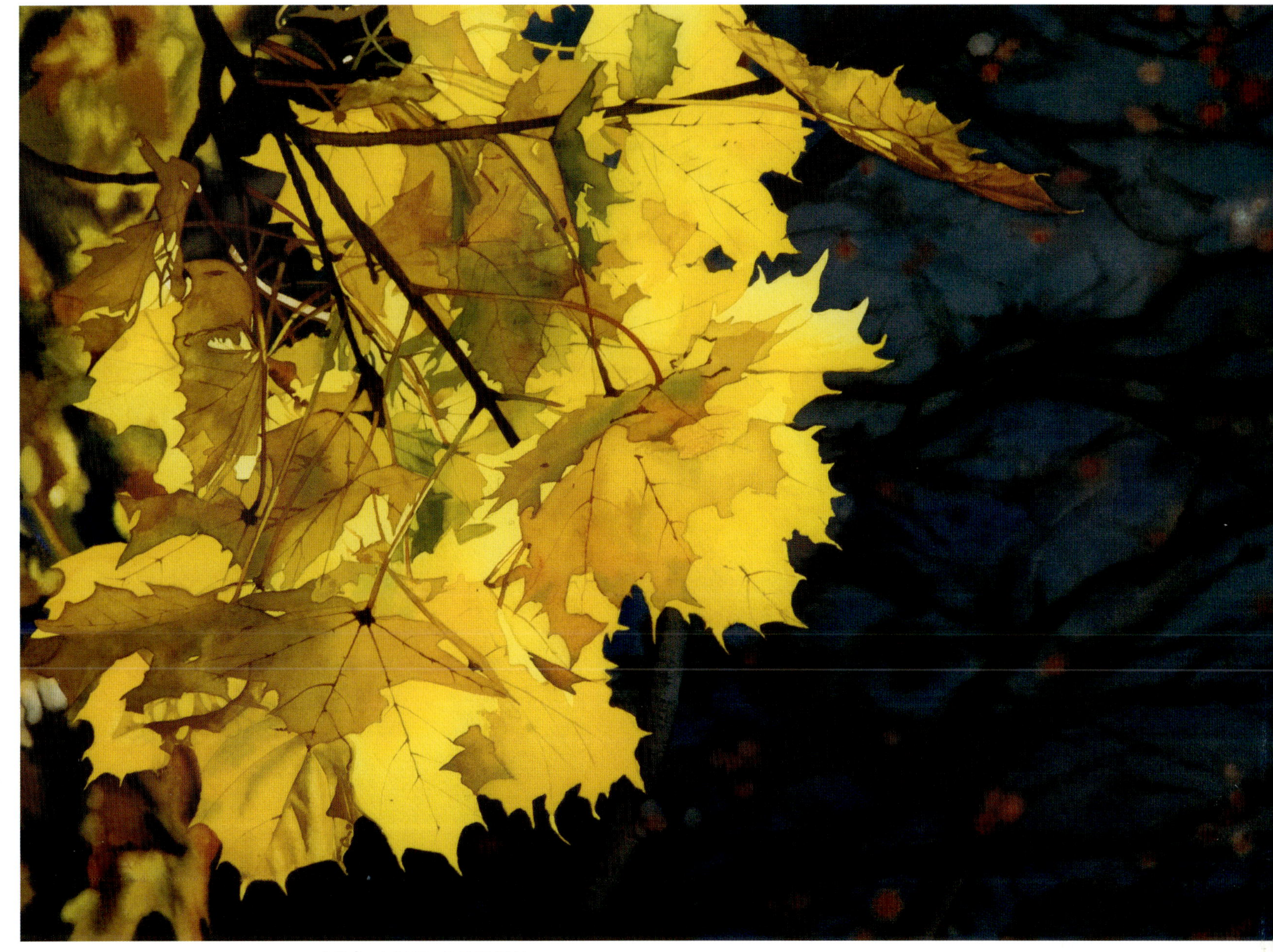

68° AND SUNNY

Heidi Lang Parrinello • watercolor on 300-lb. (640gsm) cold-pressed paper • 22" × 30" (56cm × 76cm)

I am interested in the relationship between humans and our natural environment, which I connect to the notion of reincarnation and karma. I am fascinated by the interconnectedness of every action. This painting is part of a series called *HUMANature* that expresses that karmic connection by the human-like qualities of autumn leaves. I almost always prefer to work from photographs because I like to get very detailed. It allows me to achieve a greater depth of field and gives me the freedom to concentrate on crisp (dry-brush) details, but also loose wet-into-wet backgrounds. Working this way, I need only two brushes: a no. 8 round with a perfect point and a large mop for the backgrounds.

HELIOS

Guy Magallanes • watercolor on 300-lb. (640gsm) cold-pressed paper • 27" × 21" (69cm × 53m)

This unusually tall sunflower grew in my neighbors' backyard. Fortunately for us, it followed the sun, which happened to be on our side of the fence. It was huge and sort of monstrous, not a pretty flower at all. But I looked forward to starting and ending the day with my new "neighbor." It reflected the sunlight back with such strength, I had to capture it in watercolor. I photographed it, trying to get the right angle to show the force of reflected sunlight. When the preliminaries were done, I masked off the flower and used a flat wash for the blue sky. I removed the masking and began to work in glazes on the darkest darks of the leaves, then the darks of the petals. When the painting was almost completed, I finished with a glaze of yellow for the sunflower's petals. I like to save the best for last—a reward to finish.

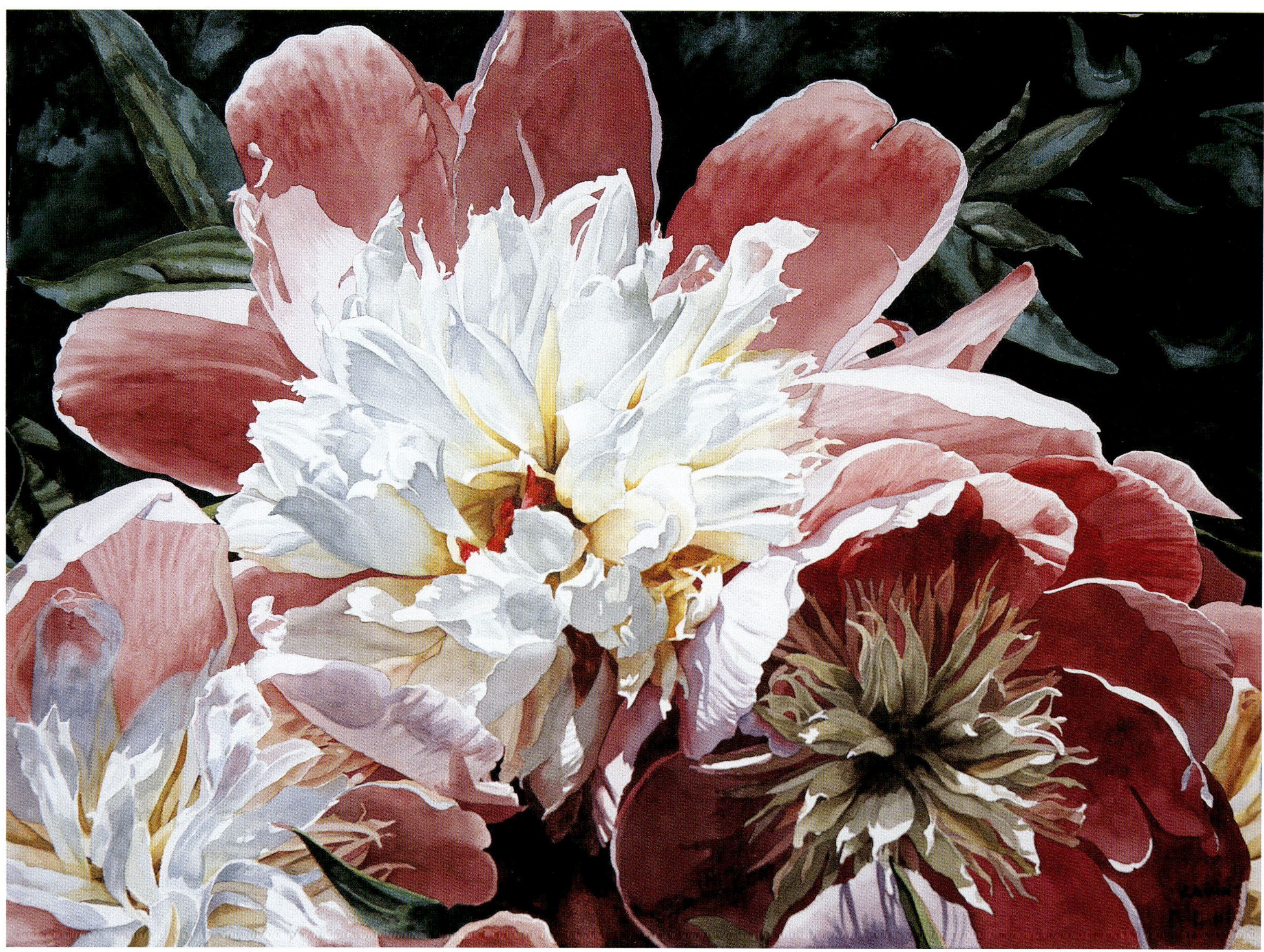

PEONY OPUS

Estelle Lavin • transparent watercolor • 22" × 30" (56cm × 76cm)

Although I paint many different subjects, I always return to flowers because painting them fills me with joy. I had photographed this particular peony at the New York Botanical Garden some years ago but had never used it. I came across it in my photo files and was again delighted by the buoyancy of life it radiated and felt I had to paint it. To capture the feeling of bright sunlight cascading over the flower, I painted the outer petals quite solidly so they would form a frame to showcase the light, effervescent center. I painted the inner shadows with pale blue to contrast with the warm pinks. The saturated colors of the lower peony support and anchor the painting.

MY PATIO DÉCOR

Alvin Joe • transparent watercolor • 28" × 20½" (71cm × 52cm)

Gardening is my passion, second only to painting watercolor. They are both magical and certainly enhance one another. I peeked at my garden through my kitchen window while sipping my morning coffee. Wow! My cactus flower plant had blossomed again. I captured its radiant beauty with my 35mm camera before these short-lived flowers (two to three days) wilted away. With my reference photo and my cactus plant inside my studio, I enthusiastically began my thumbnail sketches and created this composition. I wet the 300-lb. (640gsm) Kilimanjaro cold-pressed paper with my 2-inch (51mm) flat brush after I masked the flowers and highlighted areas. Seconds later, I attacked the background with light Raw Sienna, Cadmium Orange, Quinacridone Rose, Cobalt Blue, French Ultramarine and Indigo, with a sprinkle of salt on top of the wet floor area for visual interest.

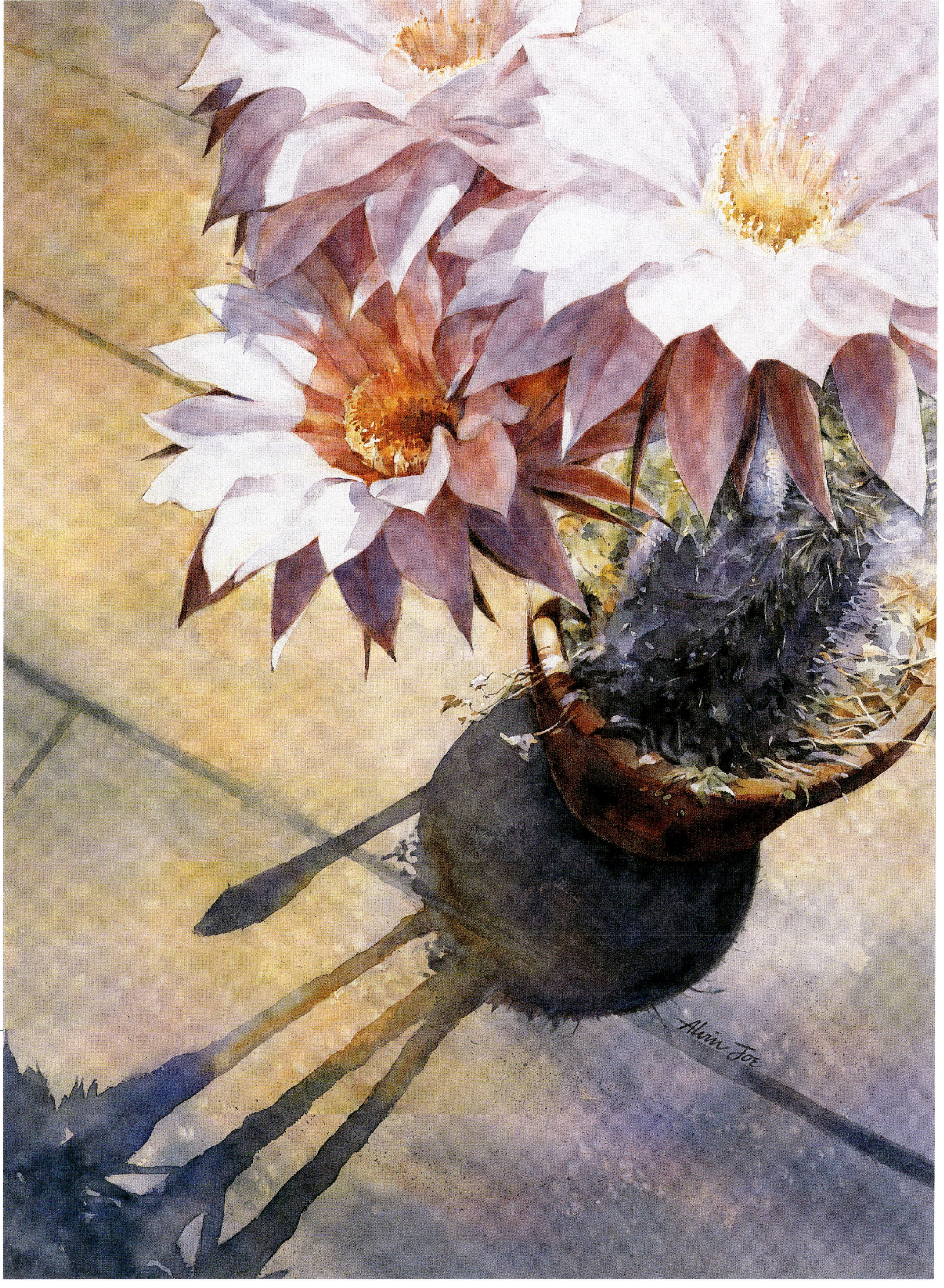

I let the poured colors speak and create the painting. Being constantly surprised by the result is my passion!

MING SHU LIN FRANZ

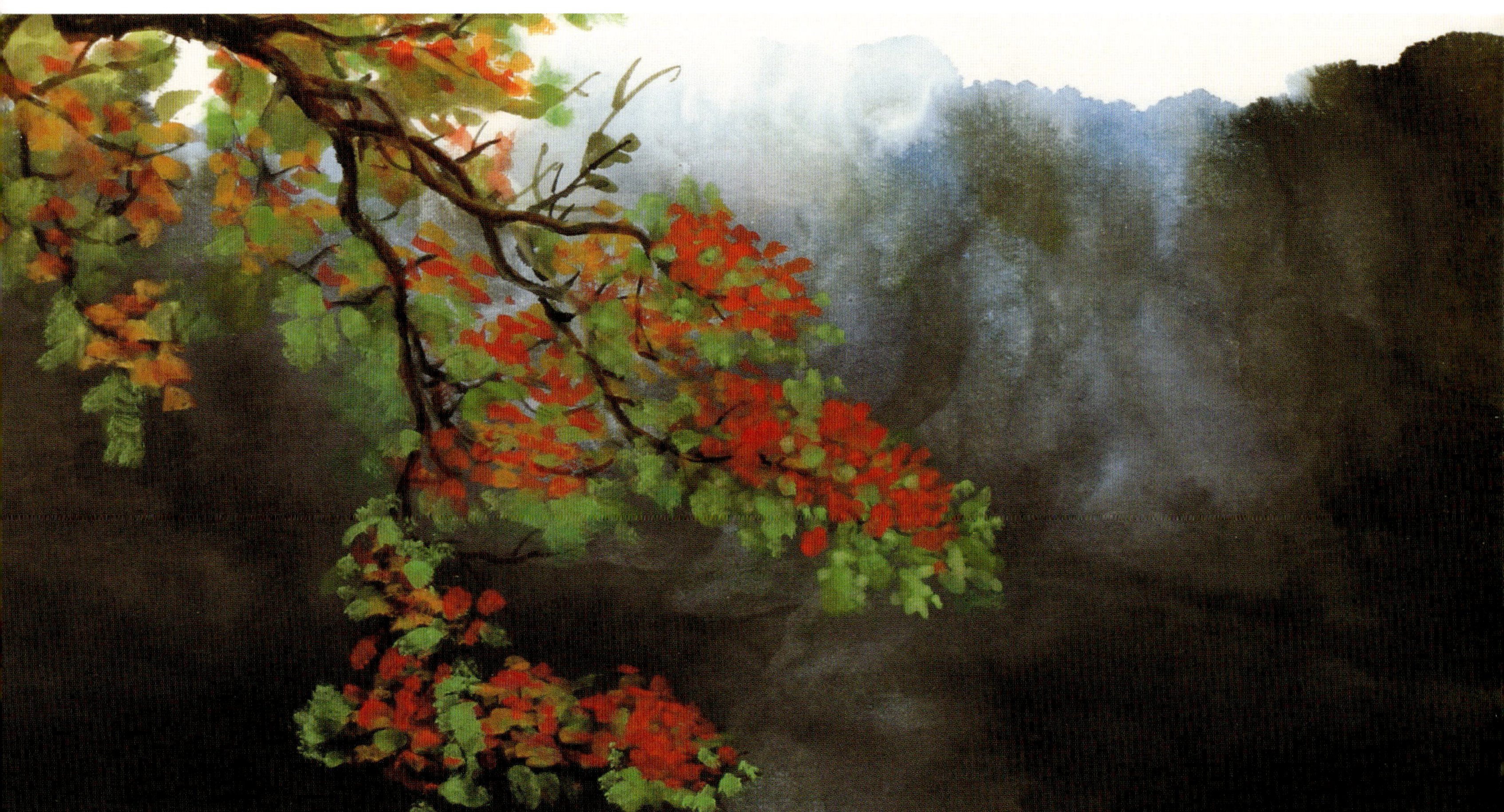

IAO VALLEY, MAUI

Ming Shu Lin Franz • Chinese ink and watercolor • 12" × 26" (30cm × 66cm)

Iao Valley, Maui expresses my love for nature and a style of painting I call "splash ink," which combines traditional Chinese brush painting with Western watercolor. I freely splashed Chinese black ink and primary watercolors onto rice paper. I looked at it from all sides for many days after it dried. The blue and black suggested mountains to me, and I remembered a photograph my coauthor Barbara Gottesman took in Iao Valley where a Royal Poinciana tree stands at the entrance. This tree with vivid orange blossoms is called the phoenix tree in China and the tree of Krishna in India. I immediately saw the branch of the blossoming Poinciana tree in my painting and finished it using bright opaque watercolors.

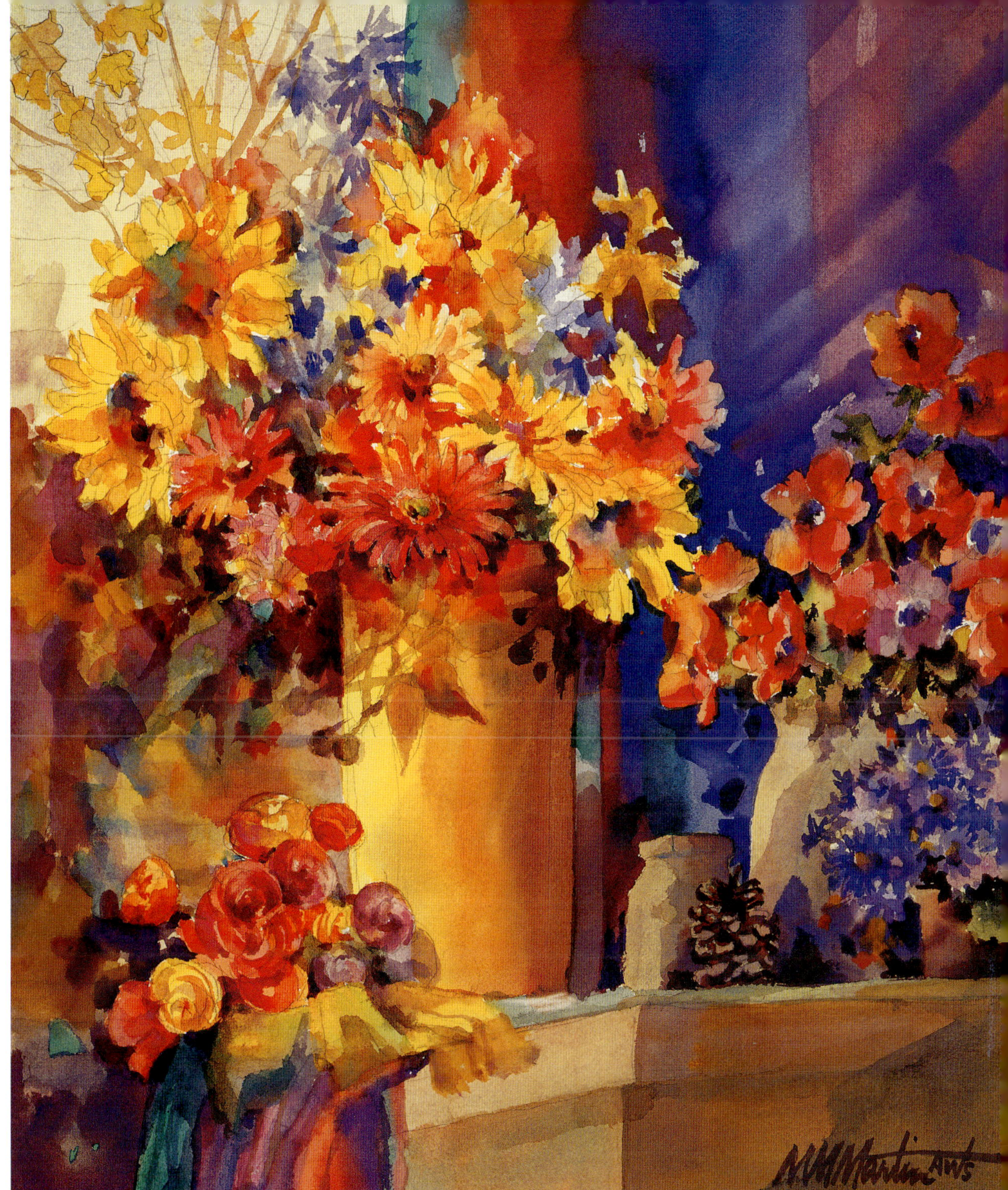

FLOWER FESTIVAL JEWELS

Margaret M. Martin • transparent watercolor • 24" × 18" (61cm × 46cm)

I have always been infatuated with the integrity, purity and sparkle of transparent watercolor. I truly love the process. This subject was one of many setups in my annual studio Spring Flower Festival workshop. A floodlight showcased the drama. The vibrant, aggressive contrasts and colors reflect my particular attraction to watercolor. Near the end of a winter season of drab grays, the bold, crisp colors reminded me of my upcoming summer garden—another passion. This painting was painted from life after doing a small value sketch, which helped me arrange the light and dark patterns. I aim for an electrifying statement with rich darks flattering pure color laid directly on dry paper with vigor.

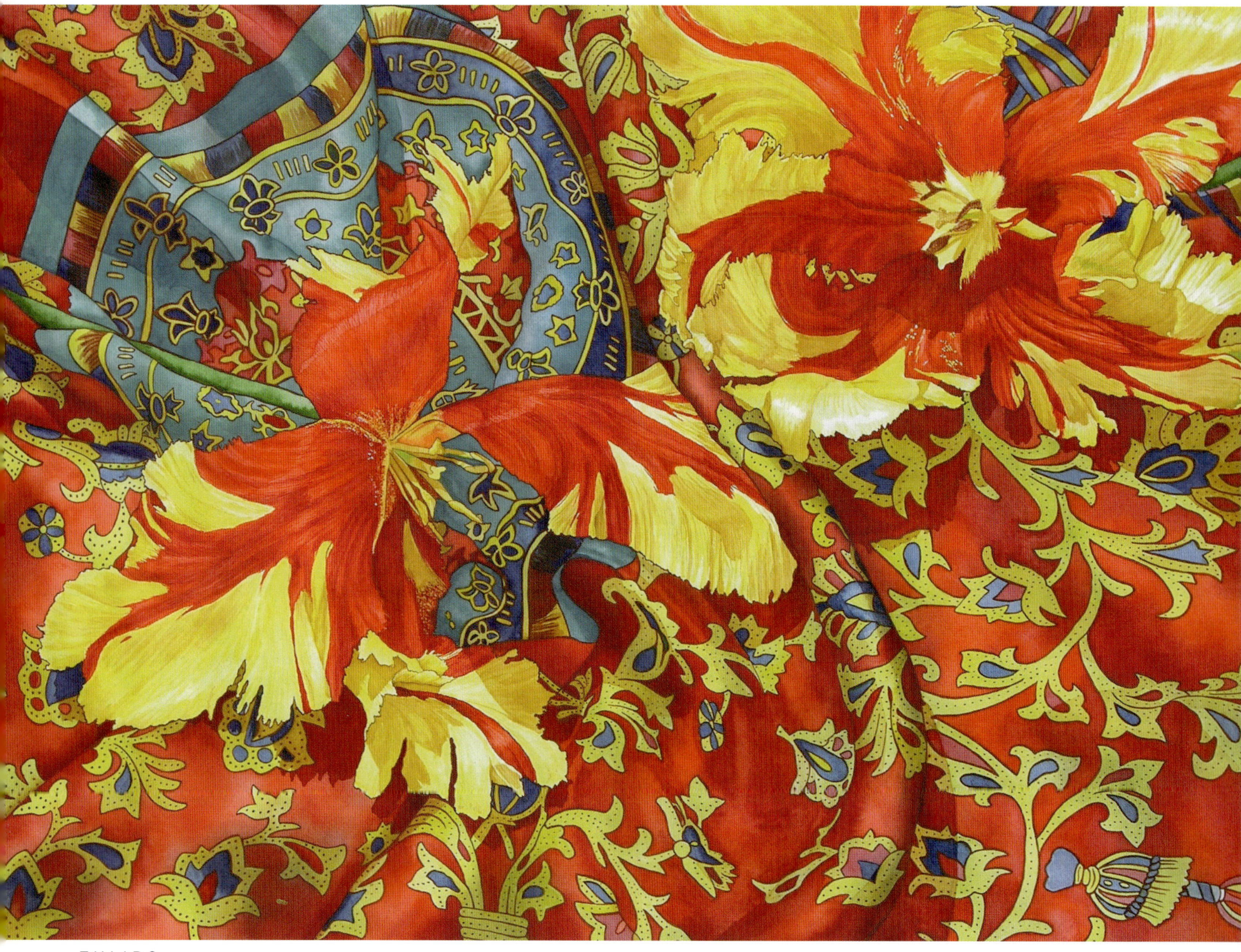

TULIPS

Brookes L. Dewey • transparent watercolor on 140-lb. (300gsm) paper • 23¾" × 32½" (60cm × 83cm)

I love watercolor—the fluid areas and the vibrant colors, along with the power of an unusual point of view with complexity. I usually set up a still life, photograph it and work from the photo because of the length of time it takes me to create a painting. When painting a scarf, I first underlay washes in gray to capture the contours of the light and shadow areas. Then I start applying layers of colors. With each additional layer, I build the intensity of the color without losing sight of the scarf's folds and valleys. Because the tulips have a very different texture from the scarf, I added color using lines that follow the structure of the flower. I built each layer with the intention of making the colors as bold and intense as possible.

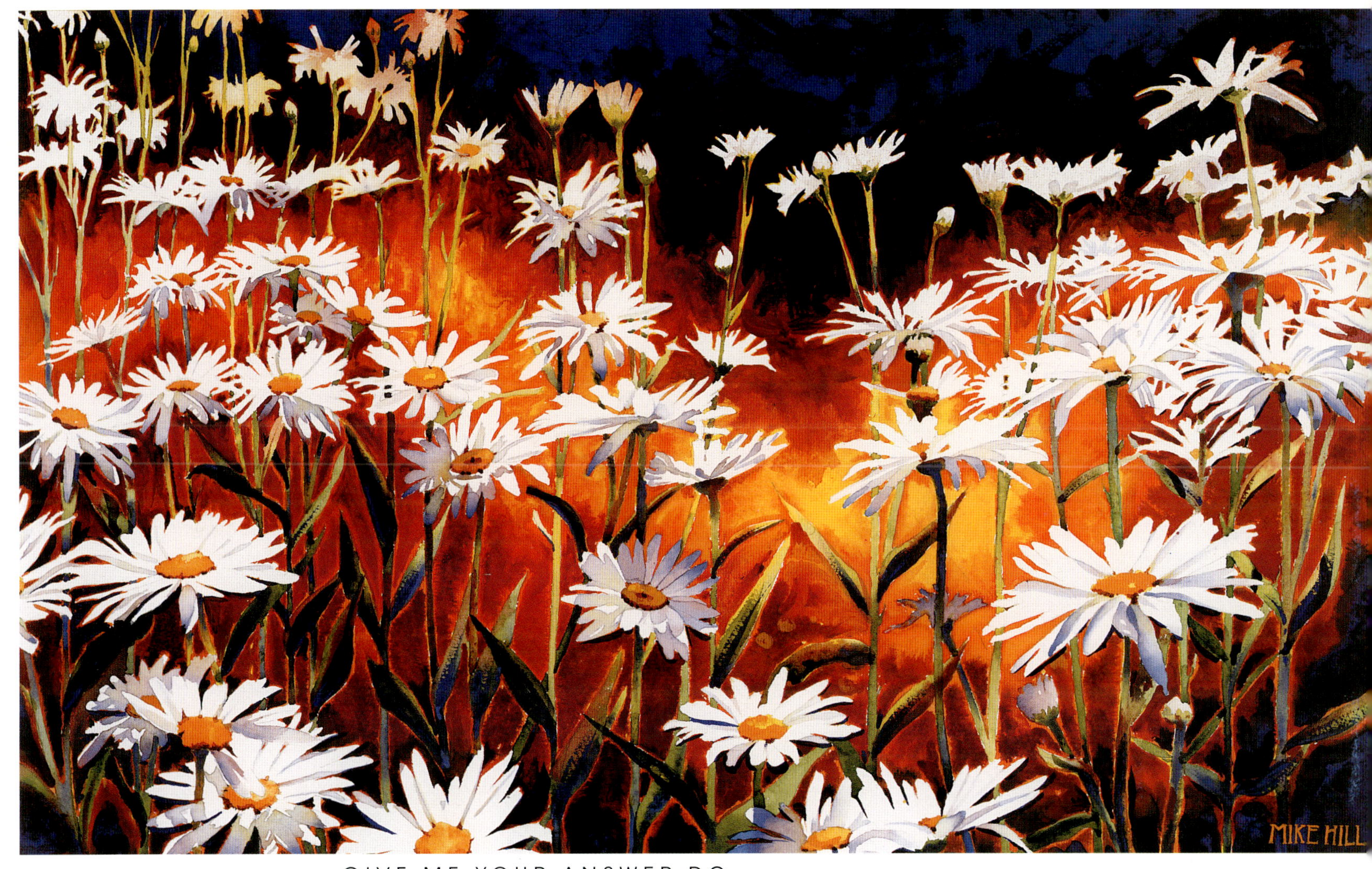

GIVE ME YOUR ANSWER DO

Mike Hill • *transparent watercolor* • 16¾" × 26¾" (43cm × 68cm)

Leaning very heavily on my imagination and a lot of feeling, I used reference photos sparingly for this painting. Daisies are a symbol of simplicity and the essence of delicacy, yet they also give us a very vibrant display. The daisy is the flower that gave us "loves me, loves me not" and the song lyric, "Give me your answer do." Chaucer called it the "daye's eye" (the eye of the day), meaning the sun. I wanted to capture the warmth of the sun and the feeling of love that we attribute to the daisy. I masked the daisies after a light wash of Cadmium Yellow and orange on the distant flowers. The background was done last by using transparent staining paints, then dropping in opaques and watching with excitement as they mixed on the dry paper.

Watercolor has been my only medium for more than forty years. Today I paint very rapidly with large brushes. When all is going well, I almost wish each brush were connected to a hose.

DON O'NEILL

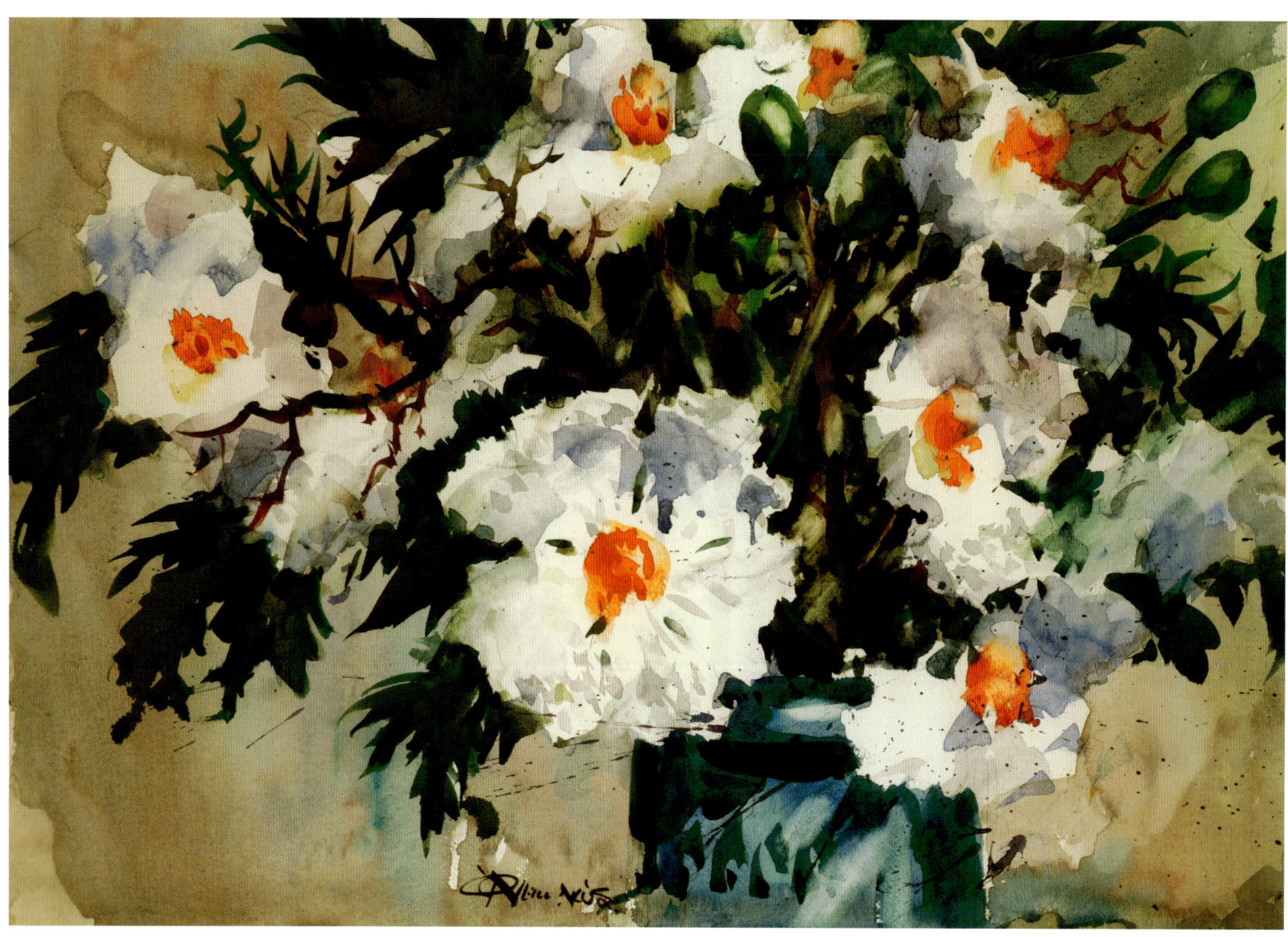

MATILIJA POPPIES IN BLUE BOWL

Don O'Neill • watercolor on 140-lb. (300gsm) cold-pressed paper • 20" × 28" (51cm × 71cm)

These Matilija poppies had to be painted with a sensitive, intellectual approach. The delicate, translucent flowers look as though they are made of crepe paper with subtle gradations of color. The pattern of the arrangement is to allow the most dominant flower to "read" most strongly. Gradually, the other blooms take their place, supporting the composition. The painting was executed in the studio from life. Matilija poppies are a natural California plant. The shrub is nothing much to admire, but the blooms are exquisite.

DAISIES IN GLASS

Elizabeth Kincaid • transparent watercolor on 300-lb. (600gsm) cold-pressed paper • 14½" × 11" (37cm × 28cm)

Daisies in Glass was painted from a photograph I took in my backyard. There is no subject like white flowers in the sun to provide a full range of values for contrast and sparkle. After masking out the daisies I painted the background wet-into-wet layering Phthalo Blue over Aureolin Yellow in many glazes of pure color. There was no color mixing done on the palette. The translucent white shapes of the petals lead the eye around the painting, and the abstract shapes of the stems within the glass provide secondary entertainment for the eye.

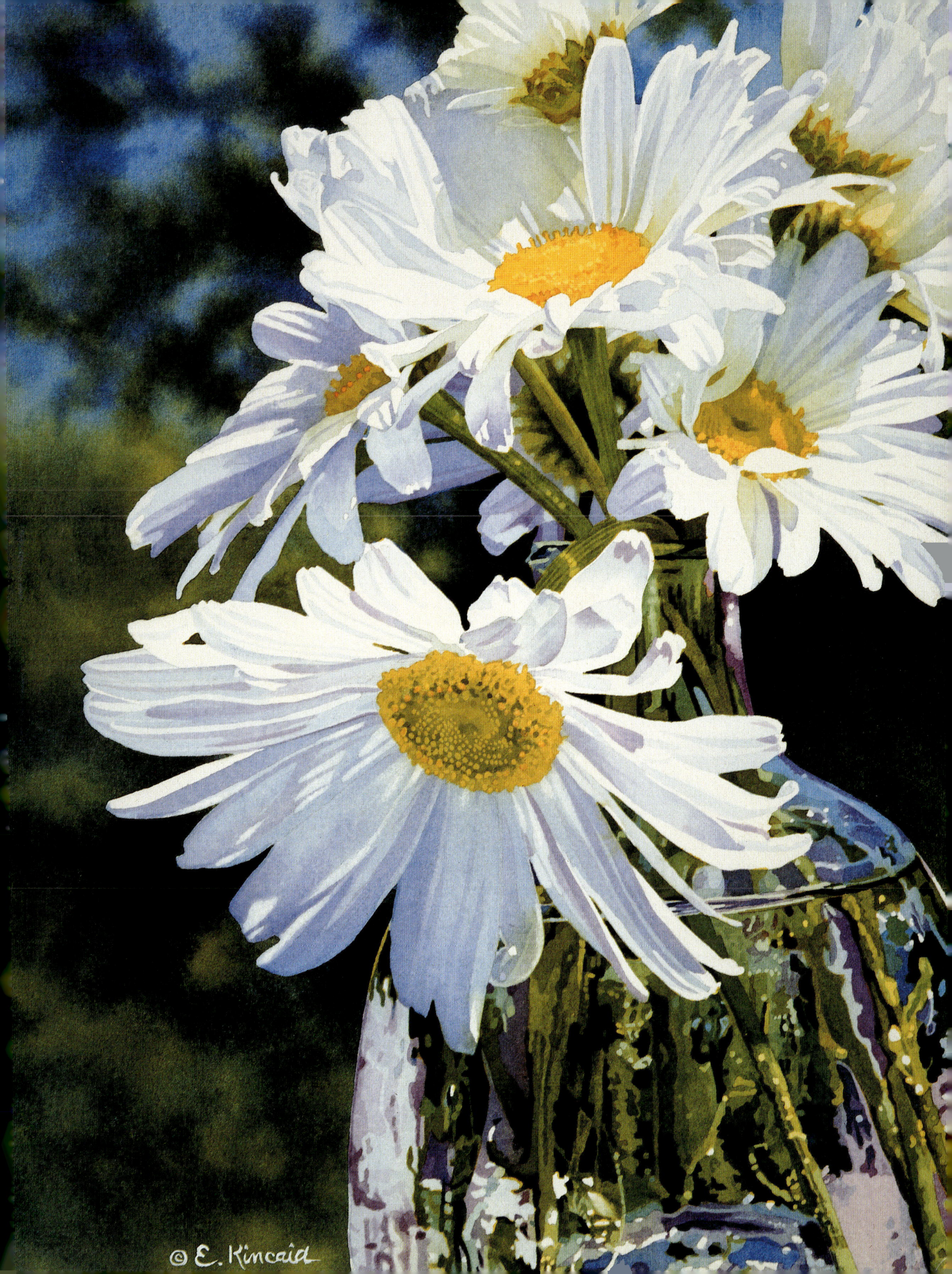
© E. Kincaid

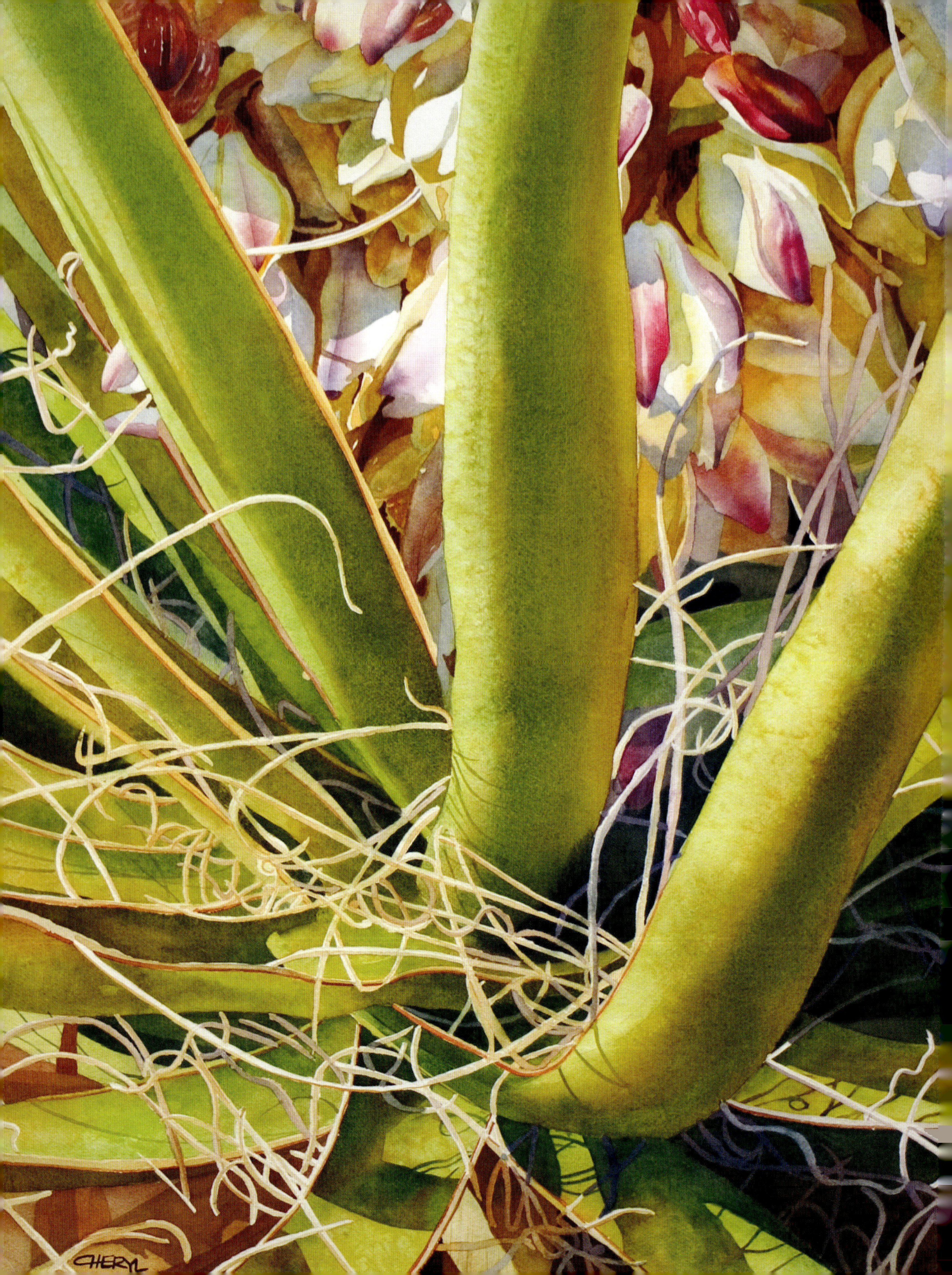
CHERYL

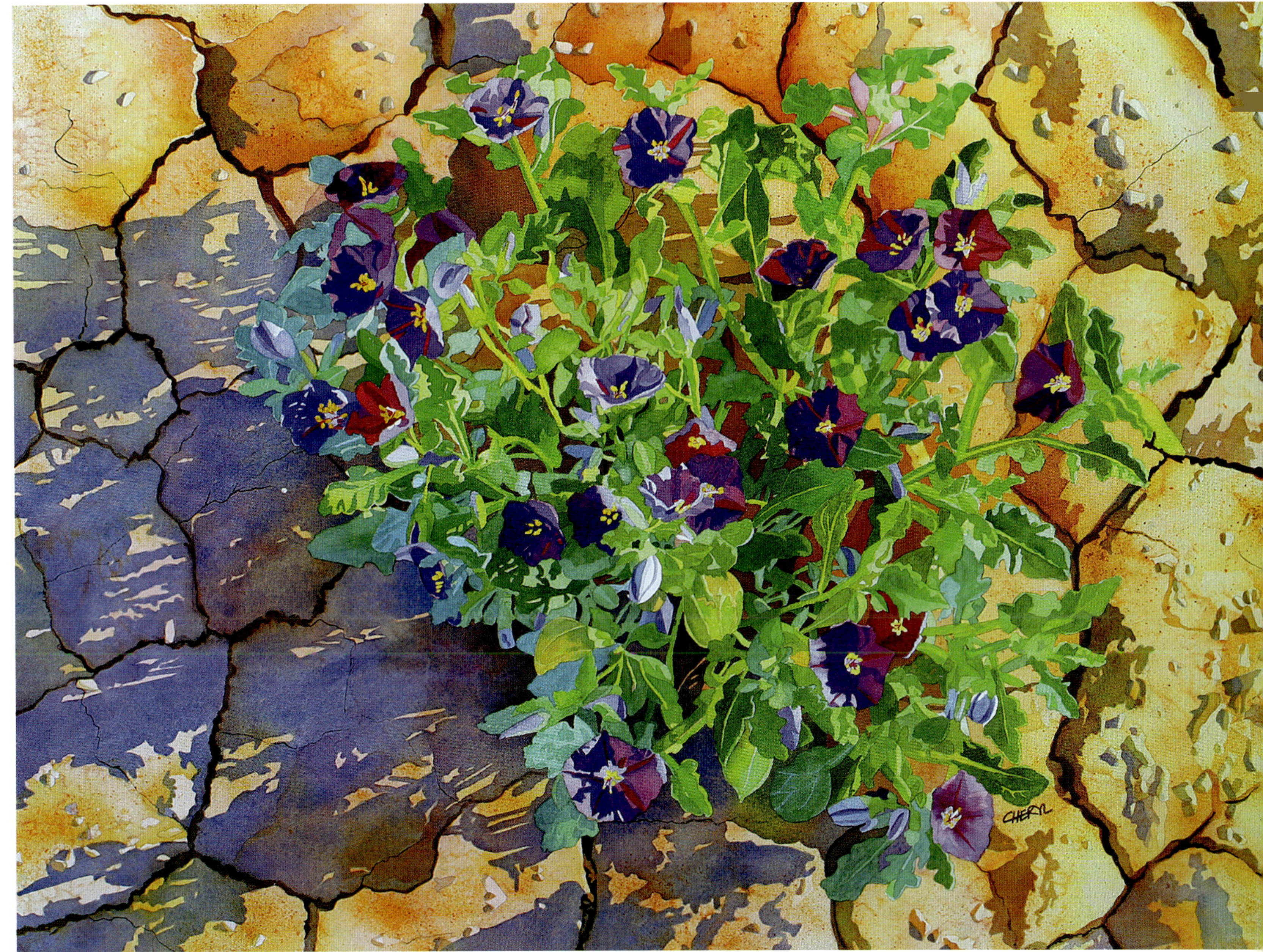

PURPLE GROUND CHERRY

Cheryl Weinfurtner • transparent watercolor on 300-lb. (640gsm) rough paper • 22" × 30" (56cm × 76cm)

TANGLES

Cheryl Weinfurtner • transparent watercolor on 300-lb. (640gsm) rough paper • 30" × 22" (76cm × 56cm)

The flowering plants that thrive in the arid Desert Southwest are juicy and vibrant. When I find them growing in impossible spaces, I have an irresistible urge to capture their essence. Clear desert skies cast colorful shadows, and the strong sunlight enhances color and texture. Transparent watercolor is the perfect medium to capture this phenomenon. I use a limited palette of staining pigments that I have selected for their transparency and ability to take on consecutive glazes. All whites are carefully preserved because I do not use opaque pigments. This technique allows light to reach the white paper and reflect back to the viewer's eye for a luminous effect. Every spring I hike remote desert trails with my digital camera, gathering reference photos that I will work from in my studio when the summer heat arrives.

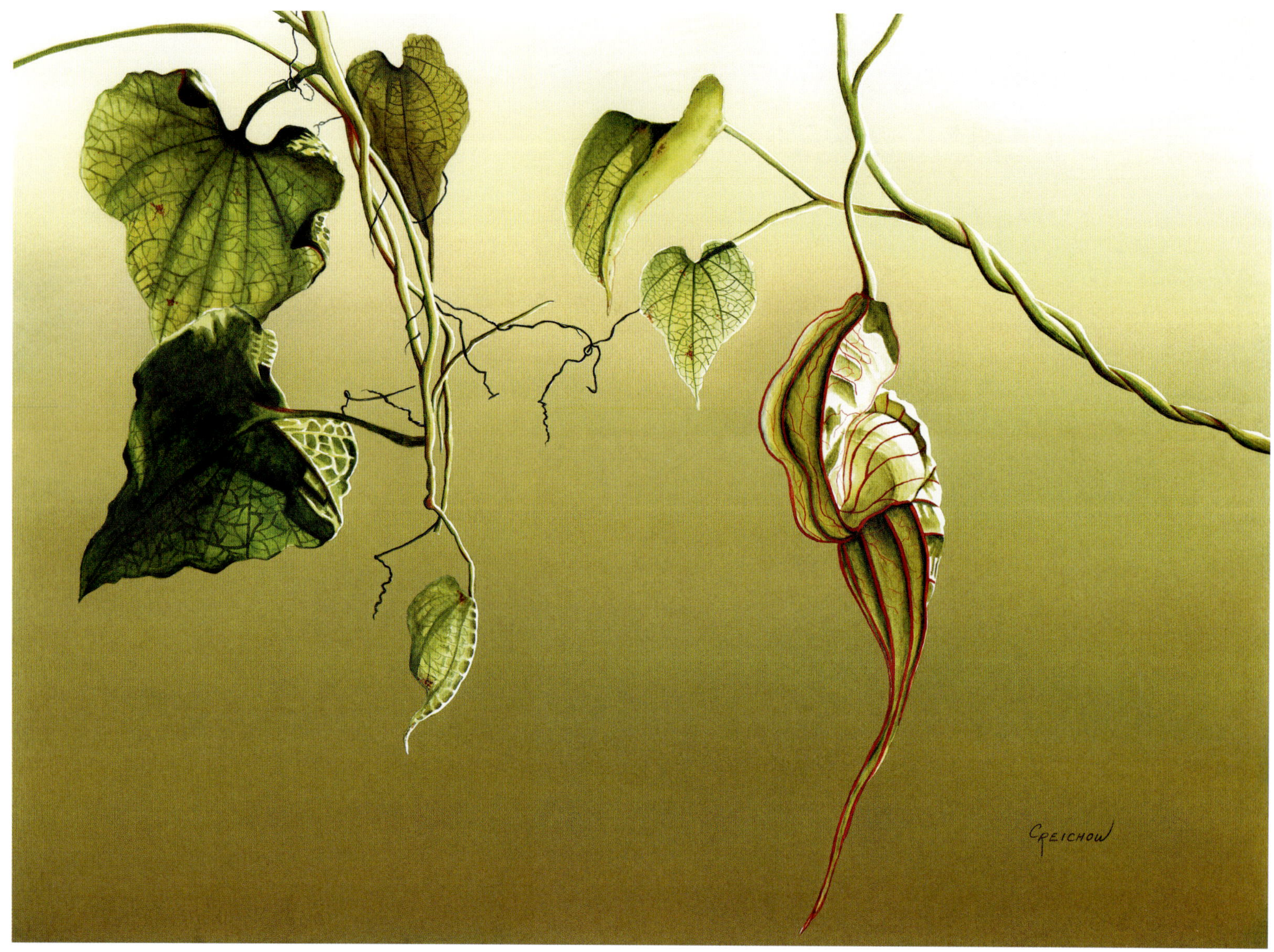

PELICAN FLOWER

Christine Reichow • watercolor on 300-lb. (640gsm) paper • 22" × 29" (56cm × 74cm)

Nature has always had a spellbinding effect on me. In my childhood, botanical stories unfolded petal by petal, blossoming from each unique plant. My passion continues to grow in the presence of the awesome beauty of nature, whether cultivated or wild. The pelican flower was photographed and sketched on-site for reference, and my goal in painting was to direct the viewer to focus on the unusual features of the plant as it connected in space across the page. To achieve this goal, I purposely eliminated background detail. I masked the plant's detail, wet the paper front and back, applied a thin layer of Aureolin with a wide hake brush, and let it dry. The process was continued layer by layer, alternating colors and building the depth of color slowly.

The process of painting puts me in an altered state of consciousness that is meditative but exciting, mysterious as well as satisfying and always pleasurable beyond imagination.

CHRISTINE REICHOW

FARM TRUCK

Robert J. O'Brien • transparent watercolor • 21" × 14" (53cm × 36cm)

Farm Truck depicts the tension between man-made objects and the steady, powerful forces of nature. I love the rustic feel of the old truck and the withered dying leaves on the vines. Light and shadow play an integral role in forming the composition, with the vines tying it all together. *Farm Truck* was painted in my studio using photo reference and value studies. I began with a very light glaze of yellow over the white area of the truck to give it a sunlit appearance. The vines and leaves were then masked. I used a combination of Winsor & Newton French Ultramarine Blue and Cobalt Blue for the truck body and a mixed gray for the shadows. After finishing the truck details, I removed the masking and painted in the vine and the leaves.

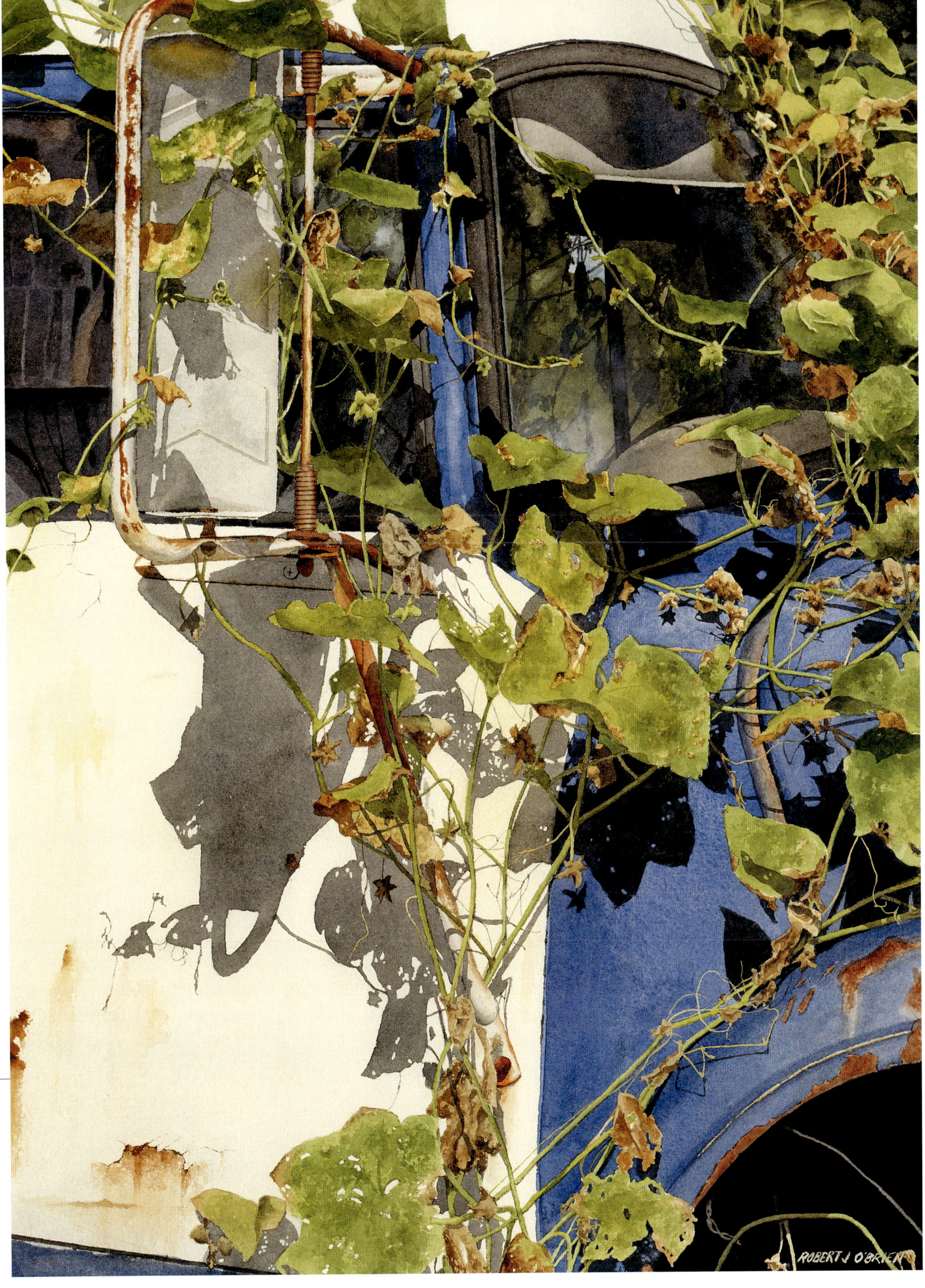
ROBERT J O'BRIEN

permissions

NEIL H. ADAMSON, AWS, NWS, FWS
5529 1st Avenue N., St. Petersburg, FL 33710
727.347.3555 (home), 727.744.9041 (cell)
nadamson@tampabay.rr.com
p. 27 *Milk Cans* © Neil Adamson, private collection
p. 27 *Tropical Sanctuary* © Neil Adamson, collection of the artist

CINDY AGAN
1201 Belmont Ave., South Bend, IN 46615
574.233.7950
cindyaganart@hotmail.com
www.cindyaganart.com
p. 67 *Napa Merlot* © Cindy Agan
p. 96 *Long Road Home* © Cindy Agan

JOSEPH ALLEMAN, AWS
PO Box 3584, Logan, UT 84323
www.josephalleman.com
p. 17 *Red Barn Composition #5* © Joseph Alleman

ROBIN SEVESTER AVERY
14322 Beacon Trace Ct., Houston, TX 77069
ravery1@earthlink.net
www.robinavery.net
p. 114 *Just Chillin' Baby* © Robin Avery

RUTH BADERIAN
390 Congress Ave., East Williston, NY 11596
rbaderian@verizon.net
www.ruthbaderianfineart.com
p. 102 *Downpour* © Ruth Baderian

ANGELA A. BARBALACE
www.angelabarbalace.artspan.com
p. 88 *The White Coat* © Angela Barbalace

STEPHEN BATES
16 Cecelia Ct., Wentzville, MO 63385
636.327.4536
mobates@centurytel.net
www.commissionedartwork.com
p. 58 *The Lady of Scituate* © Stephen Bates

ROBIN BERRY
612.824.5488
tabetberrystudio@comcast.net
www.natureartists.com/robin_berry.asp
p. 121 *Razzle Dazzle* © Robin Berry

MARCI BOONE
18 Stoney Creek Cove, Austin, TX 78734
180 Galeana 180 #8, Ajijic, Jalisco, Mexico
979.229.1599 -OR- 512.828.7539
artbymarci@gmail.com
www.marci-mjbstudio.com
p. 33 *Kissed by the Sun* © Marci Boone

CINDY BRABEC-KING
712 Ivanhoe Way, Grand Junction, CO 81506
970.242.9504
cbrabec-king@msn.com
pp. 106–107 *Hawaiian Blend* © Cindy Brabec-King

BRENDA MILLS BRANNAN
3210 Crystal Hts. Dr., Soquel, CA 95073
831.462.3214
bmillsb@yahoo.com
www.bmillsb.com
p. 45 *Dreamer* © Brenda Mills Brannan

SANDRA BRAY
3672 Copper Crest Rd., Olivenhain, CA 92024
858.756.0452
www.sandrabray.com
pp. 62–63 *Blue Vase* © Sandra Bray

CHICA BRUNSVOLD, NWS
3510 Wentworth Dr., Falls Church, VA 22044
703.256.1985
artbychica@juno.com
www.chicabrunsvold.com
pp. 118–119 *Night Blooms II* © Chica Brunsvold

DARYL BRYANT
1136 Fremont Ave., South Pasadena, CA 91030
p. 88 *San Marco* © Daryl Bryant

DAN BURT, AWS, DF, NWS
109 St. Andrews Loop, Kerrville, TX 78028-6442
830.895.3683
p. 95 *Medieval City* © Dan Burt, courtesy of Sandra Canavan Gallery, Boerne, TX

ALVARO CASTAGNET
alvaro@alvarocastagnet.net
www.alvarocastagnet.net
p. 53 *Mood of Venice* © Alvaro Castagnet

FRED CHILTON
PO Box 8436, Las Cruces, NM 88006
www.fredchilton.com
p. 25 *Cemetery at Truchas* © Fred Chilton, collection of Rosanne Camunez and Larry Lopez, Las Cruces, NM
p. 47 *Night of the Gypies* © Fred Chilton, collection of Steve and Kathleen Shubin, Dripping Springs, TX

KATHY COLLINS
Lake Forest Park, WA
kathy.collins2@comcast.net
www.kathycollinswatercolors.com
p. 22 *Columbia Gorge* © Kathy Collins, private collection, Edmonds, WA

JAIMIE CORDERO
7125 SW 95th St., Pinecrest, FL 33156-3036
786.303.5293 (cell), 305.661.8842 (studio)
wdjaimiec@aol.com
www.aquarellestudiosandgalleries.com
p. 71 *Sunrise Walk in Greenwich* © Jaimie Cordero, collection of Gary Goldfarb

LAUREL COVINGTON-VOGL
333 Northeast Circle, Durango, CO 81301
laurelvogl@durango.net
p. 55 *Gondola Basin II* © Laurel Covington-Vogl

LYNN C. DAVIS
575 Los Alamos Rd., Santa Rosa, CA 95409
mike575@pacbell.net
p. 54 *Sea Jellies* © Lynn C. Davis

MARTHA M. DEMING
9757 James Road, Remsen, NY 13438-3203
315.831.5324
mmdatmeadowtop@aol.com
www.meadowtopart.com
p. 109 *Woodsy Napping* © Martha M. Deming, collection of the artist

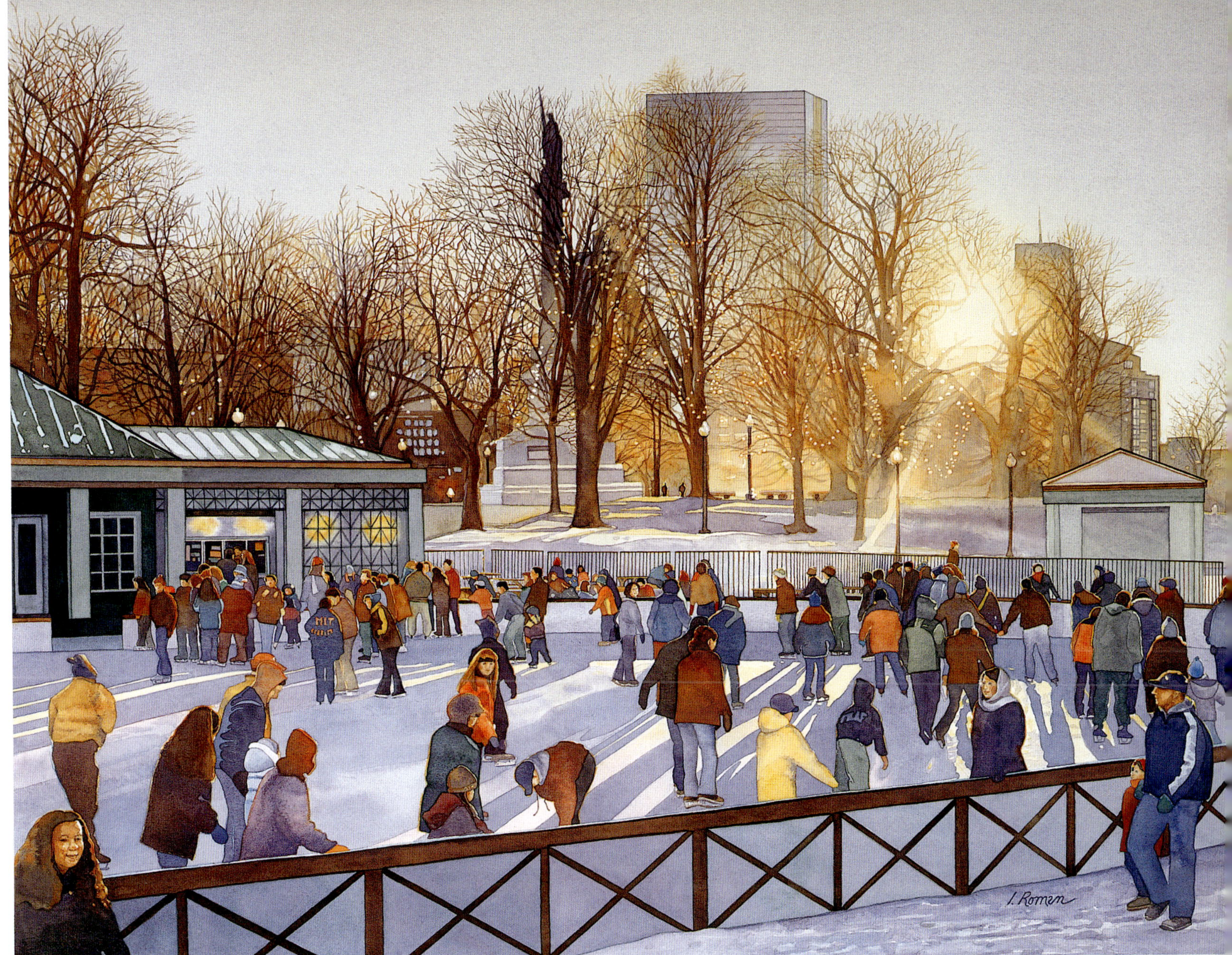

FROG POND SKATERS

Irena Roman • transparent watercolor • 25" × 28" (64cm × 71cm)

BROOKES L. DEWEY
brookesdewey@comcast.net
p. 130 *Tulips* © Brookes L. Dewey

EVELYN JENKINS DREW
721 Loma Prieta Drive, Aptos, CA 95003
831.688.7210 (home) 831.406.0052 (cell)
ejd@cruzio.com
www.ejd-design.com
p. 85 *Surf Town Run (T)* © Evelyn Jenkins Drew

SY ELLENS
326 W. Kalamazoo Ave. Suite 321, Kalamazoo, MI 49007
269.342.6326
syellens@sbcglobal.net
www.syellens.com
p. 76 *Heat of the Day* © Sy Ellens

JOYCE ROLETTO FAULKNOR
2611 Broadway, Redwood City, CA 94063
650.364.2611
www.joycefaulknor.com
p. 72 *Road King* © Joyce Roletto Faulknor

MARY LOU FERBERT
334 Parklawn Drive, Cleveland, OH 44116
p. 68 *Sea/Shore V* © Mary Lou Ferbert, collection of Maureen and Paul Ridzon

BARBARA FOX
7590 Maples Road, Little Valley, NY 14755
716.699.4145
foxbrachmann@hotmail.com
www.barbarafoxwatercolors.com
p. 40 *Arrangement* © Barbara Fox

JONATHAN FRANK
jon@jonathanfrankstudio.com
www.jonathanfrankstudio.com
p. 12 *Sustenance* © Jonathan Frank, collection of Ruth and Mark Stuenkel

MING SHU LIN FRANZ
5 Estrella Vista, Edgewood, NM 87015
505.281.4956
mingfranz11@yahoo.com
www.mingfranzstudio.com
p. 128 *Iao Valley, Maui* © Ming Shu Lin Franz

JO BETH GILLIAM
4610 81st St., Lubbock, TX 79424
806.799.4474
jobeth930@yahoo.com
p. 94 *Santa Fe Morning* © Jo Beth Gilliam, collection of Linda Gaither

MEL GRUNAU
www.mjgrunau.com
p. 78 *Potter's Tribute* © Mel Grunau

DON HARVIE
5077 Gadwall Circle, Stockton, CA 95207
209.951.1559
harvie1@aol.com
www.artistcolony.net/donharvie
p. 38 *Mommy's Hat* © Don Harvie

MIKE HILL
445 W. Powell, Gresham, OR 97030
503.516.4196
mikehillwatercolors@mac.com
www.mikehillwatercolors.com
p. 131 *Give Me Your Answer Do* © Mike Hill

GRETCHEN KRAUSE HOLESOVSKY
PO Box 1130, 32 Park Street, Belchertown, MA 01007
413.323.6377
freshair55@verizon.net
p. 74 *Dramatic Encounter* © Gretchen Krause Holesovsky

LAURIE HUMBLE
12002 Autumn Creek Dr., Houston, TX 77070
281.894.6531
lh-art@houston.rr.com
www.lauriehumble.com
p. 65 *After Dinner* © Laurie Humble

BILL JAMES, AWS, NWS, PSA-M, KA
509 NW 35th St., Ocala, FL 34475
352.694.8080
artistbilljames@earthlink.net
www.artistbilljames.com
p. 5 *Cuban Grandmother* © Bill James
p. 43 *Contempt* © Bill James

RUSTY JEWELL
116 Deer Creek Court, Easley, SC 29642
jewellart@charter.net
www.rustyjewell.com
p. 104 *Hot Seat* © Rusty Jewell, private collection

ALVIN JOE
821 Pollux Court, Foster City, CA 94404
650.341.8642 (home), 650.867.8834 (cell)
p. 13 *Lake Powell Narrow* © Alvin Joe
p. 127 *My Patio Décor* © Alvin Joe

BEV JOZWIAK
315 W. 23rd St., Vancouver, WA 98660
paintingjoz@hotmail.com
www.bevjozwiak.com
p. 30 *Shades, Shapes, and Shadows* © Bev Jozwiak
Art photographed by Art Work, Portland, OR

KWAN JUNG
kjung1@san.rr.com
p. 19 *Engagement in the Park* © Kwan Jung

ELISA KHACHIAN
artistelisa@optonline.net
www.westportartscenter.org, www.silvermineart.org, www.artplace.org
p. 79 *Three Long Stories* © Elisa Khachian, private collection

SUSAN J. KIEDIO
5817 Layor Dr., Parma Heights, OH 44130
440.845.5373
p. 35 *Hotel Lobby* © Susan J. Kiedio

ELIZABETH KINCAID
9515 NE 137th St., Kirkland, WA 98034-1820
425.823.9420
e@elizabethkincaid.com
www.elizabethkincaid.com
p. 133 *Daisies in Glass* © Elizabeth Kincaid

VALERIE LARSEN
www.valerielarsen.com
p. 113 *Horse Trials* © Valerie Larsen

ESTELLE LAVIN
6674 Hawaiian Ave., Boynton Beach, FL 33437
estellelavin@bellsouth.net
www.estellelavin.com
p. 126 *Peony Opus* © Estelle Lavin

FEALING LIN
1720 Ramiro Rd., San Marino, CA 91108
626.799.7022
fealinglin@hotmail.com
www.fealingwatercolor.com
p. 2 *Afternoon Walk* © Fealing Lin
p. 124 *Her Smile* © Fealing Lin

GUY MAGALLANES
Gallery 2611
2611 Broadway, Redwood City, CA 94063
www.guymagallanes.com
p. 112 *Duck, Duck, Goose!* © Guy Magallanes
p. 124 *Helios* © Guy Magallanes

FRAN MANGINO
1180 Smoke Burr Dr., Westerville, OH 43081
614.891.6558
midlifomama@hotmail.com
www.midlifeseries.com
p. 111 *That Radiant Glow* © Fran Mangino

SUSAN MANSELL
2718 FM 382, Ballinger, TX 76821
325.365.3642
susanmansell@hotmail.com
p. 84 *Colors of Mexico* © Susan Mansell

MARGARET M. MARTIN
69 Elmwood Ave., Buffalo, NY 14201
p. 52 *Dockside Design* © Margaret M. Martin
p. 129 *Flower Festival Jewels* © Margaret M. Martin

ANTONIO MASI
121 Brompton Rd., Garden City, NY 11530
516.742.5068
amasi@optonline.net
www.antoniomasi.com
p. 19 *N.Y. Tramway II* © Antonio Masi

MIKE MAZER
7 Holly Woods Rd., Mattapoisett, MA 02739
508.758.6216
msmmassmedorg@comcast.net
www.mikemazer.com
p. 50 *Tied Up* © Mike Mazar
p. 51 *It Ain't Easy* © Mike Mazar

WILLIAM MCALLISTER
262½ Academy Ave., Pittsburgh, PA 15228
bath392000@yahoo.co.uk
www.mcallisterpaintings.com
p. 101 *Croquet Sunday* © William McAllister
p. 105 *Burford Lamb* © William McAllister, both works courtesy of George Stern Fine Arts, West Hollywood, CA

LAURIN MCCRACKEN
1005 Picasso Dr., Fort Worth, TX 76107
817.773.2163
laurinmc@aol.com
www.lauringallery.com
p. 67 *Hospitality* © Laurin McCracken

MARK E. MEHAFFEY, AWS, NWS, TWSA-MASTER
5440 Zimmer Rd., Williamston, MI 48895
517.655.2342
mark@mehaffeygallery.com
www.mehaffeygallery.com
p. 90 *Lunch Time Light* © Mark E. Mehaffey collection of the artist
p. 91 *The Offering* © Mark E. Mehaffey, collection of Beth Patterson, AWS, NWS

DAVID MILTON
31682 Fairview Rd., Laguna Beach, CA 92651
949.415.0155
dmiltonart@cox.net
www.davidmiltonstudio.com
p. 97 *Frontier Gas Pumps* © David Milton

PEGGY MINGER-MCCANTS
18231 Fieldbury Lane, Huntington Beach, CA 92648
714.969.1225
beachdays@social.rr.com
p. 61 *Central Park No. 1* © Peggy Minger-McCants

DICK MITCHELL
24 W. Avondale Dr., Greenville, SC 29609
864.233.6629
artistmitchell@aol.com
p. 26 *Scent From Heaven* © Dick Mitchell

JUDY MORRIS
2404 E. Main St., Medford, OR 97504
541.779.5306
judy@judymorris-art.com
www.judymorris-art.com
p. 120 *Blossom, Rose, & Violet* © Judy Morris

GLORIA AINSWORTH MOUT
208-15342 20th Ave., Surrey, BC, Canada V4A 2A3
604.531.9570
gjmout60@shaw.ca
www.myartclub.com
p. 69 *Spinner* © Gloria Ainsworth Mout

TED NUTTALL
4225 N. 36th St. Unit 34, Phoenix, AZ 85018
602.253.1605
ted@tednuttall.com
www.tednuttall.com
p. 41 *Ella, San Gimignano* © Ted Nuttall, collection of Steven and Susan Spear

ROBERT J. O'BRIEN
2811 Weathersfield Ctr. Rd., Perkinsville, VT 05151
robert@robertjobrien.com
www.robertjobrien.com
p. 77 *Kingdom Camp* © Robert J. O'Brien
p. 137 *Farm Truck* © Robert J. O'Brien

CATHERINE P. O'NEILL
34 Marengo Ave., Hamburg, NY 14075
716.648.4852
kconeill@adelphia.net
p. 44 *Comes Marching Home* © Catherine P. O'Neill
p. 44 *Marching Home Again* © Catherine P. O'Neill

DON O'NEILL, AWS
3723 Tibbetts St., Riverside, CA 92506
951.686.2277
comitan@aol.com
p. 132 *Matilija Poppies in Blue Bowl* © Don O'Neill

JOANN S. OSTROWSKI
14071 Eagle Ridge Lakes Dr. #201, Ft. Myers, FL 33912-0716
239.768.6830
joannostrowski@earthlink.net
p. 108 *Tugboat* © JoAnn S. Ostrowski

PAM PAHL, ASMA, FWS
342 Charlotte St., St. Augustine, FL 32084
904.823.9703
ppahlart@aol.com
www.ppahl.com
pp. 48–49 *Three Dinghies* © Pam Pahl

HEIDI LANG PARRINELLO
25 Madison St., Glen Ridge, NJ 07028
hlang25@comcast.net
p. 125 *68° and Sunny* © Heidi Lang Parrinello

DONALD W. PATTERSON
441 Cardinal Court N., New Hope, PA 18938
215.598.8991
donpattart@mailstation.com
www.travisgallery.com
p. 25 *River Road* © Donald W. Patterson
p. 57 *Shimmering Waters* © Donald W. Patterson

JEAN PEDERSON
4039 Comanche Rd. NW, Calgary, Alberta, Canada T2L 0N9
403.289.6106
artform@telus.net
www.jeanpederson.com
p. 46 *Beyond the Borders* © Jean Pederson

CHARLES TIMOTHY PRUTZER
PO Box 49431, Colorado Springs, CO 80949
p. 59 *Buffalo on the River Letaba* © Charles Timothy Prutzer
p. 116 *Portrait of a Wood Duck* © Charles Timothy Prutzer

ROBIN PURCELL
409 Triomphe Ct., Danville, CA 94506
robin.purcell@gmail.com
925.648.0971
p. 10 *Green Day* © Robin Purcell, private collection

DAVID RANKIN
2320 Allison Rd., Cleveland, OH 44118
www.davidrankinwatercolors.com
ddrankin@sbcglobal.net
p. 117 *Naptime* © David Rankin
p. 15 *Afternoon Light* © David Rankin

MICHAEL REARDON
5433 Boyd Ave., Oakland, CA 94618
510.655.7030
mreardon@mreardon.com
www.mreardon.com
p. 82 *Pont Au Change* © Michael Reardon

LESLIE LAMBERT REDHEAD
Victoria, BC, Canada
250.984.1327
leslieredhead@hotmail.com
www.redheadstudio.net
p. 34 *The Attic Room* © Leslie Lambert Redhead

CHRISTINE REICHOW
21301 Tamiami Trail #320, PMB 225, Estero, FL 33928
239.433.3817
christine@christinereichow.com
www.christinereichow.com
p. 136 *Pelican Flower* © Christine Reichow

ALAN ROGERSON
9512 N. Central Ave., Phoenix, AZ 85020
602.678.5461
rogersonart@juno.com
www.alanrogersonart.com
p. 39 *Poor Baby* © Alan Rogerson, collection of the artist

IRENA ROMAN
575 Washington St., Canton, MA 02021
www.irenaroman.com
p. 70 *Fresh Squeezed* © Irena Roman
p. 139 *Frog Pond Skaters* © Irena Roman

ROBERT SAKSON, AWS-DF
10 Stacey Ave., Trenton, NJ 08618-3421
609.394.2460
p. 21 *Lowell Hunter's Farm* © Robert Sakson

JOHN SALMINEN AWS-DF, NWS
6021 Arnold Rd., Duluth, MN 55803
218.721.3319
salminen@cpinternet.com
www.johnsalminen.com
p. 86 *News Stand* © John Salminen
p. 87 *Brooklyn Butcher Shop* © John Salminen

DONALD SAYERS
Niwot, CO 80503
303.652.8052
p. 15 *Villas y Mar* © Donald Sayers

PAT SAN SOUCIE, AWS, NWS, WHS
11777 SE Timber Valley Dr., Clackamas, OR 97086-8388
503.698.6202
pat@sansoucie.com
www.patsansoucie.com
p. 75 *Persimmon Astringencies* © Pat San Soucie

SANDRA SCHAFFER
12700 E. 64th Ct., Kansas City, MO 64133
816.358.3609
lschaffer@kc.rr.com
www.artistsregister.com
p. 73 *Black and Blue* © Sandra Schaffer
p. 115 *Regal Bearing* © Sandra Schaffer

LIN SOULIERE
Dragonfly Ridge Studio
107 Caudle Rd., Lion's Head, Ontario, Canada N0H 1W0
519.793.4758
soulart@bmts.com
www.dragonflyridge.ca
p. 22 *Ancient Witness II* © Lin Souliere

PAM STANLEY
215 Aberdeen Ave., Corpus Christi, TX 78411
361.854.3695
pamsarts@hotmail.com
p. 14 *Sea Scape I* © Pam Stanley

RICHARD STEPHENS
28 Huntleigh Dr., Hot Springs, AR 71901
501.624.7062
rswcs7@direclynx.net
www.raswatercolors.com
p. 98 *Back Porch America* © Richard Stephens
p. 99 *Royal Street in New Orleans* © Richard Stephens
p. 100 *Fountain of Light* © Richard Stephens

JERRY STITT
1001 Bridgeway #225, Sausalito, CA 94965
jerrystitt305@google.com
p. 16 *The Corinthian Yacht Club* © Jerry Stitt, collection of the artist

SUSAN M. STULLER
2930 Barrow Place, Midlothian, Virginia 23113
804.379.1477
susan.stuller@comcast.net
www.susanstuller.com
p. 64 *Strawberry Jamming* © Susan M. Stuller
p. 143 *A Golden Morning* © Susan M. Stuller

PAUL SULLIVAN
6602 N. 82nd Way, Scottsdale, AZ 85250
sully1251@cox.net
p. 42 *Manzanita Morning* © Paul Sullivan

KEIKO TANABE
12662 Sandy Crest Ct., San Diego, CA 92130
ktanabe@san.rr.com
www.ktanabefineart.com
p. 83 *Journey Home* © Keiko Tanabe

JAMES TOOGOOD, AWS, NWS
920 Park Drive, Cherry Hill, NJ 08002
jtoogood@snip.net
p. 8 *Blizzard in the Village* © James Toogood
p. 56 *Breakers on a Rocky Coast* © James Toogood
pp. 80–81 *Blizzard on Times Square* © James Toogood
p. 103 *Blizzard on Fifth Avenue* © James Toogood

SHARON TOWLE
2417 John St., Manhattan Beach, CA 90266
310.546.1864
sharontowle@ix.netcom.com
www.sharontowle.com
p. 60 *Behind the Wheel* © Sharon Towle

KERI VANDERLAAN
PO Box 366, Silverado, CA 92676
714.649.9054
kvndrln@aol.com
p. 20 *A Gift From the Navajos* © Keri Vanderlaan

CLAIRE SCHROEVEN VERBIEST
3126 Brightwood Ct., San Jose, CA 95148
408.238.6003
aquatel@aol.com
p. 32 *Summer* © Claire Schroeven Verbiest

SOON Y. WARREN
4062 Hildring Dr. W., Fort Worth, TX 76109
817.926.0327
soon-warren@charter.net
www.soonwarren.com
p. 122 *Baby's Breath* © Soon Y. Warren
p. 123 *Yellow Daisy* © Soon Y. Warren

CHERYL WEINFURTNER
Las Vegas, NV
www.desertartist.com
p. 134 *Tangles* © Cheryl Weinfurtner, private collection
p. 135 *Purple Ground Cherry* © Cheryl Weinfurtner, private collection

DONNA JILL WITTY
jilwitty@owc.net
www.donnajillwitty.com
p. 92 *Ponte Vecchio* © Donna Jill Witty
p. 93 *Rialto Market* © Donna Jill Witty

TOM YACOVELLA
1145 Herkimer Rd., Utica, NY 13502
315.797.5863
yacovellart@aol.com
www.yacovellart.com
p. 110 *Keep Looking for a Bluebird* © Tom Yacovella

AL ZERRIES
5 Hawk Drive, Huntington, NY 11743
631.421.5497
jzerries@optonline.net
www.alzerriesart.com
pp. 28–29 *The Goddess of Denial* © Al Zerries
p. 36 *Decision* © Al Zerries
p. 37 *The Long Wait* © Al Zerries
p. 37 *The Wedding Guest* © Al Zerries

index

A GOLDEN MORNING

Susan M. Stuller • *transparent watercolor* • 21" × 29" (53cm × 74cm)